The Making of the Prefident 1789

Also by Marvin Kitman

George Washington's Expense Account

The Making of the President 1789

The Unauthorized Campaign Biography

Marvin Kitman

HarperPerennial

A Division of HarperCollinsPublishers

The Library of Congress has catalogued the hardcover edition as follows:

Kitman, Marvin, 1929–
    The making of the prefident 1789.

    1. Washington, George, 1732–1799—Humor.
2. Presidents—United States—Election—1789—Humor.
3. Presidents—United States—Election—1988—Humor.
4. Political satire, American.   5. United States—
History, Comic, satirical, etc.   I. Title.
E312.17.KS3   1989   324.973′041   88-45038
ISBN 0-06-015981-2

ISBN 0-06-091992-2 (pbk.)

91 92 93 94 95 MPC 10 9 8 7 6 5 4 3 2 1

Dedication

I live now in New Jersey, heart of the Revolutionary War battlefield. The crabgrass grows where our forefathers fought and fornicated and died for their country. Major General Lafayette, a plaque tells me, slept not far (two hundred yards) from where my crabgrass grows: "In 1780 a wing of the flying camp* under the command of Major General Lafayette encamped here."

New Jersey is now a burial ground for organized crime, whose fallen soldiers wind up near the Continental Army's dead. Jimmy Hoffa, who we locals all know is buried in the end zone, in fact the coffin corner, of Giants Stadium, may rest shoulder to shoulder with the unknown soldier of the 2nd Pennsylvania, 5th New York, or 3rd Continental Light Dragoons, who died from a chill crossing the mighty Hackensack or the Passaic, which today bursts into flames spontaneously as testimony to New Jersey's contribution to the Industrial Revolution.

This book is for you, New Jersey.

It's also for Myer Kitman, my founding father, and Rose Kitman, the founding mother. Without whom none of what follows would be possible.

---

* Forerunner of the famed Lafayette Escadrille of World War I. This cryptic phrase also may be the origin of the persisting rumor that Lafayette was gay. I will deal with this canard later.

Contents

Forward by John Cleese   VIII

Preamble   1

*Being the account of how the author first
fell under the spell of the father of his country.*

Part I: The Making of the General   13

*Being the inspiring tale of how George Washington
ran for general without knowing it.*

Part II: The Making of the General, II
(continued)   51

*Being the awesome chronicle of how the Mount Vernon Machine
got the nomination for the second-best man.*

Part III: The Making of the War Hero   93

*Being the true story of how Silent George managed to win the war,
even though the score was England 9, U.S.A. 2.*

Part IV: The Making of the Reluctant
Noncandidate   199

*Being the incredible account of the man who said,
"I'd rather sit under my fig tree than be prefident."*

Part V: Campaign '88   237

*Being the amazing saga of how the steamroller
chased George Washington over the top.*

Part VI: The Last Huzzah   275

or, the Man Who Wouldn't Be King

Acknowledgments   321

Notes   325

Bibliography   342

Index   349

Foreword

This is a very funny book. It is also, as you can tell from the historically accurate spelling of Prefident and the sixteen pages of source notes, a work of deep scholarship.

Everyone likes success stories. Marvin Kitman, having failed to become President himself in 1964 despite a good platform (the Republican Party's of 1864) and a good slogan ("I'd rather be President than write"), set about discovering how Washington managed it. The result is an inspiration to us all. First, all candidates for office should run unopposed. Second, they should not campaign. Third, they should proclaim their hopelessness and inadequacy so often that every disaster is greeted as an example of their truthfulness.

Kitman, of course, goes far beyond this. He does not shirk the dark issues of the Founding Girlfriends, the dedication Washington displayed in submitting his expense accounts, or the strategic mastery of keeping his plans from the enemy by the device of not having any. He is, of course, scrupulously fair to his hero and disputes the idea that he married the unprepossessing Martha for her money. As he points out, there was also her land.

The Making of the Prefident will, I am sure, become a blueprint for all those who want to get on in this world, or indeed the next.

John Cleese

Preamble

Being the account of how the author first fell under the spell of the father of his country.

E very four years a lot of exciting books come out about the making of the president. They are a quadrennial ritual of the American political process, sort of like the arrival of the four-year boll weevil or the seven-year itch. In 1989, it occurred to me that this country needed a change. Somebody should write about the first election, without which all the others would not have been possible. That is why I have written *The Making of the Prefident 1789.*

Please do not confuse this book with all the other making-of-the-president books. They are all imitations. You can tell mine is original by the spelling of "prefident." That is the original, true spelling. The *f*'s instead of the *s*'s were used in the old days, as in "purfuit of happineff." (A filly way to fpell, if you afk me.)

The people who write the making-of-the-president books always tell about the strategy of the candidates and what they had to do to get elected. Nobody has ever analyzed the election of 1789 in those terms. That's because they didn't think there was anything to analyze. Apparently, the writers thought Washington was elected by God. He became a hero by acclamation. And if it were not a teleological event, ordained by providence, the election was some kind of Politburo charade, a predictable victory at the polls, with Joe Stalin Washington getting 107 percent of the vote. What a slur—a slur on Washington's memory, that is.

The fact that in 1789 Washington ran unopposed and won unanimously was not a Communist plot. He won fair and square. Unfortunately, the apparent ease of his victory has cheated him of much of his glory as a politician. I hope to redress this historical injustice in this book.

How did candidate Washington get into the enviable position of running unopposed and seemingly unbeatable? I'm sure such footnotes to history now as Gary Hart, Joe Biden, Richard Gephardt, Robert Dole, Pat Robertson, General Al Haig, Paul Simon, Governor Bruce Babbitt, Pat Schroeder, and all the others who fell out of the race by tripping over things would like to know. They would have known if they had studied the Washington landslide in the first election.

Everybody who is planning to grow up to be prefident some day should study the landmark Washington campaign of 1789. It provides basic strategy for all prefidential campaigns since. Everybody running for prefident tries to recreate the conditions Washington had in his first race, i.e., being unopposed and winning unanimously. What follows is the untold story of how the Mount Vernon machine engineered the election of General George Washington to the prefidency of the U.S.

Historians always say there wasn't a race. He was elected because he was a great man? Yes. But he was even greater than they usually say.

Historians leave out the best part of the story. It is widely assumed, for example, that in 1789 Washington was the only person around who had wanted to be prefident when he grew up. As a matter of fact, the political clubhouses of the day were filled with prefidential timber. The first five prefidents, Washington, John Adams, Thomas Jefferson, James Madison, and James Monroe, to name a random selection of candidates, were all politically active during this period. Not to mention John Jay, who was always available.

In some 32,987 books written about Washington, the man, monument, and bridge, historians have not presented the real story. The Washington success story of 1789 has been ignored because of the following myths, buttressed by misconceptions and half-truth, about the leading candidate in 1789:

1. He didn't campaign.
2. He was no politician, but was an innocent, bereft of political sense.
3. He didn't have any potential sex scandals, unlike most of

the other prefidential candidates in our history, including
Cleveland, Harding, and Gary Hart.
4. He was not a man, but a marble statue.

I am going to show that none of this is true.

I see history as fun, gritty, and texturally rich in facts that apply to
real life, today, the way history used to be when I was growing up
in Pittsburgh and Brooklyn in the 1930s and 1940s.

My idea was to write a book so that even my daughter, who
thinks the founding father of the country was Barry Bostwick,
would read it. When you say "history" to her generation of ex-
hippies, they think you mean the 1960s. To most young people
today Washington is a birthday sale. Bon Jovi is better known than
some of our presidents. Who are the people everybody knows
today?

* Elvis
* Vanna what's-her-name
* Roseanne Barr
* Willard Scott

In a recent test the majority of students didn't know which
prefident was in a wheelchair.* Soon, as novelist Dan Jenkins has
observed, they'll be asked which one was the tall one with the
beard and the top hat.†

To most Americans history is not real or relevant. I want to
make George Washington at least as real as the most famous American soldier, Elvis Presley.

I first became acquainted with the general in Mrs. Jacobs'
class, the fourth grade, Room 222, in P.S. 186, in Brooklyn, to
which my parents had brought me from Pittsburgh, where I was
born. (Some parents send their kids to Switzerland "for finishing";
mine brought me to Brooklyn.)

George Washington used to look down at me every day from
a gilt-framed portrait above Mrs. Jacobs' desk. This was the famous Gilbert Stuart painting of 1796 ("The Athenaeum"). Copies

---

* Answer: Franklin D. Roosevelt.

† Answer: Rutherford B. Hayes. Also Grant, Garfield, Harrison, and, of course, Lincoln.

of it flooded the public schools of America, circa 1937, thanks to the noted art patron Congressman Sol Bloom of Brooklyn, who was in charge of the nation's celebrating appropriately the sesquicentennial of the Conſtitution. It was thought it would help improve the nation's moral tone to have schoolboys like me stare at the portrait of George Washington.

Come to think of it, he looked a lot like my grandmother, with the silver hair and the hollow cheeks of someone wearing false teeth. I didn't know much about Washington then: to me, as a nine-year-old, Washington was a baseball team in the American League.* It was also a mountain range† to the north of where I lived in Brooklyn. I remember staring at the portrait a lot during class. *What was he smiling about?* I used to wonder. He does smile. It's not a broad smile, but like Mona Lisa's, without showing teeth.

Whenever I had trouble in a spelling test, I'd look up at the Washington portrait, expecting help, some sign about whether the *i* went before the *e*. Mrs. Jacobs told us about the cherry tree, and his never telling a lie, or "lye," as he spelled it. But she never mentioned anything about what a bad speller George was. His correspondence was filled with misspellings like "blew" for *blue*, and "oyl" for *oil*, or "earl" as we pronounced it in my class in Brooklyn. (It's a good thing he didn't have a title, like "the Oyl of Mount Vernon.") I could understand why proper names like Philadelphia and Mississippi were trouble for him. But "knews" instead of *news*? And he used "sale" and "sail" interchangeably. Vanna White he wasn't.

Neither did Mrs. Jacobs tell us he was an elementary school dropout. The Washington I encountered in the fourth grade was the standard portrait of a marble statue.

The next time I thought about Washington was when I ran for prefident, excuse me, president.

You may remember my campaign for the Republican nomination in 1964, or at least my slogan: "I'd rather be President than write." I had run against Barry Goldwater, a McKinley Republican, as a Lincoln Republican. I was the only real reactionary in the race, running on the Republican party platform of 1864, so many

---

* The Washington Senators, now known as the Minneapolis Twins. This Washington was called "First in war, first in peace, and last in the American League."

† Washington Heights.

of whose promises hadn't been fulfilled. (I favored abolishing slavery, and bringing the South back into the union, a strong civil rights position for 1964.) As you recall, I lost.

After my bitter defeat, I returned to my practice as a writer. But I would never be the same. Once you run for prefident all other jobs seem second best. (Well, maybe not the vice-prefidency.) I began going to the library to read up on history and learn where Abraham Lincoln had gone wrong. Somehow in my mind I had associated my defeat with Lincoln. The country wasn't ready for him yet. I guess I was what the political analysts call "a sore loser." *

It was then that I discovered a new political role model: George Washington. What impressed me most about Washington as a politician was not just that the guy won, but he got 100 percent of the vote. He was unopposed and won unanimously! Why, even I could have won, given those conditions.

While in the library, I had a number of scholarly adventures with my new political hero, which gradually started chipping away at the marble image. First, I discovered his expense account from the Revolutionary War, which Mrs. Jacobs never told me about. Historians seem not to have appreciated it as much as I did, as a free-lance magazine writer whose expense accounts had made editors whistle in admiration.

It was first published by the Chief Clerk in the Register's Office of the Treasury Department in June 1833, under the title, "Accounts, G. Washington with the United States, Commencing June 1775, and ending June 1783, Comprehending a Space of 8 Years."

It didn't become a best-seller. My study of a man who fought a war against British tyranny on an expense account—listing all his bar bills and places he was supposed to have slept at—ensured his being not only first in war and peace but first in expense-account writing. (For details of his contribution to the art of expense-account writing, see *George Washington's Expense Account*, by General George Washington and Marvin Kitman, PFC [Ret.].)

---

* Scholars interested in further documentation should refer to the definitive work on the subject, *The Number One Best Seller* (the title, not the sales report), the first volume of my autobiography (Dial Press, 1966). Suffice it to say that now, every four years, there are postcards and letters from two or three of my supporters urging me to run again. "You can become the Harold Stassen of New Jersey," my ex-campaign manager, Victor Navasky, explained. That was a mandate from the people that I have been able to resist thus far.

He still had the marble image but the expense account was the first indication he was not just marble. This guy may have flesh and blood, I reasoned.

It was then that I decided to launch a full-scale investigation into Washington's past. For twenty-five years the subject has been a passion for me. This book is where the passion took me.

My motives, admittedly, were originally selfish, self-serving. I lost an election, and he won. How? What did he do that I hadn't?

Along the way, I wanted to know: Who was this guy and what could we learn from him? Was he actually a god whom we mortals could all take lessons from?

How is it possible that a man with no military experience becomes a general? He loses more battles than he wins and becomes a war hero?* He has absolutely no political opinions in the most sophisticated intellectual period of our history. He has no ambitions, and he wins?

The man, my working theory was, must have been a political genius, unbeknownst to himself. On investigation, my instinct, in fact, turned out to be correct. And in fact, he is even greater, smarter, more astute than anybody thought. For twenty-five years I have been thwacking away at the marble. Where other historians find underneath the marble wood, I find only gold.

I realize I may be guilty of putting George Washington on a pedestal in the pages that follow. But he is on the pedestal this time for the right reasons.

---

*Nobody likes to argue with his superiors, especially a three-star general, the first one, about strategy. But take his famous retreat through the Jerseys in 1776, which everybody learns about in school. General Washington and his men went by my house in New Jersey. There is a bas-relief statue on our corner with a plaque that reads "General Washington Went This Way." The state highway department put up signs for the Bicentennial (1976) indicating a path of retreat, two blocks past my house and through the shopping mall in Paramus. I think about the significance of that event a lot.

First of all, he went in the wrong direction. He should not have turned left (to Philadelphia) but turned right, toward the Poconos. With an army of ragged guerrillas, he never should have gone to Valley Forge but to the hills. From East Stroudsburg or Fred Waring's Shawnee-on-the-Delaware, he could have sent his men on horses (since they didn't have shoes most of the time anyway) into the outskirts of Philadelphia and harassed the British army holed up there.

As a military man myself (within the space of only two years—1953 to 1955—I rose to the rank of Private First Class, United States Army), I intend to look at Washington's war record with a professional eye. Suffice it to say now that if he had been fighting in the Civil War instead of the Revolutionary War, Lincoln would have fired him. If he had been manager of a big-league baseball team, he would never have made it out of spring training.

A Note on Source Materials

Everything in this book is factual. As a Washington scholar, I cannot tell a lie. Where one can argue with what is written, perhaps, may be in my interpretation of the facts. Like many historians, I occasionally may err.

I am not a historian—although I did get a 95 in the New York State History Regents Examination (1947). But I am an ahistorian. I have no axioms to grind. I am not constrained by thoughts of getting tenure at the university or of winning fellowships. I can go where no historian has gone before.

Traditionally, making-of-the-president books follow the candidates around to recreate the drama. Since most of the participants in the election of 1789 are dead now, or should be, I follow on the campaign trails of historians. Who knows the period better? They certainly sound more authoritative than participants about what went on then.

This is more than the standard use of respected source materials. Modern historians are characters in my story. Their way of seeing history, as McLuhan might have said, is the message. They affect the way people today think about history. In fact these writers can be called *history-meisters*, performing the function of the modern spin-meisters.

Historical spin-meisters are key players in the action, like the objective anchorman in the election coverage today, who by raising an eyebrow as a candidate promises, say, to stick to the issues, can shape our attitude toward the events. They control access to information about the past more than ever before.

Colonel James T. Flexner, in particular, colored a whole generation's views about General Washington when in 1984 CBS did a miniseries titled "George Washington" starring Barry Bostwick, based on his multivolume *Washington*. Unlike most historians who have nothing but contempt for TV, Colonel Flexner reportedly loved the miniseries, perhaps because the network consulted with him at great length before making its boring eight-hour show that turned the marble Washington into plastic.

Some historians, or spin-meisters, seem to this day to be loyal members of the Mount Vernon machine's media team. Consciously or unconsciously, they underplay or ignore the facts which do not fit into the romanticized, idealized myth of the candidate and the campaign.

*

No man except George Washington, living or dead, ever read all of Washington's letters, extant or lost. Nobody living has ever even counted them: An estimate of their number ranges from 26,000 to 40,000—a difference of 14,000 manuscripts, which is in itself an astounding fact.[1]

The periodic literature is even more voluminous: Approximately 850 articles on Washington have been published since 1900.[2] Colonel Flexner himself once estimated the number of publications and books about Washington in the catalogue of the New York Public Library by a scientific experiment. He first counted the number of cards per inch (seventy-seven to an inch), and then (back in 1965, when he started his research) measured the number of inches: thirty-seven-and-a-half. The result: 2,887. There are more now. And that, he reminds me in Appendix C of his first volume, *George Washington: The Forge of Experience* (p. 353), was only the books that had his last name in the title. He is the most heavily papered man in history. I have also read the newspapers of the day. They are not accurate for the years 1775–1779, warns Douglas Southall Freeman.

For the purposes of this book, I spent a lot of time following historians Colonel Freeman and Colonel Flexner. Their multivolume works (seven for Freeman and four for Flexner, plus a one-volume abridgement) gave me, in addition to a good overview, the standard establishment view of Washington, the man and the monument. Each grovels its way to Mount Vernon in different ways and is much admired by the Mount Vernon Ladies Association. Both books were inspirations and guides on where not to go.

For balance, I have gone to an earlier, less reverent period of scholarship. I have leaned heavily on the landmark 1927–30 reinterpretation of *Washington* by Rupert Hughes, a three-volume work which I still consider the greatest biography of Washington. William Woodward's one-volume iconoclastic Reader's Digest version of Hughes, *George Washington: The Image and the Man*, tends to judge the man by the standards for the highest office in the land set by President Warren Harding. Nevertheless, Woodward is provocative.

My view of General Greene and his happy-go-lucky wife, Catharine (Kitty), owes much to Professor Theodore Thayer of Rutgers, and George Washington Greene's three-volume biography of 1890.

Irving Brant assisted me on my Madison. Nathan Schachner, John C. Miller, and Forrest McDonald helped on Hamilton. North Callahan was my man on Henry Knox and Ticonderoga. Peter Shaw was my guide on the character of John Adams. Richard B. Morris of the City University of New York, Columbia and the John Jay Papers, and Richard B. Bernstein, constitutional and legal historian and historical consultant to the New York City Commission on the Bicentennial of the Constitution, were my midwives through "the creation" (the Federal Convention and ratification) period. My view of the critical first year of the Revolutionary War was largely shaped by Allen French of Harvard.

"Every writer who looks at George Washington," as Clinton Rossiter says[3] in *Six Characters in Search of a Republic*, "must interpret the great man for himself and fit him in his own pattern." Cheech and Chong, for example, would focus on hemp production and marketing at Mount Vernon.

I can see why everybody who comes to Washington writes three volumes. A lot happened. It pains me to skip over so many hundreds of pages of his life.

I have oversimplified some aspects of the story, sometimes. I apologize. There are some complex subjects here. Whole books have been written, for example, about the Constitutional Convention and the ratification process alone. I will write other books about them, don't worry.

I also incorporate, by inference, all the good things said about George Washington already. I want to give him credit here for the things historians took away from him: his sense of humor, his way with wine, women, and song.

Part I

The Making of the General

Being the inspiring tale of how George Washington
ran for general without knowing it.

"24th . . . Do not laugh too much or too loud in publick."

—"George Washington's Rules of Civility & Decent Behaviour In
Company and Conversation."

[1]

The making of the prefident technically took place in New York on April 6, 1789, when they opened up the ballot box in the Electoral College and counted the votes. But it actually began in Philadelphia, in June 1775, at the Second Continental Congress. The shot heard around the world had been fired at Lexington on the nineteenth of April. The British had marched back to Boston from Concord, taking terrible losses on the road. Since April the king's army had been under siege in Boston. And now the delegates were debating the question of who might lead the rebel troops surrounding the regulars.

George Washington is one of sixty-three delegates, or congressmen, elected or appointed by the thirteen states. He is not a candidate for general in the election, which is to take place after the debate. He is sincere about it. George Washington, everybody knows, never told a lie. So far as he knows, he isn't running for anything.

But he's the one wearing the uniform. All of the other congressmen are in brown homespun or black. You couldn't miss him. He's the tall, quiet gent in the resplendent outfit, someone who is watching the proceeding would know. He is a real standout.

It's hot in Philadelphia in mid-June. Muggy. Just the kind of weather the Pennsylvania mosquitos love. They are as big as the *Mayflower*.

The moist heat is unbearable. Even the mosquitos sweat in eastern Pennsylvania. Instead of the bald eagle, there is talk that the national bird should be the mosquito. They come from New Jersey, William Penn explains.

It's very close in the State House where the session is taking place. It is one of Philadelphia's noblest buildings downtown, ranking with the Alms House, Pennsylvania Hospital, and the First National Trust Bank Building, founded by some of George Washington's political associates and cronies.

The tourists would come from miles away to visit the State House and watch their congressmen in action, if the meetings were open to the public.

There is no air-conditioning. The heat is miserable. But the windows are closed. So are the doors. The managers of the Congress have ordered the doors closed for secrecy purposes. The first order of business when the session opened on May 10 was closing the doors.

The second is electing a general.

The debates of the Second Congress involving the election of the nation's first commander-in-chief, the most powerful office in the land—the stepping stone to the prefidency—are secret, banned to the press. Those who would try to prevent the press from reporting the news in a democracy today are very much in keeping with the founding fathers' thoughts on open debate. Virtually all legislative sessions were secret. Open deals openly arrived at are not in the spirit of the revolution. Secret negotiations in closed, smoke-filled rooms are already the American way. Closed doors also make it easier to avoid a draugnt, or draft.

The tall, quiet, forty-three-year-old planter in the uniform is a congressman from the Fairfax district of Virginia. He is wearing the uniform of the Virginia militia. He is a colonel. All Virginia politician-planters are called colonel or major. While Washington was a veteran of the so-called French and Indian War,* the title had as much prestige then as "esquire" does today.

Colonel Washington, like many other military men, preferred to be addressed by his military title, from his middle twenties to the time of the revolution.[1] (I felt the same way as PFC Kitman.)

The Virginia delegation of seven was the most powerful in the Congress. It had the most celebrities, along with Massachusetts.

---

* The war's correct title should have been the English-French-German-Austrian-Russian-and-Indian War of 1756–1763, or the Great North American Fur War, since the rivalry in the fur trade is what the war was really about. Europeans call it "The Seven Years War."

And Colonel Washington had finished third or second (depending on who counted; there are several results that survive) in the votes in the House of Burgesses by-elections for the Congress. Second (or third) only to Peyton (Mr. Speaker) Randolph, with ninety-eight votes. He beat out Patrick Henry, with eighty-nine.

This was the colonel's second term in office, as he had served in the First Continental Congress in 1774. The Virginia delegation this year was loaded with political heavyweights, including Colonel Edmund Pendleton, Colonel Richard Bland, and Colonel Benjamin Harrison, early Mount Vernon machine members. It also contained such parliamentary tacticians and renowned orators as Patrick (Give Me Liberty) Henry and Richard Henry Lee, soon to be a rare political foe of Colonel Washington.

The floor of Congress this hot June was the big leagues of oratory, producing splendors the ear had not heard this side of the Oxford debating union. The most gifted fencers, fence sitters, and tightrope walkers, the nimblest wits and the longest-winded tested their mettle against the best in the colonies. It was the superbowl of politicks.

Colonel Washington was a man of few words in the wind tunnel. He sat quietly in his place throughout the Congress of 1774. He always sat quietly in Congress, a habit he developed in the House of Burgesses, the Virginia equivalent of the State Assembly. A collection of the wit and wisdom of George Washington compiled from the floor of Burgesses would have made a pamphlet as thick as one on the rights of slaves.

The hottest public speakers in the colonies, specializing in insurrection, propaganda, and political philosophy, were in the seats adjoining: Samuel Adams of Massachusetts, Patrick Henry of Virginia, and Christopher Gadsden of South Carolina. But Colonel Washington never got carried away by the heat of debate.

His remarks in the Congress of 1774 were limited to "Aye" and "Nay" and "Pass the snuff." He was quiet as a Chincoteague oyster. The silent role suited him. He didn't mind debate, having sat or slept through fifteen years of it in the House of Burgesses. It's just that he didn't participate in it. With barnburners like Patrick Henry and Richard Henry Lee he preferred to play the listener.

He was not that eloquent on the stump anyway. Even on the low-pressured local Assembly level, he was no Cicero. His speaking voice was low and strained. His hands shook when he spoke. He stammered like Moses. It's a good thing they didn't have TV.

The Virginia House of Burgesses in 1758 passed a resolution commending Washington, then serving his first term in office, for his military expeditions to the West. All the best families in Virginia were in the galleries. They were to discover the freshman assemblyman's unique rhetorical style. An eyewitness recalled: "He rose to express his acknowledgement for the honor, but such was his trepidation and confusion, that he could not give distinct utterance to a single syllable. He blushed, stammered, and trembled, for a second; when the speaker relieved him . . . 'Sit down, Mr. Washington,' said he with a conciliating smile, 'your modesty is equal to your valor, and that surpasses the power of any language that I possess.' " [2]

Washington's skill as a politician was patience. He knew how to just sit there. He was never stampeded into saying something stupid, like other politicians. By never saying anything, he didn't make enemies. He didn't get distracted into areas which may have been above his head and he didn't know about: natural laws, or philosophies of government. When he had nothing to say, he said nothing, which was virtually all the time.

Whereas John Adams disliked the debates, the "nibbling and quibbling" as he called all the humble petitioning to the king, Colonel Washington may have liked it.

George Washington bore well the unbearable humid heat of the Philadelphia summer with its attendant yellow fever and smallpox, which had arrived with the delegates from New Jersey, or so the city fathers implied. But when others in the Virginia delegation in 1774—Henry, et al.—rushed back to Virginia to the House of Burgesses in the last days of the session, it was Colonel Washington who stayed on to the dreary end in Philadelphia. He held the fort, so to speak. He was, for all we know, a parliamentary procedure buff, a *Robert's Rules of Order* freak.

Or he loved Philadelphia in August.

[2]

Delegate Washington had sat quietly in his place during the First Continental Congress of '74. "No committee assignment or even presidential nods" came his way, as Colonel Freeman put it. He was a silent partner in all the congressional debates about this or that, neither resolving this or that publicly. He was shrewdly keeping his options open and his mouth closed.

Up to this point Washington's political career had been lackluster. He hadn't made a splash in the Virginia House of Burgesses during his fifteen years there. He had managed to win a seat in the House of Burgesses from Frederick County in 1758. His major recorded assignment seemed to have been on a committee to draft a law forbidding hogs to run at large in Winchester.[3]

He went to the First Congress a political nonentity and sat in courteous attention. He had heard all the debates and humble petitions and remonstrances of His Majesty's royal subjects. When the journal of the proceedings was printed, he was a big zero, appearing only on the roster of members who attended and in the listing of credentials of Old Dominion representatives.

But on the fifth day of Congress II, wearing his uniform, he was named head of the military affairs subcommittee holding hearings on defense plans for New York City, should the theater of war shift from Boston. Members included the radical superstar Sam Adams of Massachusetts, Thomas Lynch of South Carolina, and all the New York delegates. Chairman-Colonel Washington's committee eventually reported out six commonsense resolves about what to do about Manhattan, not including selling it back to the Indians.

Washington hadn't had any committee assignments until he started wearing that uniform. Whatever motivated his choice of dress, it was a smart move politically. Colonel Washington must have intuitively known how Americans love a uniform.

[3]

He was wearing his old French and Indian War (1756–1763) uniform, which he had hung up in mothballs sixteen years previously—the blue coat with red facing of the First Virginia Regiment, which he led into battle.

Colonel Freeman insists he was wearing the red and blue uniform of the First Virginia "not to remind of his soldier's background for his career was famous." It was an act, Colonel Freeman says, "as if to signify to his fellow-Delegates that he believed the time had come to take to the field." [4] But here was an ambitious young politician wearing his old army uniform to Congress among all those civilians. It was a most unusual occurrence, all political analysts would agree. Sort of like seeing "Tail Gunner Joe" McCarthy campaigning in his Air Force uniform in the 1948 Wisconsin senatorial campaign. Or Congressman Richard Nixon conducting a House Un-American Activities Committee hearing wearing his old naval Lieutenant Commander Junior Grade uniform.

He had worn this uniform only one other time—when he posed for his first portrait. This is the famous portrait of him done in 1772 by Charles Willson Peale. It's his earliest-known likeness on canvas, the one with the sword and the goget (a gilt, crescent-shaped badge suspended around the neck to indicate that the wearer was an officer, in case an enemy sharpshooter didn't know). All British officers had those two things in their portraits above the mantels and fireplaces at the family manse. But Washington's portrait also has a rifle in the background, a prop not found in the portraits of British officers of the period, who had muskets. The rifle indicated that the man being portrayed was a man of war, a little touch that would warm the hearts of media consultants today, if they had hearts. You know the one: The portrait with the hand in the tunic, like Napoleon. Peale, the Philadelphia painter, was living in Annapolis at the time. He was the fashionable painter of the hour. Everybody was sitting for him. Washington had Martha and her children, Jackie and Patsy Custis, sit too.

Perhaps there was no significance in the fact that when it came time to pose for his first portrait in 1772 he dressed himself up as a soldier. As a Tidewater planter, he could have posed with a whip or with a boot on the head of a slave. He could have been sitting around smoking tobacco or hemp. Catching or pickling herring or grinding flour were his major activities at Mount Vernon in the prewar years. So it was odd: here was a man who had put his uniform away forever after the so-called French and Indian War, when he retired to his vineyards and fig trees and his Martha. And he suddenly puts on his uniform for a portrait, the same one that he later wears to congressional sessions?

There is a look of self-consciousness in the Peale portrait that has puzzled historians. "His own embarrassment in posing gave him a measure of self-consciousness," Colonel Freeman says. It could be said that his 1772 portrait was Washington's first campaign expenditure, as his ledger indicates:

May 30.
By Mr. Peale Painter, Drawg. my Picte. £18. 4s.

Minature........*Do. for Mrs. W*   *£13.*
Ditto..........*Do. for Miss Custis*   *£13.*
Ditto..........*Do. for Mr. Custis*   *£13.*[5]

He got the family rate.

Perhaps Washington had a uniform fetish. He loved to design fancy uniforms and the accoutrements—that is, fashion accessories. It was a form of relaxation, like young girls who doodled the latest fashion creations in their schoolbooks. He designed the First Virginia Regiment uniform that he wore in Congress. When he commanded the Continental Army he designed special *ribbands* distinguishing rank in this man's army.*

His favorite indoor sport was shopping for clothes, or "cloaths," as he often spelled it.

On the other side [of a letter to his merchants in London about the political situation of the Cherokees in Virginia] is an invoice of clothes, . . . which I beg the favor of you to purchase for me, and to send them by the first ship bound to

---

* As Colonel Freeman described the fashion orders of the day: "The commander-in-chief, he announced, was to wear 'a light blue ribband . . . across his breast between his coat and waistcoat.' For the brigadiers and the major generals a pink ribband was prescribed. The badge of staff officers was green.[6] As of July 25, the pink ribband was restricted to the brigadiers. The major generals were assigned a purple.[7] Field and company officers were to be distinguished by cockades of different colors, noncommissioned officers by a strip of colored cloth on the right shoulder."[8]

this river. As they are designed to wearing-apparel for myself, I have committed the choice of them to your fancy, having the best opinion of your taste. I want neither lace nor embroidery. Plain clothes, with a gold or silver button, (if worn in genteel dress,) are all I desire . . . I enclose a measure, and, for a further insight, I dont think it amiss to add, that my stature is six feet; otherwise rather slender than corpulent.

There then followed a most astonishing list of additions to his wardrobe, which left no doubt in his London merchants' minds that they were dealing with the Liberace of the Potomac. "Half a dozen pair of Men's neatest shoes, and Pumps, to be made by one Didsbury, on Colo. Baylor's last—but a little larger than his—and to have high heels—" he wrote on May 1, 1759. "Never more make any of Dog leather except one pair of Pumps in a Cargoe unless you send better leather than they were made of before—for the two pairs of Shoes scarcely lasted me twice as many days & had very fair wearing," he complained in a follow-up letter of November 30, 1759.[9]

Yes sir, Colonel Washington was very clothes-conscious in those days. The revolutionary radical rebel was a slave to fashion.

His fondness for fine clothing went beyond his own wardrobe. Not long after his marriage, he asked for

1 salmon colored tabby [a soft plain velvet or silk] velvet of the enclosed pattern, with satin flowers to be made in a sack and coat.
1 cap, handkerchief tucker, and ruffles, to be made of Brussels lace on Point, proper to be worn with the above negligee, to cost twenty pounds.

Also in this order were "1 doz. most fashionable cambric pocket handkerchiefs," "1000 minikins," "8 lbs. perfumed powder," and "2 handsome breastflowers." The above items were for his wife, I hope.

[4]

C olonel Washington had displayed his love of uniforms twenty years before when he rode to Boston in 1756 to see Governor Shirley, the royal governor of Massachusetts who was serving as commander in chief of all the British forces in America after the death of General Braddock.

Washington had been involved in a fight with a Maryland captain who had a royal commission, which was then superior to a provincial commission like Washington's. The thousand miles to Boston to press the flesh with Governor Shirley was a long ride for a colonel to take to get even with a Maryland captain. Being a second-class officer was an open wound, a feeling of inferiority that festered.

Accompanying the twenty-three-year-old colonel on the trip were his aides-de-camp, Captain Mercer and Captain Stewart, and two servants. But it was Washington that eyewitness reporters talked about on his first military invasion of Boston in the dead of winter. It was the accessories that got them.

The colonel was wearing your basic white silk uniform, garnished with stockings of white silk with silver knee buckles and silver buckles on the shoes. The former surveyor and backwoodsman had added to the white linen stock around his neck a contraption of lace ruffles—the thing that women of the period called a jabot. It was pinned, fashion trend spotters of the day might have noted, so that it flowed over his bosom like a modern ascot. His long hair was drawn tightly back in a queue enclosed in a silk bag. To complete the military ensemble, on the shoulders he wore a cloak—one side white, the other scarlet. Over his large hands, as big as shovels, fell cuffs of white lace.[10]

Maybe Governor Shirley didn't like the colors of Washington's attendants' scarves. Maybe he should have worn the simple red and blue. But the colonel's dream of advancement in the British army did not come true. The Yankee Doodle Dandy had a long ride home.

[5]

H istorians have always said there was nothing significant about Congressman Washington wearing his uniform as the Congress debated who should be commander in chief. "His uniform cried out like a bugle," writes Colonel Flexner, "but there was nothing flamboyant about the man." [11] Had he put it on by mistake? You know how you wake up early some mornings and put on one blue sock and one brown sock. Maybe his brown homespun suit was at the cleaner's. But he apparently wore the uniform every day from his arrival in Philadelphia, on May 24, to June 15. As Colonel Freeman says, "The uniform was meant to symbolize his belief that it was time to stop jawboning with the British and take to the field." It was a radical political statement. "He was known to have been slow in accepting this conclusion that armed resistance was necessary," adds Colonel Flexner.

I'm sure there was nothing significant about the uniform. Sure, it made him stand out among the drab civilians. But it was no more unusual than Colonel North's wearing his military uniform during the Iran-Contrascam hearing in 1987. Each was consistent in his own way. George Washington never told a lie, and North apparently never told the truth. Not that he lied, he just "misspoke" or had "the wrong version of the facts," as they called it.

[6]

I n the halls of Congress that session, everybody was talking about how the tall, quiet planter in the uniform had offered to raise a small army of men at his own expense and rush them to the relief of Boston, occupied now by the ministerial troops under General Gage. The story had the ring of authenticity. Everybody knew he was the richest man in Virginia. Word of mouth described him as such. A regiment was a petty-cash expenditure to a rich man.

In those days being rich was not the handicap it is today. The Congress, which later passed a declaration of independence with high-minded words about equality, felt no general could command the respect of either his own soldiers or his enemy unless he had an independent income and social prestige. Like most plantation owners, Washington had met payrolls. They were the only Americans at the time with the managerial ability and experience in giving orders and catering for hundreds. Money talked in 1775, and George Washington was a master of nonverbal communication.

There was Colonel Washington, the congressional grapevine said, who by making the offer to finance his own private army had shown that he was ready to risk everything he had striven so hard to build. The squire of Mount Vernon was making a declaration of open rebellion. The offer to field his own army left a golden halo around Washington's powdered head.

The only thing wrong with the scenario was that he never said it, or meant it, or remembered saying it the next morning. The story was totally unfounded.

Who said it then? Nobody quite knew. It was the rumor of the year. Among the operators of the rumor mill was a congressman named Silas Deane, who wrote to his wife in Wethersfield, Connecticut, "It is said that in a House of Burgesses in Virginia on hearing of the Boston Port Bill, he offered to raise an army and lead one thousand men himself, at his own expense, for the defense of the country, were there need of it. His fortune is said to be equal of such an undertaking." [12]

Deane was a shrewd operator in Congress. As one of the earliest members of the Washington for general campaign committee, he was rewarded by being appointed member of the country's first embassy to France, where he became involved in speculation and misuse of public funds, and he is generally hailed as one of the founding political crooks of Connecticut.

A South Carolina congressman, Thomas Lynch, seems to have been the original bearer of the apocryphal thousand-man-army tale, which preceded Washington to the First Continental Congress. Mr. Lynch of South Carolina, who now, coincidentally, was serving with Colonel Washington on the armed services committee, claimed to have heard Washington make the offer in the

House of Burgesses. "He told us that Colonel Washington made the most eloquent speech at the Virginian Convention that ever was made," recalled John Adams, the congressman from Braintree, Massachusetts. "Says he [Lynch], who heard it on Aug. 31, 'I will raise one thousand men, submit them at my own expense and march myself at their head for the relief of Boston.' " [13]

The rumor of course was absurd. But John Adams, the leader of the Massachusetts delegation, believed it—or wanted to. He declared Washington's statement to be "sublime, pathetic, beautiful . . . the most eloquent speech that had ever been made in Virginia or anywhere." [14] And if a shrewd Yankee trader and lawyer like John Adams believed it, you can imagine how common people took it when it filtered down to them.

Adams is the only contemporary who recorded Lynch's report of the speech. Others might have discounted it as campaign oratory on the part of the South Carolinian, a known friend of Colonel Washington's and a first-generation member of the Mount Vernon machine.

The story was a real plus to Washington's campaign, a thousand pounds' worth of sterling publicity for him as a military leader. It told people he was rich, if they needed any reminder after just looking at him. He *was* rich. But this made him seem *really* rich. And rich knocked their socks off in the old days.

For the pro-Washington forces, the rumor was a brilliant stroke. It gave the Washington bandwagon momentum. Almost as effective as the uniform in making him noticeable.

It was a story people could relate to. As Patrick Henry said privately to two of his friends (on the second day of May 1774): "You may in vain talk to [the people] about the duties on tea, et cetera. These things will not affect them. They depend on principles, too abstracted for their apprehension and feeling. But tell them of the robbery of the magazine, and that the next step will be to disarm them, you bring the subject home to their bosoms, and they will be ready to fly to arms to defend themselves." [15]

The Washington forces knew their people. This alleged one-thousand-man army was an offer they couldn't refuse. It was either, as Dr. Sigmund Freud would later put it, an illusion of what we wanted to hear, or it was the first planted story in the media in behalf of a noncandidate or a candidate in the race for general—and prefident.

But I'm sure Washington had nothing to do with it. It was his friends' media hoax. They saw in George Washington someone they could use.

Hoax or misstatement of the truth, as we call it today, whatever it was, it couldn't have been better timed. One thousand men and it didn't cost him a thin shilling.

[7]

I t certainly gained him the limelight. The biggest celebrities of the political world were in Philadelphia these nights—Patrick Henry of Virginia, Edward Rutledge and Christopher Gadsden of South Carolina, and the Adams boys, John and his distant cousin, the mad, radical Samuel. But the hottest superstar of the season, the most talked about, the most prized and most desired at a dinner table, was Colonel Washington.

The man who had offered to arm and send a one-thousand-man army to Boston at his own expense was asked by everybody where he stood, or sat, on the issues.

At dinner that May, everybody was asking him what he thought of foreign affairs. Fashionable women behind fans, who had fought with their hostesses to be seated next to him at their lavish tables, dames, ladies, the most beautiful women in all Philadelphia, with their breasts hanging out in the current fashion, with fluttering and fans atwitter, were now asking, "Pray tell, Colonel Washington, what of the intolerable acts? . . . Will there be war? . . ." They now were turned to him for enlightenment.

His answers are not recorded in his diaries or journals. Probably he said, "No comment . . . I'll have a statement to make about that later."

What was Colonel Washington doing at these parties? What all the other sixty-two congressmen were doing—playing politicks.

This obscure assemblyman was establishing and strengthening political friendships with men of the other states. He was often seen having cheesesteaks and hoagies with Chase of Maryland, Alsop of New York, the Delaware politicians Caesar Rodney and George Read. He dined with Archibald Bulloch, who controlled the convict vote in Georgia, and Richard Henry Lee and Benjamin Harrison, a cross-section of Virginia politics. Lee was a slowly rising political foe. Harrison was among his oldest political cronies, a leader of the Mount Vernon machine at this stage.

"May 30," he wrote in his journal. "Dined at Mr. Mease's and after setting a while with the Boston gentleman, returned to my own room." The gentleman from Boston was John Adams. Some speculated that he wanted Washington's autograph for Abigail. Others were saying Adams was hatching a plot. He had a smart idea: He'd back George Washington to block the egotistical John Hancock, who had aspirations to be general. [16]

And on June 19, the last entry in the journal after the election for general took place, there is this: "Dined at Colo. Reid's. Spent the Evening at Mr. Lynch's."

Mr. Lynch, the delegate from South Carolina, was the man who had told John Adams the amazing story of Colonel Washington's offer to furnish and lead a thousand-man private army to the relief of Boston.

"He ate with people more than once only four times," explained Colonel Freeman about the master diner, Washington in Philadelphia for the Second Congress from May 10 to June 15. This shows if he was not politicking, he at least didn't have to come up with new table talk.

The colonel's favorite smoke-filled room, the tap room of the stars, was the City Tavern on Market Street, a brief walk or stagger away from the State House, to which many of the delegates regularly repaired after a long day's debate on the floor.

He had been a habitué of taverns since his days as a Virginia politician. Following his election as a Burgess in 1758, he became a regular at Anthony Hays's Raleigh Tavern. Located in downtown Williamsburg, the Raleigh Tavern (known also as Southall's) was probably built in 1735, and was the unofficial seat, or bar stool, of the legislature. The House of Burgesses, the Governor's Council (upper house), and the courts were located down the street. Here gathered all the big Whigs and earwigs of Virginia politics. They actually held sessions of the Burgesses in the Raleigh Tavern's Apollo Room, when the royal governor locked the Burgesses out. A Windsor chair, or bar stool, could be named after Burgess Washington in the Apollo Room in honor of his faithful years spent in attendance there.

He was also a regular at the Rising Sun Tavern in his mom's town, Fredericksburg, not far from the home ("Cherry Tree

Acres") where he confessed his inability to tell a lie, according to the official posthumous campaign biographer, Parson Weems, and near the Rappahannock, across which he is said to have thrown a Spanish dollar. It was one of the legendary feats his media people told about him, but I find it hard to believe Washington would ever throw money away. It was probably a book.

The keeper of the Rising Sun Tavern, George Weedon, strangely enough, wound up in the Continental Army during the war as a general. It didn't hurt to have connections.

The Apollo Room at the Raleigh was Washington's spiritual headquarters, so to speak, his political base, where he grew from an inexperienced country boy in the back rooms to one of the shrewdest of political operators. The room saw also the beginnings of the Revolution. Washington and others gathered there as eagerly to plot defiance of Parliament as to revel with the belles, play cards, or toss off the innumerable toasts of a banquet. Doctor Tyler says of the Apollo, "This ancient room saw, at one time or another, all that was brilliant and graceful in the Virginia society of the eighteenth century."

Philadelphia was a big tavern town. "As early as 1752," Bridenbaugh says, "one hundred and twenty licensed taverns did business in the city and their number increased steadily until the outbreak of the war. There was a public house to suit every price and every taste." [17]

A politician might run into a real cross section of hands to shake in a Philadelphia tavern. They were usually frequented "with a very mixed company of different nations and religions," recorded Dr. Alexander Hamilton in his *Itinerarium* in 1744. "There were Scots, English, Dutch, Germans, and Irish; there were Roman Catholicks, Churchmen, Presbyterians, Quakers, Newlighters, Methodists, Seventh daymen, Moravians, Anabaptists, and one Jew," gathered in "a great hall well stocked with flies. The company was divided into committees in conversation." Daytimes, hundreds of Philadelphians had their tea or brewskis at the London Coffee House at Front and Market streets, opened by William Bradford in 1764, which served as a general clearinghouse for business, news, and gossip, and had for sale tickets for concerts, plays, lectures, and public events of all kinds. [18]

City Tavern, where George Washington most frequently bent an elbow, must have reminded him of his legislative roots at the Apollo. Daniel Smith's inn was furnished in the London mode "at great expence by a voluntary subscription of the principle gentleman of the city" so that it was "by much the largest and most elegant house occupied that way in America." The candles were lighted in darkened wainscoted rooms. Daniel Smith's decorators did his walls with brass sconces, highly polished, in which a colonel interested in his appearance could check to see if his uniform needed straightening. The cuisine at the City Tavern featured baked oysters served hot in their shells. There were big piles of shells in the tavern's corners. The service was as good as a Tidewater planter could expect. Black waiters, it is said, appeared as if by magic at the diner's least gesture. The air was full of tobacco smoke and politics, of news and gossip; the tavern was the power place, the hot center, "where it was at" in the nation's capital-in-exile.

The City Tavern during the Continental Congresses of 1774 and 1775 is where the practice of a businessman buying a congressman a dinner for future favors began. All the important locals made it their business to be sitting at the City Tavern when Congress was in session: the city fathers like the mayor of Philadelphia, Sam Powel; the power brokers like stable owner Jacob Hiltzenheimer; the businessmen who had something to sell or buy; Philadelphia lawyers; the influence peddlers and lobbyists; and various other Michael Deavers of the day.

And what balls they had at the City Tavern. Once, during the First Continental Congress, they had a dinner for five hundred at Daniel Smith's nightery. It was called "An Entertainment Given by the City to the Members of Congress." The blow-out included a march to the State House and back, before a feast that would kill one of Jake Hiltzenheimer's wagon horses.

And according to the *Philadelphia Journal* of September 21, 1774, "More than two score toasts were proposed." Other sources say it was thirty-six toasts (including tributes to the King, the Queen, the Prince of Wales, and "The Perpetual Union of the Colonies"—that is, a perpetual union with England).[19]

Who knew what up to thirty-six glasses of wine might do to the average congressman.

[8]

We might as well discuss Washington's drinking, even though it wasn't an issue in the noncampaign for the generalship. He occasionally took a drink, but never more than a quart or two of Madeira at dinner—besides rum, punch, and beer chasers. A whiskey distiller himself, he preferred Madeira to all other beverages, but he often drank cider, champagne, brandy and vin ordinaire at dinner as well, especially after the French alliance, when surplus wine flowed into this country as tea had under British mercantilism. The amount of drinking done by people during the early days of our history is staggering. A visitor in pre-Revolutionary War Philadelphia, which still has blue laws today, kept a record in his diary of an average day's alcohol consumption: "Given cider and punch for lunch; rum and brandy before dinner; punch, Madeira, port and sherry at dinner, punch and liqueurs with the ladies; and wine, spirit and punch till bedtime, all in punch bowls big enough for a goose to swim in." [20]

During one arduous seventeen-hour, sixty-six-mile trip across Virginia, Rorabaugh says, "the stage stopped ten times, and two of the passengers had drinks at each way station: ten drinks apiece. Such habits led one foreign observer to conclude that the American stage coach stops every five miles to water the horses and *brandy the gentlemen*." *[21]

John Tower would have been right at home in this period.

Our founding fathers must have been in a state of active fermentation in colonial times getting bombed, smashed, plastered, cockadoodledooed, or whatever they called it.

Drinking had more stature in the colonial period than it does today among the Daughters of the American Revolution. It was neither a furtive sin nor a pastime. "It was sort of an athletic sport," as one historian put it. Private David How told the story of two macho Continental Army men at Cambridge who fell to kid-

---

* One wonders why there was so much publicity about tea parties in the papers of 1773–74. The media hype over the landing of some surplus tea by the East India Company, which eventually was landed in the waters of Boston Harbor by political action groups of the day such as the Sons of Liberty, was so extraordinary, one would think the Rum Distillers Lobby was trying to make it a politically seditious act to drink tea.

ding one another as to who could drink the most. This led to excessive drinking, from which one of the men died in an hour or two.[22] He must have been otherwise in poor health. Our forefathers were rated as one-bottle men or two-bottle men. Three-bottle men were looked up to with the reverence we show these days for astronauts and Pat Robertson.

Drinking increased on election days.

Colonel Washington learned early in his political career that the saloon vote was critical in American elections. In his first election in the summer of 1757, he lost. That's when he was dry. He served no liquor to the constituents. There were three candidates, and he finished a very bad third. (Out of 581 voters only 40 voted for him.)

Washington rarely made the same mistake twice, except as a general in battle. In his next election he resolved that it should be as convivial as it need be.

During the July 1758 election in Frederick County—the turning point of his political career—he received 301 votes to win his seat, and by his account books we know exactly what the election cost him:

	£	s	d
To 40 gallons of Rum Punch @ 3/6 pr. galn	7	0	0
15 gallons of Wine @ 10/0 pr. galn	7	10	0
Dinner for your friends	3	0	0
13½ gallons of Wine @ 10/	6	15	0
3½ pts. of Brandy @ 1/3		4	4½
13 Galls. Beer @ 1/3		16	3
8 qts. Cyder Royl. @ 1/6		12	0
Punch		3	9
30 gallns. of strong beer @ 8 d. pr. gall.	1	0	0
1 hhd. & 1 Barrell of Punch, consisting of			
26 gals. best Barbadoes rum, 5/—	6	10	0
12½ lbs. S. Refd. Sugar 1/6		18	9
6 galls. best Madeira Wine 10/—	3	0	0
3 galls. and 3 quarts of Beer @ 1/pr gall.		3	9
10 Bowls of Punch @ 2/6 each	1	5	0
9 half pints of rum @ 7½ each		5	7½
1 pint of wine		1	6

Charles S. Sydnor in *American Revolutionaries in the Making: Political Practices in Washington's Virginia* calculated that during that historic 1758 election, George Washington's agents supplied 160 gallons—28 gallons of rum, 50 gallons of rum punch, 34 gallons of wine, 46 gallons of beer, and 2 gallons of cider royal—to 391 voters and "unnumbered hangers on." This amounted to more than a quart and a half per voter.

This expense for "entertainment" did not shock Washington, Hughes says. The lucky candidate said his only fear was that his campaign manager, Colonel James Wood, "spent with too sparing a hand"; and he hoped that "all had enough." Evidently, as Hughes says, all had more than enough, for there was a grand rally after the election and the rum punch did its work so well that Colonel Wood, as Washington's proxy, was picked up on the shoulders of his partisans and carried about the town "in the midst of a general applause and huzzahing for Colonel Washington." [23]

Immediately after, if not immediately because of, the drunken hilarity following Washington's election, the House of Burgesses passed a law disqualifying any candidate from holding his seat who should "before his election, either himself or by any other person or persons on his behalf and at his charge, directly or indirectly give, present or allow any person or persons having voice or vote in such election any money, meat, drink, entertainment, or provision, or make any present, gift, reward, or entertainment, &c., &c., in order to be elected." [24]

So much for those who say Washington accomplished nothing in the way of legislation.

But this didn't prevent him from breaking the law, either, for the next fifteen years.

Alcohol was a "household necessarie," as he described extensive purchases of Madeira and other spirits in his account books. It was good for his health, he claimed. He had numerous scientific theories. The imbibing of certain alcoholic beverages, he explained, caused stomach aches and diarrhea. "Nothing is more pernicious to the health of soldiers, nor more certainly productive of the bloody flux," he reported, "than new cider."

Washington, the health nut, was really into Madeira, which he took as vitamin C. Madeira was a status drink in colonial days, in the category of champagne: Then, as now, it was an imported wine from the island of Madeira, off the Moroccan coast in the Atlantic. It lacks the bouquet of Shenandoah Mountain White Lightning, but it still packs power for a wine.

He does not seem to have been into vintages. In his letters to merchants, he asked for "Old Madeira" from "the best house." Connoisseurs usually ask for specific vineyards (Terrantez), or a specific year (a '69 Cossart Servial Solera or a '53 Blandy Malmsey Solera). But for Washington it was any Madeira, or sometimes port, in a storm.

According to his ledger, he went often to the liquor stores by mail. The ledgers include large and small payments ranging from the emergency purchase on March 5, 1767, of "1 Quart Whiskey 1s 3d." to the buying of a "pipe" of wine. A pipe, as Hughes explained, ranged from 110 gallons in the case of Madeira to 138 gallons in the case of port. A "butt" of wine was a somewhat similar measure, often confounded with "pipe" but likewise varying in amount according to the contents.

In 1765 he paid out:

Feb. By Mr. Searle for a Pipe of Madeira   £29. 3s
    By Maynes of Lisbon for Wine   £12. 7s
    By Mr. Searles Excha to A. Bacon
      for Pipe M: Wine   £28. 12

The next year he paid:

for a Butt of Madeira wine   £37: 14s 1

On September 3, 1767, he paid Henry Hinton:

for 1 Hhd Rum   £17. 2. 10

In 1768:

for a Butt of Ma Wine   £37: 6: 11

His orders to his merchant in London invariably included "a pipe" [87 bottles] or two of "the best Lisbon" wine, "the rich oily Madeira," as he described it, even when money was a little tight. It was the staff of life.

"Have some Madeira, my dear?" was his trademark, long before Flanders and Swann sang that song.

There were those in Philadelphia who, like John Ross (an attorney, the uncle-in-law of seamstress Betsy Ross, who falsely got credit for designing a flag later on), "loved ease and Madeira much better than liberty and strife," and declared for neutrality in the war, the roar of which (in 1775) had started with Concord and Lexington. Others, like George Washington, could have their Madeira and revolution too.

[9]

Man did not live by Madeira alone in the Philadelphia of 1775. He also danced.

Dancing was the earliest form of campaigning in the colonial period. It was a way of working the room, as we call it today, a way of pressing the flesh, if it is touch dancing the politician is doing. It was an effective way to meet the voters, even if most of the people Washington danced with were women, who, along with blacks, Catholics, Jews, and nonlandholders, didn't vote. But he didn't hold that against them. It shows you how apolitical he was. On the dance floor, Washington rose above mere partisanship.

By day the colonel was sitting in the rebel Congress that was in the process of overthrowing King George and by night he was undermining British tyranny by dancing. It was his second-favorite indoor sport, next to cracking walnuts between his fingers after dinner.

Dancing was something he learned as a teenager, one of the important social graces in Virginia, along with drinking and compounding interest. All the children of the best families learned dancing in Virginia, even on the rawest edges of the frontier. It was the custom for a number of families to engage a teacher and to give a series of house parties, in turn, with all the dancing pupils (Washington called them "scholars"). Colonel Washington had a special tutor for his stepson, Jackie, a Reverend Boucher, who was hired to teach reading, writing, and dancing.

Washington frequently mentions in his papers and letters his commitment to this form of education. Mount Vernon must have been a lively place, with half a dozen girls and their beaux piling in for a few days of wild romping under the name of scholarship. As Hughes says, the colonel often stood and peeked at them through a half-opened door, but he retired if he found that his presence checked their hilarity. They learned jigs and hugging dances as well as prim minuets, and the lessons were followed by kissing games.

The dance Colonel Washington loved most was the minuet. He was one of the Minuetmen, those rebels who were always available at any time of night or day to dance a minuet. But he was not against a gavotte or a Virginia jig, either.

He cut quite a rug and figure on the dance floor in his size 13 (EE) canal boots, very fitting for the future chief executive of the Potomac Canal Company. His large feet were in contrast to Martha's, which were said to be the tiniest appendages in the colonies. Opposites do attract.

Although clerics in early Massachusetts had denounced "Gynecandrical Dancing" (that is, jointly by the sexes) as a satanic invention, Schlesinger says, "Few people heeded this warning, since the Bible itself cited the practice without disapproval." [25]

There was nothing immoral about dancing per se. For Colonel Washington it was a form of physical expression and exercise— "Probably," according to Colonel James Flexner, "without much of any emotional or esthetic effect"—like a session at Jack LaLanne's. You could smell the sweat pouring off the athletes of the ballroom as they did their daily forty, gynecandrically whipping their pure minds and bodies into new levels of sexual disinterest.

[10]

John Adams, the Puritan from Braintree, Massachusetts, was always writing home about the appalling working conditions in Philadelphia. "A most sinful feast again" he wrote bitterly to his wife Abigail in one of his famous "Dear Abby" letters, ". . . curds and creams, jellies, sweetmeats of various sorts . . . whipped syllabubs . . . turtle and every other thing, flummery . . . Wines most excellent and admirable. I drank Madeira at a great rate." [26]

But George Washington never complained. Philadelphia, with its heavy diet of dinners and balls, drinking, dancing, and tavern-hopping, was George Washington's kind of town.

Philadelphia was the fastest-growing "matrapolis," as he spelled it, in the colonies: The population rose from 13,000 in 1740 to 22,000 in 1760, and had reached 40,000 by 1776. Bristol, then the second-largest city in England, boasted, give or take a few

Englishmen, a population of less than 36,000, according to Bridenbaugh in *Rebels and Gentlemen*, while Edinburgh and Dublin were only slightly larger: "Thus it is probably, as nearly as we can deduce from the imperfect statistics of the 18th century, that on the eve of the American Revolution, Philadelphia ranked as the second largest city of the British empire, surpassed only by the metropolis of London, itself."

The population explosion was accompanied by a building explosion. In 1776, as a result of almost continuous building, a careful count listed 6,057 dwelling houses and 287 warehouses, shops, and business establishments, most of which Colonel Washington had visited or would visit.

In the sixties, the streets began to be paved. In 1771, the Reverend Jacob Duche, who was to be the chaplain of the Congress and a Quaker City booster, spoke about the tree-lined streets which were "all well paved in the middle for carriages and . . . a footpath of hard bricks on each side next to houses. On the thoroughfare some 500 pumps supplied citizens with their water."

No colonial community had such a wonderful press. From the days of William Penn, downtrodden peasants of the German Palatinate and squeezed-by-the-laird Scotch-Irishmen had been flooded with "come to Pennsylvania" literature. By the 1770s it had all the hype of New York and L.A. combined, a city of the arts, the good life-style, the rich and famous, celebrities in commerce, arts, sciences, culture, Franklin's hometown, the best food and taverns, and anything else a country boy from the three-horse towns of Virginia could desire.

Philadelphia was founded by William Penn in 1682 as "His Holy Experiment." A master of the soft sell, Penn promoted his new town in brochures he circulated in many languages across Europe with modest claims rather than overstatement. Its major attraction: It would be a plain place. The checkerboard city plan was the model of simplicity. To the Lancaster farmers who halted their Conestoga wagons to gawk at Christ Church downtown, however, Philadelphia in the mid-eighteenth century must have seemed the quintessence of beauty and glitz or unplainness.

The pleasure capital of the colonies, as many historians say, was indolent in its leisure. The wealthy played cards with great decorum. In the drawing rooms, crystal bowls of rum and punch stood all day long awaiting any casual caller. The great ladies flirted by means of fans and handkerchiefs. On walks through the streets, they were followed by black slave boys of all ages carrying toilet cases, bonbon boxes, and an extra wrap. Inside Philadelphia houses, the rooms were lined with damask and pictures of the Fall of Troy, the candlelight, reflected by the multitude of mirrors, falling on white powdered heads bent in kissing obeisance over ladies' delicate hands.

Thomas Jefferson, who as a student at the College of William and Mary used to share the dance floor with Colonel Washington in the power Apollo Room of the Raleigh Tavern in Williamsburg, regarded Philadelphia as "a sink of iniquity." In the opinion of others, it was "a den."

[11]

Philadelphia is considered a joke today. First prize is one week in Philadelphia; second prize is two weeks. But in the 1770s nobody laughed at Philadelphia.

Your average plutocrat with monarchist leanings could really feel at home in Philadelphia. It was a genteel place with a life-style calling for city mansions and country homes, where one assembled libraries and art collections, attended playhouses and musicals, sat for portraits. As Bridenbaugh says, "All these efforts had as their ultimate objective the fastening of English standards of taste upon the aristocratic life of eastern Pennsylvania." [27] Philadelphia had the highest number of the idle rich, the snobbish, the indulgent in every extravagance of any city in America.

It was also the most decadent of the American cities, the Paris of British North America, the capital of dissipation, the center of licentiousness, the home of sensuality. There was concern about the decline in morality in American cities in 1775, as there is today. Philadelphian society, with its crowded card tables, drinking feasts, oyster parties, and excursions to horse races, balls, and the theaters, was the origin of all vice. It was denounced then by the moral minority in the same terms that were used by the puritans in ancient Assyria, Greece, and Rome, and in old England and New England.

[12]

Philadelphia was also the Las Vegas of the East, a gambling center known to attract every card shark and sucker along the Eastern seaboard out of the water. A man who had been known to enjoy a hand of cards from time to time at taverns might find glorious opportunities to whist the night away in Philadelphia Deuce Tray, Pa.

Next to social climbing, George Washington's favorite indoor sport was playing cards. He was known to like an occasional card game. Sometimes twice a day. That is why he was able to refer to himself as "a moderate" gambler. He didn't play only at the Raleigh. During the legislative session of 1774, when the Boston Port Bill and other Intolerable Acts were setting the country on fire, Washington played at Anderson's and ten or fifteen other places (taverns as well as private homes), including his Masonic lodge in Williamsburg, always apparently for money, all of which he wrote down in his journal. He seemed to have played cards on anything that had four legs.

He was known to have played a few hands on the road to Williamsburg, too. There is lore in Fredericksburg that Washington fought many an engagement by dawn's early light with the local card sharks at Weedon's Rising Sun Tavern. And he always knew exactly where he stood when Weedon and the other innkeepers blew out the candles, put the cat out, and went home. He wrote it all down in his Filofax.

Like baseball fans today who keep statistics, Washington had a page in his Ledger B titled "Cards and other Play." The games are listed like a baseball team's schedule, with entries for Mount Vernon ("home") and Williamsburg, Fredericksburg, Annapolis, Alexandria, and so forth ("away").

Analysis of the general's record at cards shows that he won twenty-seven times and lost thirty-six times. With that losing record in games, he did well to come out ahead in the profit and loss column, which is where it counts in gambling. At home his record was 5-13; away, 22-23.*

---

* For those who don't trust statistics and would rather cut the cards themselves, so to speak, the general's record in his own hand follows.

Washington's Own Account of His
(From Ledger B

Cards—& other—Play—D.[TS]

1772						
Feby.	28	To Cash lost at Fredericksburg	.3.	2	3	6
Mar.	2	To Ditto lost in Williamsburg	.3.	. . . . . .	8	9
	13	To Ditto lost in Ditto	.3.	1	0	0
	16	To Ditto . . . . Ditto	.3.	3	10	—
	17	To Ditto . . . . Ditto	.4.	. . . . . .	15	—
	21	To Ditto . . . . Ditto	.4.	. . . . . .	5	—
		To Ditto . . . . Ditto	.4.	6	10	
	24	To Ditto . . . . Ditto	.4.	1	17	6
	28	To Ditto . . . . Ditto	.4.	6	5	—
April	1	To Ditto . . . . Ditto	.4.	6	10	—
	2	To Ditto . . . . Ditto	.4.	5	—	
	6	To Ditto . . . . Ditto	.4.	6	5	—
	7	To Ditto . . . . Ditto	.4.	1	5	
	12	To Ditto . . . . . in Fredericksburg	.5.	. . . . . .	7	6
June	2	To Ditto . . . . in Frederick	.50.	1	0	0
	15	To Ditto . . . . at Home	.50.	. . . . . .	8	9
July	2	To Ditto . . . . at Ditto	.55.	. . . . . .	8	9
	15	To Ditto . . . . at D°	.55.	1	10	—
	27	To Ditto . . . . at D°	.55.	1	10	
Aug.	20	To Ditto . . . . . . in Alexandria	.55.	. . . . . .	5	—
Sept.	16	To. Ditto . . . . . in Fredericksburg	.60.	1	5	—
	30	To Ditto . . . . at Home	.60.	2	0	—
Nov.	19	To Ditto . . . . . in Williamsburg	.61.	1	0	0
Dec.	12	To Ditto . . . . at Home	.62.	. . . . . .	12	6
1773		To Ditto . . . . at Ditto	.63.	. . . . . .	8	9
Mar.	13	To Ditto . . . . at Ditto	.82.	3	10	—
	27	To Ditto . . . . at Ditto	.88.	1	10	—
April	24	To Ditto . . . . at Home	.88.	. . . . . .	7	6
Aug.	31	To Ditto . . . . Ditto	.91.	3	4	
Oct.	1	To Ditto . . . . . . at Annapolis	.93.	3	16	—
		To Ditto . . . . . in Williamsburg	.96.	3	1	—
Dec.	31	To Ditto . . . . at Home	.98.	. . . . . .	16	3
1774	..	To Ditto . . . . D°	.105.	. . . . . .	10	
May	16	To Ditto . . . . . Williamsburg	.110.	. . . . . .	15	—
	18	To Ditto . . . . Ditto	.112.	2	10	—
June	10	To Ditto . . . . Ditto	.112.	5	15	—
				£78	5	9

Losses and Winnings at Cards.
1772–1774).

Contra—C.[RS]

1772						
Jany.	2	By Cash won at Home	.3.	6	2	
Mar.	4	By Ditto in Williamsburg	.3.	....	5	
	6	By Ditto in Ditto	.3.	....	7	6
	23	By Ditto ...... Ditto	.4.	2	0	0
	30	By Ditto ...... Ditto	.4.	9	10	—
April	3	By Ditto ...... Ditto	.4.	5	15	—
June	30	By Ditto ..... at Home	.55.	4	17	0
Sept.	5	By Ditto . at Mr. Bouchar's ..	.60.	1	15	—
Oct.	7	By Ditto ... in Annapolis	.60.	13	7	—
Nov.	3	By Ditto .. in Williamsburg...	.61.	1	5	
Dec.	21	By Ditto ..... at Home	.63.	....	18	—
1773 Jany. }	5	By Ditto ..... at Ditto	.82.	1	10	
	9	By Ditto	.82.	....	14	—
April	17	By Ditto	.88.	1	5	—
	24	By Ditto	.88.	1	4	0
May	—	By Ditto ... won at Phil^a	.90.	2	5	0
Sept.	13	By Ditto	.93.	....	7	6
1774	..	By Ditto	.105.	1	8	0
Feb.	28	By Ditto ..... at Home	..	2	10	0
May	13	By Ditto . at Fredericksburg ..	.110.	1	0	0.
	18	By Ditto ... Williamsburg....	.110.	1	13	0
	23	By Ditto ...... Ditto	.112.	1	10	0
June	6	By Ditto ...... Ditto	.112.	....	9	6
	7	By Ditto ...... Ditto	.112.	1	10	0
	13	By Ditto ...... Ditto	.112.	5	5	0
	16	By Ditto ...... Ditto	.115.	1	0	0
October	—	By Ditto ... won at Phil^a	.125.	7	0	0
				72	2	6
1775 Jan.	1	{ By Ball against Play from Jany 1772 to this date }	.....	6	3	3
				£78	5	9

There hasn't been such an inspiring picture of a national leader and his inner circle's activities since Warren Harding and his cronies used to sit around the White House playing poker and planning the Teapot Dome scandal in the 1920s.*

Fortunately, Washington's gambling was no problem. He called it an "agreeable amusement." Like his dancing.

He also had his fun with prize fights. The rage in Williamsburg in Burgess Washington's time was a form of fisticuffs called "gouging," the object of which was the extraction of at least one of an opponent's eyeballs. The person whose eyeballs came out first lost the fight. He also bet on cockfights. And he loved the ponies. He was seriously into improving the breed, as they called it, as a breeder, racer, and, most frequently, a bettor. On days when he could tear himself away from legislative duties, to which he was a silent partner, he would relax at the track.

Not surprisingly, his favorite outdoor sport was fox hunting. Put Washington in a pink coat and riding to the hounds and cornering a fox and nothing could make him happier in the 1770s. There is a record of every fox hunt he went to back in Mount Vernon, complete with spelling errors, thanks to his Filofax. For January 1770, his Filofax says:

[Jan.] 10. Mr. W———n and Mr. Thruston set of home. I went a hunting in the Neck and visited the Plantn. there. Found and killd a bitch fox, after treeing it 3 times and chasg. it abt. 3 Hrs.

Ten days without hunting. Then, on the twentieth, his companion is his stepson, John (Jackie) Parke Custis, then about fifteen years old.

20. Went a hunting with Jackie Custis and catched a Bitch Fox after three hours chace—founded it on ye Ck. by J. Soals.

On the twenty-third an unusual thing occurred, bringing out the naturalist in him:

23. Went a hunting after breakfast and found a Fox at

* Interestingly, John Adams had a contempt for card playing. "It gratifies none of the senses, neither sight, hearing, taste, smelling, nor feeling. It can entertain the mind only by hushing its clamours. Cards, backgammon, etc., are genteel antidotes to reflection, to thinking—that cruel tyrant within us. They choke the desire for knowledge," he added.[28]

Muddy Hole and killed her (it being a bitch), after a chase of better than two hours, and after treeing her twice, the last of which times she fell dead out of the Tree after being therein sevl. minutes apparently well. Rid to the Mill afterwards. Mr. Semple and Mr. Robt. Adam dind here.

Hughes observed, "Doubtless the poor little thing's heart burst from fright and exhaustion." On the twenty-seventh he is tally ho-ing again:

27. Went a hunting, and after trailing a fox for a good while the Dogs Raizd a Deer and run out of the Neck with it, and did not (some of them at least) come home till the next day.

There weren't too many foxes he could chase down Walnut Street—the four-legged kind—when he moved the hunt to Philadelphia in 1775. Mayor Powel, power broker to the stars, and Mrs. Powel, about whom we will be hearing soon, however, invited him to ride to the hounds at their Gloucester Hunting Club, across the river in New Jersey. It was said to be the first fox-hunting club in the New World (established 1766).

At its meetings, George rubbed pink, finely tailored English jacket elbows with Jacob Hiltzenheimer and his cronies, a notorious group of vested interests. General Washington was often seen partying with Hiltzenheimer, who later became a principal continental agent, selling wagons to the army, or the equivalent of today's tanks, trucks, and transport. The association was as natural as George Bush's going to a football game with Lee Iacocca and the Chrysler purchasing department. The Hiltzenheimer set is remembered less for its hunting than for its manner of what Bridenbaugh described as "getting decently drunk."

Outside of duck shooting, fox hunting, horse racing, card playing, dancing, eating, drinking, and shopping and spending money—his own and especially other people's, like the taxpayers' (see his expense account for the Revolutionary War)—Washington appears to have loved the theater more than any other amusement. He went to every play, good or bad, that was produced within reach of a horse or carriage. He didn't seem to read the reviews.

The thing about the theater in Philadelphia in 1775 is that it was on the edge of the law, often being banned by the Quaker City fathers. There was something immoral, or reprehensible, about it, like going to a burlesque show in Union City, N.J., before World War II.

Indeed, they had some wild things in the Philadelphia theater—exposed breasts. But nothing you couldn't see at the finest private dinner parties and banquets frequented by congressmen.

The well-dressed woman at formal dinners, dances, and balls in Virginia society in the prewar period, social historians say, displayed what is euphemistically called ample cleavage. It was the custom for the frontless gown to be accentuated by very tight stays. The faster women were said to have rouged a nipple and exposed it in the Paris mode. The even more daring, according to one historian, often plopped a rose petal or two between their breasts, to be cultivated by some gardening enthusiast during the course of an evening's socialization. A gentleman would place the petal he had retrieved from the Garden of Eden in his brandy snifter and drink it down while the lady from whom he had plucked it beamed at the attention showered upon her.

[13]

Colonel Washington went to the theater thirty-seven times, to resume the countdown on his life; to race meets six times; to twenty-nine balls; and to five concerts and two barbecues during the less than six-year period of his diaries from January 1768 to 1774. With his heavy social calendar, he still found time to serve in Congress. His schedule of committee assignments—in 1774 zero, and in 1775 one—meant he had no duties, or practically none, to discharge; but his days and especially his nights were not wasted.

Colonel Washington went to all the banquets on the rubber pheasant circuit. He discovered and admired such young Philadelphia lawyers as Joseph Reed, and such businessmen-entrepreneurs-con men as the eloquent Thomas Mifflin, both of whom he was to later tap for important posts in his first military administration.

On these nights of becoming better acquainted with the honorable gentlemen from South Carolina or Connecticut or Madeira, the colonel also saw a lot of his old friends and respected political advisers. He was especially close to Benjamin Harrison, an early member of his brain trust and a man who was to serve a function similar to Warren Beatty's in the Gary Hart campaign of 1988.

John Adams called the man who was to be the father of one president and the great-grandfather of another "another Sir John Falstaff . . . his conversation disgusting to any man of delicacy or decorum." [29] But Harrison's defenders make him sound like a pleasant dining companion. A lover of good food, he was 6'4" tall and weighed 249 pounds. In later years, one biographer said, he tried dieting by "giving up good old Madeira for light French wines." It didn't work. Washington depended on Harrison for an occasional laugh. Not even the floor of Congress was safe from Harrison, a notorious joker of the earthy, stag party variety. He disturbed decorum when John Hancock was elected president of Congress in 1775, historians say, by picking up the Massachusetts politician bodily and depositing him in the presiding officer's chair.

Harrison the kidder was instrumental in getting Washington involved in a lot of hot water, which by the following May, in 1776, could have created a lot of flack from the press or Martha. Nobody likes to air dirty linen in a book about politics; still, Harrison the zany triggered an alleged incident of womanizing. I'm talking about the Washerwoman Kate Affair.

Congressman Harrison is alleged to have written his fellow Virginian politician-turned-general a letter shortly before a trip to Philadelphia. It opened with a brief discussion of local Virginia politics and wheeling and dealing in Congress and closed with Harrison's asking that Washington find a job for a worthy captain of riflemen from their home state. A footnote mentioned a private affair:

> As I was in the pleasing task of writing to you a little Noise occasioned to turn my Head around, and who should appear but pretty little Kate, the Washerwoman's daughter, over the way, clean, trim, and rosey as the Morning. I snatched the golden glorious Opportunity, and but for that cursed Antidote to Love, Sukey [Mrs. Harrison], *I had fitted her for my General against his return* (author's italics). We were obliged to part, but not till we had contrived to meet again; if she keeps the Appointment I shall relish a week's longer stay—I give you now and then some of these adventures to amuse you, and unbend your mind from the Cares of War.

Some historians say this was obviously a forgery, propaganda concocted by "ministerial hirelings, pensioned pens and sons of despotism" (the three worst things Whigs called Tories), designed to weaken the nation's moral fiber by revealing that Washington the monument was also Washington the man. Especially in wartime, sex makes strange bedfellows. The last passage from the letter was widely printed, from the *Boston Weekly News-Letter* (an antiwar, anti-Washington *National Enquirer* of its day) to the *Gentlemen's Magazine* of London, a monarchist *Playboy*. The general, who was quick to take offense at anything negative the press had to say about him, let this issue go by.

The Washerwoman Kate Affair may have inspired a play, which soon afterwards opened in a theater in occupied Broadway (New York). It starred General Washington and a servant girl named Kate. It was called *The Battle of Brooklyn: A Farce of Two Acts: As It Was Performed on Long Island, on Tuesday the 27th day of August, 1776 by the Representatives of Americans, Assembled at Philadelphia.* (I don't know how they ever fit that on the marquee.) The Tory playwright depicted Washington as "a whoremongering barbarian and demagogue."

What would Colonel Washington and his oldest political crony, Congressman Harrison, the lusty *tummeler* and social director from Virginia, do after a long evening of knocking back a few bottles of Madeira on the heels of the "planter's punch" they must have already swilled—not to mention aperitifs, cider and other libations; after a night of playing cards and smoking "seegars," of the finest York River and James River Plantation tobacco? *

I would like to say he went to the publick library and read a good book. What he really did was go back to his rooms and catch up on his diary writing. The record is there in such lengthy observations as the following: "14. Dined with Benj. Harrison. Lost 1s at cards." And he washed his own silk socks.

---

* Actually the colonel hated tobacco. He didn't smoke. It must have reminded him of his mother, Mary Ball Washington, who smoked a pipe at the Fredericksburg farm and in her state appearances, of which there were few. Washington saw to that. His little old cantankerous mom embarrassed him. Smoking also reminded him of the losing battle he fought with the weed as a crop. It continually bewildered him as a planter.

[14]

W hile in Philadelphia on revolutionary business, many congressmen lived at Miss Jane Port's roominghouse on Arch
Street, near Front, about five paved streets from the State House.
Miss Port's was famous for its dark halls, smelling strongly of cab-
bage. In May it was steamy and close. Miss Jane, the landlady,
magnificent in side curls and a high starched cap with purple ribbons, was always darting from a doorway, sinking to the floor in a
curtsy before some congressman or other, it is said. She rattled
brave men.

Colonel Washington preferred to sleep at the Powel house,
the home of Philadelphia's powerful mayor, Samuel Powel, and
one of his great admirers, Mrs. Powel, the former Elizabeth (Eliza)
Willing. The house is still standing, on the west side of Third
Street between Walnut and Spruce streets, number 244 (formerly
number 112).

Elizabeth Willing was the daughter of the largest Quaker fortune in Pennsylvania. Her father was one of the ten richest men in
Philadelphia. She had married *the* richest man in Philadelphia, a
real-estate king. Aside from running Philadelphia, young Powel
also owned much of it. At the death of his father, also Samuel
Powel—"the great builder," as he was known—in 1759, he had
acquired possession of more than 90 city houses (of the 6,057 in
Philadelphia mentioned earlier) and a fine country seat near the
fox hunting club in Gloucester, N.J. He was then but a student,
an undergraduate at the College of Philadelphia (later the University of Pennsylvania). On graduation, he was so well endowed with
property, education, and leisure that Powel joined a young Quaker
political inaction group, called the Society Meeting Weekly in the
City of Philadelphia for Their Mutual Improvement in Useful
Knowledge, where he studied wines, dancing and the laws of
chance at the faro tables.

Powel lost his Quaker simplicity, it was said, as he stocked his
house on Third Street after his first trip to the Continent. "Your
house is so finely situated that it looks like the habitat of a Turkish
Bashaw," George Roberts wrote.[30] While Powel was lolling in the
lap of ease and reveling in the scenes of the Italian muse, his

checkbook was active. Into the seraglio on Third Street he brought the plunder of his foreign journeys: imported furniture, original canvases and copies of old masters, marble statuary, and a profusion of objets d'art, including Colonel Washington, the most talked about congressman in 1775.

Powel was a leading Tory, and classic closet monarchist. The last of the royal mayors, Sam Powel was the first of the rebel mayors of free Philadelphia who managed to go fishing during most of the war. With 90 houses, he wasn't one of those Tories who went to England. Instead, during the war, he managed to magnificently entertain the British generals. Having Washington as a house guest at the Powels was like the aristocracy in Saint Petersburg having Leon Trotsky for the winter season during a different revolution.

The Powels and Washington, however, were people who rose above mere issues. Washington was comfortable with the Powels, and found much to admire about their home, with its fine art collection and library.

Washington did not read much on the nights when he stayed at the Powel house. Mrs. Powel was more of a cultural attraction.

Eliza was another one of those chatty women the silent military man always seemed to be getting involved with. The cultured French chevalier Jean Francois Rene de Chastellux wrote, "She talks a great deal. She honored me with her friendship and found me meritorious because I meritoriously listened to her."

Washington was an even better listener.

With Samuel Powel, they say he talked about strong central government; one of his hobbies, husbandry; and scientific agriculture. And he evidently found things to say to Eliza too.

Eliza was a strange one. She once sent a young man a pair of fur gloves, historians say, her reasoning being he had not written to her because "his Herculean hands were cold." She seems to have loved large hands.[31]

Elizabeth Willing was what today we call a political groupie. At the age of twenty-seven, Eliza had "flirtations," as they called them, with John Dickinson (the Pennsylvania Farmer himself); Richard Henry Lee of the Virginia delegation, and a Mr. Beverly of Virginia. She had a weakness for Virginian men.

Her father was Charles Willing, who established a branch of his father's English mercantile firm. Her brother Thomas Willing was partner to Robert Morris, the J. P. Morgan of the Revolution. She was first cousin to Peggy Shippen, the socialite wife of Benedict Arnold, a woman who was soon to have an identity crisis and who seduced everybody in sight, taking a shot at Alexander Hamilton and possibly even General Washington as they were learning of her husband's perfidy at West Point.

Eliza Willing Powel was a beautiful, tall, supersophisticated, very rich woman, who coquetted with the general in the gay and bantering way he enjoyed; she teased him*; as the historians say, she inspired him to sallies of wit. Her cosmopolitan manner kept him amused. She played games and danced divinely. And so of a night, whenever he could tear himself away from his pressing legislative duties, Washington could be found in the Powels' ballroom, working out with Mrs. Powel on the best hardwood floors old Quaker money could buy.

---

* In one of her letters to Washington she teased him about his "continence to the ladies" (March 6–11, 1787, manuscript, Mount Vernon Ladies' Association of the Union).

Part II

—

The Making of the General, II
(continued)

*Being the awesome chronicle of how the
Mount Vernon Machine got the nomination
for the second-best man.*

[15]

O n June 15, after sitting through thirty-seven days of a heated convention that was not always taut and gripping, a period in which he managed to sow some Quaker oats while sewing up the nomination, George Washington, forty-three, was unanimously chosen to be commander in chief of the rebel forces raised and on duty in the ten miles of trenches and redoubts outside Boston. Political lightning had struck. It was a major—if early—step to the prefidency.

The rising young politician-planter from Virginia had won what was then the most powerful office in the land without campaigning, as he imagined. It's true he wore a uniform every day. That is not what we would call a low profile today. But it could have been more blatant. He could have sat with an American flag on his desk or around his shoulders. It was a post he didn't ask anyone to nominate him for. It could be said, as Charles Francis Adams once observed, that he nominated himself. Unconsciously.

And now he, in what must have been the biggest surprise of his life, had been handed the highest honor his not-even-founded-yet new country could bestow.

Returning to his rooms on this historic night, he wrote in his diary: "15. Dined at the Burnes in the Fields. Spent the evening on a Committee." Among the committee business on the agenda that night were numerous toasts to the victorious noncandidate: "The Generalissimo," as one went. George Washington had heard his first huzzah.

If Washington was guided by Providence, as historians say,

53

then that is the end of it. Finis. It had to be. Political lightning struck this piece of wood, and the rest is history, as they say.

Still, I was fascinated by how it happened, how the Congress had picked a man like the inexperienced Washington, who hadn't worn a uniform in sixteen years, except to sit for a portrait, until the congressional sessions, who had zero experience in a large war or anything more than a skirmish or maneuvers with militia, jobs which he always quit for one reason or other. He had threatened to resign or resigned seven times from his two major posts before he was thirty.

George Washington had been chosen out of all the distinguished soldiers the colonies had, including those who had bloodied the British at Concord and the so-called Battle of Bunker Hill* and had sealed them up in Boston: generals Ward, Putnam, Heath, Spenser, Lee, to give a random selection, plus those without press agents or historians to remind us of their names. How was it possible that this one tall, quiet planter had been chosen to deal the cards in the new country's first united action?

He certainly wasn't the nominee on the basis of his war record. Let's look more closely at the war record.

[16]

Heroes, like sandwiches, are made, not born. George Washington was appointed a buck major in the Virginia military establishment on November 6, 1752, when he was still twenty. He didn't start at the bottom, as I did in the U.S. Army 201 years later. And he rose through the ranks to become colonel.

Washington's military background is an example of the basic old American principle of starting at the top. Why start at the bottom, where it's always so crowded, when there is always room at the top?

---

* It took place, of course, on the adjoining Breed's Hill, the first of many mistakes the media made in reporting the war, but perhaps the most inexplicable. It's not as if they were reporting Hill No. 692 versus Hill No. 693.

Some people would call George Washington's early military career an example of nepotism. I call it "pull." He had connections. And it taught the young Washington a lesson in politics. "It is not," my mother once told me, "who you know, but what you know." She was wrong about that.

"Pull" had a lot of power in the old days. George Washington received his majorship as a gift at twenty, like a bar mitzvah present. ("Today you are a major in the militia.") It came to him through the political clout of his devoted half-brother, Lawrence Washington. When Larry, who formerly sat in the chair, became terminally ill, he resigned his post in the colony's militia, more or less on the understanding that George would be appointed in his place. In other words, he inherited his army job.

The Washington seat in the Virginia militia seemed to include the adjutant general's office. Larry Washington had also been an AG. So George also started out as a twenty-year-old adjutant. Talk about being born with a silver oak leaf in your mouth.

The state was divided, for military purposes, into four quarters, and there was an AG for each quarter. The adjutant general's office was an amateurish, ornamental officer's sort of office, the equivalent of playing war. AGs were expected to oversee the militia of their districts. He was appointed to the Southern District, composed of several distant counties. And the next year (1753), through political jockeying, his jurisdiction was transferred to the Northern Neck (his home counties).

There was some protest about one so young being appointed, especially one with no military knowledge whatsoever.

Age should not be held against Major, or Majorette, Washington. After all, at twenty-two Alexander the Great was in Asia decimating the Persians; at twenty-four in Egypt; at thirty in India. At seventeen Charles XII of Sweden, with four hundred horsemen, shattered six thousand Russian cavalry and annihilated an army at Narva. At twenty he entered Warsaw and captured Cracow. At twenty-six he crossed the Vistula on the ice and made borscht of the Russians.

I myself was only twenty-five when the government finally accepted me as a draftee, starting a distinguished career in which I fought communism by serving as a sportswriter at Fort Dix, N.J. By that time Washington had already started the French and Indian War.

So don't knock youth.

Anyway, Washington was studying military tactics. He had

bought five books. He was studying a manual of tactics with Major Muse, one of the fellow AGs. Also, the art of fencing with Jacob Van Braam, a Dutchman. Muse and Van Braam had been army buddies of Lawrence Washington's (Cartageña campaign) and had been engaged by him to teach George the basics of soldiering, of which he knew absolutely nothing when luck gave him the plum of the adjutancy. Van Braam was to be the young Washington's interpreter on his first major mission in the war to come.

Twenty was a big year for George. Not only did he get his big break in the militia, he also became a Freemason. He had been accepted as a Mason on November 4, 1752, in the lodge at Fredericksburg. He loved uniforms, as I've suggested, so the Masons' gloves, aprons, and other apparel must have appealed to him. Also the secret closed meetings. The Masons were an apolitical group, of course; many of the delegates in the Continental Congress that elected George Washington general were Masons. Washington eventually belonged to three Masonic lodges. He was making all the right moves, even as an adolescent.

He was a rising young man who would have been on the U.S. Chamber of Commerce top one hundred young go-getters in the colonies on the way up list. At twenty he had a commission with the rank of major and a salary of one hundred pounds a year for a part-time job. (That was good money for a young surveyor.) And he was, as Rupert Hughes put it, in uniform. Washington was about to begin being Washington.

[17]

The first turning point in Washington's military career took place when Lieutenant Governor Dinwiddie got involved in a real-estate dispute with the French in 1753. They had been poaching on land owned by the Ohio Company in the western part of Virginia, and the lieutenant governor of the Commonwealth was furious.

The Ohio Company was building a fort at the confluence of

the Allegheny, Monongahela, and Ohio rivers, which was soon taken over by the French and called Fort Duquesne, then by the English and called Fort Pitt, and is now held by steel millionaires' heirs and called Pittsburgh.*

This called for an expedition, especially in the light of the reports that there were squatters on the land already. The ownership situation had to be explained to the French, who were of the opinion they owned the land. A messenger was needed to deliver a letter of protest for the record. Also, Dinwiddie wanted his messenger to check out the lay of the land, note what kind of fort the French had built, and so on. To go West, young man, he chose the boy major, Washington.

It was a smart choice. The young major was ambitious, fearless, and by now skilled in backwoods travel, from numerous surveying trips in the so-called Western lands. He had been studying military tactics, fortifications, and fencing. He was an outdoorsman by trade (a surveyor), a tough, hardy man of action. But also a gentleman, a cavalier, a self-made aristocrat who knew how to dress and dance, who could exchange courtesies and military etiquette with the French. Any minuets in the woods, he would be able to hold his own.

Major Washington in October 1753 rode off to warn the French, near Lake Erie, to get off the Ohio Company's land in the name of the King of England—or else! His message from Lt. Governor Dinwiddie read, in part, that "the lands up on the River Ohio in the Western Parts of the Colony of Virginia are so notoriously known to be the Property of the Crown of Great Britain,

---

* My grandmother, the one who looked like Washington, used to live on Dinwiddie Street in the Hill District, then a Jewish neighborhood on the edge of downtown Pittsburgh. It was a short street connecting two main avenues. It began at Fifth Avenue and ran, or walked slowly, straight up the hill—to use a surveyor's term, a 100-percent grade—for about an eighth of a mile. The street ended up at Centre Avenue, at the top of the hill, not far from the historic shrine where Willie Stargell's ribs place was later located. Every summer during the Depression my parents sent me from Brooklyn to Dinwiddie Street. It was like going to camp.

All those years I thought the word *Dinwiddie* meant a very hilly street that knocked the wind out of fat little well-finished boys from Brooklyn. You had to walk up Dinwiddie Street a lot on hot summer days after getting off the streetcar line at the bottom of the hill. It was some climb when you were a city boy from Brooklyn, where the largest hill was Crown Heights.

Washington himself may have slept at my grandmother's house, though she never bothered to put up a sign. He at least stalked the redskins in the area. Of course, by the time I was born the only redskins they talked about in Pittsburgh were the football team in Washington. And the only violence I saw was steelworkers throwing beer cans at Howard Cosell's face on "Monday Night Football."

that it is a matter of equal Concern and Surprize to me to hear that a Body of French Forces are erecting Fortresses and making Settlements upon that River within his Majesty's Dominions." [1]

He returned safely with a polite reply, warning the English off the French territory in the name of the King of France. Sadly, they claimed the same territory. Possession, their theory went, was nine tenths of the law, at least.

To resolve the stalemate, the now promoted Governor Dinwiddie sent out his man Washington a second time on Ohio Company business: this time to recapture the fort at the confluence, which the French had taken from the English carpenters employed by the Ohio Company.

He ordered Washington to enlist two hundred men, train them, equip them, and then go out and "finish and compleat in the best Manner and as soon as You possibly can, the Fort w'ch I expect is there already begun by the Ohio Comp'a. You are to act on the Defensive, but in Case any Attempts are made to obstruct the Works or interrupt our Settlem'ts by any Persons whatsoever You are to . . . make Prisoners of or kill and destroy them." [2]

All this was easier ordered than done. In the first place, Washington had never drilled a soldier or been drilled in a company. He had merely studied under private tutors, and had to learn on the job. Dinwiddie, they said, must have been in a frenzy to send a raw kid out there to face the trained soldiers of France, the best army in Europe at the time. There was nobody to say, "You can't send a kid up in a crate like that!"

In the course of his travails and travels, the young, inexperienced Washington would wind up leading an army of 350 mostly shiftless idlers, men who were underclothed, underfed, and underpaid (8 pence a day), a command that had been nominally under a Colonel Fry, who had fallen off a horse and killed himself before the expedition left. He committed suicide, some said.

In his first encounter in the woods with the French, Major Washington had not waited for war to be declared but had fired into a band of French scouts claiming to be an embassy (ambassador) to the English. In the group was a peace messenger, as Washington had been on his last visit, with a letter from the French governor.

It was his first victory. But then it turned out that the man he had killed was a young monsieur named De Jumonville, "l'ambassadeur" who was delivering the letter. Later, the French, under the dead man's brother, were to trap Washington in a little stockade called Fort Necessity, and after a siege made him surrender and secured his signature to a capitulation, twice confessing the assassination of M. De Jumonville.

The only thing is Major Washington didn't read, write, or, most importantly, understand French, and actually had denied both the assassination and the confession.

It is not fair to say that George Washington started the French and Indian War. That was a century-long series of wars. But Voltaire, among others, had written of George Washington as a contributing cause of the last phase of the war, a laurel indeed.

[18]

The thing that impressed me about Washington's debut as a soldier was what he did at a place called Great Meadows, near Little Meadows, not far from the Youghiogheny River in the Monongahela valley, near the present Uniontown, Pennsylvania, not far from where my Aunt Ida used to live.

Major Washington was responsible for the planning and erection of the fort which he called Fort Necessity, a good name eventually. For it was here, on July 3, 1753, that he of necessity repaired to, being chased, after his disastrous killing of Ambassador-at-Large De Jumonville, by a superior force of French and Indians, led by Ambassador De Jumonville's brother.

The site had been described by Major Washington in a letter to Governor Dinwiddie, whom he corresponded with almost hourly, it would seem by the correspondence files, as "a convenient spott." He "made a good Intrenchment" and "by clearing ye Bushes out of these Meadows, prepar'd a charming field of an Encounter."

I went there on a visit to my Aunt Ida in Uniontown—the fort is now part of a National Park site—and whistled in admiration at the great "spott" he had picked out for ye "Intrenchment." My God, if I had done that as a PFC, they would have sent me to Ft. Leavenworth.

The site he selected was the bottom of a valley by a side of a creek with higher ground all around it.

Even as a PFC, I could see that the French and/or the Indians, hiding in the surrounding woods at higher elevations, could watch the interior of the fort at all times. He couldn't have picked a worse "spott."

Three sides had higher ground with heavy tree cover, approaching close to the stockade. The topography was all wrong. The place was unfit for defense. And it was here "the buckskin general," as the French called him, elected to make his last-ditch stand.

Into "ye good Intrenchment" the amateur major rushed his Virginians (and some North Carolinians), who had to stand off twice their number of French and Indians behind the trees above them. The French got into the woods and started throwing lead down on them. As if things weren't bad enough, it started to pour. Even a moderate rain, with water draining into the basins from the surrounding slopes, would have turned the fort quickly into a muddy pond. The heavy rain put many of the muskets out of order. Dead and wounded wallowed in the mud, historians say. Food was lacking, but rum was plentiful. All about the fort drunk soldiers reeled and fell, either dead drunk or dead dead from the French and Indians' rifles.

After nine hours of siege during a heavy storm, Washington was forced to surrender Fort Necessity. Military experts today say that the raw acting colonel made every conceivable military error save one: capitulating, thus saving his men from drowning. Even Napoleon would have surrendered, given the circumstances.

[19]

Thus ended Act One of acting Colonel-Major Washington's prewar record. Despite the Fort Necessity disaster, Governor Dinwiddie was right in selecting the kid as his representative to invite the French to vacate the land owned by the Ohio Company.

This organization, as everybody knows, was a speculative land concern formed to buy and sell Western lands. Among its holdings were the rights to 500,000 acres around the confluence of the Monongahela and Allegheny rivers, forming the Ohio.

It was not well known that among the nineteen honorable gentlemen of the colony who were Ohio Company stockholders was Governor Dinwiddie. He first became a stockholder in a private capacity in 1747. And then, putting on his other hat, in his official capacity as the chief executive of Virginia, he gave his own company the 500,000 acres of land in the Ohio valley. The beauty part of the deal, as I have observed, was that the land was not necessarily the governor of Virginia's to give away, because of the French prior claim. (The French based their claims to the territory on exploration and occupation, which usually held up in courts of law of that day.)

It is not well known, either, that among the other stockholders of the Ohio Company was George Washington.*

It was shrewd of Governor Dinwiddie to have sent someone into the woods who had a financial interest in delivering the message. However, Washington's interest apparently was in conflict with French interests.

If the French stayed where they were, the Ohio Company would be wiped out, and with it young George's dreams of enormous riches and countless acres. The French could make the grant from the king of England, countersigned by the royal governor of Virginia, a worthless scrap of paper.

He was, in effect, caught in the middle of a stockholders fight, an unfriendly take-over bid.

Reinforced self-interest: the best kind of interest. Today we would call it corruption. But it was not corrupt by the standards of the time. The public/private distinction was still under development. But even if it was corruption, it smelled better in the old days. And at least the American public got something from the shady land development schemes—the Middle West.

Owning land wasn't a corrupt act in Washington's day. They thought it was a positively noble act for a man to buy land. Voting

---

* The Washington family was prominent in the management of the company. Half-brother Lawrence was especially active as its president. Also involved in the affairs of the company was half-brother Augustine Washington. His brothers' stock became part of George's portfolio on their deaths. Young George had every right, as a stockholder, to be furious about the encroachments of the French swine on his property.

was even based not on literacy but on owning property. The Mount Vernon machine was later to advocate giving the vote only to the landed gentry. It meant they would keep up their property. As John Jay said, "Those who own the country ought to govern it."

[20]

Despite his disastrous first campaign in the Pennsylvania veldt, the boy major found himself a popular hero in Virginia, the most widely talked about superstar of the French and Indian War. Maybe it was his way of placing the blame where it belonged, on other people. No one went unblamed—it was a shortcoming of a governor, or an Assembly in not equipping his troops. Predating President Roosevelt's New Deal, he was always saying his men were ill clothed, ill housed, and ill fed. His men were always naked and short of grog. It was appalling.

He also had a vivid way of describing battles. After the debacle at Fort Necessity, he had written a letter to his half-brother Augustine (Jack) and tacked on this footnote: "P.S. I fortunately escaped without any wound, for the right wing, where I stood, was exposed to and received all the enemy's fire . . . I heard the bullets whistle, and, believe me, there is something charming in the sound."

Somehow the remark made the colonial papers and was widely reprinted, even in the *London Magazine*. Horace Walpole, then in the royal exchequer, tells the story:

> In the express, which Major Washington despatched on his preceding little victory [the skirmish with M. De Jumonville], he concluded with these words,—"I heard the bullets whistle, and, believe me, there is something charming in the sound." On hearing of this the King said sensibly—"He would not say so, if he had been used to hear many."[3]

Already, at twenty-two, George Washington's name was on the lips of his most sacred majesty, King George III.

George Washington did not rest on his laurels. The veteran of Fort Necessity volunteered for duty with General Braddock, who was leading a British expeditionary force into the Pennsylvania woods to recapture Fort Pitt from the French in April 1755. He had no commission in the Braddock campaign. Recommended by Benjamin Franklin, he served as an unpaid aide-de-camp and advised General Braddock on fighting in the woods against the French and Indians, things he knew so well. He was the one who told him to divide his army in two. The general went ahead into the woods outside of Pittsburgh, with half of the 2,200 men, while the remainder, including Washington, brought up the rear a day or two behind. When Braddock's advance force was attacked by a small detachment of Franco-Indians and turned on its heels, it ran smack into the rear guard in the middle of the dark woods. It probably was not the best advice Washington could have given, all things considered. But strategy was not his suit. Suits were.

Still, he was very brave and courageous in the mess that followed, riding around on a pillow, trying to rally Braddock's divided army. He was recovering from dysentery at the time.*

Colonel Washington wisely decided at this juncture to quit—while he was still alive. He hung up his sword forever, as he put it, and retired to his plow at Mount Vernon to pursue careers in real estate and politics, and his most important quest of all, besides the pursuit of the dollar, Martha.

---

* Hugh Mercer described how he first met Washington, during Braddock's Massacre. According to the nineteenth century historian George Washington Greene, Mercer said he had seen him "ride backward and forward over the fatal field of the Monongahela, untouched by the bullets that were striking down some comrade with every fresh discharge from the deadly rifles of their unseen foe, until, of all the gallant band of officers who had marched out that bright morning in the pride and fullness of their strength, he was the only one who came from the battle unwounded. Mercer could also tell how, spent with exertion and loss of blood, he had hidden himself under the trunk of a fallen tree, over which one of the victorious Indians had passed in pursuit of him: what a refreshing draught he had drunk from a little brook, the first refreshment since the dawn of that disastrous day; and how, in the extremity of his hunger, he had killed and eaten a rattle-snake, and fancied it a delicious morsel." [4] Captain Mercer later rose to general on the staff, and could always be counted on as a reliable source by most historians.

[21]

A nd so twenty years later in Philadelphia the strategist of Fort Necessity and Braddock's Massacre was being favorably mentioned as a candidate for America's first general in a global war against the British Empire. But it was not as if the tall, silent real-estate mogul/planter didn't have any opposition. John Hancock was also running for the office.

The Hancock-for-General movement was headed by John Hancock. His polls were showing him in the lead. He had paid for them.

The wealthy, Harvard-educated merchant was no shrinking tobacco plant like Colonel Washington. The noted tea smuggler from Boston had some real support among the New England delegation members, some of whose transportation he had paid. He had even paid for the new suit on the back of Sam Adams, the Boston Bolshevik.

Hancock's stock had risen when he was elected unanimously to head the Congress after Peyton Randolph returned to Virginia. The flamboyant entrepreneur-politician with the glorious signature was being mentioned as a serious possible successor to the ailing General Artemas Ward as commander of the forces raised outside Boston.

"Mr. Hancock himself has an ambition. Whether he thought an election a compliment due to him," John Adams wrote to Dear Abby, "and intended to have the honor of declining it or whether he would accept it, I know not." [5] Adams privately was against the elegant radical Whig El Prefidente's aspirations.

There is a tendency to scoff at Hancock. Since the death of his father Hancock was the head of one of the top families in Boston. Socially he was unimpeachable. At thirty-seven, he was vain and immaculate with a taste for beautifully tailored and elaborate clothes.

They say he was too foppish, too elegant, too much the dandy to be a general. I'd be willing to match Colonel Washington's wardrobe, item by item, against Hancock's any day in the leadership race for best-dressed radical Whig.

Hancock, to continue with his political assets, was richer than

George Washington, if that's possible. Colonel Washington may have had more on paper, with his land, slaves, and Martha's dowry. But Hancock was already a rich merchant-shipowner and insurance man when he had, at twenty-eight, inherited the mighty fortune from his uncle Thomas Hancock.

He also was a lover of good wines, particularly Madeira. Whereas Washington was famous as a consumer of the stuff, Hancock was a well-known smuggler of it. Madeira, tea, you name it, John Hancock smuggled it. He was one of the founding cigarette-boat-runners.

Not that there was any stigma attached to smuggling then. Nine tenths of the country's merchants were smugglers, historian David A. Wells says. One quarter of all the signers of the Declaration of Independence were possible contraband traders. So few merchants were paying any duty at all in the custom house in Boston, eyewitnesses recall, that it was a favorite dozing place. And John Hancock was the prince of tariff-law breakers.

At the hour the shot heard around the world was being fired at Concord, Hancock was supposed to be before the Admiralty Court in Boston in a suit for $500,000 in penalties, alleged to have been incurred by him as a smuggler. His counsel was, of all people, John Adams, the William Kunstler of his time, a very able attorney whose flair for left-wing causes was "tolerated."

Hancock's conflict of interest and character as a shady businessman was at least equal to Washington's, which would appeal to the commercial element in the electorate. The corrupt mercantile vote was split.

Smuggler, yes, but one thing you could say for Hancock, he was not a slaveholder. Give him a better record on civil rights than Washington.

He was also a better speller.

Someone described Hancock as a young man whose "brains were shallow and pockets deep." So he wasn't Sir Isaac Newton. So he wasn't the sharpest tack in the shoe of the empire. Neither was Colonel Washington. But, unlike Hancock, George Washington: 1) knew his limits and 2) knew whom to consult and whom to listen to. Valuable gifts (cf. Machiavelli).

The up side of Hancock's candidacy was that he actually paid for a private army already in Boston. In 1773 Hancock underwrote with a grant an independent cadet company complete with a band. It played "Yankee Doodle" and other top-forty songs of the day at official functions.[6]

The Boston Cadets, as Hancock's drum and fife and bugle corps was known, traditionally served as the governor's militia guard of honor at official functions. Captain Hancock, as British military historian Michael Pearson points out with disgust, "had used this very unit to take over the tea ships." [7] They went in their other uniform, disguised as Mohawk Indians.

Captain Hancock's cadets were much more substantial contributors to the war effort than George Washington's media hoax thousand-man expeditionary force.

And not only that, but Hancock's money paid for organizing and underwriting the activities of the leading political education group of its day in Massachusetts, the Sons of Liberty. They were sort of a pressure group, a political Guardian Angels. But Hancock was not a man who stood around listening to, or making speeches at, the Liberty pole.

The Sons of Liberty also had starred in the big social event of 1773, a masquerade ball, the previously mentioned Boston Tea Party.* Few appreciate what that event was really about.

The British had repealed the Stamp, Paint, Paper, and Glass acts, thanks to mob activities. The tea tax was left in place as a British statement of defiance: "We have the power/authority to tax you. What will you do about it?"

The bungling East India Tea Company, which, as a result of various governmental and corporate blunders, had a surplus of seventeen million pounds of the leaves, was on the brink of bankruptcy and sought to unload its stock. [8] The company planned to open the equivalent of Seven-Eleven stores to sell tea fast, starting with Boston. Eliminate the middle men. Cheap tea. This would leave merchants like Hancock stuck with all their overpriced tea.

Hancock was alarmed at that. It wasn't that he wanted people to stop drinking tea; he only wanted them to stop drinking the East India Company's cheaper tea. This sounded like a job for those well-known lovers of liberty and democratic procedures, the Sons of Liberty. After the Indians were through dumping, the price of Hancock's tea actually went higher because stores had nothing to sell afterwards.

Hancock's money and Sam Adams's brains made the Sons of Liberty what they were. The Sons' three major democratic activi-

---

* The dumping of tea in the Wilmington, N.C., harbor in 1774 was just as outrageous as the Boston tea party. But, as David Brinkley of ABC News and Wilmington, N.C., has explained, "all the historians are from Massachusetts."

ties were tarring and feathering, riding people out of town on a
rail, and smashing furniture, houses, and heads of dissenters. They
were the Nationalist Socialist Party of the day, or perhaps the Ku
Klux Klan. But they were very effective politically. They encouraged unanimity and harmony by reducing differences of opinion
on political issues.

Unlike Washington, Hancock was on the cutting edge of the
Revolution. They could hang him at any time. He operated where
it was dangerous. His rich neck was on the line. The Brits, in fact,
were on their way to get him and Sam Adams when Paul Revere
made his famous ride, immortalized in Longfellow's poem and one
of the best media hypes of all time.

The British weren't coming for Washington. He was not a
thorn in their side.

While Washington was dancing, playing cards, slumping over
a bottle of Madeira, or sitting silently in the House of Burgesses,
Hancock was almost in the trenches at Lexington. As Scheer and
Rankin report in *Rebels and Redcoats,* based on eyewitness accounts:

> "When Revere trotted up and demanded entrance, Sergeant
> Munroe said the family had retired. Adams and Hancock,
> after receiving Devens's warning that a British patrol was
> asking for 'Clark's' and appeared to be headed toward
> Lexington and perhaps Concord, had sent a warning to
> leaders in Concord and then had settled down for the night,
> asking Munroe not to disturb them by any noise in the yard.
> " 'Noise!' shouted Revere. 'You'll have noise enough
> before long. The regulars are coming out!'
> "John Hancock heard the commotion in the yard and
> recognized Revere's hearty voice. From the house he called,
> 'Come in, Revere. We are not afraid of *you!*' "

Both Hancock and Sam Adams ushered him in, Scheer and
Rankin say, eager to know the events that had brought him riding
to their door at midnight. "His news shattered the peace of the
household. John Hancock's formidable old aunt and his fiancée,
pert, pretty Dorothy Quincy, were also guests of the minister and
his wife. They all crowded noisily about Revere, while frail, dan-
dified John theatrically proclaimed he would take up a gun and
join the Lexington Minutemen if they opposed the British
march."[9]

This was Paul Revere, the noted copper pot man, the Federal

Express of his day; he delivered news flashes as Sam Adams's favorite messenger. That was why he rode around the countryside shouting "the British are coming." What did he really mean by saying "the British are coming"? Why would he say *that?* Everybody was British back then. Did he say, perhaps, "The Yiddish are coming, the Yiddish are coming"? Now, *that* would have been news.

Revere was the busiest man in Boston media circles. As soon as Sam Adams heard about the shooting of the people by the government troops in Boston on March 5, 1770, his first words were "Get me Paul Revere, the engraver!" A picture of the Boston Massacre was made—at once.*

The massacre did not turn out, in the end, as well as the radicals had expected. The soldiers were tried in a Boston court, and, to the credit of the leading patriots, every effort was made to give them an unbiased trial. John Adams volunteered to defend them. All were finally released.

Only six people died in the unfortunate incident. The Braddock massacre, with 841 killed, was a *massacre* massacre. As they said in London, "Give Adams a skirmish and it becomes a massacre."

With the Adams machine behind him, or in front of him, Hancock was sure he had a shot at becoming general before he had his last huzzah. It's not as if the Colonies didn't have any real general available for the post. Artemas Ward at forty-eight (in 1775) was already a general and commander of the Massachusetts troops around Boston. He was of Pilgrim stock, also a colonel of militia in

---

* Everybody has seen Paul Revere's engraving. It's one of the most popular of the revolutionary period etchings, soldiers in close neat ranks firing a volley into the crowd of decent-looking, sober citizens minding their own business. A dog stands in the foreground, contemplating his navel. Under the engraving there is a poem, beginning:

Unhappy Boston! See thy Sons deplore,
Thy hallow'd Walks besmear'd with guiltless Gore

It was a grossly inaccurate picture, including a fictitious sniper from an upstairs window. Nevertheless, copies of the picture were Faxed to every Son or Stepson of Liberty in America. If Britain ever needed a publicity agent, she needed one at that moment.

Sam also called for his poets and muses. The ballads were ground out at once. And the journalists. The headline writer suggested calling it "A Short Narrative of the Horrid Massacre in Boston!" Troops were shooting men down like dogs! (Prose was coordinated with photo opportunity by Adams.) A picture editor chimed in, "Right! Put a dog in the picture to show the contrast! Shot down like dogs! No, no—not a black-and-white picture! Put red in it; soldiers' coats must be red! The negro? Leave him out . . . no, put him in, but make him white! It won't do any good to have a negro in it when it gets to South Carolina!" [10]

the so-called French and Indian War, and he knew what the men of New England could do as fighters. He was very popular locally, and believed that God was on the side of the rebels and New England particularly.

Massachusetts was supplying the largest number of troops. Should not the Bay Colony name one of its sons as a leader? Should not the rebels be under an officer thoroughly familiar with the people and the militia of the region? asked Colonel Freeman. Ward met that requirement. But his political enemies said Ward's health would not permit a long campaign.

Also in the race was General Israel Putnam, "Old Put," the hero of the so-called Battle of Bunker Hill. Old Put was the one who gave those instructions about when to shoot. He may have said "Don't fire, boys, until you see the pupils or retinas of the eyes."

He had a reputation as a fierce fighter. Several papers in 1775 had an item describing General Putnam as "the American Cincinnatus," referring to the Roman farmer-patriot-warrior. The blurb reported that when Putnam learned of the Battle of Lexington at his farm in Redding, Connecticut, "he was following his plough"; giving one plow horse to his servant, he rode the other, armed, to Boston.[11]

That answer to the call to duty was worthy of a poem by Longfellow, but it never came. Old Put didn't have the right media connections.

And then there were the competent ones, the technocrats, the professional soldiers, the actual working generals, who did not have any other plows and fields to harrow or slaves to count. Most noticeable among those who had thrown their tricornered hats into the ring was Charles Lee.

At forty-four, Lee was an eccentric aristocrat who was the candidate most widely traveled, most widely schooled, most widely experienced, and with the best actual war record, if you're looking at qualifications. Commissioned in the British regular army as a boy, according to custom, he had come to America in 1755 with the 44th Foot, one of the Irish regiments in Braddock's army, eventually rising to lieutenant colonel. Rather than vegetate in the American jungle, he went off to fight against Spain on the Iberian peninsula. Peace bored him. The military adventurer and soldier of fortune went off to Warsaw to fight in the civil war in the Polish army, with Stanislaus Poniatowski, the king of Poland and former lover of Catherine the Great. As a Polish major general, he next went off with the huge Russian army in Moldavia to fight in another civil war. Fighting (in civil wars) was his middle name.

Charles Lee was no raving beauty. About 5'8" in height, he was an unhealthy-looking, thin, spindly, ugly bloke who resembled a Cincinnatus only in that he had a Roman nose of enormous size. Some eyewitnesses thought it a deformity. Riding a horse, he looked like a scarecrow, they said.

He also was slovenly, unshaven, and unwashed. The image he projected was of a man who had just stepped out of the trenches, even in peacetime. He dressed down, so self-consciously it may have been an affectation, a marked contrast to the always well-groomed Colonel Washington. As the unwashed slob, he was making another kind of political statement. Exactly what it was is still not clear.

"The General is a perfect original," wrote Dr. Jeremy Belknap, an eighteenth-century minister and historian, "a good scholar and soldier; and an odd genius, full of fire and passion and but little good manners; a great sloven, wretchedly profane and a great admirer of dogs, of which he had two at dinner with him, one of them a native of Pomerania, which I should have taken for a bear." [12]

There were always arguments about whether he had two or three dogs at table with him. James Thacher, who served with him, said merely that "a number always followed him." Others described it as "a small pack." Any man who travels to war with his dogs can't be all bad, any dog lover would agree.

There was no doubt that Charles Lee actually preferred the company of his dogs to men. As he explained, "to say the truth I think the strongest proof of a good heart is to love dogs and dislike mankind." [13]

Aside from dumb animals, Lee loved Shakespeare, and talked dogmatically about Rousseau and the rights of man, as well as Swiss democracy. He also thought highly of the undisciplined patriot soldiers. Though he lost his temper frequently and hit them over the head, he authored an important, cutting pamphlet explaining why the raw American militiamen could fight more effectively than polished British regulars. More than campaign propaganda, it was the blueprint for winning a guerrilla war in less than eight years.

Lee was the best writer running for general. He was as biting as a Pomeranian, and his acid wit was sharper than a Doberman's tooth. His hobby was writing satirical letters, poetry, and pamphlets with a radical bent. His achievements with barbed pen and tongue included, when he returned to England after service with Catherine the Great's army, insulting George III in person.

As Walpole says, when George III granted Lee an audience in order to receive a letter from Stanislaus of Poland, and began to apologize for his inability to offer Lee military preferment, the latter stopped him short by coolly observing: "Sir, I will never give your Majesty an opportunity of breaking your promise to me again." [14]

He quit on the spot and retired as a half-pay officer. He was an amazing character. He was also opinionated, rude, and had a hot temper. The Iroquois Indians had named him "Boiling Water," and it didn't take much for him to whistle like a kettle. One day soon, during the coming war, his aide Lieutenant Benjamin Craft was to note in his journal: "Stephen Stanwood for saucy talk to Gen. Lee had his head broke. The general gave him a dollar and sent for the doctor."

He talked continually, unlike George Washington. He was compulsively verbal and dirty-mouthed, and would dominate any forum no matter how small. They tell of a ride in Washington's phaeton on the way to the front, with Lee and Schuyler crowded into the space during a rainstorm. A bizarre mixture of profanity, radical politics, and military stories and experiences came pouring out of the sloppy and unwashed general. The fastidious Schuyler is said to have fainted.

Lee was haughty, cheeky, supercilious. The exact opposite of George Washington, about whom a Boston newspaper reporter, seeing him for the first time, said, "Modesty marks every line and feature on his face."

Republican culture placed a premium on humility, as Schwartz says. Many military men were given to public self-deprecation. Washington knew what sort of demeanor the public expected of its leaders. He never misread the public he was working for and whose good opinion he always sought.

Charles Lee eventually was to have the war's worst PR, second only to Benedict Arnold, the ex–New Haven druggist-bookseller, and the British cause in general. Lee got blamed for a multitude of judgment calls that could have gone either way, and he was on the short end of all of them. The rebels had all the media geniuses and manipulators from Sam Adams to Paul Revere, and later the Mount Vernon machine's Hamilton and Madison.

But Lee had nobody except himself. And he was his own worst enemy.

Unlike Washington, Lee campaigned openly for the job as commander in chief, starting in 1774. He and his dogs attended the sessions of the Congress so religiously there were those who thought Lee was the delegate from . . . they were not sure where. Poland? He curried favor and cadged drinks, while he chewed everybody's ears off about his excitement over Swiss "democracy" (a dirty word in 1774–75) and guerrilla warfare.

He had even gone to the trouble of reducing the stigma of his being foreign-born—there were many others in the new country—by buying a plantation, like Washington's. The Lee place was "over the mountains" in Berkeley County. Lee visited Mount Vernon, talked of war and liberty over a few bottles of Madeira, and wound up borrowing £15 from the host.

Lee also became involved in land deals, borrowing another page from Washington's account book. He had a magnificent scheme, which even a Washington could admire, in which he and fellow stockholders flattered the Prince of Wales by promising to call their new empire out west New Wales. He was becoming Americanized.

Despite his obnoxiousness, Lee still had political support in Congress; Elbridge Gerry and Joseph Warren favored Charles Lee. But if he was disqualified because of being foreign born, they looked with favor on their second choice, "the beloved Col. Washington." [15]

Richard Henry Lee of the Virginia delegation (no relation), who was never much thrilled with Washington, also was among Lee's early supporters. Sam Adams, and perhaps John Adams himself, would have voted for Lee, if they didn't have other codfish to fry.

Lee never sold himself short. He even came up with the wrinkle, in accepting his job as major general, that Congress should pledge that he would be indemnified for any financial loss during the war. [16] Ingenious. The first federal disaster insurance.

Even Colonel Washington would have voted for Charles Lee if it had been a free and open convention. At the time of his appointment he wrote: "He [Charles Lee] is the first officer in military knowledge and experience we have in the whole army. He is zealously attached to the cause, honest and well meaning, but rather fickle and violent, I fear, in his temper."

[22]

I t had been a long way from the floor of the Great Meadow valley and the waters of Fort Necessity to the floor of Congress, where George Washington now stood, twenty years later almost to the day. He was the front-runner in the race for general of the army, a race that he wasn't even making, as far as he knew. He had hung his sword up forever, forgotten boyhood dreams of military glory and advancement. This was one young soldier who would fade away.

He was not now, nor had he ever been, a candidate for the commander in chief's job. He had given no orations on the floor which might call attention to himself. Or lose votes. His colleagues would have been thunderstruck if he had. Not doing anything "politickal" or special here in Philadelphia, honing a style of speechifying he developed in fifteen years at the Burgesses: Speak softly and dress loudly. Say nothing and stand tall.

He also seems to have added to his nonlegislative duties while attending sessions in Congress, attending church more than was usual down home in Virginia. His valuable diaries say that on one Sunday (in October 1774) he visited a Quaker meeting in the forenoon of a Sabbath, and Duche's church in the afternoon, inspected a hospital, "dined at the Tavern with the Virga. Gentn, etca"; next day "spent the afternn. with the Boston Gentn," dined at the Governor's Club and with the Pennsylvania Assembly, and went to a ball afterwards, then to another Episcopal church. On the third Sunday "to the Presbyterian Meeting in the forenoon and Romish Church in the afternoon," and dined at a tavern; "drank Tea with Mrs. Roberdeau," daughter of a New York clergyman.[17]

And here was a man who didn't even believe in God, some of his political enemies said, paraphrasing his own minister, who had been complaining about the way Washington never mentioned the word *God*—he did use *providence* regularly—didn't come to take sacrament, or do this or that. He was big with the deist vote, however.[18]

The non-candidate was also doing his homework. He had

bought those "5 books-military*," as he put it in his ledger (paid £1 12s.), while the Congress was debating the election of a general. "He saw the arm of fate," as Colonel Flexner interpreted it, "swinging in his direction."

Meanwhile, back in Virginia, the preelection Mount Vernon machine had been stirring up the pro-Washington sentiment. As early as January 12 the *Virginia Gazette* published this news item:

> In spite of Gage's flaming sword
> And Carleton's Canadian troop
> Brave Washington shall give the word,
> And we'll make them howl and whoop.

As Washington continued insisting he was not a candidate—and if such a nomination came, it would be through "no desire or insinuation," as he phrased his noncandidacy statement form—word leaked out that he was under consideration for general.

"George Washington might not have been ready for America," said Barry Schwartz, "but America was ready for him."

Among his many admirers in the State House as the Congress continued its nibbling and quibbling was John Adams, the country's first king maker, or prefident maker.

All of the talk about accommodation with His Majesty had shortened the temper of the congressman from Braintree. He thought it was time the colonies and the Congress supported the New England troops investing Boston. The shrewd leader of the Massachusetts delegation had been conducting a talent hunt on the floor since May, and he led the fight for the Virginia colonel. It was the pudgy partridge of a lawyer who went into the snuff-filled back rooms and set up the nomination for George Washington for general. As early as May, the official campaign manager was writing one of his Dear Abby letters to Abigail Adams praising Washington's military committee work. The year before he had hardly noticed him sitting there in the delegates' seats.

He had never been impressed by the colonel's upstairs floors. But Boss Adams had come a long way in his political thinking. The hero of Fort Necessity, the minuteman, the dandy planter foperino was the best man for the job, by George.

---

* One of the volumes was Field Marshall Count Saxe's *Plan for New Modelling the French Army, Reviving its Discipline and Improving its Exercise in Which are Shewn the Advantages of the Roman Legion.*[19]

There were political considerations, not just his good looks, real-estate holdings, and number of slaves. They needed a balanced ticket to run the war against the British.

The Puritan Yankee intellectual Congregationalist congressman had qualms about a Southern Virginia Episcopalian who may have gambled, drank, hunted foxes, and tipped washerwomen too lavishly—all things against his principles—but he squared it with his New England conscience by recognizing that a commander-in-chief from the South would clinch adoption of the army. It would be no longer a New England army exclusively. New England feared being isolated. And he also knew that only a Southern general would be able to bring Southern men into the field.

Which member of the Mount Vernon machine happens to have explained that fact of life to Adams is not known yet. But he spoke of the pressure: "The intention was very visible to me that Colonel Washington was their object, and so many of our staunchest men were in the plan, that we could carry nothing without conceding to it." [20]

Another potentially embarrassing problem to Adams, the ramrod behind the Washington-for-general plan: it was never publicly known, and was carefully covered over by those insiders who knew it, but the Massachusetts and New England delegations were divided on Adams' man. As Adams wrote: "Mr. Hancock and Mr. [Thomas] Cushing hung back, Mr. [Robert Treat] Paine did not come forward, and even Mr. Samuel Adams was irresolute. Mr. Hancock himself, he explained, was planning to vote for himself. To the compliment he had some pretensions, for, at that time, his exertions, sacrifices, and general merits in the cause of his country had been incomparably greater than those of Colonel Washington. But the delicacy of his health, and his entire want of experience in actual service, though an excellent militia officer, were decisive objections to him in my mind." [21]

John Adams only had eyes for George Washington now. But he ran into another pocket of resistance in the least likely place. As he explained in his diary, "In canvassing this subject out of doors, I found, too, that even among the delegates of Virginia there were difficulties. The apostolical reasonings among themselves, which should be greatest, were not less energetic among the saints of the ancient Dominion than they were among us of New England. In several conversations, I found more than one very cool about the appointment of Washington, and particularly Mr. [Edmund] Pendleton was very clear and full against it." [22]

Adams thought the leader of the Southern opposition was Edmund Pendleton! How shrewd. Eddy Pendleton was a close associate of Washington's, a friend, a confidant, the lawyer who drafted his will before he shared a coach ride from the Northern Neck to Philadelphia, his political mentor in the House of Burgesses, and soon to be a Washington speech writer. With enemies like him, Washington didn't need friends.

In fact, all the opposition Adams seemed to have detected were Virginians who came up in Washington's coach.

How naïve Adams was.

Pendleton was so artful. Washington had indeed asked him to oppose the nomination. He had induced his friend and fellow delegates to argue publicly against him, as the pressure on him continued to mount. Imagine—setting up the opposition yourself, chaired by your closest friends and advisers. An ingenious move, by a man who probably once again had no idea of what he was doing.

As Colonel Freeman summarizes the mystery of the anti-Washington movement at the convention, "Pendleton's opposition is of record[23] but the grounds of it nowhere have been stated. David J. Mays, who has been working for some years on a biography of Pendleton, is of the opinion that Pendleton took his stand for a New Englander rather than against Washington because Pendleton believed it proper to have the operations directed by a man from the threatened region. This may have been the fact. On the other hand, Pendleton had been Washington's private counsel in important matters, such as the Dunbar case . . . he was the man Washington selected at this very time for drawing up his will. No matter how independent the mind of either man, personalities were weighty in the Congress and in the politics of the time. Pendleton scarcely would have opposed the advancement of his friend and client had he not done so at Washington's instance."[24]

Adams, the floor manager for Washington, campaigned vigorously for his man, "the modest and virtuous, the amiable, generous and brave George Washington," as he called his candidate in a letter to Dear Abby in June 1775. But first he had to sell him to his country cousin.

Sam Adams, who was nominally a Hancock man, was as different from John Adams as Cindy Adams is from Franklin Pierce Adams among newspaper columnists. As Scheer and Rankin describe them:

John Adams was thirteen years younger [than Sam] and profoundly different: logical, cautious, self examining, and scrupulously honest. Most of his life had been spent on the family farm in the beautiful, rocky country just outside Braintree, ten miles south of Boston on Boston Bay. He lived, off and on, in Boston, and became much more the successful lawyer than the husbandman, but inevitably he was drawn back to the rugged farmhouse at Braintree.

To his intelligent, knowledgeable wife, Abigail, and his children, he was passionately devoted. Unlike Sam, he could not leave their well-being to chance: providing well for their health, comfort, and schooling was his whole life. He was a thoughtful revolutionary, an architect rather than a destroyer, an adherent of gradual change rather than of sudden upheaval. This . . . plump, bald, round-faced, snub-nosed little man of thirty-nine was as forthright as he was honest. This great believer in confederation, this adroit statesman, sat in Philadelphia's muggy June heat, because he had reached his decisions the slow, painful way and was ready for a new world.[25]

Samuel Adams was a radical, a hothead, the great PR man for the revolution, and politics had given him a convenient excuse for escaping his family responsibilities. The cause was everything. He never went home, abandoning his wife and children in the little house on Purchase Street, which badly needed repair. Often there was not enough cash for food, a fact that did not seem to worry this strange, dedicated political ascetic.

"Sam Adams was also Chief Incendiary of the revolution," as Governor Hutchinson of Massachusetts called him in his letters home to the ministry, a tough, cunning, full-time professional politician. He was the founding rabble-rouser, the leader of the rabbleoisie. He really believed in the revolution. He was a rebel with a cause, the workhorse of the radical wing of the Whig Party, the engineer of the locomotive of rebellion. He was the first of a new school of eighteenth-century revolutionaries who unbeknownst to himself was drawing up the blueprint of the French Revolution, a quarter of a century later.

Making revolution was the one thing he was good at; everything else he failed at. He was the opposite of Washington, having no head for business. The first thousand pounds his father loaned him he lost. He was good at losing. Very slowly he elevated himself from town scavenger to tax collector of Boston. As various historians say, it was here that he showed what a really first-class loser could do when given a free hand. In a few years his accounts as tax collector revealed shortages. He was so notoriously honest that nobody accused him of stealing the money. Investigation uncovered the fact that his shortage had come about through his failure to collect tax arrears which had been charged against his office. In time he and his friends managed to repay part of the shortage, which was, after all, technical and legal rather than actual. He was so easy-going, soft-hearted, and impractical that what with dipping into his collections for small personal sums, intermingling public and private funds, ignoring delinquencies, and neglecting his records, he was discovered at the end of ten years to be in arrears nearly seven thousand pounds.

Fortunately, just as he faced jail for defalcation, passage of the Stamp Act diverted attention from everybody's favorite tax collector's shortages, and he swept into power as a radical member of the Massachusetts House of Representatives and quickly rose to supreme leadership.*

Sam Adams controlled two Boston mobs, and he could still organize a riot whenever he chose, as he had on the day of the tea party. Then, having created the news, he could spread it fast in a form that was often untrue and always emotionally loaded, through his correspondence committee network. He was clerk of the Assembly of the colony of Massachusetts, troublemaker *extraordinaire*, a man who was one step from being an outlaw, who if it hadn't been for the revolution would have been in debtors' gaol as an embezzler or commingler of public funds. And he was the conscience of New England who had to be turned around. What to do? Boss Adams did what was necessary. The two distant cousins met on that fateful day outside the doors of the Congress. As Cousin John remembered it:

> Full of anxieties concerning these confusions, and
> apprehending daily that we should hear very distressing news
> from Boston, I walked with Mr. Samuel Adams in the State
> House yard for a little exercise and fresh air, before the hour

---

* I am in debt to Rankin and Scheer and Woodward for this audit of Sam Adams's career as a steward of public monies.

of Congress, and there represented to him the various dangers that surrounded us. He agreed to them all, but said, "What shall we do?"

I answered him that he knew I had taken great pains to get our colleagues to agree upon some plan, that we might be unanimous; but he knew that they would pledge themselves to nothing; but I was determined to take a step which should compel them and all the other members of Congress to declare themselves for or against something. "I am determined this morning to make a direct motion that Congress should adopt the army before Boston, and appoint Colonel Washington·commander of it." [26]

Cousin Samuel brushed aside the flies that followed him around Philadelphia. He was all for the Congress adopting the army. But Colonel Washington as the nominee for general was out of right field. He argued passionately that it was a New England army, a people's army, and Washington was a wealthy aristocrat from Virginia. Would his appointment dampen enthusiasm for the revolutionary cause?

"It is just because he is from Virginia, and aristocratic and wealthy, that I propose to nominate him," said Cousin John, in substance. "There is nothing that the revolutionary movement needs quite as much as it needs aristocracy and wealth; and above all it needs Virginia and the South."

Samuel Adams was as astute in politics as he was democratic in opinion. His cousin did not have to explain any further. Astuteness was considerably stronger than democracy at that moment.

"And I expect you to second the nomination," said Cousin John.

He didn't have to break his arm. Cousin Samuel, who understood politics, was probably worrying most about his puppet Hancock's reaction to the bad news. Would it crush the sugar daddy of the Massachusetts revolutionary movement? Well, you can't make an omelette without breaking some *oeufs*, as the great chef Brillat-Savarin was soon to observe.

There were other power brokers to consider as well as Hancock. The revolutionary movement—especially the army around Boston—had grown entirely too democratic for the taste of the wealthy landowners, lawyers, and merchants who composed the

Congress. "The heads of the mobilities* grow dangerous to the gentry," Gouverneur Morris had written the year before, "and how to keep them down is the question." Morris was an aristocratic revolutionist in the John Jay mold. In another letter of the same period he exclaims with a note of fear that "the mob begins to think and to reason."

Something had to be done about it. In Congress it was felt that the best remedy would be to place a rich man at the head of the army. Gouverneur Morris, a member of the Mount Vernon machine from New York, didn't have to be convinced.

The New York Provisional Congress had already written to its delegates with instructions: The ideal commander-in-chief should not only be a man who is an experienced soldier but he should be so wealthy that he would communicate luster to his duties rather than receive it from them. It seemed to many of the delegates, looking around, that the opulent Washington, sitting there every day in his uniform, was communicating a good deal of luster. He was the great nonverbal communicator.

And so it was that, on June 14, when Congress assembled, John Adams, leader of the floor fight for Washington, rose from his seat to his full 5'6". As he recalled:

> . . . and in as short a speech as the subject would admit, represented the state of the colonies . . . I concluded with a motion, in form, that Congress would adopt the army at Cambridge and appoint a general; that though this was not the proper time to nominate a general, yet, as I had reason to believe this was a point of greatest difficulty, I had no hesitation to declare that I had but one gentleman in my mind for that important command, and that was a gentleman from Virginia who was among us and very well known to all of us, a gentleman whose skill and experience as an officer, whose independent fortune, great talents, and excellent universal character, would command the approbation of all America and unite the cordial exertions of all the Colonies better than any other person in the Union. . . .[27]

This may have been the first "man-who" speech in which the name isn't mentioned until the end, a political tradition that survives in conventions to this day.

---

* *Mobility* was an eighteenth-century word meaning "the common people," in distinction to *nobility*.

Two things happened during Adams's man-who speech.

John Hancock, as head of the Congress, was in the chair when John Adams got on his feet to start his commander in chief nomination speech. He was on the edge of his chair, raptly agreeing as Adams ticked off the virtues that a new general must possess. "Gentlemen," Adams continued, "I know these qualifications are high, but we all know they are needful in this crisis in this chief. Does any one say they are not to be obtained in this country? In reply, I have to say they are; they reside in one of our own body—"

John Hancock was all smiles. He puffed like a peacock about to score.

"—and he is the man whom I now nominate—George Washington of Virginia."

John Adams wrote that he had never seen anyone's expression change as quickly as Hancock's changed that day. "Mr. Hancock, who was our President, which gave me an opportunity to observe his countenance while I was speaking on the state of the Colonies, the army at Cambridge, and the enemy, heard me with visible pleasure; but when I came to describe Washington for the commander, I never remarked a more sudden and striking change of countenance. Mortification and resentment were expressed as forcibly as his face could exhibit them. Mr. Samuel Adams seconded the motion and that did not soften the President's physiognomy at all." [28]

"Mr. Washington," as Adams wrote a few lines earlier, "who happened to sit near the door, as soon as he heard me allude to him, from his usual modesty, darted into the library room."

What a sight Colonel Washington must have been when he realized whom they were talking about. All legs and arms, the tall gentleman in the uniform bolted through the swinging doors like a skittish colt, beating a hasty retreat, a maneuver that he would be executing frequently in the years ahead.

Was the general-elect's surprise simulated? They had talked about the acceptance before Adams rose. A shrewd politician like Adams wouldn't risk getting egg on his face, being turned down, after all the machinations. He wasn't whistling or dancing in the dark when it came to picking Washington.

And yet the nominee now seemed genuinely stunned, surprised, startled enough to bolt out of the room. This was political theater at its best.

Such modesty, many thought and wrote in their notebooks and diaries. A man runs out of the room . . . flabbergasted they nominated him, picked him out; as John Adams is delivering the man-who speech, the man-who himself realizes 'tis he they are speaking of. *Moi?*

Of course, it could be argued, the truly modest person you're not even aware of. He is being so modest he blends into the wallpaper. You don't know he is trying to be modest. But it was a spectacular performance.

He went out; he stayed out; but after adjournment he, of course, was told of what happened. According to Colonel Freeman, John Adams paid high tribute to Washington and predicted that the choice of the Virginian would be approved by "all America" and would be a means of uniting the efforts of the colonies more cordially than would be possible under any other leader.

Boss Adams went into action again in the smoke-filled back rooms that night, or as he put it:

> The subject came under debate, and several gentlemen declared themselves against the appointment of Mr. Washington, not on account of any personal objection against him, but because the army were all from New England already, had a general of their own [Ward], appeared to be satisfied with him, and had proved themselves able to imprison the British army in Boston, which was all they expected or desired at that time. . . . The subject was postponed to a future day. In the meantime, pains were taken out of doors to obtain a unanimity, and the voices were generally so clearly in favor of Washington, that the dissentient members were persuaded to withdraw their opposition.[29]

It was all over but the huzzahing. The next day Washington again modestly absented himself. The Congress resolved that a general be appointed to command all the forces raised and to be raised outside Boston in defense. Thomas Johnson of Maryland rose and officially proposed Washington.*

No other name was put forward.

The election was unanimous.

---

* Johnson, it appears, was another good friend of long standing of the former Colonel Washington. The man who placed his name in nomination was eventually to be one of the three commissioners appointed by Prefident Washington for setting up the Federal District of Washington, a project of great interest to Prefident Washington and his friends, many of whom owned the land the city was built on or the ferry franchises across the Potomac.

[23]

eneral," a delegate said politely greeting Washington as he
G arrived for dinner at Burns's Tavern (a.k.a. "Burns in the
Fields")* the next day, handing off his cloak. It was the first time
history records his being addressed by the *word*. He didn't look
around to see whom the congressman was talking to. He didn't
say, *"Moi?"* He seemed to know, even though the congressional
session where the business had been transacted earlier in the day
was secret.

There is no record of dancing on the tables at the taverna on
the Schuylkill. It was a small working dinner with Dr. Cadwa-
lader.[31] And then there was a night session of a committee, drafting
rules and regulations. He was helping to set up the army, his army.
He also had to burn the midnight oil working on his acceptance
speech. He had decided not to do one of his off-the-lace-cuff
speeches for formal notification of his election the next day.

As for many a winning candidate with honors bestowed by a
convention in pocket, Washington's acceptance speech was written
in his hotel room by dawn's early light, an activity in which he was
aided by Edmund Pendleton. It was one of Washington's most
memorable speeches of his early political career. And was probably
written in its entirety by Pendleton. The only known copy of this
address, apparently the manuscript used by Washington on the
floor of the Congress that morning, is in vol. 152, "Papers of the
Continental Congress," Pt. I, p. 1, Library of Congress. "With the
exception of a single interpolation," Colonel Freeman continues,[32]
"it is in the autograph of Pendleton."[33] Fast Eddy, the admiring
Colonel Freeman says, "wrote more readily than Washington did."

Pendleton! Washington's ghost writer? The erstwhile leader
of the Stop-Washington-for-General movement, his speech writer?
The noncandidate's lawyer, who drew up his will? *Mon dieu*. What
a coincidence.

---

* Colonel Freeman says the *Diary of Jacob Hiltzenheimer*, p. 205, gives the historic site
of Burns's Tavern as Tenth Street. J. T. Scharf in his *History of Philadelphia*, vol. 1, p. 476,
fixed the location on Ninth, above Arch. Eberlein and Hubbard in their *Diary of Independence
Hall*, p. 260, stated that it was on the Commons, around Tenth and Vine Streets. That's
what happens from all that drinking: the taverns themselves moved like pink elephants.[30]

The next morning at the State House the Congress convened. John Hancock looked down from the chair at the man who had won the post that he himself had coveted, yearned for, and, for a moment there yesterday, thought was within his grasp. The session is graveled. The delegates take their Windsor chairs.

The despondent Hancock solemnly announces the good news: "The President had the order of Congress to inform George Washington, Esq., of the unanimous vote in choosing him to be General and Commander-in-Chief of the forces raised and to be raised in defence of American liberty. The Congress hoped the gentleman would accept." [34]

This time the colonel doesn't run out of the room. He stands, bows, whips out the acceptance speech from his back pocket, and reads the words written in Pendleton's hand:

> Mr. President: Tho' I am truly sensible of the high Honour done me in this Appointment, yet I feel great distress from a consciousness that my abilities and Military experience may not be equal to the extensive and important Trust: However, as the Congress desires I will enter upon the momentous duty, and exert every power I Possess In their Service for the Support of the glorious Cause: I beg they will accept my most cordial thanks for this distinguished testimony of their Approbation.
>
> But lest some unlucky event should happen unfavourable to my reputation, I beg it may be remembered by every Gentn. in the room, that I this day declare with the utmost sincerity, I do not think of my self equal to the Command I am honoured with.

It is a brilliant address. Modest, with humility, and politically astute. Not only does he tell his constituents that he is unqualified for the task ahead, they should expect nothing from him. He is making no promises about a job he never wanted.

It was a strange way to kick off a war. "Ho, boy, have you guys made a mistake." Disarming, to say the least. It's a strategy known as "covering one's ass."

From his earliest days as a soldier, in the Fort Necessity and Braddock campaigns, he demonstrated his concern and skill in protecting his rear, not to mention his flanks, from all censure and criticism. He was diligent in worrying about his reputation. With letters and paid newspaper stories (read, for example, his rebuttal to the *Centinel's* attacks on the debaucheries on the Virginia frontier), he smote his enemies tooth and eye. He had the genius, even in his twenties, to realize the importance of the printed word in public opinion.

He was, in a sense, not only making history but writing (or rewriting) it at the same time. He shrewdly did not rely on mere events or the telling of them. Participants die. But speeches last forever, preserved by industrious historians like me. He was never one to leave to posterity the judgments about him. He was working on his image as he went.

In the next few days the diffident general-elect expanded on the theme of incompetence and its pitfalls; he was to write furiously to everybody who had a mailbox, it seemed, to relatives and friends and political associates, predicting the worst that could happen. "From the day I entered up on the command of the American armies," he wrote sorrowfully to his friend Patrick Henry, "I date my fall and the ruin of my reputation." [35]

A tendency toward pessimism is displayed. But it was a master stroke in terms of PR. He openly told everybody about his darkest secret—his military incompetence. He was not the world's best general, as anybody knows who has looked at his war record. He promised them nothing. And he more than fulfilled the promise. In fact, he tells them to expect nothing. They didn't call him Honest George for nothing.

But there is one more paragraph in his inaugural military address which historians and patriots dwell on more, another disclaimer, that was to play an important role in the future of defense spending.

[24]

As to pay, Sir, I beg leave to Assure the Congress that as no pecuniary consideration could have tempted me to have accepted this Arduous employment (at the expence of my domestt, ease and happiness) I do not wish to make any proffit from it: I will keep an exact Account of my expences; those I doubt not they will discharge and that is all I desire." [36]

No pecuniary consideration . . . "proffit" without honor from it . . . Pendleton or Washington? Whoever wrote it, magnificent! The offer reeks of personal sacrifice. And what better time to sacrifice for one's country than at the start of a war. It's a lesson for the public. Time for everybody to hitch up their velvet britches, take a notch in the silk sash, do their bit for the war effort.

The general-elect was waiving the salary of $500 a month the Congress had voted. He was working for no pay. Zero. He only wants his new country to pick up his expenses. Imagine fighting a war against tyranny on an expense account!

When Washington declined with thanks to accept pay for his military services, the act was hailed as a monument to patriotism. John Adams, for one, almost fainted upon hearing the last paragraph. He had not been so moved in the Congress since overhearing the sentiment about Washington's readiness to send a one-thousand-man army to Boston. At the time Adams was worried that Congress would consider extravagant the rest of the army payroll he had been hammering through committee. Generals Ward, Lee, Putnam, and Schuyler were to get $166, or £75, a month—when they got it. Brigadier-generals were rated at $125 a month, and so on down to captains at $20; lieutenants, $13⅓; privates, $6⅔ a month. And all were "to find their own Arms and Clothes,"* which was even harder to do than to find their pay.[37]

This concept was not totally original. Paul Revere handed in an expense account for the famous ride to alarm the countryside that the British were coming. Henry Longfellow did not mention it in his poem, full of inaccuracies but a superb puff piece for the midnight rider.†

It takes away none of the luster of General Washington's achievements in the field. He is still, according to the standard source on the subject,[38] the founding father of the expense account. Revere is the grandfather.

His enemies, the naysayers, however, pooh-poohed Washington's sacrifice. It was a snobbish action, they said. It immediately set him off from everybody who *needed* to get his pay. They said he was, after all, one of the richest men, if not the richest, in the colonies. The money was a drop in the barrel.

---

* Except for General Washington, whose haberdashery bills were put on his expense account.

† Revere's chit for that and other efforts in the patriots' cause can be seen at the Massachusetts Archives and Commonwealth Museum at Columbia Point in Boston.

In fairness, it should be pointed out that his wealth was largely on paper, based on crops and land, therefore uncertain and dependent on vagaries. He was land-poor, always in debt, as we shall see, always short of hard cash to meet his daily needs. He even had to borrow money from some Alexandria businessman in 1789 to get to his inauguration, a potential conflict of interest that never interested the first Congress's ethics-in-new-government committee.

The refusal of pay, then, was a genuine sacrifice. Nevertheless, it should be pointed out he had never previously gotten paid for going to war. He served without pay when he served Lieutenant Governor Dinwiddie in the stockholders' war for the Ohio Company and when he was on General Braddock's staff as a consultant on fighting in the woods. The fact is that planter-aristocrats never accepted a paycheck for anything. How did you pay a planter-aristocrat—by the hour? Like a day laborer? And what is the going rate for being the father of a country?

To this day, many Washington admirers believe that his services to his country were entirely uncompensated for. It was a sentiment widely stated before the publication of the expense account in 1837. "Here was no mercenary view of private emolument," exclaimed Charles Atherton, a New Hampshire lawyer. "His services were unbought. They were free will offerings at the altar of patriotism." [39]

It is inaccurate to suggest that during the war Washington lived in the style to which he had grown accustomed after marrying the richest woman in Virginia, Martha (Megabucks) Custis. He did not exactly share the spartan conditions of his men, as historian John Ferling has put it: "Headquarters normally was in a modest dwelling in which Washington allotted to himself one or two small rooms." Whereas John Adams may have thought his candidate's bill for fighting the war against British tyranny was going to be a petty cash item, it may have inspired the later Stealth (B-2) budget.

The shrewd Adams never dreamed he was underwriting the Washington-for-Prefident movement.* Congress, in effect, by accepting Washington's no-salary deal, was authorizing the taxpayers

---

* Adams never did understand expense accounts or the basic principles thereof. He later went to Paris, in 1778, as a diplomat, a member of the American embassy to France, on a government expense account and made quite a nuisance of himself. He went around the embassy hassling the head of the delegation, Benjamin Franklin, and our old friend Silas Deane, a founding peculator, about the amount of money they were so lavishly throw-

to pay for all his campaign expenses. All the ink and goose-feather quills that went into the letters, all the paper, sand for blotting, postage, all the secretaries, poets, portraitists, all the dinners and express riders, spreading his words and legends. He was building a war record he could run on—and everything was, in effect, tax deductible. Sitting presidents do the same thing. It wasn't until 180 years later that Congress officially got around to approving federal underwriting of campaigning expenses, which Washington was anticipating by having taxpayers pay his own expenses. George Washington's picture on the dollar bill is wonderfully appropriate.

John Adams became more and more depressed by his support of Washington for general. By 1777 he was standing up in Congress, leading the opposition against a proposal to allow Washington to choose his own general staff. And in a speech on the floor he dared to criticize the general, who was already bucking for demigod status.

"I have been distressed to see," Adams said, "some of our members disposed to idolize an image which their own hands have molten. I speak here of the superstitious veneration which is paid to General Washington. Although I honor him for his good qualities, yet in this house I feel myself his superior."[40]

Soon Adams would be questioning Washington's intelligence. "The great Character," he roared, "was a character of Convention," created by all those who "expressly agreed to blow the trumpet of panegyric in concert. . . . That Washington was not a scholar is certain. That he was too illiterate, unlearned, unread for his station and reputation is equally past dispute."[41] Benjamin Rush outdid Adams's bitter assessment by telling of a friend who once noticed that Washington, after making a purchase, was unable to count his change.[42]

That is an obvious falsehood, a base canard.* No matter how limited General Washington's mind would prove to be—"His

---

ing around. Adams scrimped and saved on his expenses, and argued that the free-spending freedom fighters Franklin and Deane should be less wanton and profligate. Didn't they realize there was a war on? He won the enmity of Franklin and Deane, and everybody else, for his pain and economies. He worried himself sick about the waste of the public's money on government business. And the government soon turned on him. When he was appointed ambassador to the Court of Saint James, after the war, Congress cut his salary by one fifth.

* It is not true that a base canard is a duck with a low voice.

mind was great and powerful," said Thomas Jefferson, but that mind, he added, was not "of the very first order. . . . It was slow in operation, being little aided by invention or imagination but sure in conclusion"[43]—George Washington, I'm sure, always counted his change!

Adams had begun to question the media hype for Washington which he himself had started in 1775. He was beginning to think that Washington was, whatever providence decreed, and whatever he said in '75, not the best man.

Adams had two flaws as a politician. He was sensitive and he had a conscience, qualities that will usually prevent anyone from climbing to the top of the greased pole of American politics today. He was always checking his emotional temperature, looking around for cause and effect. "What hath I wrought," he asked himself about Washington. As Hughes writes:

> John Adams was, in a very real sense, Washington's creator.
> If afterwards he came to fear that he had played
> Frankenstein and manufactured a monster who might devour
> the republic; if he came to be revolted by the groveling
> idolatry the public felt for this general who somehow won
> almost no battles; if Adams dreaded that the adulation
> Washington received might, and must, waken royal dreams
> in that lofty head, this was only natural in one who had read
> so much history and had found few or no men whom power
> and reverence had bowed down under a sense of
> responsibility and meekness.[44]

Adams had been Dr. Frankenstein in making Washington the general, and he was to spend years trying to dismantle the electrodes. As Adams was always to find, he was no match for Washington. "George Washington's mind operated on complex levels," as historian Richard B. Bernstein was to say, "and Adams was on one level—honest."[45]

He had created a monster, but it wasn't as bad as Adams made it out to be. With the power Adams injected into him, he didn't run amuck. With the army behind him, he could have become a dictator, a Caesar, but he never did. Adams created the right monster, at the right time. Think what shape this country would be in, for example, if Jefferson had become the first prefident. We'd be the biggest of the banana republics, with revolutions every four years and fence-to-fence farms from coast to coast.

Adams, of course, was on the lunatic fringe of American politics in the late 1770s, daring to be anti-Washington. He became unhinged, I believe, in Paris. While Washington spread his feathers like a peacock under the eyes of belles at balls his wife didn't attend, John Adams went to pieces away from Abigail during his five-year stint as a diplomat. Poor Adams was badly shaken, I believe, by being forced night after night to dine with French mam'selles in deep-cut gowns. With only his Puritan conscience for company in his hotel room, he developed severe migraines—*le headache*, the medical term in France. A model for future Pulitzer Prize winners in letters, suddenly Adams would go three or four months in Paris without writing a single letter home. While tangling with Franklin and a normal Puritan's sex problems, Adams was suffering from what psychoanalysts today would call severe depression.

[25]

I t is not clear from the remaining evidence whether there was, at the conclusion of the acceptance speech, a spontaneous demonstration in Washington's behalf. There undoubtedly was applause, Colonel Freeman says. A polite padding of gloves and a few "Hear, hear, you alls" from the Virginians. In fact, none of the letters in Burnett's record of the proceedings even mentions the acceptance speech, which was treated as an extemporaneous remark, not worthy of ink.

Hancock, the runner-up in the race, made peace. "I shall sign his commission tomorrow," the disgruntled avowed candidate said in his concession speech, delivered to Elbridge Gerry back home in Massachusetts. "He is a fine man." Life goes on. Eventually Hancock also wrote to Washington asking for a place in his army. "I am determined to serve under you, if it be to take the firelock and join in the ranks as a volunteer." Hancock compromised by getting married instead, sublimating his martial for marital instincts until 1780, when he fulfilled his promise—briefly—appearing in Rhode Island in a colorful uniform.

Meanwhile, Washington prepared to ride into battle by writing a few more humble letters which show himself aware of the political horsetrading that had made his election possible. He wrote to Martha's brother-in-law, Colonel Bassett: "I am now Imbarked on a tempestuous ocean, from whence perhaps no friendly harbor is to be found. . . . It is an honor I by no means aspired to. It is an honor I wished to avoid . . . but the partiality of the Congress, added to some political motives, left me without a choice. May God grant, therefore, that my acceptance of it, may be attended with some good to the common cause, & without injury (from want of knowledge) to my own reputation." [46]

He wrote in the same modest, humble tone to his fellow officers of the Fairfax militia companies, the weekend warriors from whose ranks he was graduating:

Gentlemen: I am now about to bid adieu to the companies under your respective commands, at least for a while. I have launched into a wide and extensive field, too boundless for my abilities, and far, very far, beyond my experience. I am called by the unanimous voice of the colonies to the command of the Continental Army—an honour I did not aspire to: an honour I was solicitous to avoid, upon a full conviction of my inadequacy to the importance of the service. The partiality of the Congress, however, assisted by a political motive, rendered by reasons availing, and I shall to-morrow set out for the camp near Boston. [47]

He was always at his most eloquent when saying how incompetent he was in military matters. He excelled in putting himself down. It was his *shtick*.

About this time, too, he wrote his brother-in-law, Burwell Bassett, about his dream of establishing on some of his wilderness lands at the confluence of the inaccessible Kanawha and the impenetrable Ohio a refuge so remote that "no enemy would think the loot worth the labour of the journey." In "the worse event," as he explained in a dark letter about the future, his lands would "serve him for an asylum." [48]

This secret escape plan was hardly a personal vote of confidence. All in all, the general-elect seemed to have some doubts about his qualifications. Hence, he took steps to preserve his neck in case he lost.

There was an element of risk, psychological and real, in the whole Revolutionary War caper. With his own and his army's limitations, he might very well lose, and be hung as a treacherous, disloyal rat.

Not even his worst political enemies doubted his courage and fearlessness, demonstrations of which were always broadcast through the nation, like Edward R. Murrow's reporting from the rooftop in the London blitz. Washington had a readiness to risk his "precious and valuable life," as one of the encomiums from the battlefield reporters called it.[49]

And then there is my own theory. The call to duty was an excuse to get away from Martha. I'm not saying he wasn't devoted to his wife. But his whole pattern of going away every season—to sit on the Burgesses or in Congress, where he did nothing much— is as orderly and predictable as the departure of those love birds, the swallows from Capistrano. Jefferson managed to stay at home during the war. It was not totally necessary even to go to Congress or to run for general, a job he himself avowed he was nowise qualified for.

The defeatist, pessimistic talk about his abilities left the new commander in chief in an enviable political situation. If he lost a battle, well, he had told them so. If he lost enough of them, he would lose the war, and be hanged.

The prefidential bandwagon was on its way. The next stop: Boston.

Part III

The Making of the War Hero

Being the true story of how Silent George managed to win the war, even though the score was England 9, U.S.A. 2.

[1]

Three days after his election, the general-elect left downtown Quaker City with his major generals (Lee and Schuyler) in Washington's new carriage, the limo of its day for the Virginia gentry, purchased on his new expense account, accompanied by the Philadelphia Light Horse. Adams was in the delegation from Congress riding with their choice for Generalissimo. As the entourage made its way to the Pennsylvania Turnpike, on the way north to the front, he might have been in a mixed mood about events, as was so often the case with Adams.

As the general-elect's carriage crossed the Delaware, and the Light Horse and the congressional delegates turned back to the business of running the country, Adams could have been regretting something. The new nation had elected a general, unusual for its time and today. What Adams might have brooded about was the second half of his legislative program. Adams had advocated the election of all general officers by the Congress—annually.[1] It was a plan of government in a new democracy that would understandably not be popular at headquarters.[2]

As Washington continued northward to the front as commander in chief, people were now traveling many miles just to look at him. This tall, silent real-estate tycoon from Virginia had become instantly the most prominent man in America. He was the colonies' first superstar.

And when they saw him, someone in the general's legion of admirers was sure to jot down a poem. One of the popular versifiers-correspondents reported on observing the new general go by:

> . . . With manly gait
> His faithful steel suspended by his side,
> Pass'd W—shi—gt—n along, Virginia's hero.

(The poet, Dr. Solomon Drowne, added a daydream that the outcome of the war would be determined in a single manly battle between W—shi—gt—n and George III.[3])

The news of Washington's election, meanwhile, jarred the War Office in Whitehall out of its bureaucratic slumbers. Ministers and clerks flipped through old files looking for Braddock's reports, in which he may have mentioned the name of Washington, trying to analyze his character and elicit clues to his forthcoming style of fighting. Who was this man who they could have had in their own army? "A very deserving gentleman," Lt. Governor Dinwiddie had written the ministry in Washington's behalf as he wheeled and dealed for a commission in the regular army in the late 1760s before he married Martha. Who was this war hero, as the public thought, who only twenty years ago had surrendered at Fort Necessity to save his men from drowning because he had built the fort in the middle of a riverbed and it started to rain? Who *was* this aristocrat in velvet britches who led a revolt to overthrow the aristocracy, the leader of the people's army of the people's republic, the rebels?*

In the beginning, they wouldn't even call our rebel general by his rightful title. When Admiral Lord Howe of the British Navy made his first move to negotiate peace with our commander-in-

---

* The rebels didn't like to be called "rebels." Although *rebels* was a customary term for those taking part in a rebellion, the noun pained many Americans. "Britain has most unjustly pronounced us rebels, and treated us as such," the Reverend Jacob Green, minister of the Presbyterian Church in Hanover, New Jersey, complained in 1776. In the same year, Captain Alexander Graydon found *rebel* "extremely offensive to my ear . . . however appropriate it might be."

The word *rebel* sounded seditious, radical, un-American. And we still don't like it today. In modern press usage, rebels are usually the bad guys. Our papers today would have called the founding fathers "the Bolsheviks." For synonyms they might have used "Reds" or "Communists."

The rebels were also called, by Nicholas Cresswell, a British visitor who had arrived in the colonies in 1774, "Sleber"—rebels, in reverse. The good guys in his journal of his visit were called "Sgnik Sdneirf," in his pre–James Bond transparent code reference to the "King's Friends," or Tories.

The slebers would have preferred *liberators*, but settled for *patriots*.

I, myself, like the word *oppressed*.

The British settled for *banditti*, or *dirty bandits*.

chief in Cambridge the next month (August 1775), as Michael
Pearson says,

> He sent a lieutenant over to the town in a longboat under a
> flag of truce, but the rebel commander refused to receive the
> letter the officer carried because it was addressed to George
> Washington Esq. with no reference to his status as general.
> Two days later, delivery was rejected even of an answer to a
> letter of his own because it was not properly addressed.
> Ambrose Serle, the admiral's secretary, was incensed. "We
> strove as far as decency and honour could permit . . . to
> avert all bloodshed . . ." he scribbled angrily in his journal.
> "And yet it seems to be beneath a little paltry colonel of
> militia at the head of a banditti of rebels to treat with a
> representative of his lawful sovereign because it is impossible
> to give all the titles which the poor creature requires."[4]

"A little paltry colonel of militia" was considerably less than
"his Excellency," which is what Americans called George Washington. He didn't mind that.

General Charles Lee, the satirist-general, got some good
laughs out of the tendency of the republicans to adopt resounding
titles of the monarchy. On September 19 he wrote to Dr. Benjamin
Rush:

> I condemn with you the barbarous, dangerous custom of
> loading the Servants of the People with the trappings of
> Court Titles. I cannot conceive who the Devil first devis'd
> the bauble of Excellency for their Commander in Chief, or
> the more ridiculous of His Honour for me—Upon my Soul
> They make me spew—even the tacking honorable to the
> Continental Congress creates a wambling in my stomack—
> What cou'd add dignity to the simple title of the Continental
> Congress of America, as long as they do their duty? And the
> instant They grow corrupt or slavish from timidity all the
> rumbling sounds of honorable, serene, mighty, sublime, or
> magnanimous, will only make their infamy more infamous.[5]

One who probably didn't mind the monarchist claptrap was
"Lady Washington," as they called Martha. She seemed to revel
in that appellation. It was the least she should get in return for
being discommoded so much by her husband's latest adventure in
politics.

[2]

I n 1775, when George Washington was riding to war, most Americans did not want a revolution. They had to be cajoled into it. A super sales job by Sam Adams and the radicals, though admittedly King George and his ministers were a great help. Our king (remember we were all British in 1775) was a little unbalanced at the time. His majesty's policy of blundering his way to Yorktown has been lately attributed to porphyria* but that didn't kick in until later in George the Mad's regime. His mental derangement was one of the rebels' secret weapons in winning the war.

As Marcus Cunliffe says, the majority of Americans were still Sgnik Sdneirf—Tories—or if not outright Tories, they were, in Washington's phrase, "still feeding upon the dainty food of reconciliation." One third of the nation supported Sleber, or the Washingtonistas (patriots). Of that one third, what percentage preferred liberty or death is not known. I suspect many were moderates on the death issue. One third of the people were for the king (Tories). And one third were for neither side (neutral). These figures, courtesy of John Adams, did not include the "don't cares," and the "don't knows," who had to be considerable. They didn't have TV news on the frontier. The apathy vote must have been significant.

The "people," we can be sure, were not as high on the revolution as historians and patriotic societies later claimed. What did the revolution mean to the average man? A story is told about John Adams bubbling over with revolutionary passion as he returned from the Continental Congress. Riding along a country road, he met one of the common herd. In his democratic fervor Mr. Adams drew the fellow into conversation, and found that the man was "grateful" to Mr. Adams and to the Continental Congress for the changes they had wrought in society. "There are no courts of justice now in this province," he said, "and I hope there will never be another."

For one who believed in the rule of law, was a leading member of the bar and a regular in attendance at the courts of justice,

* Not only did George III have blue blood, but blue urine, according to *George III and the Mad Business* by Ida Macalpine and Richard Hunter.

Adams was made very gloomy by this idealist. When he reached home, he wrote his reflections:

"Is this the object for which I have been contending, said I to myself, for I rode along without any answer to this wretch. . . . If the power of the country should get into such hands, and there is a great danger that it will, to what purpose have we sacrificed our time, health and everything else?"

The one third who supported the war included romantic idealists, those who sincerely resented British tyranny, and born rebels. Sam Adams rebelled against anything. He would have been a troublemaker in Utopia.

The division between patriots and Tories went through all levels of society. Even the "don't knows," "don't cares," and fence-sitters were divided. Some of the common people who would have been expected to support the revolution liked the king because he protected them from the landlords and lawyers, who were among the biggest supporters of the revolution.

There were many issues, of course, afflicting the other oppressed, those of Washington's class. The Washingtonistas were against "taxation without representation." It was the slogan of the revolution. What was this representation they were always talking about?

First of all, most Americans were not represented in their own legislative assemblies. Women were not represented, to name a large group at random. Those who didn't go to the established church in South Carolina, Georgia, Pennsylvania, or in any colony in New England (except Rhode Island) couldn't vote.

How amazed the British were about the fuss we were kicking up about the representation issue. It's not as if British citizens were somehow *better* represented in Parliament. Liverpool, Leeds, and Manchester did not have one representative, while some tiny hamlets had two. Certain individuals of title had several representatives. The Duke of Norfolk had eleven! Not one Englishman in fifty possessed a vote. In all Scotland there were only 3,000 voters. The rotten borough system could be smelled in New Jersey.

The breach between the mother country and the revolting children was over taxation. Ye stamp acts and other Intolerable Acts (especially various tax bills) were levied in order to pay for defense costs of the French and Indian War. This led to the demand of "no taxation without representation," by those on whom those petty taxes fell—the rich. The average guy didn't have to buy that many stamps to put on official documents.

The American rich people also suffered from being slighted by their counterparts in England. They wanted to be treated like English aristocrats. They were second-class rich here.

Of course, George Washington represented more than just the rich people in his club, the moneyed classes, the top rank, the very rich. The ex-paltry colonel banditto was a land developer, a man of vision who was excited by the opening up of the West, some of which he already owned. His holdings included some forty miles of land on both sides of the Ohio River. He was a visionary schemer and planner who was investing in canals and steamboats, probably thinking of railroads and airplanes. He was also a captain of industry, the owner of a flour mill, a whiskey distillery (spiritual home of Mount Vernon Rye), chief executive of an agribusiness that stretched over five plantations. His industrial empire included a company town and a store, providing social welfare services (food, medicine, and recreation) to his 235 full-time employees, the slaves.

Basically his profession between the two wars was getting rich. And nobody worked harder at it. In colonial life, there was not much room for idle men or women. They all worked hard accumulating capital, as Washington did. He was a representative of those men of fortune. His industry had been fruitful and it multiplied. He was a role model to everyone who was trying to improve his material situation in life. He was a symbol of getting ahead. Everybody in colonial times was doing business with and to each other. The prevailing idea was to get the best of one's neighbors, if possible, by selling something, starting with land—at a large profit. At this George Washington was the greatest, a man everyone rallied behind. Every speculator and land jobber was his friend. The founding shady businessmen were for him. Like all generals who were also politicians, Washington had a circle of friends from business who profited from his making war. Well, Grant and Eisenhower were not as clean as a houndstooth, either.

[3]

W ho was this forty-three-year-old man who represented one third of the people but was rapidly becoming beloved by all, the chairman of the board, riding into battle carrying the hopes of all Americans, but particularly of the Van Rensselaers, Beekmans, Schuylers, Livingstons, and the rest of the gentry?

George Washington was not born in a manger, nor a log cabin, but in a small house on a plantation at Bridge's Creek, Virginia, on three different days, or so it would seem.

He was born on February 22. Or February 11, old style. Or maybe it was the third Monday of every February. The reason we get everything wrong about George Washington's birthday was explained by Hughes:

> Wise men had long known the inaccuracy of the popular opinion that a year is always 365¼ days long, and, as far back as 1582, Pope Gregory had lent his authority to a revision of the old calendar. But anti-Catholic England did not accept the Gregorian correction until 1752, by which time it was necessary to add eleven days to all Old Style dates to bring them up to the sun. New Year's day was simultaneously changed from the 25th of March (the Day of the Annunciation) to the first of January. Hence we find the date of Washington's birth put with an ambiguous double numeral, as February 11, 1731/2.[6]

None of this would have mattered to George Washington. To his dying day he thought of himself as born on February 11, whatever the calendar said. In the last two Februaries of his life he wrote in his diary under February 11 that he went up to Alexandria to attend "an elegant Ball and Supper at Night," "in commemmoration" of his birthday.[7]

What would he think of the current style of celebrating his birthday on the third Monday of every February as Presidents' Day? He would celebrate three times, if I know my George Washington. He liked parties.

The plantation where all of these birthday celebrations started was in Westmoreland County. The Washington birthplace was a mile-wide plot bordered by Pope's Creek on one side and Bridges' Creek on the other, a thousand acres of wood and bottom land, with the house facing the Potomac. Many years after his father moved away the plantation was called Wakefield. The house burned down in 1779, without a picture ever being made by campaign graphics people of the national shrine.

He was "a poor boy." By "poor," I mean compared to his neighbors. He grew up next to the Fairfaxes. The Fairfaxes owned the Shenandoah Valley—all of it. Also the Northern Neck, from the upper Potomac River to the Rappahannock (twenty-one counties were later made of the Fairfaxes' 5,400,000 acres). It was more land than in my entire state of New Jersey.

It led to a feeling of social inferiority in the young Washington, and a pattern of keeping up with the Fairfaxes that was to keep those big feet of his climbing upward on the social ladder.

Little is known about his childhood. This is strange, in the light of how much is known about the rest of his life. Every inch of ground he plowed, every fruit tree or bush he planted, or slave he bought, is counted, enumerated. Yet he wrote nothing of his childhood. His childhood consisted of his father's asking about the cherry tree. It wasn't until the sixth edition of Parson Weems's posthumous campaign biography—*A History of the Life and Death, Virtues and Exploits of General George Washington* (1800)—that the brazen account of the cherry tree affair was invented.

Although he was a celebrity in his twenties, after the French and Indian War, isn't it strange that nobody remembers anecdotes about the young Washington? "Let me tell you about . . ." this exploit or that, or "Remember the time George and I were horsing around down at Madame Fifi's in Williamsburg. . . ." It is as if a vacuum cleaner had gone through his life and tidied up.

Of course, a marble god casts no shadow. But the man appears to have cast no shadow on mere mortals or anybody else's life. It's frustrating. I want to know what he really said when his father asked him which son of a bitch here cut down that cherry tree? Was the father of the father (to be) of the country like Bill Cosby's father? Where did George get his monumental sense of humor from—his father or mother?

We know, despite the thousands of books following Weems's whimsy, as much about Washington's boyhood as about Shakespeare's, and/or Marlowe's, i.e., almost nothing.

*

But we do know some things. His formal education was limited. The elementary school dropout's shaky spelling and grammar did not hurt him politically. Everyone's spelling and grammar were shaky. His geography also seemed quaint. In a school copybook, George listed "Colofornia" as one of the "Chief Islands of North America," together with "Icelands, Greenland, Barbados and the rest of the Caribee Islands."[8] Many in Virginia thought that California was an island.

The whole colony may have been geography impaired. One Virginia leader reminded the Board of Trade in London that his colony's western lands stretched as far as "the South Seas" (the Pacific Ocean), "including California." Under the Virginia charter, Virginia arguably *did* extend to California.

He was not a reader, like Adams. Nor was he a boy of ideas, as Jefferson was. But he was good in math. Washington was a boy of money and action. His intellectual pursuits were bookkeeping rather than book reading. He was fascinated less by Hobbes, Hume, and Rousseau than compound interest and debentures. He was very good at counting things. He once noted in his diary[9] that he had calculated the numbers of each grain there were in bushels of various grasses. His highest figure was for timothy: 13,410,000.

Pshaw, says Colonel Flexner, assuring us that he didn't actually count the whole bushel. "But he enumerated how many there were in a small fraction of a bushel and then multiplied."[10] This takes away nothing from the achievement. Clearly his was the kind of mind that was not going to write sonnets or quartets for a living when he grew up.

As a teenager, he liked to draw maps. He was one of those kids whose parlor tricks included drawing up for house guests, with his new surveying tools, a plan of a turnip field.

As a poor boy, at thirteen, with the death of his father and with a mother who didn't understand him, and being a number-two son—Lawrence, the half-brother and the number-one son, was sent to England for schooling (it was the age of primogeniture)—George stayed home and had to learn a trade. Whereas other presidents and politicians became lawyers, he was a surveyor. To this day he is the only surveyor ever to become chief executive.

The Fairfaxes influenced his choice of careers. Lord Fairfax, who came over to Virginia in 1746, needed some land surveyed, the Blue Ridge parcel (the Shenandoah Valley), and he gave the job to his relative, young George William Fairfax, who lived next door to George Washington. The boy next door applied for the job of assistant surveyor and was accepted.

The pay was magnificent for a sixteen-year-old. "A Dubble-loon is my constant gain every Day that the weather will permit my going out and sometimes Six Pistoles." At that time a double-loon was the equivalent of about $7.20, and a pistole was worth $3.60, approximately. He didn't squander it at discos. He bought land.

In 1748, about the time of the Fairfax surveying expedition, he wrote a letter to a friend about one of his love affairs. A draft of the letter was found in his workbook recording his survey of the Fairfax estates. It is too boring to repeat, except for the parts where he gets to the girls. Two of his heartthrobs were Mary Cary (Sally Fairfax's sister) and the famous Low Land Beauty:

> My place of Residence is at present at His Lordships' where
> I might, was my heart disengaged, pass my time very
> pleasantly as theres a very agreeable Young Lady Lives in
> the same house (Colo George Fairfax's Wifes' Sister) but as
> thats only adding Fuel to fire it makes me the more uneasy
> for by often and unavoidably being in company with her
> revives my former Passion for your Low Land Beauty
> whereas was I to live more retired from young Women I
> might in some measure eliviate my sorrows by burying that
> chast and troublesome Passion in the grave of oblivion or
> etarnall forgetfulness for as I am very well assured thats the
> only antidote or remedy that I shall be relieved by or only
> recess that can administer any cure or help to me as I am well
> convinced was I ever to attempt any thing I should only get a
> denial which would be only adding grief to uneasiness.[11]

First of all, who was this "Low Land Beauty" who must have told him to go throw himself across the Rappahannock? Nobody knows, though half a dozen Virginia families still claim an ancestress who was the very beauty from the lowland.* And, as Hughes has said, none of them can prove it.

---

* Some say it was Mary Bland of Westmoreland. She married a Henry Lee. But Lucy Grymes has more support for the honor, according to Hughes. She lived in Richmond County on the estate called Morattico. Her father, Charles Grymes, was the son of John Grymes of Grymesby, "on the Piankatank where the bullfrog leaps from bank to bank."

As this paragraph from the Low Land Beauty letter explains, "Whereas was I to live more retired from young Women I might in some measure eliviate my sorrows by burying that chast and troublesome Passion in the grave of oblivion or etarnall forgetfulness"— he's finished with women. Forever. He's going to become a monk. And he's all of sixteen.

Then we come to another in his secret teenage arsenal of Cupid's darts, the love poem, this one a truly deadly weapon, the acrostic:

From your bright sparkling Eyes I was undone;
Rays, you have; more transperent than the Sun,
Amidst its glory in the rising day
None can you equal in your bright array;
Constant in your calm and unspotted Mind;
Equal to all, but will to none prove kind,
So knowing, seldom one so Young, you'l Find.

Ah! woe's me, that I should Love and conceal
Long have I wish'd, but never dare reveal,
Even though severely Loves Pains I feel;
Xerxes that great, was't free from Cupids Dart,
A*nd all the greatest Heroes, felt the smart.

"No teenager ever took his puppy love so seriously," explained a historian well on in his years. There is nothing more serious, he doesn't seem to realize. I still haven't gotten over mine.

In the prewar years, before he got his act together, Washington had compiled a record with the chicks that would have been statistically impressive (0–9). He was famous for asking 12- or 13-year-old bimbos to marry him. None accepted. Jilted was his middle name in his hapless teens.

She threw away the chance to marry the father of his country and married another Henry Lee of Stratford. (Everybody seemed to marry a Henry Lee.) She became a famous mother and grandmother, numbering among her children Lighthorse Harry Lee, who was a favorite of Washington's, and among her grandchildren, Robert E. Lee.

A still more likely Low Land Beauty was Betsy Fauntleroy. We know that she rejected Washington at least once, for he says so himself. As Hughes reports, "She was descended from the famous cavalier Moore Faunt Le Roy, a Huguenot who was the proprietor of a great tract on the Rappahannock."

* The FRANCES ALEXA young George was singing about was never officially identified. She was said to be a member of the ALEXANDER family, who had a plantation near Mount Vernon. Some love historians say she was his first recorded passion.

Let me tell you what a dork he must have been as a teenager.

During the summer of 1751, Washington went swimming in the Rappahannock near his mother's home, and while he frolicked in the waves, two women stole his clothes. For this they were arrested and tried; one of them turned state's evidence and the other received fifteen lashes on her bare back.

The case is thus recorded in the order book of 1749–55, William Hunter being one of the county justices:

> 3 Dec. 1751. Ann Carrol and Mary McDaniel Senr. of Frederickburgh, being Committed to the Gaol of this County by William Hunter Gent, on Suspicion of Felony & Charged with robing the Cloaths of Mr. George Washington when he was washing in the River some time last Summer, the Court having heard Several Evidences Are of Oppinion that the said Ann Carroll be discharged & Admitted an Evidence for our Lord the King against the said Mary McDaniel.
>
> And Upon Considering the whole Evidences & the prisoners defence, The Court are of Oppinion that the said Mary McDaniel is guilty of petty Larceny, whereupon the said Mary desired immediate punishment for the said Crime & relied on the Mercy of the Court, therefore it is ordered that the Sheriff carry her to the Whipping post & inflict fifteen lashes on her bare back, And then she be discharged. [12]

Washington was not in the country during the trial and the punishment. He had sailed for Barbados in September. Otherwise he probably would have married her.

It was at the end of his career as a teenage werewolf that he happened to notice Sally Fairfax, who made the others seem as nothing. She was a sophisticated older woman who could speak French and dance, looked exactly like Jaclyn Smith, and took matronly interest in the awkward, gangly surveyor who wrote mad, passionate (for him) love letters to her during the French and Indian War.

The typical average Englishman George Washington grew up wanting to be was Lord Fairfax. He was a cousin of the George William Fairfax who owned Belvoir, the plantation next to Mount Vernon, and whose daughter had married Lawrence Washington. The nobleman was a bachelor in his fifties when he took up residence at Belvoir and met young Washington. Princeton historian and later president Woodrow Wilson says, in his airy, romantic prose, that Lord Fairfax was "a man strayed out of the world of fashion . . . a man of taste and culture, he had written with Addison and Steele for the Spectator."

George was more at home in the saddle than in the drawing room. But Fairfax took a shine to him. The overgrown lad could ride magnificently and shoot well. He was a terror with the foxes, and a disaster with the ladies. All of which Lord Fairfax liked in a young man.

Young George Washington, the historians say, was also dependable, forthright, and honest. He said very little. He did not ask the keen and searching questions which make wealthy elderly gentlemen uneasy and wonder what the world is coming to. He was not a pain in the ass. No doubt Lord Fairfax liked that, too, in his protégé.

At sixteen, he had much to learn about society—but at least he knew it. Hanging around with the Fairfaxes, the awkward, gangly, rough-hewn surveyor's apprentice next door picked up a patina of manners and a polish of liquid gold.

He left his widowed mother and moved in with his married half-brother Larry at Mount Vernon. In the library, he found *Youth's Behaviour, or Decency in Conversation Amongst Men* by the Englishman Francis Hawkins, the Mr. Manners of his day. He saw the shortcomings, the gaffes, the difference between the saddle and drawing room, between life at Mount Vernon and the Fairfaxes. In one of his school copybooks, he wrote in neat handwriting 110 "dont's," which he titled "Rules of Civility & Decent Behaviour in Company and Conversation."

There is something refreshing and charming about a teenager who wrote so carefully in his copybook the distillation of centuries of good manners, the English gentleman's guide for getting along and ahead. He memorized such don'ts as "Spit not on the fire . . . especially if there be meat before it."

I especially love this rule: "If you yawn, do it not loud but privately; and speak not in your yawning, but put your handkerchief or hand before your face and turn aside."

And:

* Sleep not when others speak.
* Put not off your cloths in the presence of others, nor go out your chamber half drest.

* If others talk at table be attentive but talk not with meat in your mouth.
* When in company, put not your hands to any part of the body, not usually discovered.
* Shew nothing to your friend that may affright him.
* In the presence of others sing not to yourself with a humming noise, nor drum with your fingers or feet.
* Let your countenance be pleasant but in serious matters somewhat grave.
* Run not in the streets, neither go too slowly nor with mouth open—Go not shaking yr arms—kick not the earth with yr feet—go not upon the toes or in a dancing fashion.

Locke's *Essay Concerning Human Understanding* it's not. But unlike teenagers who just grow, he had a game plan, rules to follow. He may not have been to the manners born, but with his usual perseverance, dedication, and goal-directedness he would learn every one of his rules until they were part of him. And he abided by his rules of civility, too. These are the rules that shaped the Washington character. Those few hundred didactic words say as much about what makes the man tick as multivolume biographies.

George Washington had the great qualities of confidence, courage, perseverance, and fortitude. Also great instincts. There is a kind of radar he seems to have been following, a radio beam, his unconscious. Whatever shortcomings he may have had as a young adult, he was rectifying them step by step. His unconscious made the right choice in ways to go on the path of life.

And above all, he had good luck, without which all of these qualities wouldn't have been worth a farthing.

Look how lucky he was in marriage.

[4]

George first met the Martha of his dreams at the home of his friend Major Chamberlayne on the Pamunkey in May 1758. He was en route to Williamsburg on important military business. Chamberlayne, an old militia buddy, had ridden down to the ferry to meet George and invite him to tarry. He mentioned a house guest, Mrs. Daniel Parke Custis. *The* Mrs. Custis, the rich widow who had inherited a lot of slaves and land? The very same. George decided he had time to stay for supper.

After a long discussion, I'm sure, of military fortifications and strategies, they reach the Chamberlayne manse, a large, airy house, as it's described, with its cool green blinds softening the hard whiteness of its walls. Under the veranda's tall, leisurely columns, there is a flutter of ladies and fans. The servants stand at the horses' heads and stable boys are astir. Washington hands his riding gloves to his servant, Bishop; the gravel of the curved driveway crunches under his feet.

"Mrs. Custis, may I present my friend Colonel Washington"—pause—"of whom you have doubtless heard?"

Violins up.

Yes, Mrs. Custis nods, who has not heard of Colonel Washington, the war hero, and his exploits in the wilderness. He had danced and . . . dined widely. He was so tall, brave, and handsome. She was impressed. He was, of course, in uniform. He looked marvelous in red, white, and blue.

Mrs. Custis was a hotly contested prize in the Virginia social wars. Many a swain had been on his knees pitching the plump little widow. The hands of wealthy widows were sought, kissed in adoration, then as today. George, of course, was a veteran at this sort of thing, but he was batting 0-for-9 by the time he met Martha.

During the long afternoon of their historic first meeting, historians say, he and Mrs. Custis sat alone in the parlor of the Chamberlayne mansion. There are no transcripts or wiretaps of the negotiations. But it must have been some campaign speech he made, filled with "mah little debenture" and other such endearments.

On his way back from Williamsburg, after handing in his sword, he made a detour at the home of Mrs. Custis on the York River. Immediately thereafter, the engagement was announced. You can't lose them all.

It was, on paper, a good deal for Mrs. Custis too. She had a manager for her estates and slaves. Also her children's. The only domestic skill that she had was sewing. She loved doing needlework. Martha spent the year 1760 making pin cushions from her wedding dress. She also made place cards in the form of tiny ladies, each skirt being made from a piece of wedding frock.

She admitted that she did not have brains enough to take care of all of this, as Hughes says, and her lawyer had advised her to "employ a trusty steward, and as the estate is large and very extensive . . . you had better not engage any but a very able man." [13]

She had found him. And he had found her.

[5]

What did George and Martha have in common? They couldn't wear each other's pajamas. He was a foot taller than her. But she was eight months older—at least. George liked older women, almost as much as younger ones. And she could play the spinet well enough to give lessons. What was the attraction? Was it her double chin? The plump bod that grew wider, especially during the war? The little feet? Or was it the little snood she wore, which I'm told was the fashion of the day. "She wore a high cap," Colonel Freeman says, "because she probably wanted to look taller." It emphasized her broadness instead. "Her lips," Colonel Flexner adds, "were pulled under, almost completely hidden." Her hazel eyes were sad, not happy. She looked lost. Her light-brown hair was drawn back from a high forehead, straight back. Combed down behind to cover the tip of each ear. She had a mole on her right cheek, and a hooked nose, strong, with high nostrils.

Reports varied over the years about what the widow Custis really looked like.

The French General Chastellux said, "She looked like a German princess."

A Hessian prisoner of war considered her "pretty." But he may have been bucking for a pardon.

A Frenchman said, "She is small and fat. Her appearance is respectable; she was dressed very plainly."

Suffice it to say, she was not Vivien Leigh as Scarlett in *Gone with the Wind*. Actually, Martha looked like, to cite another great lady in history, Dorothy Killgallen, with her pointy little chin. For a picture of Martha, along with some of the other pinups in General Washington's footlocker at Valley Forge, see pages 258–259.

George did like Martha's personality. She was described as "a gay little woman, but not frivolous.[14] The gaiety of good health, good nature and a small mind," Chastellux says. "And her manners were simple in all respects." "Nobody," adds Colonel Flexner, "could remember anything she had ever said, but remarked on her affability and charm."

She was domestic and chatty, full of talk about stitchery (one of her specialties), household details, and, in later years, grandchildren. She made people feel good talking to her.

There was a streak of romanticism in her. She was like the sort of rich, young, suburban wives who sit in their expensive suburban Williamsburg-style houses watching soap operas on TV. In Martha's day, the escapist fare consisted of novels filled with daring lovers, the gothics with rogues who abducted the young, gorgeous, and voluptuous, and married them without their consent.

Her only weakness was her excessive fondness for caps and finery, feather boas, ostrich plume scarves, tuckers, and lace flounces. And her dependence on others for entertainment. She hated being alone.

She was a homebody, afraid of travel and strange places and guns. Though she hated guns, she loved the sound of fifes and drums, preferring it "to any music that was ever heard." She was no problem. No pest. Not one of those women who questioned a man about his decisions—the silent little woman at his side at home, even when he was away. When George said, "Come to the front," she went. When George said, "Stay at home," she stayed.

Among her other virtues, the historians say, was ample common sense, except maybe where her two children were concerned. She worried herself sick over the children. Not without reason— Martha Parke Custis (Patsy) had epilepsy and John Parke Custis (Jackie) died of a cold (swamp trench fever) after a few days at Yorktown in '81. George had gone eight years without a scratch or a day off for illness. The Washington stock was stronger than the Dandridge-Custis.

Martha's greatest asset, Colonel Freeman says, was her unfailing discretion. She was the perfect politician's wife. Never talked to the press, never opened her small mouth, no careless talk about what her man was thinking or talking about in his sleep. Nobody ever said, "Guess what Lady Washington told me today at tea about Alexander Hamilton and the Marquis de Lafayette having an affair?"

And, of course, Martha could have been good in bed. There is nothing about that in his diaries and journals, either.

[6]

George Washington married Martha Dandridge Custis on January 6, 1759, at the White House, as Martha's place on the banks of the York River was called, after which a happy honeymoon was spent at the well-furnished other Custis home, on the banks of the Pamunkey.

Washington was almost twenty-seven years old and Mrs. Custis was twenty-eight. Governor Fauquier, who had received George's sword, was among the guests, and the house hummed with the power elite of Virginia.

George did not wear his uniform at the wedding. He towered over the little bride with the pointy chin. In his wedding costume he resembled a Gainsborough portrait. As Hughes saw him, he wore a suit of blue cloth, the coat lined with red silk, and trimmed with silver. Beneath was an embroidered white satin waistcoat. His knee breeches were fastened with buckles of gold. His stockings were of the finest. His huge feet were in shoes buckled with gold. He wore at his side a straight dress-sword. His hair was powdered. On his hands were white gloves that can still be seen in the Masonic Museum of Alexandria. They are monstrous.[15]

Martha, they say, wore a white satin quilted petticoat, over which there was a heavily corded white silk overdress. This is the outfit she later spent the year giving away as wedding souvenirs. She also wore pearl ornaments. Her tiny shoes had diamond buckles.

What a catch for George, socially. His unconscious, which always did the best for him, had chosen well.

In one of his down moods, John Adams said Washington never would have amounted to much if he had not married Mrs. Custis's money.

It is not true, in my opinion, that George married Martha for her money. There was also her land, slaves and Bank of England stock. Her portfolio was a major turning point in his career. It was an opportunity to fulfill his boyhood dreams of owning a proper plantation, of living a life he could grow accustomed to. The American dream of being rich. Remember this was a poor boy, who was obsessed with making it in childhood, and constantly reminded of his inferior status, keeping up with the Fairfaxes next door. This was a class-conscious society. Those Brits to this day can make you feel bad about your lack of class.

Martha's fortune was the secret campaign fund all presidential candidates dream about. It gave Washington the freedom to think big, to rise above petty things like asking for salaries, working for a living, which distract so many great men from their destinies as leaders. It gave him freedom of action, and the peace of mind to lead a long-winded revolution. Poorer men wouldn't have played the waiting game with the British army, dragging it out eight years. Few could have afforded such an extended uprising. The wolf would have eaten their starving children.

It sounds a little sleazy, disreputable, but lots of the founding fathers married for money. Alexander Hamilton made such a fortunate union with Elizabeth Schuyler of the Schuylers, who owned half of New York State. According to Clinton Rossiter, in *1787: The Grand Convention*, among the framers of the Constitution who had similarly married well were John Dickinson, Rufus King, Jared Ingersoll, George Clymer, Thomas Fitzsimmons, and Charles Pinckney.

Even closer to home, Washington's favorite half-brother, Lawrence, had also married money. He had the good fortune to marry one of the neighboring rich-widow Fairfax women, Anne.

It's not nice to count other people's money, my mother told me. But let's look at Martha's holdings to see what else Washington, at almost twenty-seven, might have seen in this small dumpy woman of twenty-eight, with her dark eyes, sharpish nose, pointy chin, and tiny feet, who didn't like to dance, and who came with a family of two spoiled brats, one of them with epilepsy.

Martha Dandridge Custis, at the time she married George Washington, brought to the wedding an estate of about 15,000 acres (7,500 acres of cleared land, 7,500 acres of timber land), plus town lots and several plantations and houses in downtown Williamsburg, as well as 300 slaves and cash and securities. The interest alone on Martha's Bank of England stock in 1786, according to Colonel Freeman, amounted to £4,168. Her total cash and securities as she went down the aisle were estimated in the neighborhood of £100,000. That was a good neighborhood in 1758.

Under the laws of colonial Virginia, a wife's property became the husband's through the act of marriage. So the estate of the late Daniel Parke Custis which had been left to her became George Washington's. But there was more. Not only had he married a rich widow, but one whose husband had died intestate. That means the management of the two children's money also fell to Colonel Washington. By law, he became administrator of two minifortunes, and the value of the estates doubled in the seventeen years of his administration (1759–76).

It was hard work. Martha's son, John Parke (Jackie) Custis, inherited 15,000 acres of land in various counties; they were farmed by slaves under the watchful or not watchful eyes of overseers who had to be overseen, or were leased to tenants who paid their rentals in shares of the crop. The crops themselves had to be harvested, sent to warehouses, shipped to England and the West Indies, and the money received for them kept track of, invested, and so forth. All of this was before computers, before modern banking. A man could lose his lace shirt.

Such was the financial acumen and trustworthiness of his stepdaddy manager that Jackie Custis, by the time he reached maturity, was the richest spoiled young man in Virginia.

None of what Washington achieved would have been possible if Colonel Custis hadn't gone to the trouble of marrying the eighteen-year-old Martha Dandridge and accumulating the largest fortune in Virginia before he died. He deserves some recognition from our patriotic societies as the founding sugar daddy of the country.

The secret Washington campaign fund, raised by Custis and laundered through Martha, would have been especially interesting to the character cops in the press today as it pertains to the Bank of England stock. There was the appearance of conflict of interest in the conflict. As soon as Colonel Washington put on the uniform at the Continental Congress, in July, he should have put his—or their—Bank of England stock into a blind trust. Congress was blind in this as in many other ways when it came to its new military weapon, General Washington.

The infusion of Martha's capital into Washington's financial empire was needed. For at the time of his marriage his own financial picture was murky. He was well to do, of course. He owned forty-nine slaves and about five thousand acres of land in his own name—cleared and uncleared. But his estate and Mount Vernon had become badly run down during his absence of three years, trying to make a name for himself as the country's leading amateur soldier during the campaigns against the Indians and French. In 1757 he wrote to his London agent—he was then on the frontier—that he did not know whether he had any tobacco to ship or not, and added, "I am so little acquainted with the business relative to my private affairs that I can scarce give you any information concerning it." [16]

His mismanagers had allowed buildings to collapse, and stock had disappeared. "Corn crops had been so meagre and hogs had been bred so carelessly or had been stolen and devoured in such numbers when bred—that Washington would have to buy provisions and feed to carry his family and his livestock through the winter." A situation intolerably humiliating to any good farmer, as Colonel Freeman says.

What complicated his financial situation was a slight cash-flow problem. This seems inconsistent with his growing wealth; but it must be remembered that his wealth was principally in land. He was always hard up for ready money. A tendency toward lack of frugality, or what we call today overspending, as we shall see, didn't help the budget.

[7]

At Mount Vernon, Martha's closest new neighbors are at Belvoir, the home of Mr. and Mrs. George William Fairfax, possible heirs to Lord Fairfax's trillions. Mrs. Fairfax is better known as Sally Fairfax, the first founding secret girlfriend.

The owners of the Belvoir and Mount Vernon plantations were not only neighbors but "best friends," as Colonel Freeman says. They exchanged ideas as readily as they lent sugar or borrowed shingles. If Colonel Washington had business with Colonel

Fairfax, he could ride over to Belvoir and transmit it in not much more time than would be required to draft and copy a letter. And you know how much George loved to ride, not to mention write letters.

Colonel Freeman says that in a short time Martha was on the friendliest footing with Sally Fairfax, and was exchanging news and notes. And perhaps even gossip about who was fooling around with whom in the neighborhood?

How convenient. George now had his wife and closet girlfriend lined up neatly, side by side, on his surveyor's map of the Potomac quadrant.

Sally does not look like Martha at all. She is thin and intellectual, whereas Martha is plump and a housewife. Sally is a dancer and Martha, shortly after the wedding, became a wallflower. Sally runs around. People still talk about the swath she cut through Braddock's headquarters in Alexandria before the massacre. Nobody would ever say Martha fooled around, not even a nonadmirer like me.

The plot of this Potomac soap opera, as historians see it, is as follows:

He wrote to Sally now and then. And as Marcus Cunliffe puts it, "perhaps to fall in love with her. It seems certain from his letters that he liked her very much, valued her friendship."

His letters to her don't compare with President Harding's love letters to Nan Britton, whom he made love to in the closet of the White House, amongst the galoshes, but they were pretty steamy for him (and for 1757).

'Tis true I profess myself a votary to love. I acknowledge that a lady is in the case; and further, I confess that this Lady is known to you. Yes, Madam, as well as she is to one who is too sensible to her charms to deny the Power whose influence he feels and must ever submit to. I feel the force of her amiable beauties in the recollection of a thousand tender passages that I could wish to obliterate till I am bid to revive them; but experience, alas! sadly reminds me how impossible this is, and evinces an opinion, which I have long entertained, that there is a Destiny which has the sovereign control of our actions not to be resisted by the strongest efforts of Human Nature.

You have drawn me, my dear Madam, or rather I have drawn myself, into an honest confession of a Simple fact.

Misconstrue not my meaning, 'tis obvious; doubt it not, nor expose it. The world has no business to know the object of my love, declared in this manner to—you, when I want to conceal it. One thing above all things, in this world I wish to know, and only one person of your acquaintance can solve me that or guess my meaning—but adieu to this till happier times, if ever I shall see them; the hours at present are melancholy dull—

Be assured that I am Dr. Madam with most unfeigned regard. Yr. most obedient, Most Obliged Hble. Servant, Geo. Washington.[17]

Misconstrue not, this is a masterpiece of writing between the lines. It was as subtle as a wagon train going through the virgin woods. The wily Sally misconstrued anyway. She evidently pretended to misunderstand—her letter has disappeared, a historical misfortune—and Washington wrote to her again on September 25, 1757: "Dear Madam: Do we still misunderstand the true meaning of each other's letters? I think it must appear so, tho' I would feign hope the contrary, as I cannot speak plainer without—but I'll say no more and leave you to guess the rest."[18]

His letters to Martha, in comparison, sound as passionate as a government weather report. Here is one that he wrote from the front a month after his engagement to Martha, which went back to Tidewater in the same delivery with "the votary of love" missive to Sally F:

My dear: We have begun our march for the Ohio. A courier is starting for Williamsburg, and I embrace the opportunity to send a few words to one whose life is now inseparable from mine. Since that happy hour when we made our pledges to each other, my thoughts have been continually going to you as another self. That an all powerful Providence may keep us both in safety is the prayer of your ever faithful and affectionate friend, Geo. Washington.

He could have delivered that as the state of the union address in the House of Burgesses.

In the spring of 1759, when George brought his new wife home, Martha couldn't have known about his playing post office with the vivacious, flirty older woman next door. One wishes he was a bug on the wall to have been privy to the first meeting, when the tall, gracious George introduced the very slender, willowy Mrs.

Fairfax to the plump, tiny persimmon, Martha, while George William Fairfax, Lord Cuckold, stood in the background. Hughes says, "Her husband must have been either mercifully sheltered by the usual husband's blindfolds from any suspicion of his friend George's secret love-letters, or, if he knew, he must have been grateful to Martha for capturing and restraining this firebrand 'darling of Virginia.' " [19]

We know about the exchange of visits between Mount Vernon and Belvoir. The diaries show, as it has been said, "an incessant intercourse." The Fairfaxes were at Mount Vernon for dinner or the night, Hughes says. "The Washingtons were at Belvoir for the hunt or for dinner or for the night. What, most of all, must Sally Fairfax have felt? Was she able to take it as a huge joke? or did she care so much for the Washington she had raised from a pupil to a lover that she was glad of his next-best happiness, and resolved to do nothing to mar it, everything to enhance it? What did she and George say to one another when they were alone by chance, as they must have been innumerable times?" [20]

But Washington was not self-destructive. He would never get caught in a bedroom by enraged husbands, like Mount Vernon machine lieutenant Gouverneur Morris. He wasn't like Alexander Hamilton, his boy prodigy, who was later in the Mrs. Reynolds affair caught in a blackmail trap. Washington didn't do anything to mess up his career. He had his eye on the main chance at all times. He could have ridden himself out of the picture here by coming out of the closet and actively pursuing Sally Fairfax. What could the two love birds have done: run off to a Barbados love nest, and lived a beachcomber existence?

Sally was George's best friend's wife, his fantasy (what Freud* was to call later the My Gal Sal Syndrome).

Do we need further evidence of how smart and on his side George's unconscious was? Well. Sally never did become Lady Fairfax. George William Fairfax expected to inherit his uncle's title and vast estate, but apparently there had been a rumor back home in England that George William Fairfax was a Negro. The family thought that Sally's husband, who was born in the Bahamas, was a "darkie," as they put it then. In 1760, the potential heir and the secret love in George's armoire left Belvoir to press his claim in the mother country, and never returned.

---

* Dr. Horatio Freud.

There was doubtless a farewell dinner, as Hughes says: "Doubtless Washington toasted each of his guests and perhaps when he stretched out his glass to Sally Fairfax, she followed a pretty custom of the day; perhaps her long, slim fingers lifted one petal from a rose at her breast and let it fall into his brimming wine. As he raised the glass and the petal smote his lips, his eyes upon her must have had much to say. Sally, no doubt, smiled back triumphantly in her manner. She had conquered herself as well as him. Martha watched them both, no doubt, having learned from gossips or guessed from countless little clues many things that we cannot know. And she doubtless smiled also. After all, she held Mr. Washington. She probably liked Sally a little better for going abroad." [21]

At an auction in 1774, George bought the coverlets, bolsters, sheets and pillows, and other bedroom furnishings from Belvoir. [22] What would his shrink have made of that?

[8]

Three months after the wedding in January, 1759, and the honeymoon at Martha's estates on the York and Pamunkey, the happy couple were settled into Washington's seat at Mount Vernon. They were very happy together. She called him "old man" and he called her "Patcy" (as he spelled it).

The first thing he did was count the servants. This was the military side of him, mustering the staff, taking charge of the troops. With Martha's personal domestics added, there were more servants than there was work to be done, as Colonel Freeman says. "For the household, he and Martha allowed eleven; Breechy, the waiter,* had an immediate assistant, when needed, in the person of Mulatto Jack, who officially was the 'jobber.'† The cook, Doll, commanded Beck as a scullion. Jenny was to do the washing, and

---

* In modern establishments, of course, he would be termed the butler.

† This term for the modern "handyman" accorded with good eighteenth-century usage.

Mima the ironing. Besides Sally, her maid, Mrs. Washington used Betty as a seamstress. The boy Julius was chosen to wait on Jackie; the juvenile maid for Patsy* bore the name Rose. To keep an eye on these youngsters, black and white, and to do their sewing was the exclusive assignment of Moll."†

Besides the eleven in the house, there were seven on the home plantation (Mount Vernon), eleven working at trades, nine at Muddy Hole, ten at Dogue Run, and seven at the mill. That's a lot of people—a total of sixty-eight—in 1759, when three was a crowd.

At the same time, Colonel Washington embarked on a gentrification program at Mount Vernon. The house is at this point of time a fix-it-upper. With the equivalent of a home improvement loan from the bank of Martha, he began fixing it up. His hobby was decorating. As a bachelor, even while sitting around the campfire during the French and Indian War, his thoughts always turned to home. "The Floor of my Passage is really an Eye sore to me," he wrote to John Augustine Washington, then employed as caretaker of Mount Vernon. "I would therefore take it up if good and Season'd Plank could be laid in its place."

The first target was the bedroom, as befitted the newlyweds. The ceiling was eight feet high, and Washington brought in a bed seven and a half feet tall. He also had picked the wallpaper himself. Blue. Martha was then allowed to decide on furnishings and draperies, which she decided should be blue and white. A cornice, or "cornish," as Colonel Washington spelled it, of "papermache," or one covered with "blew" or blue and white cloth, was required for each window.

In the large downstairs room, there were places for eight ornaments of chimney piece and wall. His requisitions for filling these openings were as orderly as any general's requisitioning of supplies for a battle. The list to his merchants in London was titled "Directions for the Busts."

---

* Not Patcy (Mrs. W.), but the stepdaughter.

† The total of eleven does not include the weaver, the five carpenters, their boy helper, and the four tanners on Washington's roster of "Servants in and about the house." This list in the Custis Papers, Virginia Historical Society, is undated but, as Colonel Freeman says, to judge from the age of the little Negroes assigned to "wait on" and to play with Jackie and Patsy, it was prepared as soon after the Custises came to Mount Vernon as suitable selections could be made. No doubt, most of these houseservants had been employed similarly at the White House. The carpenters specifically are mentioned as "tradesmen belonging to estate."

It included: "One of Alexander the Great; another of Julius Caesar; another of Charles XII. of Sweden; and a fourth of the King of Prussia. N.B. These are not to exceed fifteen inches in height, nor ten in width. 2 other Busts, of Prince Eugene and the Duke of Marlborough, somewhat smaller; 2 Wild Beasts, not to exceed twelve inches in height, nor eighteen in length. Sundry small ornaments for chimney-piece."

This adventure was something of a bust. It took an interminable time to get anything from London, and usually the orders were not properly filled. In his case, Washington's London agents sent filigree poetic statues—graces or nymphs or something; as Woodward says, "mere sentimental trash not at all to his liking." [23]

It's well known that Washington was first in war, first in peace, etc. But he was also first in interior decorating and gardening. He was always redoing Mount Vernon. In the middle of the war for independence he found time to write to Lund Washington, his estate manager, to plant more locusts: " . . . across from the new garden to the spinning house. . . . Let them be tall and straight bodied and about eight or ten feet to the first limbs. Plant them thick enough for the limbs to interlock when the trees are grown, for instance, fifteen or sixteen feet apart." [24] And so forth, over several pages.

[9]

A nother of George's hidden talents was buying things. He showed leadership in this field, as soon as he assumed command of Martha's affairs, firing off this salvo to her late husband's merchant bankers:

> To Robert Cary and Company, Merchants, London
> Williamsburg, 1 May, 1759
> Gentln.,
> The inclosed is the minister's certificate of my marriage
> with Mrs. Martha Custis, properly, as I am told,
> authenticated. You will, therefore for the future please to
> address all your letters, which relate to the affairs of the late

Daniel Parke Custis, Esqr., to me, as by marriage I am
entitled to a third part of that estate, and interested likewise
with the care of the other two thirds by a decree of our
General Court, which I obtained in order to strengthen the
power I before had in consequence of my wife's
administration.

There follows an amazing shopping list, including:

> 1 Tester Bedstead 7½ feet pitch with fashionable bleu
> and white curtains to suit a Room laid w yl Ireld. paper—
> Window curtains of the same for two windows; with
> either Papier Mache Cornish to them, or Cornish covered
> with the Cloth.
> 1 fine Bed Coverlid to match the Curtains. 4 Chair
> bottoms of the same; that is, as much covering suited to the
> above furniture as will go over the seats of 4 chairs (which I
> have by me) in order to make the whole furniture of this
> Room uniformly handsome and genteel.
> 1 Fashionable Sett of Desert Glasses and Stands for
> Sweetmeats Jellys &c—together with Wash Glasses and a
> proper Stand for these also.—
> 2 Setts of Chamber, or Bed Carpets—Wilton.
> 4 Fashionable China Branches & Stands for Candles.
> 2 pair of fashionable mixd. or Marble Cold. Silk Hose.
> 6 pr of finest cotton Ditto.
> 6 pr of finest thread Ditto.
> 6 pr of midling Do. to cost abt 5/
> 6 pr worsted Do of yl best Sorted—2 pr of wch. to be
> white
> N.B. All the above Stockings to be long, and tolerably
> large.
> 1 Suit of Cloaths of the finest Cloth & fashionable colour
> made by the Inclos'd measure.—
> 6 pr Mens riding Gloves—rather large than the middle
> size.
> Order from the best House in Madeira a Pipe of the best
> Wine, and let it be secured from Pilferers.

He was one of those men who enjoys shopping for their wives.
A negligee gown, some hose and shoes, "of smallest fives"—
gloves, satin pumps, "a neat pocket looking glass," and a lady's

black furred riding hat with a white feather, and other such "necessaries." Nothing embarrassed him.

It's not for nothing that department stores hold sales to honor Washington's birthdays, all three of them.

George Washington has not received credit for being a leader in the mail order catalogue shopping field. His lists and letters to Robert Cary & Co., the Nieman-Marcus of its day, should bring tears to the eyes of every yuppie. He had a consuming passion. The most awesome achievement in the newlywed's incredible shopping spree was his buying by mail in June, 1768, a new chariot.

> My old chariot having run its race, and gone through as many stages as I could conveniently make it travel, is now rendered incapable of any further service. The intent of this letter, therefore, is to desire you will bespeak me a new one, time enough to come out with the goods (I shall hereafter write for) by Captn. Johnston, or some other ship.
>
> As these are kind of articles that last with care against number of years, I would willingly have the chariot you may now send me made in the newest taste, handsome, genteel and light; yet not slight, and consequently unserviceable; to be made of the best seasoned wood, and by a celebrated workman. The last importation which I have seen, besides the customary steel springs, have others that play in a brass barrel and contribute at one and the same time to the ease and ornament of the carriage. One of this kind, therefore, would be my choice; and green being a color little apt, as I apprehend, to fade, and grateful to the eye, I would give it the preference, unless any other color more in vogue and equally lasting is entitled to precedency.
>
> In that case I would be governed by fashion. A light gilding on the mouldings (that is, round the panels) and any other ornaments, that may not have a heavy and tawdry look (together with my arms agreeable to the impression here sent) might be added, by way of decoration. A lining of a handsome, lively colored leather of good quality I should also prefer, such as green, blue, or &c., as may best suit the color of the outside.[25]

Like the capitalists of today, he must have his costly limousine. In September, his chariot, sweet chariot—which coincidentally was just like the one Betsy Fauntleroy's family owned—had finally arrived, its body green and gilt-edged, shipped to him at a cost of £133.

Two years later he complained that he had been cheated, "the wood so exceedingly grien that the panels slipped out of the mouldings before it was two months in use—Split from one end to the other."

George's new life with Martha can be summed up in one word, C-H-A-R-G-E! He charged everything he ordered from merchants to his account. Instead of using MasterCard or Visa, he consigned his tobacco or other cash crops to his creditors, which they would sell as his agents. The difference he had to pay, or send more tobacco to cover.

Despite all the accounts, perhaps because of them, he was always in debt. What George had stumbled on serendipitously at Mount Vernon was the principle of living over one's head.

And the future prefident of the country was dunned regularly. His merchants in London introduced the concept of charging interest on credit purchases as Visa and MasterCard do today. Washington was indignant.

> I shall now in consequence of your other letter . . . beg leave to inform you, in terms equally sincere and direct, that it is not in my power I should add in a manner convenient and agreeable to myself, to make remittances faster than my crops (and perhaps some few occasional sums which may fall in my way) will furnish me with the means; but if notwithstanding, you cannot be content with this mode of payments you have only to advise me of it and I shall hit upon a method (tho' I would choose to avoid it) that will at once discharge the debt, and effectually remove me from all further mention of it; for I must confess, I did not expect that a correspondent so steady, and constant as I have proved, and was willing to have continued to your house while the advantages were in any degree reciprocal would be reminded in the instant it was discovered how necessary it was for him to be expeditious in his payments.[26]

There were those who criticized the way upper-class Virginians like Washington (Jefferson, Madison, and Monroe were also big deficit spenders) were drowning in debt and extravagance. Patrick Henry, for one, attacked "the wanton spending of the planter class" in a speech in the House of Burgesses. He was always voting against proposals aimed at permitting rich debtors to mortgage their lands to pay for luxuries. "What sir," he demanded, "is it proposed then to reclaim the spendthrift from his dissipation and extravagance, by filling his pockets with money?"

But to Washington's credit as the proto-yuppie, no matter how bad his financial plight at Mount Vernon, even when he was appalled by the size of his debt, he didn't stop spending extravagantly.

[10]

After George Washington was drafted in Philadelphia, he didn't get on his white charger and ride back to debt-plagued Mount Vernon to tell Martha the good news. After partying for three days, he finally wrote a Dear Martha letter:

> My Dearest: I am now set down to write you on a subject which fills me with inexpressible concern, and this concern is greatly aggravated and increased, when I reflect upon the uneasiness I know it will cause you. It has been determined in Congress that the whole army raised for the defence of the American cause shall be put under my care, and that it is necessary for me to proceed immediately to Boston to take upon me the command of it.
>
> You may believe me, my dear Patcy, when I assure you in the most solemn manner that, so far from seeking this appointment, I have used every endeavor in my power to avoid it, not only from my unwillingness to part with you and the family, but from a consciousness of its being a trust too great for my capacity, and that I should enjoy more real happiness in one month with you at home than I have the most distant prospect of finding abroad, if my stay were to be seven times seven years. I shall hope that my undertaking it is designed to answer some good purpose. You might and, I suppose, did perceive from the tenor of my letters that I was apprehensive I could not avoid this appointment, as I did not pretend to intimate when I should return. That was the case. It was utterly out of my power to refuse this appointment,

without exposing my character to such censure as would have reflected dishonor upon myself, and have given pain to my friends. This, I am sure, could not, and ought not to be pleasing to you, and must have lessened me considerably in my own esteem. I shall rely, therefore, confidently on that Providence which has heretofore preserved and been bountiful to me, not doubting but that I shall return safe to you in the fall.

There follow many paragraphs to his dearest Patcy, sentimental endearments and nothings about land sales, Bank of England stocks, and the drafting of his will by his arch political enemy, Colonel Pendleton, and a suggestion that she move into Alexandria or visit with her friends while he founds his country.

"In short," he wrote, "my earnest and ardent desire is that you will pursue any plan that is most likely to produce content, and a tolerable degree of tranquility; as it must add greatly to my uneasy feelings to hear that you are dissatisfied or complaining at what I really could not avoid."

He closes with a tender adieu:

"P.S. Since writing the above I have received your letter of the fifteenth and have got two suits of what I was told was the prettiest muslin. I wish it may please you. It cost 50/ a suit, that is 20/ a yard."

One wonders, while reading this often-quoted—it is considered by patriots as one of the great love letters of all time—what might have happened if he hadn't accepted the office that the Congress forced on him, as he described it to his dearest Patcy.

"I decline, kind sirs," he could have said. "Tho' I be much flattered by the honors. As I told my wife Martha (Patcy) just yesterday by Pony Express, it will cause her uneasiness. I assure you in the most solemn manner, so far from seeking this appointment I have used every endeavour in my power to avoid, because of my unwillingness to part with my dear wife and my family. She doth fear being alone. Not to mention the job being too much for me to handle at this juncture in time."

Martha Washington could have changed the course of history, by writing him, "Now you come home, George, or I go to Reno." But Martha Washington was one of those "Yes, dear" women. She worried about her children. She left affairs of the state to her "old man."

*

George had been away from Martha since May 4. It was some consolation for Martha, in June in Mount Vernon, to have her old man's word he'd be back in the fall. A promise he fulfilled six years later, and then only for two days. The nonpolitical Washington was becoming a real politician.

[11]

Now the fighting aristocrat was in the saddle. This way to Boston . . . 325 miles.

Actually, he was in his chariot. The yuppie general bought a new one on his expense account, a light phaeton, purchased from Dr. Renaudet of Philadelphia.[27] He has sent his old green one, the one with the split panels, back to Mount Vernon as a keepsake for Martha, to remember him by. He has also bought four new horses as accessories.

He was, as people were saying in June 1775, David facing Goliath (the British army). But he had none of David's cockiness going into the ring. He was no "harum scarum, ranting, swearing fellow," as one of the delegates to the Second Continental Congress who had put him on the white horse with his vote saw him. Washington did not promise victory. He did not rattle his saber. "Lest some unlucky event should happen," he warned, "I beg it may be remembered by every gentleman in this room that I, this day, declare with the utmost sincerity, I do not think myself equal to the command." [28]

Try stitching those words on a flag: *Not Equal to the Command.* Those are fighting words for a moderate. He might as well have said: "Don't Tread on Me Unless I'm in the Way."

He was a David, too, who needed basic training. Here was a man who, sixteen years before, had never dealt with groups of men larger than 300; he was now taking command of an army 16,000–20,000 strong, or weak. He had never used cavalry. He had some strange ideas about artillery. But he believed in it, and pulled it along with him wherever he went. And he couldn't afford to trust his own judgment. It was not very good.

The morning line on Market Street as the Washingtonistas rode out of the Quaker City on June 23 was bet on the big fellow— and twenty-four points.

As he rode to the front to take charge of the people's revolution, the common people were already hailing him as a war hero. Babies were being named George Washington in 1775.[29]

Odes and poems were being written about the war hero who hadn't fought a battle.

George Washington certainly looked like a hero, which is the same thing for some people. To the common folk he could do no wrong. He communicated something to them. He never lost that magic whatever he did, or didn't do, during the war. Of course, the American people at this time were not the most sophisticated. At this point in time they were especially being manipulated right and left by slogans and propaganda about tyranny and oppression. Sam Adams was writing the book on the semantics of populist rebellion, the basic principles of which were to work in France, Cuba, and China in later centuries.

As Arthur Schlesinger, Sr., has written:

> The stigmatizing of British policy as "tyranny," "oppression" and "slavery" had little or no objective reality, at least prior to the Intolerable Acts, but ceaseless repetition of the charge kept emotions at fever pitch. Even the coupling of vows of loyalty to the King with denunciations of the ministry and Parliament helped to reconcile the timid to acts of opposition which might otherwise have alienated them. On the other hand, soul-stirring words like "liberty," "freedom" and "independence," though at first they connoted nothing more than the status the colonies had enjoyed before 1763, came in time to pack a revolutionary meaning.[30]

Freedom? The Hessians, who were to arrive in this country when Washington was taking over, wondered about this. A career soldier with His Excellency Lt. General Baron Wilhelm von Knyphausen's regiment, forty-four-year-old Captain Wiederholdt, had come to America to fight because, with Europe temporarily at peace, America was where the action was. *Amerika?* "What a paradox," Herr Wiederholdt wrote in his journal. "Why were these people, so well treated, enjoying so much freedom, ungrateful enough to rebel against their king? Why, while they ranted about freedom and liberty, did they treat their black slaves worse than animals were treated in Germany?" [31]

[12]

On July 2, the Washingtonistas arrived at the front. His Excellency had said, in effect, after his election, "I will go to Boston," and here he was. It had taken El George ten days in his brand-new chariot to travel the 325 miles to the rebel lines circling Boston. Daniel Morgan, commander of a company of sharpshooters from Virginia, and his ninety-six men reached the front—traveling 600 miles—in twenty-one days. And they *walked*. Captain Michael Cresap's riflemen from western Maryland walked the 550 miles to Cambridge in twenty-two days, calling over twenty miles a day "a pleasant march."

It had been a long, hard ride for the general and his "family," as he called his inner circle of advisers. Major Thomas Mifflin, thirty-three, one aide-de-camp, was a wealthy, handsome speculator, established in Philadelphia society, a golden-tongued orator who wrote speeches for the general. Also a silver-fingered operator, Major Mifflin was to rise to quartermaster general and become an embarrassment of riches as one of the founding crooks.

Colonel Joseph Reed, the other A.D.C., was a Philadelphia lawyer, thirty-four, a skilled writer, very smart, a diplomat. He was to serve as the general's first letter writer.

Also in the general's party were the two vice generals elected by Congress, Major General Charles Lee, the satirist-soldier, and Major General Philip Schuyler. One of the fighting landlords of New York, his estates included the North Bronx. And all the land to Albany.

The general and his family had been delayed reaching the front by official business. There had been a few parties along the way.

The first in a series of organized spontaneous demonstrations in behalf of the general-elect broke out in New York City. It had never been a big Washington town. Politically, it was pro-loyalist. The king protected the lower class from the wealthy landholders like Schuyler and Wall Street lawyers, who tended to be Washingtonistas. Where the rest of the nation was split, according to the Adams formula, $\frac{1}{3}$-$\frac{1}{3}$-$\frac{1}{3}$, New York was 60-40 Tory.

There were many people, of all ages and sexes, who had come to see and greet their new general. As Colonel Freeman says, "Washington never had faced a like ceremonial on comparable scale. Philadelphia's generous reception and grateful farewell were small affairs when set against the welcome that awaited him and Lee and Schuyler."

At the ceremonies that followed, the equivalent of a formal press conference, well attended by the press, politicians, and city fathers and sons, formal addresses were delivered and received. The New York radical elite wished him well, hello, and good-bye. Festivities were finally concluded with a "thank you, Your Excellency."

On the same evening, at nine o'clock, Governor Tryon (the royal hated governor and representative of His Majesty the King) landed at the Exchange and was welcomed by Judge Jones and the rest of the Supreme Court, the Clergymen of the Church of England, all the dignitaries. Judge Jones goes on:

But strange to relate! yet strange as it is! it is nevertheless a fact, that those very people who attended the rebel Generals in the morning, and conducted them from place to place with repeated shouts of approbation, congratulated them on their respective appointments to such principal commands, in so virtuous an army, upon so important an occasion; wished them joy of their safe arrival in New York, prayed God to bless their "great and glorious undertaking," and to grant them success in all their measures in the management of "so great and necessary a war," a war undertaken (so they asserted) for the sole defence of the just rights and liberties of mankind. I must again say, strange to relate! these very men, who had been not five hours before pouring out their adulation and flattery, or more probably the real sentiments of their souls, to the three rebel Generals, now gone and all joined in the Governor's train, and with the loudest acclamations, attended him to his lodgings, where with the utmost seemed sincerity, they shook him by the hand, welcomed him back to the Colony—wished him joy on his safe arrival, hoped he might remain long in his Government, enjoy peace and quietness, and be a blessing to the inhabitants under his control. What a farce! [32]

But these are no less spontaneous or disorganized outpourings of emotion for or against than we have on the sidewalks of New York and in the political arenas everywhere today.

More demonstrations and banquets in New Haven, Hartford, Windsor, Springfield. "Time must not be lost on display and formal etiquette," Colonel Freeman says.[33] "He had to press on to Boston." Those thirty-nine-toast dinners were slowing him down.

There was some reason for haste. Reports had reached His Excellency on the road between Philadelphia and Trenton that a big battle had taken place at the front. Bunker Hill. Breed's Hill, actually. The British had won the battle. "A few more such victories," a British officer explained, "and we will be undone." General Howe was in such a state of shell shock having lost so many of his best troops, he shied away from fighting the rebels for a year afterwards.

An American general on the scene might have quickly followed up on that Pyrrhic victory, with another Pyrrhic victory or two that week which might have changed the war, and brought the boys and men home for Thanksgiving Day. But the general had other fish to fry and turkeys to roast.

The trip to the front established the style of travel by Washington from 1775 to 1789. Every trip was a campaign trip, war or no war.

It was not his fault. The founding fathers were a political people. They gloried in the ceremonials of politics—long Fourth of July speeches, parades, musters, and the like. And Washington was always ready to play the game. It gave him, a shy person, the chance to be formal and grave and shy, with all due modesty.

A professional soldier might have galloped to take over his troops. But Washington was a politician, albeit an unconscious one, slowly conducting a victory procession through the cities, meeting with other politicians, making friendships, cementing ties for a postwar election period he did not even know was coming.

Now it was time for the Washingtonistas to roll up their lace sleeves and get to work to win the war.

[13]

July 2. A quiet Sunday afternoon. The general-elect and his military family rode into Cambridge, a quiet, ivy-covered college town. More quiet because it's the Sabbath. Everybody is in church or feeling guilty about not being there. There is no celebration. Sabbath in New England, Washington will find, is more somber than in Virginia.

The general bivouacs on the Harvard campus. His first headquarters is across the Yard, in the "prefident's house," built by Harvard College in 1726 for its chief administrative officer. The general is cramped, even though the Harvard prefident, Samuel Langdon, has moved into one room. His flatmates are General Lee and his disgusting dogs. His second headquarters is now at the Craigie House, later the home of Longfellow, where he wrote his odes to Paul Revere and other classics in the same room where Washington earlier stayed (without Lee).

The next morning, at nine o'clock, Washington officially took command of the army on Cambridge Common, although local residents believe it was under the so-called Washington elm. His first orders called for "returns" (that is, a count of the troops under his command). He was told by the senior officers at Cambridge that from 18,000 to 20,000 men were on the lines,[34] but nobody could say for sure. With his mathematical mind, Washington demanded the precise number. It was characteristic that his first military action should be counting noses. The previous command could never get an exact count. For days it went on. He became obsessed with the inability to get everybody to stand up and say "Present. . . ." "Could I have conceived," he wrote later, "that what ought and, in a regular army, would have been completed in one hour, would employ eight days?" Washington, an innovation as a general, had a unique army in military history.

The upside of not knowing exactly how many men were on the lines in the ten-mile semicircle from Prospect Hill, the American left wing, to Dorchester Heights, the right wing, is that neither did the British. Spies were active. A piece of paper with the exact number would have quickly found its way into General Gage's pocket. The not knowing probably scared the British as much as Washington.

The figure eventually returned was 16,600. This was an extremely large establishment for the times, larger than the peacetime population of Boston, and almost as many citizens as resided in New York.*

Inside Boston, Washington confronted less than half the number of "the ministerial troops," as the king's regulars were called before the break in relations with their British cousins (the Declaration of Independence). General Gage had lost a thousand of his small force at Bunker/Breed's Hill in dead (212) and wounded (846). The wounded then were just as good as dead, even better.† They often didn't recover from wounds inflicted by balls made of rusty nails and old scrap iron, the state of medicine being what it was.

Whatever the numbers, 16,000 or 18,000 to 20,000 troops, when General Washington finally confronted the rabble, he was appalled. As he wrote to his half-brother in Virginia, "I found a mixed multitude of People here under very little discipline, order or Government." He discovered that "some men lived in tents, made from now useless sails from seaport towns." The Reverend William Emerson reported others lived under boards and sail, stone and turf, and birch bush.[35]

The camp outside Boston that summer resembled a large county fair, a huge rural nonstop cookout, a hunting and fishing camp. The crowd was interracial (it wasn't until later that Washington tried to discourage blacks from serving in his army). Many had beards and hair tied in a ponytail. There was singing and smoking and tall-storytelling going on. Alcohol was the substance abuse of choice. Many were stoned, plastered, bombed out of their gourds. But this was an intense time for many of the idealists in this crowd. To judge by all the diaries and journals I have read, Cambridge in 1775 was something like the 1963 March on Washington, or Woodstock 1969.

After the news about Concord had spread, men had come running from a distance of three hundred miles in shirtsleeves, in bits and odds and ends of antique uniforms; they wore cocked

---

* According to *A Century of Population Growth*, vol. II, New York had a population of 21,863 in 1771, and Boston 15,520 in 1770.

† It took two men to carry each wounded from the battlefield.

hats, red worsted caps, caps of beaver fur. For equipment, they brought whatever they could carry. Arms included old family heirlooms, flintlocks, smooth bores, guns longer than the men— some seven feet long, heavy enough to need a wagon to carry them—and without bayonets. In their packs many carried whatever they could throw together, gunpowder mingled with bacon and biscuits.

These were not the just-a-minutemen. They had come together without compulsion, every man of his own free will. No draft, no bounty, no nothing. These were born rebels, some of the most idealistic young people in the nation. They had left their plows, their farms, their fields and wives untended. They had left their studies at Yale and the College of Rhode Island (Brown) to fight for freedom, whatever it meant to each man.

For some it was like a big summer camp for adults—a place where they could go without wives and responsibilities, or tests to take at school. Others were shrewd Yankee opportunists out to make a fast continental dollar off the crowd of 16,000 to 20,000 who showed up for the rebellion against authority. It was a true cross-section of radical America they had outside Boston.

Into the alcoholic haze that must have hovered over the plains of Cambridge like a pink elephant, General Washington rode on his white horse. On August 19, 1775, E. Clarke's diary reports, the general proclaimed to the men that he planned to discourage "vice in every shape." High on his list of reforms was the reduction of the use of liquor by the patriots.

Washington, the distillery owner and noted consumer of six packs of Madeira, must have been of two minds about alcohol, like Gorbachev is about vodka. But a story is told of the temperance-minded general overhearing some drunken soldiers having an inebriated debate in the yard outside his headquarters. He rushed down the stairs and into the courtyard and personally pasted a few of the brawlers with his own meat hooks.

At Cambridge in 1775, he made being drunk and disorderly a crime punishable by whipping. Michael Nash, according to General Washington's "Orderly Books," got drunk and received fifty lashes.

Seventeen-year-old David How, who had been a leather worker in Methuen, Massachusetts, before he answered his country's call to duty, reported in his journal the discovery of "a man found Dead in a room with A Woman this morning. It is not known what killed him."[36] Liquor *couldn't* be blamed for everything, whatever new temperance advocate General Washington said.*

With all the drinking going on during the founding of the nation, one wonders how many understood the consequences of their actions. It's too bad we couldn't give our patriot fathers Breathalyzer tests retroactively. Historians could have called *this* the Whiskey Rebellion.

In his moral crusade of 1775, the general warned his hippie army that henceforth he expected them to respect property, particularly gardens. They were to take baths. But outdoor bathing was forbidden, as the general ordered, "at or near the bridge in Cambridge, where it has been observed and complained of, that many men, lost to all sense of decency and common modesty, are running about naked upon the bridge, whilst passengers, and even ladies of the first fashion in the neighborhood are passing over it, as if they meant to glory in their shame."

It is not in the record whether the women of Cambridge next complained about the men *not* bathing in front of them.

Not that the men had so many cloathes to take off. As General Washington had written to Congress,[37] many men were almost naked because they had lost their clothing at Bunker Hill and "had not received that which the provincial Congress had voted them cheerfully."

Washington had found the New Englanders "dirty and nasty," although Benjamin Thompson thought this derived not from their normal habits but from the fact that they had no women to do women's work and the men were too proud to do their own washing.[38]

The most disgraceful thing in the people's unwashed republican army, as far as Washington could see, was the relationship between the officers and men. There was almost no distinction between them. Egalitarianism was rampant in Cambridge.

He didn't approve of the way the militia picked their officers. Your average company in the hippie army consisted of the men of a neighborhood or town; the officers were neighbors and comrades

* The highball, I mean highlight, of the antipartying movement in the patriot army occurred during an actual battle. At Fort Lee, next year, which the patriots abandoned without a fight, two hundred rebel drinkers were found inside the fort, abandoned by their mates midparty. The patriots, having broken out the officers' bubbly, invited the occupying British to hoist a few, and were rudely marched off to a prison ship on the Hudson. Washington was not the only party pooper.

who had been elected to the post. A private from New Jersey[39] has described the mode of procedure: the men were "sworn to be true and faithful soldiers in the Continental army, under the direction of the Right Honorable Congress. After this we chose our officers. . . . When on parade, our 1st lieut. came and told us he would be glad if we would excuse him from going, which we refused; but on consideration we concluded it was better to consent; after which he said he would go; but we said, 'You shall not command us, for he whose mind can change in an hour is not fit to command in the field where liberty is contended for.' In the evening we chose a private in his place."[40]

Washington thought this voting was a military disaster, apparently forgetting he himself had been elected. He was not elected by his men, but by Congress, a distinction that mattered.

The elective process was not foolproof. Some of the popularly elected militia officer-politicians did not precisely distinguish themselves at Breed's Hill. Discipline depends upon those in command. What could be expected of a company whose captain ordered his men to march into battle at the hill, "promising to overtake them directly" and never appearing until the next day?

One of the first issues on which the commander and his men disagreed was saluting. The small *d* democrats who dropped everything to fight for freedom in 1775 refused to salute officers, who were, after all, "not infrequently his intimate friends, or even his inferiors, men who devoted their time to local militia organizations and had become familiar with drill and tactics while he perhaps was busy with other matters."[41] Privates could not understand why they should salute such neighbors in camp, or why they should ask permission to go beyond the lines.

The general said he was sickened by the way his officers were fraternizing with the ranks. Reading through the court-martial records, one sees that a Lieutenant Whitney was tried and convicted of "infamous conduct in degrading himself by voluntarily doing the duty of an orderly sergeant." Joseph Reed, of the "family," reported that a cavalry officer was found guilty "for unconcernedly shaving one of his men." It didn't matter that he may have been a barber back home who was afraid of losing his touch. Washington was determined to give his junior executives a sense of dignity.

He dealt just as firmly with the enlisted men. The first court-martial of a man in the ranks was for stealing eleven geese. There was no excuse for petty crime, even hunger, and the fellow was convicted. The hippies were also found guilty of swearing, whoring, and the equivalent of not obeying KEEP OFF THE GRASS signs.

The general hadn't given up his orderly life at home, his slaves, his plantations, his peace and contentment, his Madeira, his Martha, for this ragtag democratical motley crew.

Washington found the mostly New England army before Boston "stingy, grasping and peculating," as Rankin and Scheer say. "But perhaps he did not sufficiently take into consideration that the bulk of them were common men whose pittance pay was important to the well-being of their families at home." [42]

There was a geographical, social, and class gap in the people's army that the aristocratic Washingtonistas had inherited. But it was nothing a little discipline could not cure. Spare the rod, spoil the soldiers, as the olde saying goes. Washington hit them with everything except his Philadelphia rod. *

General Washington was an earnest advocate of flogging for almost every offense from disobedience and dishonesty to playing cards.† Corporal punishment of thirty-nine lashes was considered stern discipline in a volunteer army composed of Minutemen and

---

* A surveyor's instrument.

† For more serious crimes, an offender sometimes had to "ride the wooden horse." As this was described to me by a military historian, "The patriot was tied a-straddle of the sharp edge of a board or some similar peaked device, raised about six feet off the ground, and weights were put on his feet. The physical effect was something in the nature of a split, though, of course, the weights were never heavy enough actually to split the patriot in two. Usually he would faint after a few minutes, though some of the hardened veterans could stick it out for an hour."

Whole regiments participated when an offender was made to run the gauntlet, an innovation in the American army's penal code which didn't last. Usually the brigade was drawn up in two lines to form a narrow lane, sometimes a half mile long, through which the culprit ran naked to receive lashings from switches held by his comrades.

For the crime of robbery, it was the gallows or the firing squad. Washington had to use the death sentence more sparingly than he might have liked. Otherwise he would have had to fight the war almost alone.

Ebenezer Wild, in his Revolutionary War journal, refers to a variation which kept the army in a state of suspense. The doomed men were marched to the place of execution to the strains of the "Dead March," each one with his coffin borne before him. The brigade was then paraded, with the guilty men in front, where they could be seen by all. The death sentence was read in a loud voice. Graves had been dug. The coffins were set beside them, and each man was commanded to kneel beside his future resting place in Mother Earth while the executors received their orders to load, take aim, and—

At this critical moment a messenger appeared with a reprieve, which was read aloud, Bolton says. He adds, "This last, all-important act in the series was omitted often enough to strain the nerves of everyone present by leaving the result in doubt until the last instant."

farm boys. To remedy this softness on crime, Washington introduced sergeant punishment. Looking through his Orderly books, one finds punishments of one hundred lashes, or even three hundred. On some occasions he added, "to be well washed with salt water after he has received his last 50." [43] Saltwater was sloshed over the wounds supposedly to guard against infection. Or maybe because it stung.

Washington's draconian tactics caused dissension. New Englanders said they were being dismissed for being New Englanders. As North Callahan says, "It was felt by some of the New England soldiers that Washington was partial to the Southern men, some even saying that he had several Easterners court-martialed in order to fill their places with his fellow Southerners. There were men from the South, however, who charged that there was a disproportionate number of New England officers, especially from Massachusetts, in the patriot army. Now, these Southerners said, 'Since our cause is a common one, we ought to have equal opportunity for command.' " [44]

In a few weeks Washington wrote to Richard Henry Lee, "I have made a pretty good slam among such kind of officers as the Massachusetts government abound in." [45]

The court-martial arts is what the new Washington army outside Boston excelled at this summer that the people's revolution went sour. Before Washington took command, men talked back to their officers, and came and went as they pleased. Under his direction this laxity was soon stopped. Offenses no longer went unpunished. His vigor in enforcing discipline has always been given high praise by military historians. The new army felt, besides the lash of his tongue, the lash of his lash.

It may have been some consolation for the patriot flog-ees to know that the general was not the only flogger: inside Boston the British army, Washington's role model, also flogged. They were just as bad, if not worse.

[14]

D iscipline is the soul of the army," George Washington wrote. And the first reliance of a commander had to be on a body of well-trained troops who would do what competent officers directed, added Colonel Freeman.[46]

What did this soulless, undisciplined army do that was so bad before Washington? Was it so disgraceful that perhaps the less said about it the better? Fairness impels one to say that this disgraceful army, led by a fat, unhealthy general, Artemas Ward, who had gout and had trouble mounting and sitting on his horse, had bottled up the 8,000 British troops in Boston, commanded by four of England's best generals, for nearly three months.

This was the same soulless, undisciplined motley crew that had given England's best troops if not a beating, a solid thwacking, a cuffing about at Breed's Hill that they remember to this day.

The former British regular, General Lee, expressed astonishment that "1,500 of the most disorderly peasantry, without a single officer to command, had been able to commit such execution on 3,000 very good regular troops under the command of the very best officers, in the British service." Who would believe the British casualties at Breed's Hill had been a stupendous 1,054 out of 2,400?

And that was after the havoc wrought by these soulless, undisciplined farmers and mechanics at Concord and Lexington on the 700 British soldiers who marched back to Boston. When the last shot that was heard around the world was fired, the British had suffered 273 casualties (73 killed, 174 wounded, and 26 missing, a rate of nearly 20 percent). They had just barely missed being cut off and annihilated at Charlestown Neck.[47] And these were the men at whom Washington was to direct his energies over the next months to pry them apart, break them down, so he could reassemble them, like Tinkertoys with parts that don't fit.

For some reason not apparent in the military annals, the Continental Army, after being trained and disciplined and given soul, a process that is now about to start, often did more poorly on the battlefields. Sometimes I think Washington didn't understand his men.

The original army was a free-floating experience to them. They hadn't read Marshall Saxe on the rules of war. They couldn't comprehend the importance of marching in straight lines on parade grounds. All they came to Cambridge for was to stand behind trees and stone fences and kill British soldiers. The strategy had worked brilliantly at Concord. At Breed's Hill, they had patiently and silently waited until the British were forty yards away—they had sharp eyes—and had done their thing. "Where companies of Grenadiers had stood," the British historian Trevelyan wrote, "three out of four, and even nine out of ten in some places, lay dead or wounded in the long grass." A Scotsman living in Virginia two months later blamed the slaughter of June 17 on the fact that the Americans actually "took sight" when they fired.

General Washington's plan was to turn his rabble into a highly polished, regimented, good-marching, Anglo-Saxon army. He was determined to hammer the farm boys, students, and weekend warriors from the militia companies into automatons who would fire by platoons. "Hyde Park tactics," as they were called. Friction was bound to occur.

In 1775, Philip Freneau, the poet-reporter, portrayed the American soldier's manly disdain for military dress. He was

> No fop in arms, no feather on his head,
> No glittering toys the manly warrior had,
> His auburne face the least employ'd his care,
> He left it to the females to be fair . . .[48]

The appearance and unmilitary bearing of the men must have depressed Washington, not to mention their alternate life-style. But the original army was hailed for its idiosyncratic style. What the war was about was American individualism—the freedom to dress and to shoot at the enemy in their own way, as they always did. The poets knew it.

The troops quickly tired of the degrading nature of army life. In September 1775 a sergeant was tried for "disrespectful reference to the Continental association" (Congress) "and drinking General Gage's health." He was put in a cart with a rope around his neck and drummed out of the army for life.

Most of the hippies weren't due to go home until the end of the year. The terms of the Connecticut militia ran out on December 10, 1775. "Some of the soldiers sought to anticipate their freedom by going home early," Commager and Morris write in *The Spirit of Seventy Six*. Faced with a sharp reduction in his forces now—seven thousand militiamen from Connecticut alone were due to phase out in December—the high command of the Washingtonistas addressed a number of emotional appeals to the troops to re-up. "We was ordered to parade before the general's door, the whole regiment, and Generl Lee and General Solivan came out," recalls the Connecticut soldier Simeon Lyman in his diary entry for December 1.[49] "General Lee made a speech to the men. The first words was, 'Men I do not know what to call you; [you] are the worst of all creatures,' and flung and curst at us, and said if we would not stay he would order us to go on Bunker Hill and if we would not go he would order the riflemen to fire at us, and they talked they would take our guns and take our names down." One of Lyman's buddies was explaining the advantages of not re-upping. "The general sees him and he catched the gun out of his hands and struck him on the head and ordered him to be put under guard."

As Washington's views on law and order became better known, the rate of enlistments declined. When the enlistments expired, the recruits would listen to no one. "We have found it as practical to stop a torrent as these people when their time is up," the commander-in-chief told his aide Joseph Reed.[50]

Fortunately, General Washington was not a strong cause-and-effect man. Just as he saw no effect of his wearing his uniform in the Congress, so he saw no effect of his management of affairs in the army. It was all due, in Washington's opinion, to the mercenary, low in public spirit, the money-grubbing, speculating, peculating, degenerate New Englanders. He forgot for the minute that they didn't have to be at the front. At the end of the year he got a whole new army to whip, beat, and toilet train.

[15]

A standing army needs action to take its mind off the petty details of administration, such as counting heads, tailoring of uniforms, and cuisine. But this was a sitting army, which hadn't had a major battle since the commander-in-chief took over in July.

The troops were getting restless. And so was their general. Standing pat, keeping the enemy surrounded, was not enough to satisfy Washington's military mind, as Colonel Freeman says, "or his conscience, as a steward of public money." He considered it as shameful as it was militarily unsound and humiliating to have close to 19,000 men eat their heads off and do nothing but drill, mount guard, and wait behind parapets.[51]

The impact of it all cast deep gloom upon Washington, and he wrote Joseph Reed: "Such a dearth of public spirit and such want of virtue, such stock-jobbing and fertility and all the low arts . . . I never saw before and I pray God's mercy that I may never be witness to again. . . . Could I have foreseen what I have experienced and am likely to experience, no consideration on earth should have induced me to accept the command."

General Washington was very belligerent in the Council of War meetings, held regularly at his headquarters, as suggested by Congress. The committee meetings of generals were designed to serve as a check on a commander who might lack certain military skills, a deficiency he had hinted he might have. While the two armies glared at each other in Boston, General Washington advocated "a surprize invasion of Boston Neck by means of boats, cooperated by an attempt upon their lines at Roxbury." He told his co-generals that it would be "hazardous, but did not appear impractical."

The man who had planned and engineered the stunning Fort Necessity coup, in his first military action of the war, was planning the equivalent of the D-day invasion of Normandy. The Council of War voted down the idea.

Washington gave in on this issue in September, then again in October. In the winter, he pushed for an attack across the bay on ice. He was to continue advancing his amphibious land-sea attacks with an army that he seemed to doubt could remember anything more complex than "one if by land, two if by sea" to the end of the siege. His amphibious landing scheme would have ended the war, unfavorably for our side.

If the general had me on his staff, in charge of operations (G-3), I would have advocated a more conservative form of attack. "Your Excellency, Sir," I would have said, "use your riflemen to pick off the British one by one. Go with your strong suit."

The sensation of the camp had been the mighty riflemen, those woodsmen who came from beyond the Delaware in their hunting shirts, leggings, and moccasins. They had marched across the nation, such as it was then, without Madeira, toasts, and press conferences. And all along the way of the long walk to Cambridge folks had turned out to cheer the sinewy, awesome men with the long rifles, tomahawks, and hunting knives, and had marveled at their deadly marksmanship. One American wrote a friend in England that Pennsylvania "has raised 1,000 riflemen, the worst of whom will put a ball into a man's head at the distance of 150 or 200 yards; therefore advise your officers who shall hereafter come out to America to settle their affairs in England before their departure." [52]

Having all those real sharpshooters from the Pennsylvania and Virginia hills just sitting on their thumbs, that's no way to beat the British! That's why I will remain PFC forever, and why George Washington was a general. What I didn't understand is that the riflemen were a nuisance. They tended to waste ammo. They sometimes missed. This vexed His Excellency very much, all his historians say.

These "shirtmen," as the Washington family called the rifle companies, were not the most disciplined in the army. They had marched to Boston as self-contained bands of fighting men, as Colonel Freeman perceived them, "and they saw one duty and one only: That was to kill the British, precisely as their fathers and elder brothers had slain the Indians, by stalking them." The way the riflemen operated is as follows: As soon as they had established their camps, they began to slip through the line of guards and to make their way toward the British outposts. Some went alone; a few crept forward in pairs. Whenever they saw a "lobster," as they were now calling the Redcoats, they would take a shot at one, regardless, it seemed to the riflemen's critics, of range.

The riflemen were chewed out by General Washington for this pop-popping at extreme distance. They should shoot less, he ordered briskly (August 4), to reduce what he saw as the endless waste of powder. [53]

If it had been up to General Washington, the Minutemen never would have been called out at Lexington and Concord. There was a powder shortage then. He kept writing to Congress about the ammo problem. Shortages of powder and shot were alarming and not half of the men coming in could be given a musket. Benjamin Franklin, in Philadelphia, wondered why Washington did not resort to bows and arrows, a weapon which he thought had certain advantages over the slow-loading musket, including not needing powder. [54]

One day in August, a messenger brought Washington word that the magazines had only thirty-five half-barrels of powder, enough for no more than nine rounds per man. Washington was so shocked by the disclosure "that he did not utter a word for half an hour." Rush orders to New York, Philadelphia, and Elizabethtown soon relieved the situation, but still not enough powder arrived to permit the Americans to send more than token shots into the British lines.

On investigating the powder situation, General Greene found that not a little was being wasted and some stolen. The men had a yen to fire their guns whenever a chance occurred, wild geese being a favorite target. "It is impossible to conceive upon what principle this strange itch for firing originates," he wrote. In general orders he warned that all soldiers found firing without orders would be tied up and whipped. As a further precaution, he directed officers to limit the number of cartridges to ten to twelve rounds per man (British troops were furnished with sixty) and to put them in the hands of the men only when necessary.[55]

While the general amassed powder and shot, and sought to discourage firing at the enemy as cost ineffective, everybody waited. It was now a race against time, to see if the army would come up with an offensive plan—or die of old age, whichever came first.

[16]

Washington solved his own morale problems by bringing Martha to Cambridge in November as a Thanksgiving Day present to himself. Actually, he was a bit surprised at her arrival. Washington had written Martha prior to October 13 to come to Cambridge if she cared to make the journey, and he had erred in thinking she would not do so because of the lateness of the season, Colonel Freeman says. But he had also thought the war would end by the winter.

His gift from home, which the general put on his expense account,[56] arrived on December 11. Traveling at the public's expense, Martha did not settle for economy- or business-class. As one eyewitness said, Lady Washington "arrived in state . . . the splendid coach and its four horses; the postillions in white and scarlet; the harness buckles with Washington's arms engraved on them . . . all whirling through the forlorn camp."

The equipage and its escort stops at the Craigie house—Washington's headquarters—and Martha descends. As Woodward says, young officers in their best blue and buff stand bareheaded under the cold sky, bowing and mumbling polite words. "Jackie Custis comes with his mother . . . Jackie and his slender wife, a girlish creature who had nestled among pleasant adjectives all her life. Martha is in silks and furs; she is small, but her manner is that of the *haute noblesse*."[57]

Washington's protégé Major General Nathanael Greene, the ex-blacksmith from Rhode Island, was in Cambridge at the time. (In 1774 Greene had been a private in the Kentish Guards, and within a year he was the general of all Rhode Island's armed forces. His meteoric rise was attributed to political connections and assiduous study of books about war.) The day after Martha's arrival General Greene wrote home to Catharine, his wife, that Lady Washington had arrived at camp; she must put on her best frock and leave Coventry, Rhode Island, and come to Cambridge. Kitty Greene didn't need much encouragement. She was a Revolutionary War buff.

Kitty Greene, the former Catharine Littlefield of Block Island, was now pushing twenty-two. She had been married to Nat Greene for a year. She was vivacious, beautiful, slim, and she had a yen to travel, which probably came from having been born and raised on Block Island. Some said she was an airhead, but she knew French and loved to dance.

And so Washington and Kitty Greene met in Cambridge. History does not record the circumstances, but it was the beginning of a very special friendship. He surely found her attractive. She was trim, bubbly, a beauty who could banter and play the coquette, a great dancer. Mrs. Greene was a younger version, it is said, of Sally Fairfax, the girl of his dreams. But Sally was trapped in England by the war, and Kitty was not.

Kitty's flirting enlivened Camp Cambridge,[58] where previously one of the major recreations had been Lee's dogs. The first night in Cambridge, Lee had Scanda, his best friend, the huge Pomeranian, doing one of its stupid pet tricks, sitting on a Chippendale chair, offering its paw to Abigail Adams.

Martha befriended Kitty. "An intimacy sprang up between Kitty and Mrs. Washington which, like that between their husbands, ripened into friendship, and continued unimpaired through life," Kitty's grandson, George Washington Greene, later wrote.[59] Martha had a heart as big as all outdoors.

In 1776, Kitty would name her firstborn George Washington Greene. Several years later, Nat and Kitty's second child, a girl, was named Martha Washington Greene. Kitty was very sensitive to other people's feelings. How ingenious to placate Martha in this way.

The Madeira flowed like wine that fall in Cambridge as the general and his lady had for dinner the very social Greenes, Nat and Kitty, as well as every major Massachusetts politician. Congressmen visiting the battlefield all paid their respects at the Washington table. He was forming friendships that would help him through the dark days ahead.

[17]

B ack at the front, Washington had to do something. Carpers were calling him a do-nothing general. Weeks and months went by, and he made no attempt to drive the British out of Boston.

Washington and his army would probably still be outside Boston today if not for Henry Knox, my favorite bookseller. General Washington first met the man who was to be the hero of the Boston siege on one of his many inspection tours of the lines. "Yesterday as I was going to Cambridge," Knox wrote his wife, Lucy, in an undated letter (probably on July 13, 1775, according to Allen French[60]), "I met the Generals who beg'd me to return to Roxbury again which I did when they had viewed the works. They expressed the greatest pleasure and surprize at their situation and apparent utility, to say nothing of the plan, which did not escape their praise."

Harry Knox was proud of his works, for he had designed and supervised their construction. He seemed to know a lot about defense and fortifications, despite his youth and the fact that he was a bookseller in civilian life. Actually the latter was an asset. The stout convivial Boston shopkeeper read voraciously all the books in his racks about the science of artillery, which he discussed with British officer customers in his store; he also was brilliant at applying what he read. He actually seemed to understand the principles intuitively.

The lines at Roxbury obviously impressed Washington, who had once built a works in a valley which put his defensive position surrounded by hills and in the middle of a riverbed. He soon named this confident young bookseller to the post of artillery chief of the armies of the United States. Upon his appointment, Knox looked around and asked, "Pray tell, Your Excellency, but where are the cannon?" Henry Knox had an idea for getting some.

Washington and Knox were to become close friends in the war ahead, despite differing personalities. George was grave and pessimistic of nature, always doubting his abilities. Harry was jolly and cheerfully confident. Everything seemed possible with Harry Knox.

When Knox asked Washington in his humorous way where the artillery was, the commander had to reply that there was none to speak of. The general lamented of the lack of cannons, without which nothing could be done. Then Knox broached a grandiose scheme:* "I will bring you a train of artillery," he said. There were at Ticonderoga uncounted numbers of cannons, captured by Ethan Allen and Benedict Arnold in their twin attacks on the British fort earlier that spring. Knox told Washington of his daring plan to rescue the cannon from their inactive status in the north woods. He would be the engineer of the artillery train.

"So be it," the godlike Washington responded.

---

* Most historians give Knox the credit for the plan of bringing the cannon back from Ticonderoga. But the original idea came from Benedict Arnold, the ex–New Haven bookseller-druggist and the co-liberator of Ticonderoga, in the days before the swine came out of the closet. Few give the traitor credit for anything anymore. Allen French gives credit where it is due, in a footnote.[61]

[18]

I t was a tale of heroics that will live in the annals of teamsters, military strategists and of bookstore managers. It made Washington crossing the Delaware seem like punting on the Cam. Unfortunately for Henry Knox's reputation, nobody made a painting of him leading one of his 82 teams of oxen 350 miles in the dead of winter all the way from Fort Ticonderoga to Boston. Or wrote a poem about it.

Historians argue as to just how many guns were brought from Ticonderoga in Knox's icy odyssey through the north country. Freeman says 66; Spaulding, 55; Perry, 78; and the Commonwealth of Massachusetts says in its 1925 House Document Number 219 that there were 58 pieces, mortars, howitzers, and coehorns. A coehorn is a type of small mortar named after its Dutch inventor, Baron von Coehoorn.[62] Mortars and howitzers, as is better known, were named after Jeremiah Mortar and Sam Howitzer. The inventory of Knox himself sets the number at 59, as do Alexander C. Flick[63] and North Callahan. I'll go with Harry's (Henry's) inventory.*

* Mortars and Cohorns, December 10, 1775

		Dim. of bore	Ft. & Ins. of length	Weight	Total w'ht
Brass	2 Cohorns	5⁷⁄₁₀	1-4	150	300
	4 do.	4½	1-1	100	400
	1 mortar	8½	2-0	300	300
	1 do.	7½	2-0	300	300
	8				
Iron	1 do.	6½	1-10	600	600
	1 do.	10	3-6	1800	1800
	1 do.	10¼	3-6	1800	1800
	3 do.	13	3 (average)	2300	6900
	6				
		Howitzers			
Iron	1	8	3-4	15. 2. 15	15. 2. 15
	1	8¼	3-4	15. 2. 15	15. 2. 15
	2 (16)				

How does one move 66, 55, 78, or 59 cannon, including 13-inch mortars, plus 24 boxes of ammo and flint over 350 miles of woods, water and mountain? With difficulty. It began with Knox going to Fort Ticonderoga to eyeball the several hundred pieces stockpiled, with his trained eye "to chuse" the best of the artillery. Knox's choice included some that would warm an artillery maven's heart: the 24-pounder, the 21 eighteens and twelves. Among his favorite mortars were three of the 13-inchers, short massive things, according to Allen French, averaging more than a ton apiece.

Now all that had to be done was to haul these beauties to Lake George, ferry them across by boats and scows, and then carry them by road to Albany, four times crossing the Hudson on the way. Then straight ahead, over the Berkshires, and down the road a piece to Boston.

The roads from Albany to Springfield were not then widely praised. Travelers suffered great hardship, especially in the winters. There were no houses along this route for a distance of forty miles, North Callahan says.[64] They were traversing roads "that never bore a cannon before nor ever have borne one since." At their best they were gullied or usually at this time of year covered with snow and ice, praise God.

Knox's secret plan for whipping Mother Nature was to drag his cannon by "slay," or sleigh. He had worked out the logistics in his "Inventory of the Cannon" of December 10, adding a codicil, "Instruction for their Transportation":

Let the touch-holes and vents of all the mortars and cannon be turned downwards. Observe that 2 pairs of horses be [put]

		Cannon			
Brass	8 3 pounders	3½0	3-6	350	2800
	3 6 do.	3⁷/10	4-6	600	1800
	1 18 do.	5½	8-3	2000	2000
	1 24 do.	5¹¹/12	5-6	16. 3. 18	1800
Iron	6 6 do.	3⁷/10	9-7	2500	15,000
	4 9 do.	4⁴/10	8-4	2500	10,000
	10 12 do.	4¾	9	2800	28,000
	7 18 do. (dbl fortif.)	5½	9	4000	28,000
	3 18 do.	5½	11	5500	15,000

To[tal] can.	43		Total weight	119,900
Mortars	16			
	59			

to between 2 or 3 thousand weight, and 3 or 4 pair for the 4000 weight, and 4 span for those of 5000 weight. The one span will take above 1000 weight. They are to receive seven £ per ton for every 62 miles, or 12s. per day for each span of horses. Write to me by every slay the quantity that is upon that slay. When a number of slays go off together, one letter will serve for the whole, mentioning the cannon that each have particularly, and the people's names. All to be delivered at Springfield or Boston.

It was, to use typical British-American understatement, tough sledding, a big challenge for a big man. At 25, Knox was as tall as Washington: 6'3". But he weighed in the high 200s.* Knox's size was part of folklore. A notorious punster of the period, Mather Bayles, worked one of his verbal gags into a prominent pop song ("The New England Palm-Singer"). He reportedly told his corpulent bookseller friend, Henry Knox, that "I never saw an [Kn]ox fatter in my life." [65]

He also had one of the biggest voices in the colonies, to go with his appetite. Colonel Henry Knox's voice at the Battle of Trenton was, as one soldier would recall, "a deep bass," and at McKonkey's Ferry it was "heard above the crash of the ice which filled the river." Knox—now at his fighting weight of 280—was using his deep bass to direct the river crossings, across and back, across and back. [66]

Knox's martial bearing was not diminished, either, by a maimed left hand. He carried a handkerchief on marches, North Callahan says. And in battle? Few mention his handicap.

The first step in Operation Big Schlep was to bring the Knox 59 down Lake Champlain in "battoe" (*batteaux* are two-masted light, bottom-shallow scow-like craft suited for lake travel) and "gundaloes." Like his idol, General Washington, Knox would never win a spelling bee. However spelled, the "battoe" and "gundaloes" were small, with a tendency to sink when loaded.

"It is not easy to conceive of the difficulties we have had in getting the cannon over the lake," Cheery Harry wrote to Gloomy George, "owing to the advance season of the year and contrary

---

* He weighed 280 pounds at the end of the war and we all know how they were starving at Valley Forge. If not for that, he might have weighed 320. Is the 280-pound figure historians give him caused by inflation, which was rife by 1781? Gilbert Stuart's portrait of Major General Knox, posed alongside a beloved artillery piece, depicts a corporation the size of a volleyball up front. Successful portrait painters usually show the subject's thinnest side.

winds. Three days ago it was very uncertain whether we should have gotten until next spring, but now please God they must go."

As Knox pulled away from the shores in his flagship gundaloe as the sun was setting behind Ticonderoga, everything was going smoothly until the scow that carried many of the 59 pieces of artillery hit a rock and sank. The vessel turned out to have been only partially sunk at Sabbath Point on the hidden rocks. They were able to bail her out and refloat the cargo.

Then contrary winds started. The Knox party wound up having to row continuously, for six and a half hours one day, to make any progress with 119,900 pounds of cannon, howitzers, mortars, and coehorns. Exhausted, they had to break their journey, winding up all frozen except for feet next to the fire. The next day they finally made Fort George by "rowling very hard."

The first day Knox and his flotilla of land cruisers pushed off for Albany they managed to go two miles, then the horses quit. They refused to budge. The sleds were stuck. It now became a human struggle, historians and Knox's journals say, the horses having to be left behind and the men proceeding on foot. Knox now had "to undertake a very fatiguing march of about two miles in snow three feet deep, through the woods, there being no beaten path." Arriving fatigued and famished at the home of a Squire Fisher, the little group gratefully partook of a "fine breakfast" and accepted the loan of some horses which took them the rest of the way to Albany. They reached it in the afternoon, "almost perished with the cold." Unfortunately the guns were still stuck on the icy trail. So Knox spent the next four days with General Philip Schuyler, planning for more men, horses, oxen, and sleds. The soldiers from Ticonderoga and the civilians Knox had already hired were plainly not enough to get the guns to Boston. By December 31, Knox & Co. recruited 124 pairs of horses with sleighs so the caravan could slide on.

Knox's train pulled into Albany after seventeen days, just about when he had told His Excellency he would be arriving in Boston. The Hudson River, which had to be crossed four times from Lake George to Albany before they headed east into Massachusetts, was expected to be no problem. They'd drag the "slays" across its frozen surface. But then a "cruel thaw" now visited Knox and his train. On New Year's Day 1776, a subsidiary project had to be started. Team Knox had to travel up and down the Hudson River cutting holes in the ice, in order to strengthen it by flooding it and allowing more ice to freeze over to support its train of guns.

Knox was sitting down to dinner with General Schuyler on January 4 when alarming news arrived. One of his largest cannon had just fallen through the ice into the river at Half Moon, or Lansing's Ferry, near the present town of Waterford. This could have ruined an ordinary man's appetite. Historians say Knox immediately sprang up from the table and rushed to the hole in the ice.

Knox, being Knox, probably finished his roast lamb, probably the whole one, before he sprang upon his "slay" to direct the salvage operation.

By dusk he was in Half Moon, North Callahan says. He chewed out those in charge for their careless manner of hauling the cannon across the river, then he made sure that the "drowned cannon" was retrieved. "His criticism may have been more impetuous than justified, however, for an account of one of those engaged states that, as a precaution, a long rope had been attached to the tongue of the first sleigh, the other end to the horses pulling the big gun across the ice. A teamster with a sharp hatchet walked alongside, ready to cut the rope to save the horses, should the heavy gun crash through. Halfway across, it did, and the 'noble 18 sank with a crackling noise and then a heavy plunge to the bottom of the stream,' despite the efforts of men and horses. Fortunately, the water at this point was not very deep and the recovery was therefore less difficult than it might have been." [67]

On the leg of the journey through Albany, Knox was luckier. The townspeople, who'd never seen such big guns, turned out to help slide the pieces across the river. As Knox summed up the joint military-civilian operation: "8th. Went on the ice about 8 o'clock in the morning and proceeded so cautiously that before night we got over three sleds and were so lucky as to get the cannon out of the river, owning to the assistance the good people of the city of Albany gave, in return for which we christened her— The Albany." [68]

Now they faced the mountains. On January 10, the slideathon reached "No. 1," as Knox called a peak in the Berkshires in his diary, "after having climbed mountains from which might almost have seen all the kingdoms of the earth.

"11th. Went 12 miles thro the Green Woods to Blanford. It appeared to me almost a miracle that people with heavy loads should be able to get up and down such hills as are here, with any thing of heavy loads." [69]

And then there were the hazards of the excited crowds that

congregated along the way. In Westfield, Massachusetts, only a few of the residents had ever seen a cannon, North Callahan says, much less scores of big ones being sledded over the drifted snow. This mass curiosity soon became a problem. The people crowded into the road and insisted on examining and fondling the guns. The cannon groupies tried to guess how much the different pieces weighed, as it was said, none having any good conception of the correct answers. A few, of more scientific turn of mind, measured the length to the muzzles, and the circumference at the breech.

The populace was drunk with excitement. Also with alcohol. The new patriots plied the teamsters with great quantities of cider and whiskey. They even gave the cannons something to drink. In their "enthusiasm," according to historians, the merry teamsters even took their turns at fondling and measuring the guns—as if they had not seen them before. Then they were pushed aside by the merry residents, by turns wishing to handle the guns and to show their hospitality, saying "they would be darned if it was not their treat."

After the Knox traveling cannon show reached Springfield, it was all downhill to Boston. Except another terrible thaw struck, and the cannon sank into the mud. Knox was able to get fresh yokes of oxen but discovered a new problem. Most of his teamsters were walking out. There was a jurisdictional dispute.

As North Callahan says:

> Most of his teamsters were from New York and were, of course, some distance from their homes. This fact, coupled with the increasingly difficult sledding conditions, discouraged many of the men and made them wish to return home. Had the weather been more favorable, Knox might have persuaded them to remain, as he had done before; but with the snow almost gone, the cannon lying forlornly in the mud by the roadside, he could hold out to them little promise of better conditions. So he released the New York men, and depended on those of Massachusetts, and the soldiers, to get the guns the rest of the way.[70]

As soon as temperatures plunged, and the ground froze again, Knox and the cannon slid on to Framingham. There on January twenty-fifth, John Adams observed them and noted in his diary: "Thursday, about 10 A.M., Mr. [Elbridge] Gerry called for me and we rode to Framingham where we dined. Colonel Buckminster, after dinner, showed us the train of artillery brought down from

Ticonderoga by Colonel Knox." There are few details of the rest of the journey, from Framingham to Cambridge, Callahan says. Knox may have left some of the heavier guns at the former location until Washington should send for them, taking the lighter ones along for immediate placement on the American fortifications.[71]

It had taken fifty days for the "noble train of artillery" Knox had promised Washington to chug through the state. And all the while, with 59 cannon, weighing 119,900 pounds and requiring 82 yoke of oxen, requiring vigorous beating of the bushes and sundry recruitment drives, the commotion went undetected by the British. It suggests at least a flaw in His Majesty's secret service. What was General Sir William Howe doing while the Eighteenth Century Limited slid into home plate? As we shall see, Billie Howe had other irons in the fire.

While on the road with the cannon, Knox's colonelcy appointment from Congress came through. He had finally arrived as a professional soldier. Along with the train, Washington received a bill for Colonel Knox's expenses on the Ticonderoga trek. It amounted to 520 pounds, 15 shillings, 8¾ pence,[72] according to North Callahan's calculations, about $2,500 in modern money, for expenses for himself and his brother and a servant (at 3 pounds per day for 70 days). Although this was nearly twice the original estimate, it was a bargain for such an extraordinary trip, compared to some of General Washington's bills during the same period. And they didn't pay the needy young officer with a growing family and an enormous appetite for three years![73]

Today in honor of the incredible feat there are thirty granite monuments along the Knox Route in New York state, from Fort Ticonderoga to Hillsdale at the Massachusetts state line, and an eight cent Henry Knox stamp issued in 1985. It's not enough for the real hero of the breaking of the siege at Boston, and the man who kept alive George Washington's chances in 1789.

[19]

O n the evening of March 4, only 240 days after he began worrying about his reputation, the general finally went into action at Dorchester Heights.

It was now time to put the second phase of the Free Boston Now—or Soon—movement into effect. Knox's cannon, resting or rusting at Framingham, were to be moved into position east of Roxbury, about a mile on the western extremity of a long, irregular peninsula called Dorchester, containing a series of hills, including Dorchester Hill, or Nook's Hill, which Washington spelled pro phetically "Nuke's Hill." Dorchester had the strategic advantage of looking down on downtown Boston.

By one of his characteristic oversights, General Howe had neglected to occupy this hill, though, as Colonel Freeman says, heavy cannon placed there could sweep the inner harbor. He had a lot of other things on his mind, faro tables and Mrs. Loring, to name two of them.

"The enemy," explained Lieutenant Samuel Webb in his diary on March 1, "are erecting two batteries on Mount Whore-dom [Mount Horam, next to Beacon Hill] against ours on Lech-mere Point and the one on Cobble Hill, known by the name of Putnam's Impregnable Battery. The fortifications our worthy general was planning to erect on this Point would enable us to cut off the communications between the town and their out works on the Neck, at the same time annoy the ships and town."[74]

The idea which Washington had in mind, as Allen French says, was almost as old as the siege. Howe had forgotten it, but not Washington. Very early the Americans had cast their eyes upon Dorchester Heights, and they had planned to take it in June but took Breed's Hill instead. Washington was taking up his predeces-sor's old idea, but the plan was no longer easily executed, now that the ground was frozen. Not even in a long winter's night could earthworks be thrown up, as Washington had learned by the slow work at Lechmere Point, lasting from November till late in Feb-ruary. The British would never allow him leisure to finish the works, once the attempt was discovered. Yet, as at Bunker/Breed's

Hill, the fortifying had to be done in a single night, and the question was, how?

The problem was solved by Rufus Putnam, who got it from reading a book (*The Gentleman's Compleat Military Dictionary*, Boston, 1759). Putnam, General Israel Putnam's cousin, made the suggestion that the breastworks, since the ground was frozen to a depth of eighteen inches, could be made by fascines, bundles of sticks, held in place by wooden frames called chandeliers and gabions (wooden frames filled with dirt). The general bought the idea.

Preparations for fortifying Dorchester Heights, as Thayer says,[75] were now pushed with great dispatch. Quantities of powder, cannon shot, lumber, bales of pressed hay, barrels, and other material were gathered at Dorchester below the heights to be fortified. The bales of hay were to be set up along the low stretches of Dorchester Neck to prevent the enemy from raking the approaches to the heights with shot and shell. Barrels were to be prepared, filled with earth, to be rolled down from the higher hills in the case of attack. "The Hoops should be well Nail'd or else they will soon fly, and the Casks fall to Pieces."

On February 27, Washington's general orders sent quakes of excitement and fear through the troops. "As the season is fast approaching when every man must expect to be drawn into the field of action, it is highly necessary that he should prepare his mind." The troops should remember that they were engaged in "the cause of virtue and mankind," and also that every man who skulked, hid, or retreated without orders, "will be instantly shot down as an example of cowardice."

As Lieutenant Webb remembered it, "Our worthy commander in chief (in orders a day or two past) has in the most pathetic terms told the soldiery that on our present conduct depends the salvation of America; that in all probability e'er long we shall be called to the field of battle; that he is confident his troops will behave as deserves the cause we are contending for; but that in all army's their are those who would flee before a much smaller number, and that should any such be found sculking or retreating before the enemy without orders, they must expect instant death by way of example to others."[76]

Called in from the community, French says, were carts with their teamsters, entrenching tools, and quantities of marsh hay. All were assembled for an undertaking whose success depended on secrecy, skill, and speed.

On the third, Washington wrote General Ward reviewing the preparations. A blind should be thrown up along the causeway from Roxbury to Dorchester, "especially on the Dorchester side, as that is nearest the Enemy's guns." Two hundred and fifty axmen would soon fell the trees for the abatis; but the number of men to get the abatis in place, and set the chandeliers and fascines in position, he left to Ward. Seven hundred and fifty men, posted on the lower hills near the water with sentries between, would cover the workers.

All these arrangements were smoothly executed; but first the enemy (whom Washington suspected of intending to forestall him) had to be misled—"amused" was the eighteenth-century term—with a bombardment.

The rebels told themselves that the size of the balls and shells caused British surprise, but unfortunately, as French says, one of Knox's thirteen-inch mortars and three of the ten-inch size split, from improper bedding or too strong charges. On Sunday night there was another cannonade, and on the night of Monday, the fourth, came the heaviest of all. For that night Knox reported firing 144 shot and 13 shells, an amount minuscule compared with the slightest of barrages in any police action today. Abigail Adams, listening from Braintree, called the sound one of the grandest in nature, "of the true species of the sublime." But it was mostly noise, and fortunately for the inhabitants of Boston, few were killed or even wounded. Nevertheless, this cannonading accomplished its purpose. The British, whose pride, if not body, was hurt, fired more frequently and noisily than the Americans, and did not hear the sound from Dorchester.

And then it was B-day. Bofton (as they spelled it) or buft. The men he had described in his letters back home to Virginia as "exceedingly dirty nasty people" did a most fantastic thing. Under the cover of darkness the night of March 4, the rebels, led by General John Thomas, finally went over the top.

"Working feverishly through the night," according to Commager and Morris's communiqué (in *The Spirit of Seventy-Six*) on the battle, "the Americans threw up their timber wall, cut down fruit trees to form an abatis in front of the timber, and in front of these placed their stone filled barrels, useful in defense and dangerous on offense." Then the ragged Continentals dragged 43 cannon and 14 mortars up the heights.

First to start for Dorchester Heights was a covering party of 800 riflemen and musketeers. They were followed by General

Thomas and 1,200 troops with entrenching tools. Behind them came more than 300 ox carts, loaded high with bales of hay, fascines, frames, barrels, and all. During the night most of the carts made three or four trips. A low-lying fog hid the hills from the sight of the British while on top of the heights a bright moon shone to light the work for the Americans. Providence, or Mother Nature, smiled on the enterprise.

By dawn's early light, when the British woke up, they couldn't believe their eyes. Wrote the Reverend William Gordon, a spectator: "Gen'l How [sic] was seen to scratch his head and heard to say by those that were about him that he did not know what he should do that the provincials (he likely called them by some other name) had done more work in one night than his whole army would have done in six months." [77]

What Howe actually wrote is striking enough to show how much he was amazed: "They could not have employed less than 12 or 14,000 men that night. Besides the assistance of the Devil himself."

In Boston the surprise was complete. Troops and civilians gazed in astonishment at the two forts, raised, wrote an officer, "with an expedition equal to that of the genii belonging to Aladdin's wonderful lamp." Howe's cannon was wheeled out; it opened fire on Dorchester Heights but for naught—the elevation was too high. The balls struck the hills below the forts. Troops then labored to get more height by burying the rear wheels. More reports, but the balls still did not reach. After some hours the effort was abandoned, Colonel Flexner reports, but not until it was too late to achieve anything on the noon tide.

A counterattack was planned, using the famous Gage-Howe how-to-whip-the-cowardly-rebels strategy: a frontal assault, like the one that had almost wiped out their entire army at Bunker/Breed's Hill the previous April.

The British were waiting for night, and a favoring tide; but night brought another "surprize." "A Hurrycane," wrote Timothy Newell, a Selectman of Bofton, in his diary, "or terrible sudden storm." Gordon is more explicit in his letter. He went to bed early, "But when I heard in the night how amazingly strong the wind blew (for it was such a storem as scarce any one rememberd to have heard) and how it rained towards morning, I concluded that the ships could not stir, and pleased myself with the reflection that the lord might be working deliverance for us and preventing the effusion of human blood." Some of the transports were driven ashore, and boats would be pounded to pieces in the surf on Dorchester beach. Howe wrote in his orders: "The General desires the Troops may know that the intended expedition of last Night was unavoidably put off by the badness of the Weather."

Battle canceled because of rain, the record books should read.

The next morning (March 7) Howe's council of war decided it wouldn't be necessary to actually fight the battle. War to the British was like chess. When they saw that the Americans had seized control of a position that gave them command of the Boston area, it was tantamount to checkmate—by a pawn. This round was not the king's. The transports were moved in to the wharves, and the loading of equipment and stores was begun.[78]

[20]

What the British didn't realize at the time was that there was a third phase of Washington's amazing battle plan. Still to come was his big haymaker, the blockbuster, the key element, what he considered the most important step. Dorchester Heights was just a feint, a diversion, something "to amuse" the enemy. He was planning, yes, an invasion of Boston by sea.

He had Greene and Sullivan waiting in the boats. Four thousand fresh men were poised on the banks of the Charles River for a signal from Cambridge, relayed through Roxbury to Dorchester or vice versa, on receipt of which a fleet of boats, preceded by floating batteries, was to cross the Back Bay and assault the town.

First the beachhead around Fenway Park was to be softened up by three "floating batteries" (platforms each carrying one 12-pounder, which rowed into position, presumably without molestation from the amazed Redcoats). Then Sullivan's men would hit the beaches at the Powder House and overwhelm "Bacon" (Beacon) Hill and Mount "Whoredom."

This was Washington's fourth plan for assaulting Boston, and it had the complexity that was to be the hallmark of all his assaults. It assumed near-impossible precision in the synchronization of several separated advancing units. The British, as Colonel Flexner says, "any one of whose officers would have been sent to a lunatic asylum for such a plan, had not the slightest inkling of what Washington intended. The surprise would have been as complete as the time it took to row a mile permitted. This would have been Washington's greatest hope: the regular army mind was not at its best in improvising reactions to what their training told them could never happen.

"Yet the odds would have been greatly against the American assault," Colonel Flexner continues. "The patriots would have had to cross a mile of open water into the mouths of British cannon. Had all succeeded in getting ashore, they would have been 4,000 against the 3,600 Howe had left to garrison Boston. Only if the columns aimed at different points did not stray but succeeded in joining up according to plan and then successfully broke down the British barrier at Roxbury, would the patriots have had any real numerical superiority. And, as was to be proved again and again in the next few years until it became the basic rock on which Washington built his strategy, the raw Americans were no match in close combat for professional foes trained in maneuvering under fire and in the use of bayonets." [79]

The great storm of March 5 and 6, 1776, was one of the most crucial events in the making of the prefident, 1789. Had the "hurrycane" not stepped in, as even Colonel Flexner concedes, "there would have been such a battle as the Continental Army actually engaged in only once, at Fort Washington, when the entire American force that was engaged fell to the enemy. In all other battles, the patriots had access to escape routes through which, if they found they could not stand up to the trained European regulars, they could run for safety. But the troops Washington had intended to land in Boston could never have regained their boats. They would have been trapped. They would either have had to annihilate the British or be themselves entirely defeated." [80] It would have made the Boston Massacre look like a tea party. George Washington would have managed to snatch defeat from the jaws of victory.

There are some who say Washington didn't realize the effect of all he had wrought in his plans for the Knox-Ticonderoga and Dorchester maneuvers. He didn't understand massed artillery's tactical impact. As Colonel Flexner says, "Washington had not realized how grievously guns on Dorchester Heights would terrify officers well trained in artillery warfare."

On the morning of March 16, the British and loyal people of Boston sailed away. A fleet of nearly 100 ships carrying more than 10,000 people, including 1,100 Tories ("the boat people") was bound for the British naval base at Halifax, before the hero of Boston could do any real damage—to them or his own army.

But where were the British in all this? How is it possible they didn't hear Washington's 3,000 men digging in? At least one man heard the racket upon Dorchester Heights.

At that very hour, in Boston, Lieutenant-Colonel Campbell reported to Brigadier-General Smith that "the rebels were at work on Dorchester heights."

Allen French says, "how strange a duplication of the story of Bunker Hill, and how significant that the news should come to Smith of all men! He had been dilatory on the nineteenth of April at Concord, and he was to be lazy at the taking of New York. The news required instant action; but action and Smith were irreconcilable terms. The report may never have got past him to Howe. Certainly nothing was done in Boston, not a cannon turned on Dorchester, not an infantryman called from his bed. On the hills the carting, the picking, the shoveling continued uninterrupted, with 3,000 fresh men changing places at three in the morning . . . with digging and heaving, ramming and making firm."[81]

The British commanders had been drinking toasts the night before when they had received a report that the enemy were active on Dorchester, Colonel Flexner says. However, the officers had gone to sleep contentedly, sure that whatever the yokels were up to could be handled easily the next day.[82]

Another school of thought says Howe himself had heard the reports. But he apparently refused to be hurried from his game of faro or the company of a certain femme fatale named Mrs. Loring. "It is hard to believe that after the savaging he had endured at Bunker Hill," says Pearson, "he could have happily left the matter until the next morning. But that is what he did."[83]

This neglect was to happen over and over during the war. General Sir William (Billie) Howe was to play a key role in the making of the prefident, by not finishing the stumbling, puzzled, often befuddled Washington off in the eight or nine decisive engagements that he neglected to consummate in the coming New York–New Jersey campaigns of 1776–78. As Sir Henry Clinton writes:

Had Sir Wm. Howe Fortified the Hills around Boston, he could not have been disgracefully driven from it: Had he pursued his victory at Long Island, he had ended the Rebellion: Had he landed above the lines at New York, not a man could have escaped him: Had he fought the Americans at Brunswick he was sure of victory: Had he cooperated with the Northern Army, he had saved it, or had he gone to Philadelphia by land, he had ruined Mr. Washington and his Forces; But, as he did none of these things, had he gone to the D———l, before he was sent to America, it had been a saving of infamy to himself and indelible dishonour to this Country.

So, let's pause to examine this gift from Providence, the gods had strewn along Washington's path.

Howe was a strange man, very tall, dark, brooding with thick eyebrows, ample black hair and a flat wide nose that gave a coarseness to features that were said to be otherwise handsome. Historians say he was a convoluted, complex character, an intelligent and shrewd military tactician; as he had proved at Bunker/Breed's Hill, he had great courage and his men and most of his officers held him in high respect. But he was withdrawn and taciturn.

General Howe's basic fault was a puzzling apathy that seemed to cloud his judgment. Very often he was slow to go to battle. Sometimes this was due to the fact that he was waiting for men or supplies, but he seemed to have an instinctive tendency to delay aggressive campaigning. There was a weariness about him, as though the slightest effort required strength of will. His dispatches dealing with the postponement of attack through lack of stores or equipment carry little of the impatience that would have nagged many other commanders. On the contrary, there is almost a sense of relief. For "Billie" Howe, there was always time.

His idiosyncratic conduct of military affairs later was attributed to Whig tendencies. He was accused of being a fellow traveler and supporter of the American rebel cause, dating back to his service as a Member of Parliament for Nottingham. The soldier-politician also was widely thought to be the illegitimate son of King George II. Others said he was just plain indolent.*

As busy as Howe was with military affairs, he still had time

---

* For the best discussion of the fascinating Billie Howe story, see Ira D. Gruber's *The Howe Brothers and The American Revolution* (New York: Atheneum, 1972).

for community affairs. He was not so apathetic about his battles at the card tables. Dame Fortune smiled, or, more usually, turned her back on him. He had better luck with the other ladies of Boston. At forty-seven, he was what a contemporary called "a ladies' man" . . . fine-figured, full six feet high and well-proportioned . . . his manners were graceful and dignified.

His inactivity at the front didn't prevent him from laying siege to one of the fine women of Boston, Mrs. Elizabeth Loring. A generously endowed beauty, she was known in reports of the day as "a brilliant and unprincipled woman," "the flashing blonde," and, to staff officers, "the Sultana." She was a superstar in Boston society whose praises were sung in the gossip columns of the day. Francis Hopkinson, the noted first flag designer, immortalized Howe's alliance with the lady in his popular quatrain "Battle of the Kegs":

> Sir William he, snug as a flea,
> Lay all this time a snoring,
> Nor dreamed of harm as he lay warm,
> In bed with Mrs. L———g.[84]

Nobody likes to accuse a lord of being remiss of duty, but it was widely said that what distracted Sir Billie was Mrs. L———g. Howe appeared, as one historian put it, "to have been personally most comfortable in his easy relationship with Mrs. L———g, whose share in ruining his career is not difficult to estimate."

But even the most priggish historians today admit that Lord Howe was s———p—g with Mrs. L———g. He was the victim of our nation's first under-the-covers agent. She was the nation's first secret weapon, the sex bomb.*

Elizabeth Lloyd Loring on her back did more than most Daughters of the Revolution standing up. It was His Excellency's flirt who was responsible in 1778 for General Howe's sea voyage

---

* In Philadelphia in 1778 a loyalist poetaster wondered why Sir William, with nearly 20,000 men, did not attack nearby Valley Forge. He tried the power of song to light a fire under the British high command:

> Awake, arouse, Sir Billy,
> There's forage in the plain,
> Ah! leave your little Filly,
> And open the campaign.
> Heed not a woman's prattle,
> Which tickles in the ear,
> But give the word for battle,
> And grasp the warlike spear.[86]

from New York to Philadelphia, a circuitous forty-seven-day trip—
which, in England, was credited with "making the Americans a
present of Burgoyne's army," and of the French alliance. It was
said that he "played at bo-peep with the rebels" and his voyage to
Chesapeake Bay was called "circumbendibus." John Bernard, the
actor, when he visited America in 1797, said that the reason for the
"perverse and fatal" voyage was "that Mrs. Loring, being at this
time in as critical a condition as the country, required the benefit
of sea-air, and her wish was law!" [85]

No woman did more for the cause. Elizabeth Loring, the
rebels' S-x Bomb, was married to Joshua Loring, Jr., the distinguished scion of an old Boston family high on the social scale who
doesn't get mentioned too often in family histories. Through his
new army connections, Mr. Loring rose—rather suddenly—to
commissary of army prisons in Boston. Then New York, then Philadelphia. The Lorings and Howe were quite a ménage à trois, as
they slept their way across the war zone. It turned out to be a
lucrative post for Loring. As Judge Jones, the Tory legal correspondent, wrote, "Joshua Loring fingered the cash, while the general
enjoyed madam."

His penal administration is widely noted in the histories of the
period. Ethan Allen, when a prisoner in New York, said of him (in
his "Narrative," pp. 106–7), "This Loring is a monster!"

One of his reforms as a commissary of prisons was the reduction of food from once a day to once every other day, thence to
once every so often. This nutrition plan increased the amount of
profit he made per day. But from the diaries of prisoners we learn
that the system did not work well with the wounded Americans.
As the surgeon Leach reported:

The poor sick and wounded prisoners fare very hard: are
many days without the comforts of life. Dr. Brown told me
that they had no bread all day and the day before. He spoke
to the provost, as he had the charge of serving the bread,
who replied, "let them eat the heads of nails, and knaw the
planks, and be d--d." The comforts that are sent us by our
friends, we are obliged to impart to these poor sufferers, and
feed the soldiers and others with rum to carry it to them by
stealth, when we are close confined and cannot get to them.
They have no wood to burn for many days together to warm
their drink, and dying men drink theirs cold. Some of the

limbs which have been taken off, it is said, were in the state of putrifaction, and not one survived amputation.

Probably because of the severity of their wounds, twenty (two thirds) of the prisoners were dead by the middle of September. Loring was a real sweetheart.

Another scheme of his was more wholesale and bold. French says, quoting a survivor, "Many goods of the inhabitants have been plundered by sheriff Loring, and brought to the prison-house.— They made a vendue of them in the prison-house, Loring the vendue master; the provost, his son and Dyer (deputy-provost), the bidders—a most curious piece of equity."[87]

Thus was another Boston fortune amassed.

Mark Antony, legend has it, might have conquered Rome but for Cleopatra's abandonment of him in the sea battle at Actium. Howe had his own Cleopatra, Mrs. Loring, the beautiful gambler who lost three hundred guineas a night without a qualm.[88] And helped Washington win a great victory at Boston.

You can worship and salute your Boston Brahmins, your Cabots and Lodges, your Longfellows and Shortfellows, your transcendental poets, your Mercy Warrens and Phillis Wheatleys and other heroines who march to different drummers. I'll take Mrs. Loring, the nation's true liberty belle.

[21]

General Washington was on a winning streak. He was 1–0 against the British Empire. True, it was a default. The Brits took their marbles and went home without a shot fired in anger, except by Colonel Knox's artillerymen. (American casualties were light: two dead and five wounded from exploding cannon.)*

Congress voted General Washington a gold medal. Struck in Paris, his head was on one side, and Boston on the reverse, with

---

* Smallpox wreaked more damage in the British camp inside Boston than rebel guns.

Washington on horseback in the foreground and a British fleet everywhere in the background. Around his head was this inscription: "Georgio Washington supremo duci exercituum adsertori libertatis, Comitia Americana."

Around Boston on the first Congressional Medal of Honor was this: "Hostibus primo fugatis Bostonium recuperatum XVII Martii MDCCLXXVI."

Continuing the avalanche of Latin, Harvard made him a Doctor of Laws—"Georgium Washington, Doctorem utrius Juris." [89]

The Massachusetts Assembly praised his military achievement in a formal address (in English).

But Dr. Washington didn't rest on his laurels. As a unit of 1,500 men with smallpox liberated Boston, the generalissimo led the bulk of his army on to New York, where the war was about to turn nastier.

Even though he hadn't actually fought the British yet, Dr. Washington's popularity was soaring.

Oddly, though, the victory did not rouse martial enthusiasm among the people. There was no flocking to his standard. The "sunshine patriots" were leaving the army in 1775 at an alarming rate. Even before Tom Paine coined the term in his pamphlet, written in 1776, it was winter at the recruiting office. If Washington was such a charismatic figure in the war, and in the founding of the country, why didn't they flock to his cause? Other charismatic military figures in other countries had that effect. People seemed to have fallen in love with Washington the man, but not the cause. Our ancestors certainly weren't prepared to die for their country, or anything else.

At least the poets rallied to Washington's side. One of the first to venerate him was Phillis Wheatley. The first of the black poets—she was born in Africa and was brought to Boston in a slave ship at the age of seven in 1761; at nineteen her first volume of poetry had been published in England—she joined the arts-for-Washington bandwagon with a letter written from Providence, Rhode Island, on October 26, 1775: "I have taken the freedom to address your Excellency in the enclosed poem, and entreat your acceptance, though I am not insensible of its inaccuracies. Your being appointed by the Grand Continental Congress to be Generalissimo of the armies of North America, together with the fame of your virtues, excite sensations not easy to suppress."

The overheated sensations, combined with a love for big words and the pomposities and artificialities of the period, are faithfully recaptured in the first Wheatley campaign poem. She sings:

> Celestial choir! enthron'd in realms of light,
> Columbia's scenes of glorious toils I write.
> While freedom's cause her anxious breast alarms,
> She flashes dreadful in refulgent arms . . .[90]

Despite his being tied up whipping and training the hippies, he found time to write a letter thanking his excited supporter. The generalissimo said he was ready to publish the poem himself, "with a view of doing justice to her poetical genius," but in all modesty he couldn't.

His favorite poems nowadays were the ones that spelled his name right. He didn't go for the hidden symbolism of the acrostics like "FRANCES ALEXA." He liked the ones that came right out directly dedicated to him. He knew the value of poetry as political statements and publicity.

His tent flap was always open to visiting bards. Even at Valley Forge, he always found time to encourage the arts. The Yale poet Timothy Dwight (a chaplain attached to General Samuel Parsons's brigade) asked permission to dedicate to the general his epic-in-progress, "The Conquest of Canaan." Silverman says Washington had not seen the poem, but he wrote back to Dwight from camp, returning encouragement as well as consent. Nothing, he said, could please him more "than to patronize the essays of Genius and a laudable cultivation of the Arts and Sciences, which had begun to flourish in so eminent a degree, before the hand of oppression was stretched over our devoted Country." *

While people may not have been whistling "The Conquest of Canaan," the pop musicians were also at work for Washington. A few months after Washington received his commission, Barry Schwartz says,[91] there appeared the immensely popular "New Song," whose very first stanza made use of the new military commander as an emblem for the colonies' martial sentiments: "Since WE your brave sons, insens'd, our swords have goaded on, / Huzza, huzza, huzza, huzza, for WAR and WASHINGTON."[92]

---

* Dwight worked on the poem as long as Washington worked on his expense account, completing the first draft in 1776, and finally publishing it in Hartford in 1785, dedicated, as were all his works, to Washington: "Commander in chief of the American Armies, the Saviour of his Country, the Supporter of Freedom. And the Benefactor of Mankind." The politically astute Dwight later became president of Yale.

The colonial man doesn't live by poetry alone. Civic celebrations, including poetry, oratory, illuminations (the first slide shows), fireworks, and newspaper hosannas, gave proof long before the war was won that George Washington had become the savior of his country.

The practice of naming the newborn after him accelerated. With the exception of certain saints, as Hughes says, no human being has had so many human beings of all colors and races named after him. One of the earliest so named was probably George Washington Robinson, son of Colonel Robinson of Dorchester, baptized on the first Sabbath in August 1775. On the last Sabbath of October, George Washington Appleton was baptized at Andover. There was no dearth of children coming along who would carry the burden of having to live up to their namesake.

To be fair, they also named babies after John Hancock and James Warren. The Whigs were shameless, using every technique and propaganda tool possible, from pseudonyms in the papers to the baptismal font, to remind the masses who the heroes were.

The selling of George Washington continued. "George Washington," or just "Washington," began appearing in an endless list of towns, counties, creeks, institutions, and articles of merchandise. "Fort Washington" and "Washington Heights" appeared on Manhattan Island in 1776. Shortly afterwards, counties in North Carolina, Maryland, and Virginia and towns in North Carolina and New Hampshire were named after the American commander. In 1781 Washington County was formed in Pennsylvania. In 1782 the college in Chestertown, Maryland, was renamed Washington College.[93] There was a trend here, the experts said.

Then they started celebrating the birthday—long before his death and not to promote department store sales. As early as 1776, Washington's birthday was a sacred day, so much so that the *New York Argus* disparagingly referred to it as America's "Political Christmas."

Meanwhile, the campaign portrait business was booming. Lafayette bought one to send home to his wife's château in the Loire. Hancock desired one for his sweetheart.

While Washington was at Boston the highest honor was paid. As Hughes says,[94] there began that endless array of his spurious portraits. Joseph Reed sent him a ferocious mezzotint made out of fancy by Alexander Campbell, who represented him sword in hand advancing to battle, and Washington commented ironically: "Mr. Campbell, whom I never saw, to my knowledge, has made a very

formidable figure of the Commander-in-Chief, giving him a sufficient portion of terror in his countenance."

In 1779 the Pennsylvania legislature hired Charles Willson
Peale to dash off a picture of Washington to be hung in the statehouse, "for the expressed purpose of promoting public morals." [95]
The legislators hoped that contemplation of the general's countenance might "excite others to tread in the same glorious and disinterested steps which lead to public happiness and private
honor." [96] When Peale finished the job, the public approved and
presumably set about improving their morals. Unfortunately, however, the painting was badly defaced by "one or more volunteers
in the service of Hell." [97]

Freeman's Journal, which reported the dastardly act, did not
say how it was defaced. Was a mustache added? Or a scurrilous
slogan like "The illegitimate father of his country"?

The venerational odes to Washington prominently displayed in the
nation's press in 1776 helped brainwash the public's mind about
the once-glorious beloved king. As Schwartz says,[98] they attributed
his former qualities—his "great soul," "godlike virtues," and "in-
born greatness"—to the new hero. Americans had lost a monarch
but gained something better: a demigod.

Along with the symbolic assaults—the removal by angry
crowds of the king's coat of arms from courthouses, churches,
taverns, and shops; and the destruction of royal portraits and
statues—came the ultimate malediction: "God bless Great Washington; God damn the King." [99]

The most wonderful thing the Mount Vernon machine had
going for it was the prevailing belief that victories such as Boston
were made possible by God. A victory, Schwartz says, inspired
confidence, largely because the press and pulpit saw a religious
significance to them. "One source of the revolutionaries' confidence lay in their obedience to God. A religious vocabulary voiced
many of the calls to serve in the Continental Army and to promote
its cause. . . . God intended His punishment of war-makers only
for Britons, and He entrusted its execution to Americans. . . .
This explanation obviously allowed only one outcome—American
victory." The prevailing belief in providential intervention made
God a co-pilot. It rendered every occurrence on the battlefield a
manifestation of the Divine Plan.

Washington's role in this legend of "providential interven-

tion" was understood in terms of an important aspect of the prevailing covenant theology. Specifically, Schwartz says the story of
the Israelites' exodus from the land of Egypt provided Americans
with a model of their own experience with England, enabling them
to transform a complicated geopolitical struggle into familiar religious terms.

"It seemed foreordained, at least in hindsight, that someone
would play the leading role in the American Exodus drama. When
Washington emerged, he was the most plausible Moses." [100]

Oyy. As if he didn't have enough troubles, he was now the
American Ben-Gurion.

[22]

I t's 1779. March. The Washingtonistas are in the hills of New
Jersey, where guerrillas should be. They are bivouacked in
Middlebrook. Morristown. Basking Ridge. Pluckemin. [101] Fox
hunting country to this day. Social New Jersey. It has not been a
good war since General Washington left Boston, undefeated and
untested in the spring of 1776. In New York, in May, he unveiled
his secret strategy of winning the war: by losing all the major
battles except the last one.

As a general, Washington had a few shortcomings. He sometimes lost battles by leaving his left flank unprotected. Sometimes
his right flank was open. And sometimes it was the center of the
line. His left flank exposed, as in the Battle of Long Island (August
27, 1776), enabled the British to ride up an undefended Flatbush
Avenue.* At Brandywine he lost by leaving the right flank unprotected. In Westchester he lost by being weak in the center of the
line. At Germantown he lost because of reliance on too complicated a battle plan. The British never knew which mistake General
Washington would make. It kept them continually off-balance.

---

* It didn't help either that he split his army between New York and Brooklyn and
failed to use his cavalry for reconnaissance, which led to being taken by surprise through a
flank attack.

At White Plains (October 28, 1776), General Lee saw serious flaws in Washington's deployment of the troops, according to the historian John Shy in *George Washington's Generals*, "and recommended a movement northward to the next ridge line. Washington agreed, but immediately received a report that British troops were preparing for an attack. There was no time to deploy, and Washington could only alert his command and tell his generals, rather lamely, 'Do the best you can.' Their best was not good enough to hold a faulty position and the American army was again driven back."

"Do the best you can" was among the better strategies evolved by the rebels' general staff. Testing these original theories led to the terrible winter of 1777–78 in Valley Forge, followed by the less publicized one in Middlebrook in 1778–79, when it snowed as much as in Switzerland.

[23]

The Generalissimo had gone into the wilds of New Jersey that bitterly cold winter of 78-79 with his "family," which included his most innovative contribution to the art of war, the awesome secretarial pool.

General Washington wrote or had written for him a lot of letters. At times Washington, almost rivaling Julius Caesar, was able to keep five men busy writing letters at his dictation, or suggestion, or for his approval. Sometimes it seemed there was more action in his pen-and-ink brigade than on the battlefield. His few critics were saying that he got too involved in paperwork, recruitment, acquisition, or supplies and weapons. Nothing was too unimportant for him to say "Take a letter, Al, Aaron, or Caleb."

Twenty-five volumes of wartime correspondence (more than any other American officer ever produced) attest to his greatness in this field. The rattle of his sword, not the scratching of his pen, was what the revolution needed, some misguided wretches argued.

What they didn't understand is, rain or shine, battle or not, the war of letters went on. Washington's HQ was a smoothly operating campaign machine. His five secretaries were the equivalent of a press office in a political HQ, all interconnected, for the greater good of the country, someday, at the public's expense. There were the letters home to his constituents—the congressmen who elected him. He diligently explained what their general was doing for them, always solidifying his position with the powers-that-be, never mocking the "right honorables" as the other soldiers did. He also wrote regularly to the governors of the nearby states, conducting what amounted to foreign relations with independent chief executives of states.

Among the family members in 1776 was Aaron Burr, appointed as aide-de-camp and amanuensis to the general after his brilliant and brave campaign with Arnold in Quebec. Burr wasn't delighted with his new assignment. He thought Washington was a bad general and an honest but weak man. Burr said "he knew nothing of scientific warfare, and could therefore give not instruction of any value to a young soldier burning to excel in his profession. He thought the general was as fond of adulation as he was known to be sensitive to censure, and that no officer could stand well with him who did not play the part of his worshipper."

He lasted six weeks. Burr said he objected to the drudgery of the job. Washington is said to have objected to him on moral grounds.

The general had a lot of trouble getting good secretarial help—and keeping them. Most members of his family grew restless for military activity or for escape from the apparently somewhat oppressive atmosphere about the commander in chief. Many of them quarreled with him and wounded him in various ways, either at once or in after years.

It was not until March 1, 1777, when Providence sent him a gift from heaven in the diminutive form of Alexander Hamilton, that his secretarial worries ended.

Hamilton was just twenty-two, a captain in Knox's artillery, and he had been recommended by General Greene. Born out of wedlock in the West Indies, he emigrated at seventeen and entered King's College (now Columbia). At 5'7" he was of average height but was slight of frame. He was a boy genius, well read in the science of government and economics, opinionated and cocky. Character assassins today might say he was a cross between Roy Cohn and an early Alex Keaton of "Family Ties." Unlike Roy Cohn he was honorable; unlike Keaton he was brilliant. He was a leading conservative thinker, but was a conservative revolutionary. His enemies for a time would say he wrote most of the famous speeches and letters supposedly written by General Washington. But Washington was just as good at rewriting Alexander Hamilton as Alexander Hamilton was good at writing for the general. The boy ghostwriter also had his falling outs with the general. He was hurt and outraged by Washington's refusal (at first) to give him a field command. Unlike Burr he never broke with him for long. He always came to his senses in time to climb back on the prefidential bandwagon.

The model family member, an idolator for the idol, who adored the general and worshipped the ground his horse rode upon, was a young man of nineteen who often rode on one side of Washington during this period, in a splendid uniform and with the aloofness of an assistant to a god. He was a French volunteer, recently arrived in America, by the name of Marie-Joseph-Paul Yves-Roche-Gilbert du Motier, Marquis de Lafayette. His friends and later namers of streets, towns, counties, universities, and flying squadrons called him Lafayette.

General Washington had met the red-haired, blue-eyed boy at a dinner at Philadelphia's City Tavern, where so many hungry military adventurers came to advance their careers in the rebel army. He was a modest wealthy aristocrat married to an heiress of the de Noailles family, well connected to the palace at Versailles, who once said of himself, using the imperial third person, "Upon him the eyes of Europe were affixed." [102]

For Washington, who had no French, and the marquis, who was learning English quickly, it was the start of a beautiful friendship, like that of Rick and Louis in *Casablanca*. The boy marquis had absolutely no military experience, so Congress started him out at the bottom—as a major general. It was an honorary title, they said, like "colonel" in Virginia. Washington didn't hold *le kid*'s lack of experience against him. He offered him an honorary aide-de-camp job in the family. The marquis was bursting with enthusiasm. He explained he was in America "to learn about *la guerre*." And with no conventional military knowledge to unlearn, as Colonel Flexner puts it, "Lafayette became, with sensational rapidity, one of Washington's most successful military pupils."

It was the old older-man-and-his-boy-major-general-from-the-decadent-French-court story. Lafayette was to explain to the teen-age wife he had left behind in the Loire château that Washington, "surrounded by flatterers or secret enemies . . . finds in me a sincere friend, in whose bosom he may always confide most secret thoughts, and who will always speak the truth." Unlike other young men Washington had encouraged, unlike Hamilton and Reed, Lafayette never turned on his patron. His affection became to Washington a poultice for loneliness. The childless general and the French aristocrat who had been orphaned at the age of three came, as they both boasted, to fill the roles of father and son. Washington spoke of Lafayette as "the man I love," later to be the title of a Gershwin song. [103]

They were very close during the war. Dewy-eyed historians write about how "they slept together under one cloak among the dead [after the Battle of Monmouth, June 1778]." One blushes still today to read the exchange of military communiqués between the two officers.

On July 4, 1779, after his protégé had gone to France on furlough, Washington wrote, "When, my dear Marquis, shall I embrace you again? Shall I ever do it? —or has [sic] the charms of the amiable and lovely Marchioness—or the smiles and favors of your Prince, withdrawn you from us entirely?" [104]

On his own in the mess at Morristown, he wept unashamedly when speaking of his affection for the absent boy major-general. Washington wept again when the marquis answered his letter. He answered in haste:

> Your welcome favor of the 27th of April came to my hands yesterday. I received it with all the joy that the sincerest friendship could dictate, and with that impatience which an ardent desire to see you could not fail to inspire. I am sorry I do not know your route through the State of New York, that I might with certainty send a small party of horse (all I have at this place) to meet and escort you safely through the Tory settlements between this place and the North River. . . . I most sincerely congratulate you on your safe arrival in America, and shall embrace you with all the warmth of an affectionate friend when you come to headquarters, where a bed is prepared for you. Adieu, till we meet. Yours.

On May 10, 1780, Lafayette reached Morristown and, Hughes says, "doubtless seized Washington in his arms and kissed him on both cheeks." They repaired to headquarters, where Lafayette told the great news he had brought: the French were coming—two fleets were on the way. "It was enough that he had brought himself," Hughes adds.[105]

Reports filtered in from the combat zones about the meetings of these two. Outside of Yorktown in 1781, Saint George Tucker, a Virginia officer who became a judge, wrote: "At this moment we saw the Marquis, riding in full speed from the town, and, as he approached General Washington, threw his bridle on his horse's neck, opened both his arms as wide as he could reach, and caught the General round his body, hugged him as close as it was possible, and absolutely kissed from ear to ear once or twice as well as I can recollect with as much ardour as ever an absent lover kissed his mistress on his return. I was not more than six feet from this memorable scene."[106]

Washington and Lafayette embracing and hugging—what is this, the Turkish army? These overt displays of affection were bad for morale. Other officers were getting jealous, Brand Whitlock says.[107] All of which raises the inevitable questions: Was Lafayette straight? Was Washington? Were they, as newspaper reporters might have wondered, gay? They were certainly merry. But were they having a homosexual relationship? Of course not. All that kissing and smooching and hugging was normal in male friendships of that time, like football and basketball players hugging and patting each other on the ass today. The attraction could have been that the marquis was a *oui* man who never uttered a word of criticism for Washington—in English or French. The general could do no wrong in all the years they were such good comrades-in-arms.

[24]

The family became very close at Valley Forge. They survived the bitter winter of 1777–78 by drinking and dancing and speaking French. The veterans of Valley Forge might be collectively called "the Happy Valley Forge set," anticipating the British expatriates in Kenya two hundred years later, banded together by their isolation and intimacy.

The Happy Valley Forge set, the history books say, often met at each other's quarters, and sometimes at General Washington's lodgings, where the evening was spent in conversation over a dish of tea or coffee. The only entertainment was singing, according to the French volunteer Pierre Etienne Duponceau, who had left the fleshpots of Paris to enroll in the patriot cause as the valet-secretary to Baron von Steuben, the Prussian D.I. at Valley Forge. "Every gentleman or lady who could sing was called upon in turn for a song."

Valley Forge sounds like summer camp.

The closeness of the inner circle became even closer at the Middlebrook headquarters during the winter of 1778–79. In January 1779, at Middlebrook, all eighteen of the general's aides were stricken with colds. The family that plays together gets sick together.

The life-style of the family was summed up by Elijah Fisher of the commander-in-chief's guard in a description of a day's activities:

> We Selebrated the Independence of Amarica the howl army parraded . . . the artilery Discharged thirteen Cannon we gave three Chears &c. At Night his Excelency and the gentlemen and Ladys had a Bawl at Head Quarters with grate Pompe.[108]

"To Bawl," in Revolutionary War terms, was to drink enough Madeira and other libations to knock out a horse with "grate pompe."

Every schoolboy knows about Valley Forge of 1777–78. But little is taught about the suffering that went on at Middlebrook and Morristown in the winters of 1779–81. The spirit of the Spirit of '76 crowd is captured in one of the "bawls" thrown by the Happy Valley (Forge) set at the quarters of Colonel and Mrs. Clement Biddle in Morristown during the winter of 1780–81. Biddle was forgemaster general under General Greene. Marian Sadtler Hornor describes one such bawl.[109] The highest-ranking officers and their wives attended. Headed by General Washington, the guest list also included General Greene and his Kitty, George Olney, a relative of General Greene and his right-hand man in the business of providing for a hungry army, and his wife, Deborah, a Providence matron. It wasn't until a year later that details of how they "bawled" emerged.

Mrs. Olney heard malicious whispers concerning her conduct

at the party, Hornor says, and accused Mrs. Greene, her erstwhile friend, of circulating what she mildly termed "a very extraordinary story." As Mrs. Olney's scandalous behavior was reported at every tea table in Boston, Wethersfield, Providence, Morristown, and Philadelphia:

> The men, jolly over their wine, started horsing around. A scuffle ensued between the men and women in Biddle's parlor. Mrs. George Olney was heard to say to General Washington, "If you do not let go of my hand, sir, I will tear out your eyes or the hair from your head; and that tho' you are a general, you are but a man." [110] Immediately afterwards, the general was seen rushing out of the parlor with a red face.

When Mrs. Olney began hearing the story from friends in Boston, Wethersfield, Providence, Morristown, Philadelphia, wherever Kitty Greene traveled, she accused Kitty of spreading the tale. As if that wasn't bad enough, Mrs. Olney said, it wasn't true. "You did say," Kitty wrote back, "you would tear his hear [hair]." If it were not true, why, asked Kitty, did General Greene take the Olneys into the next room and tell them that Washington was offended? And that they should apologize? Mrs. Olney's version, Thayer says, [111] was that George Washington left the group in the parlor because they wanted to get him intoxicated.

"Bawling" also included dancing. It was in Middlebrook that terrible winter of 1778-9 that General Henry Knox and his equally rotunda Lucy Flucker Knox hosted a grand celebration of the French alliance. General Washington opened the ball at the Jacobus deVeer house in Pluckemin by taking a turn with Lucy Knox, who by now weighed as much as George Washington. "Everybody allowed the ball to be the first of the kind ever exhibited, in this state at least," Knox reported in a communiqué from the ballroom. "We had about 70 ladies all of the first *ton* in the state, and between three and four hundred gentlemen. We danced all night—an elegant room. The illuminating fireworks, etc. were more than pretty."

It was at these soirees that the general also worked out with Lady Stirling, the wife of the phony nobleman, General Lord Stirling, and her daughter, Lady Kitty Alexander, and her companion, Miss Nancy Brown, the distinguished ballerina. And Mrs. Biddle, of the partying Colonel Biddles. "And," as one eyewitness reminisced, "some other ladies whose names I do not recall."

Mrs. Greene, Mrs. Olney, Mrs. Lucy Flucker Knox, Mrs. Lady Stirling, et al. were part of a patriotic organization I call George's Angels, his dancing partners who helped fight British tyranny by dancing the long, lonely nights away.

Dancing was rampant in the Middlebrook/Morristown war zone. Captain Samuel Shaw wrote in his diary, "Three nights going till after two o'clock have they made us keep it up." Shaw, who later became the first secretary general of the Society of the Cincinnati, was one of the thirty-four officers in the military elite or dancing assembly, which met at Colonel Biddle's (of the Main Line Biddles) house.

Later, at Middlebrook during the darkest days of the war, the high command of the Washingtonistas held the Dancing in the Dark Ball, at which the general appeared in black velvet, with his black belt and dancing pumps. The foreign officers were in golden lace, an excess that Washington later deplored.

Black velvet was the uniform of the day. I'm sure these were black velvet rags, knowing the condition of the enlisted men since Valley Forge.

In March 1779, at Middlebrook, General Greene wrote to Jeremiah Wadsworth, "We had a little dance at my quarters. Mrs. Greene went three hours with his Excellency without sitting down. Upon the whole we had a pretty little frisk." [112]

At the conclusion of the night of the big frisk—when his wife and Washington danced three hours without stopping—Gen. Greene was shipped out on a secret assignment, by command of the general. So quickly, as he explained, that he didn't have time to say "goodbye" to Mrs. Greene. Talk about a coincidence. Three hours without stopping, and sending the husband off to the front on a secret mission? A most strange business. I'm surprised the Washington establishment historians haven't investigated it more.

They often cite Washington's amazing achievement of dancing three straight hours without stopping with Mrs. Greene. But they fail to ask questions such as, what kind of dancing was this, vertical or horizontal? Was anybody else dancing at the time?

And what was Martha Washington, who had arrived in camp from Virginia, doing during those three hours? Knitting a scarf for the boys at the front?

Dancing in those days was a commitment. It was rare to dance three hours with one partner. Most of the time, they danced with multiple partners. So much so that they needed a dance card to keep track of their schedule, like an appointment calendar. Washington's ledgers are filled with items about every time he went fox hunting, played cards, or bred a dog, but nothing is found of what it was like to dance with his most trusted officer's wife for three hours. Did it slip his mind?

Well, there is nothing in his diary about Mrs. Olney either. Or Lucy Flucker Knox, with whom he opened the big ball at the Middlebrook Camp Country Club. Or Lady Stirling . . . or Eliza Willing Powel . . . or Mrs. Biddle . . . or Mrs. Benedict Arnold, the notorious Peggy Shippen . . . or Mrs. William Bingham . . . or Washerwoman Kate . . .

What the general was doing with Mrs. Greene at this little frisk was building troop morale, starting with his own. It was consistent with the provisions of his general orders, which called for improvement of morale and working conditions, which had been declining under his leadership. He specifically encouraged parties and celebrations. As his contribution to the war effort he had allowed himself to unbend to the extent of dancing three hours without stopping with Mrs. Greene.

As attentive readers will recall, she originally had come to the front at Cambridge in 1775, pursuant to orders received earlier from her husband, General Nathanael Greene. He had written home to his wife in Rhode Island that "Lady Washington had moved into headquarters to brighten the drabness of Army life." Mrs. Greene was instructed to bring her best frocks and join the troops on the ramparts forthwith. She became the number-one camp follower of the war. Her greatest accomplishment along these lines occurred in 1776, when she followed Nat to New York, just as General Howe was arriving with reinforcements.

[25]

What was Kitty Greene doing in New York in 1776 with her trunks of dancing shoes and party dresses? The British had come. On June 29 they arrived in the harbor off Staten Island in 138 ships, carrying General Howe, Mr. and Mrs. Loring, and the king's army. The flotilla looked like a forest of masts anchored off the Staten Island ferry dock, wrote an eyewitness on Staten Island in his diary.[113] "I thought all London was afloat." In July the general's elder brother, Admiral Howe, would join him with yet another army, in a huge armada of 150 ships. Two more fleets were on the way.

The putrid fever (typhoid and typhus and smallpox) had arrived in New York in July. General Heath (who, a historian says, "undoubtedly put the number too high") estimated that by August 10,000 lay sick.* "In almost every barn, stable, shed, and even under the fences and bushes, were the sick to be seen," he recalled. During this trying period, Washington lost more men from the fevers than were to die from British bullets in the approaching battle.

For the first time in the war Washington's generalship was under fire. He had been soundly beaten in his first pitched battles on Long Island. War had turned out to be different from fox hunting, the derby, pitching horseshoes, and the other competitive sports in which he excelled. The army was poorly managed, historians say. The wilds of Jamaica, Queens, and the hills of Crown Heights and Flatbush Avenue, heavily timbered, broken by narrow passes, were perfect for guerrilla warfare tactics. But General Washington with his Hyde Park mentality was doing fortifications, works, and straight-on battle plans, with left and right flanks or the center of the line left open. It's too painful to go into the details.

Washington's strength as a general, oddly enough for one so open and honest, was deception, cunning, sudden surprises, sneak attacks—as at Trenton later in 1776, getting the cannon up the heights at Dorchester that night, and escaping from Brooklyn Heights with his whole army while Howe was snoring with Mrs. Loring. He had poured fresh troops into a trap caused by his not understanding what had been happening on the battlefield on Flatbush and DeKalb Avenues, in downtown Brooklyn. The evacua-

---

* Greene, Professor Thayer says,[114] attributed the sickness in the army in New York partly to a diet of too much fresh meat. To remedy this, he tried to get more vegetables, fruit, and milk. All meat was to be roasted rather than boiled. Believing cleanliness essential for good health, he sought to have his men well supplied with soap with which to keep washed, shaved, and dressed in clean clothes. As an additional precaution, he refused to allow his soldiers to stay in swimming more than half an hour or to swim in the heat of the day.

tion that night was a marvelous achievement, a Dunkirk of the Gowanus. But why would he then stay in New York?

New York was undefendable. It was an island surrounded by water filled with British ships. But that didn't stop "the Blockhead," as Clinton called him. Defending the undefendable, putting all your eggs in one basket, twice in a row. It's important to remember, as Colonel Freeman says, that in the second year of the war he was "engulfed in a fog."

The psychohistorians don't tell us why Washington was in a fog. Nerves? An anxiety attack? Private reasons? Dark psychological things? Could it have been the presence of Kitty Greene?

Now, I'm not saying that he and Kitty Greene were carrying on in New York. There's no evidence that they were, just as there was no record she may have been visiting with Aaron Burr, Alexander Hamilton or Benedict Arnold. Still, Mrs. Greene created some talk by returning to New York when the wives of other officers were leaving. As Henry Knox wrote on July 8, 1776, to Mrs. Knox,[115] after he had raced his Lucy back to Connecticut as soon as they saw the masts of the fleet over South Ferry: "Mrs. Green's return was a vast surprize to us. . . . My Lucy . . . acted right in not returning to this place. As to Mrs. G's husband being happy to see her at all times and in all places . . . he would have rather lost his arm than have seen her here at this time. . . . He was over here [not in New York] at the time she arrived and would not believe she was coming until he saw her."

Coincidentally or not, General Washington, as Colonel Freeman puts it,[116] had "Martha started homeward [on June 30] because New York under hourly threat of bombardment and attack manifestly was no place for her." And General Greene had been sent off by his general to study the lay of the land around Fort Washington, and the "defences," as far away as Westchester.[117]

As a result, Mrs. Greene didn't actually see her Nat for some time. It would not be the last time the commander-in-chief separated his good friends the Greenes. It happened again the following year. As General Greene explained in a letter to "my dear angel": ". . . Gracious God, how much I wish to come to you! . . . But the General will not permit me to go. I have had exceedingly hard duty this spring. The General keeps me constantly upon the go. The love and friendship he has for me, and the respect and kindness he shows me, goes a great way to alleviate my pains. I am as well loved and respected in the army as I can wish; but notwithstanding the honors of war, and the love and respect of men, I feel a blank in my heart which nothing but your presence can fill up. There is not a day or night, nay, not an hour, but I wish to fold you to my heart." [118]

I must also point out that it was during the New York campaign in 1776 that General Greene emerged as Washington's favorite general. Washington decided to pull out of Manhattan Island in November, leaving an entrenched fortification on the northern part of the island called Fort Washington, garrisoned by 2,800 rebels. The failure to abandon it is unfathomable. It was isolated, remote from the rest of the patriot army, and of no strategic value. It had been built originally to prevent British shipping from going up river and cutting American communications. The plan had not worked well; the British kept coming and going past the fort as if it were a tourist attraction, a navigational aid like the little red lighthouse underneath the George Washington Bridge today.

The fort was located on Washington Heights, a four-mile ridge running from the Hudson River to Harlem Heights. General Washington, with his taste for the grandiloquent, called it "Mount Washington." But it was not, whatever one called it, the Himalayas.

One would have thought he would make his last stand farther down the coast on the East Side, at Bloomie's, but he picked Fort Washington, its base at the corner of 164th and 165th streets by the North River (now Hudson) and Broadway, where Columbia Presbyterian Hospital is now. It was surrounded on three sides by the enemy and on the fourth by water.

All of Manhattan was vulnerable, as I've said, especially Fort Washington. All Howe had to do was land his forces in Riverdale and pull the noose. Howe had naval superiority. The Continental navy at that time was not into guarding coasts; it preferred privateering, which was the fastest way to make a buck during the war. Men were deserting Washington's army to join privateers.

In July, General Greene was inspecting Fort Washington, seeing to its defenses. This remarkable piece of strategy was expected to produce another Breed's Hill. For here the patriots were behind breastworks, on a height, and they could fire down on the enemy once they saw the whites of their eyes. So it seemed to Washington and his co-genius Greene as Washington kept pouring his well-whipped and disciplined army into the breastworks of this impregnable bastion, the Maginot Line of Manhattan.

The Hessians had landed in the New York area in August in

their heavy all-season uniforms after a terrible journey from Hesse-Cassel. They had been so tightly packed on the decks of the transports arriving in New York, it was said, "An officer had to give orders for the troops to all turn at once so they could get comfortable." [119] The Hessian Grenadiers, under Baron Wilhelm von Knyphausen, had distinguished themselves at the Flatbush and Bedford passes in the battles of Long Island and White Plains, and on November 16, 1776, they enhanced their growing reputation as ferocious fighting men during the attack on Fort Washington. It was said they stuck bayonets in the backs of the men in front, a kind of early radar guiding system in battle.

In the final charge on Fort Washington, a Hessian diarist noted, "not a shot was fired." The grenadiers relied as usual on the bayonet in chasing the Americans into the fort. They charged forward as a body, screaming and holding their bayonets forward and parallel to the ground. The awesomeness of such charges was enhanced by the grenadiers' getup. Their coats of blue wool were almost covered with broad belts. They wore towering brass-fronted headgear that made even short men appear tall. They dyed their mustaches with the same concoction used for blackening their shoes. Their long hair, according to a contemporary description, was "plastered with tallow and flour and tightly drawn into a long appendage reaching from the back of the head to [the] waist." A Hessian soldier tells what happened next: "We took positions in a ditch that the Americans had dug around the fort, and here we were ordered to stop our advance. The Americans had outrun us but now they were commanded to consider themselves prisoners of war. General Knyphausen ordered that the fort had to capitulate within two hours." [120]

The Knyper's eight thousand men overran the impregnable fort in three hours.* The Hessians marched the rebels back to Joshua Loring's prisons.

For the first time, criticism of Washington began to appear in the army itself. "We have alarm upon alarm—Orders now issued, & the next moment reversed. Wd to heaven Genl. Lee were here is the Language of Officers and men," wrote Colonel John Haslet, a man who had stood unflinchingly with Stirling against the king's troops at Long Island. William Duer, a member of Congress,

---

* Fort Washington was renamed Fort Knyphausen, but the new name never caught on in Manhattan. Neither did Knyphausen Heights. Or the expression "win one for the Knyper."

though not so critical as Haslet, hoped Lee would soon arrive from the South. Washington was a great general, he said, but he needed the help of his best officers at this time. Regardless of what others thought, Greene's confidence in his advocate remained unshaken.[121]

"Don't be frightened," he wrote to Governor Cooke of Rhode Island, "our cause is not yet in a desperate state."[122]

Lee had advised Greene and Washington to abandon the fort; it was undefendable. After walking around the area today, I can see why. With the enemy on three sides and the water on the fourth, there was no place to go.

The general had a lot of faith in Greene to let him put his army in that place. The Americans were a running army. They needed room to scatter and then re-form. It was one of their greatest tactics, what we called "bugging out" in my army days. When in doubt, Washington's army ran away. This confounded and irritated the British. They could never win, and the Americans would never admit they had lost. You had to catch them first. But at Fort Washington, under Washington and/or Greene's guidance, they got caught. Except for the escapees, including Greene and Washington, who were on the New Jersey side in Fort Lee.

The fall of Fort Washington, with a third to half of the American army, was the blackest defeat in our military history. It resulted from Washington's continuing to see the war as a static conflict of forts and set-piece battles. Instead of penning up his men in a fort, he should have stationed them behind every bush and tree in (soon-to-be) Central Park, and told them to pick off the British one by one.

There were those in Congress who blamed Greene for what happened in the Fort Washington debacle. The leader of the Put-the-Blame-on-Greene movement was General Washington, also his staunchest champion. As the chorus of criticism swelled, Colonel Flexner explains, "Washington could not defend himself by insisting that no blunder had been made. Always oversensitive to situations which might take away from that public esteem which he desired as his sole reward, less sure than ever that he possessed the military skills requisite to his station, Washington did not generously shoulder the blame. He pushed the blame off on Greene."[123]

Actually, Greene had tried to convince Washington to burn the city before it fell into the hands of the enemy. Citing history, he wrote, "Remember the King of France, when Charles the

Fifth, Emperor of Germany, invaded his kingdom, he laid whole provinces waste, and by that policy he starved and ruined Charles' army, and defeated him without fighting a battle." Furthermore, he argued, two thirds of the property of the city and suburbs belonged to loyalists, so why should Washington put himself in jeopardy by attempting to defend it? [124]

The Hessians struck while Washington was dithering. He "was so exhausted, so puzzled and depressed that he did not find it in his heart to give peremptory orders," Colonel Flexner admits. [125] Again, the fog.

Making Greene the sole engineer of his "blackest defeat" reveals another aspect of Washington's character, the ability to put the blame where it belongs, on others. Always blame someone else was one of his unwritten rules of civility. That way whatever happened was never his fault.

I don't want to dwell too long on his deficiencies in planning and intelligence for battles. After all, the British master plan for winning the war in the New York area against Washington was, according to documents and maps now in the War Office archives in London, to sail the fleet, with the whole British army on board, up the Saw Mill River and invade Westchester, thus splitting the colonies in two. They have the navigational charts to prove it is feasible. Those of us who drive up the Saw Mill River Parkway today must marvel at the thought of the mighty British armada sailing up that spit of water, the Saw Mill River, a driblet to nowhere.

So Greene was made the scapegoat of the Fort Washington debacle. But Washington, great statesman that he was, forgave him. Instead of banishing him to Siberia or sending him down the river, he nominated him for quartermaster general, a cushy post for anyone who liked to travel and get rich in the army. Washington had a soft spot in his heart for Greene—or was it his wife?

Greene remained fiercely loyal to His Excellency. His trust in Washington was awesome. No matter what bad things were being said in the years of the Big Fog (1776–77), Greene supported him, as did Kitty. They were a mutual admiration society—all three of them loved Washington.

[26]

Greene's appointment as quartermaster general took place in the midst of the social-athletic season at Valley Forge in the winter of 1777–78, when Kitty was reigning as the fun girl of the year. The Greenes' temporary residence in the old Derrick Van Veeghteen farmhouse was always filled with laughter and music, the closest thing they had at Valley Forge to a disco. Von Steuben's valet-aide Duponceau called it "the favorite resort of the foreign officers." Kitty not only spoke French but understood it. She dazzled the foreign officers with her command of *le français* and contemplated Racine and Voltaire with the Marquis de Lafayette.

The Greenes' *cercle français* was interrupted when the commander in chief needed a replacement for the eloquent but corrupt Thomas Mifflin, the previous quartermaster general, who was retiring a wealthier ex-soldier.

The quartermaster buys supplies for the army: food, shoes, hay for the horses, wagons and tents, scrapple and hoecake, everything an army needs to function. It's a peach of an assignment, especially if one likes to travel. A man is constantly on the go, rounding up supplies. But it keeps one away from one's dear angel.

The job was a plum in other ways. It was lucrative. The custom in the quartermaster corps at the time was that a commission of 1 percent went to the quartermaster general on every purchase. In other words, he got a royalty of 1 percent on every piece of straw the horses ate, every slice of hard tack or filet mignon the enlisted men were served in the mess hall, every brewski they drank. One percent here, 1 percent there—it adds up. By the end of Greene's first month in office, as Thayer says,[126] expenditures had exceeded four million dollars in continental currency (less than half that sum in specie). And this was "but a breakfast for the department," said Greene, smacking his lips.

Thayer says that Greene was a man who admired wealth. He wrote in February 1778, "Money becomes more and more the American's object. You must get rich, or you will be of no consequence." Thayer adds, "But consideration for Washington and the pressing needs of the army also went into the making of his decision. Greene convinced himself, at least, that these were the real reasons for accepting the offer and perhaps he was right."[127]

They were soon saying the new quartermaster general was avaricious and greedy, corrupt and dishonest, with an unusual tendency to giving advantage to friends and relatives. He was blinded by temptation. This was ridiculous, of course. Greene, as he was to prove, was an average American. He only did what other patriots in similar situations facing equal temptation did—he got what was coming to him.

As quartermaster general, Thayer says,[128] "Greene had a flow of money coming to him from his commission, which soon reached enviable proportions. This income he invested in shipping, privateering, iron manufacturing, and real estate. He was too preoccupied with army duties to handle the investing himself which he left to friends to perform."

At first, Greene was just into good old-fashioned honest corruption, the usual placing of orders with companies—not only the ones he had relatives in but others, in which he was an investor. But he expected from these companies no overcharging or sale of inferior goods, by God! Thayer assures us.[129]

With the flow of capital increasing daily, Greene soon became a major venture capitalist in the colonies, investing in a number of risky deals. He was a major money man for the outfitting of privateers, which attacked the British for private profit. Some historians, though, piously point out that not all Greene's ships were profitable. But enough of them were that he could take a flyer in real estate.

Greene's investments in real estate, Thayer says, included purchases of land along the Passaic River in New Jersey and up along the Hudson in New York. In Rhode Island he purchased Patience Island in Narragansett Bay at a cost of $4,700 in specie. The island, it was said, could support twenty-five cows, six oxen, four horses, one hundred sheep, and eighteen hogs.

By the end of his reign as quartermaster, Greene and Congress were at war. He was about as popular as Benedict Arnold. His enemies in Congress accused him of dishonesty, and there were serious insinuations that he was enriching himself. The clamor increased, even after he left the job under a cloud. But one man never lost confidence in the money-hungry Quaker from Rhode Island.

A vacancy occurs in the high command. The army of the south

needs a commander. The previous one, General Horatio Gates, has had a setback at the battle of Camden, South Carolina (July 27, 1780). The man who had once been proposed as a candidate to be the next commander-in-chief by the Conway Cabal, a grassroots movement to overthrow Washington, left the battlefield on the fastest horse in the army. Gates didn't stop riding until he reached Charlotte, sixty miles distant.[130] Since he was sixty miles ahead of his men, it looked bad.

General Washington's nominee for the post: General Greene. How happy Mrs. Greene must have been.

It had taken some doing to get Greene this great honor of being shipped out to South Carolina. Army commands had to be approved by Congress, where Greene wasn't too popular at this time. There had been a major debate about the appointment. The military procurement ethics scandal lingered. The leader of the legislative floor fight and arm-twister-general for Greene was none other than General Washington. He lobbied hard for his friend as a replacement for General Gates, mounting a massive letter campaign to Congress on behalf of Greene. This was part of his usual diplomatic relations with the legislative branch. He was the ambassador to Congress during the war, master politician that he was. Usually Congress served as a rubber stamp, adopting his suggestions as its own.

Why would Washington want Greene to go to South Carolina? He was a great general, of course. In the words of Henry Lee, "a very highly trusted councellor of the commander-in-chief, respected for his sincerity, prized for his disinterestedness, and valued for his wisdom." Scheer and Rankin say Greene seldom showed brilliance, but he had much of Washington's capacity for enduring. His wife, Kitty, may also have had something to do with it.

[27]

The Greenes' life in the army was filled with comings and goings, missed connections. So many times Kitty the angel is flying to the front, but duty is calling her husband elsewhere, PDQ. Reading the Greene letters is like studying the habits of migratory birds in the mating season.

At the time of his appointment, Greene was at West Point in 1779, recovering from the bruises on his reputation inflicted during the excess profits debate in Congress, and anticipating a cushy, quiet, idyllic, romantic winter with his dear heart, Kitty. After Arnold had fled, Greene asked Washington for that post, and it had been assigned to him, temporarily. Nine days later, Greene received a letter from the commander-in-chief informing him of his appointment to succeed Gates in the faraway Southern department. Greene asked for a few days at home to settle his "domestic concerns" and to recover from a high fever. Then he wrote another letter:

> My dear Angel,
> What I have been dreading has come to pass. His Excellency General Washington, by order of Congress, has appointed me to the command of the Southern Army, General Gates being recalled to under[go] an examination into his conduct. . . .
> I have been pleasing myself with the agreeable prospect of spending the winter here with you, and the moment I was appointed to the command I sent off Mr. Hubbard to bring you to camp. But, alas, . . . I am ordered away to another quarter. How unfriendly is war to domestic happiness.[131]

Washington pressed him to leave for South Carolina. He must fly at once. "Fly" was an expression used loosely in the travel writing of the day. A trip from Haverstraw or Fishkill, New York, to Charleston, South Carolina, could take three weeks, as the crow flies.

Greene told Washington the source of his domestic concern. "I wrote to Mrs. Greene to come to camp, and I expect her here every hour. Should I set out before her arrival, the disappointment of not seeing me, added to the shock of my going southward, I am very apprehensive will have some disagreeable effect on her health, especially as her apprehensions were all alive before there was the least probability of it. My baggage sets out in the morning, and my stay here shall not be more than a day longer, whether Mrs. Greene arrives or not." [132]

Tough noogies. Greene's request for a short leave to prepare for a very long journey was denied. Within the hour that he received the note, General Washington had shot back a telex, or its equivalent: "I wish circumstances could be made to correspond with your wishes . . . but your presence with your command as soon as possible is indispensable . . . I hope to see you [at head-quarters in Preakness, New Jersey] without delay." Even as the frustrated Greene set out upon the road to Preakness, he glanced over his shoulder in the anguished hope that his dear angel would catch up with him before he left for the South. She may have tried, but she failed.

The next day, Greene hurried to Fishkill, having heard that Kitty was about to reach that village. He rode out as far as Peekskill, the historians say, on the chance of meeting her coming in. The road was empty, and the few travelers he encountered were sure they had not passed her along the way. Back at West Point, he sat down to compose one last farewell letter, to be entrusted to the colonel of the garrison and forwarded to her as soon as her whereabouts could be learned, a letter which, Thayer says, he knew would be read in a storm of tears and anger.

My dear Angel—

I am this moment setting off for the southward, having kept expresses flying all night to see if I could hear anything of you. But as there was not the least intelligence of your being on the road, necessity obliges me to depart. As I shall ride very fast, and make a stop of only one or two days at Headquarters, and about the same time at Philadelphia, it will be impossible for you to catch up with me. Therefore, whatever things you have for me, you will please to forward by the express who will await you.

I have been almost distracted, I wanted to see you so much before I set out. My fears of being ordered southward was what made me hurry away Hubbard at such an early hour. God grant you patience and fortitude to bear the disappointment. My apprehensions for your safety distress me exceedingly. If heaven preserves us until we meet, our felicity will repay all the painful moments of a long separation. I am forever and forever yours, most sincerely and affectionately, Nath. Greene.

Au revoir, Fishkill and Kitty.

Catharine Greene was temperamental, a high-strung filly. General Greene was afraid of her reaction. What would a woman scorned, who feels abandoned, neglected, uncared for, a hot-tempered flirt, do in the Haverstraw-Fishkill area? Play Parcheesi for the rest of the winter? Fortunately, when the bereaved angel finds her hubby is gone, perhaps forever, a friend of the family remains to console her. A dance or two, maybe after hours? The general, who a few months earlier at Middlebrook danced three hours with her without stopping, could explain the military situation to her in person.

And what happened to Kitty? Why had she missed her husband? Where was her escort, Mr. Hubbard? "The mystery of her delay remains to this day," Professor Thayer says. He blames the habitual failure of communications in those chancy times and the frequent miscarriage of letters sent out in the vicinity of enemy patrols.

Last-minute adjustments could also have explained her itinerary. Forewarned by Mr. Hubbard that Nat was off to the wars, she may have stopped off to visit with General Anthony Wayne, who was in residence at headquarters in Preakness, New Jersey, at this time. Nat's angel had flirted with General Wayne at Cambridge in 1775. Mad Anthony, too? Generals were her hobby.

The irony of Washington's hustling Greene off to South Carolina in the middle of the night for a 780-mile journey was that when Greene finally got to Philadelphia, he cooled his heels nine days before he could "fly" to the South. He was nine days delivering various messages for the general to congressional committees. Hurry up and wait—the army hasn't changed.

It is most peculiar that Washington chose as his principal military adviser a thirty-four-year-old businessman and forge operator. Greene was a pretty good general for an anchorsmith, but nothing compared to a general with the background of Lee. It's interesting that Washington—having access to a trained soldier, a man who had actually fought and led troops in the European wars (Poland,

Spain, the Russian front), the best military mind in the colonies, who advocated tactics that would have ended the war faster, which he ignored—would turn to the advice of Greene instead of Lee.

But Lee had a personality problem. He didn't suffer fools gladly. He was blunt. He was the man who said that the reason Fort Washington was defended was its name, and conversely, the reason Washington abandoned Fort Lee without a fight was because of *its* name. Thus beginning a retreat which might not have been necessary if General Washington had followed Lee's advice in Cambridge and and started fighting a guerrilla war.

Although he was a regular army man in training, Lee understood a basic principle of leadership: make the most of what you have. When you're stuck with men who can shoot squirrels between the eyes at seventy-five yards, don't make little tin soldiers out of them. He recognized the American spirit more than Washington.

Rifle fire by the untrained and undisciplined Minutemen had made mincemeat of twenty-one companies of Britain's crack troops in the colonies at the time—Grenadiers, the tallest, most heavily armed of infantrymen, and light infantry, the agile flanking troops of the regiments—on the march back from Concord to Boston. It was murder. They were sitting ducks in the road.

The regulars were poorly adapted psychologically to deal with the New World fighting. They had been terrorized by the withering fire from behind stone walls and trees. The sharpshooters had left them in a state of panic on the road back to Boston. Only the action of a group of junior officers, teenagers, had calmed the regulars down enough to make the long march which left their tongues, and many bodies, in the dust. The next meeting, at Bunker/Breed's Hill, left them in a further state of shock, a major reason the regulars didn't venture out of Boston often during the siege of 1775.

Lee understood the economics of the war better than Washington. The king, who was cost conscious, couldn't keep replacing troops ad infinitum.* Remember, a major cause of the war was the

---

* The king had trouble getting British subjects to fight in America. The Landgrave of Hesse-Cassel, who reputedly had a hundred children to support, sold 20,000 mercenaries to George III, for some £3,000,000.[133] The king's other German relatives, including the Prince of Brunswick-Lunburg, chipped in 4,300 men for £160,000. Eventually the family sold him some 30,000 German mercenaries at a total cost of £4,700,000. Of these, Commager and Morris say, some 12,000 were killed or stayed in America (deserted).

It cost the king £257 to transport each soldier to America. Every soldier killed repre-

king imposing taxes to help defray the costs of the French and Indian War.

Washington would have been uncomfortable with a real military genius like Lee in his tent—and vice versa. It is sometimes said that Lee was a disaster in the field, especially at Monmouth, where the supposedly brilliant Lee appears to have botched things completely. General Washington had to ride out into the field to give him a foul-mouthed tongue-lashing that was so eloquent the fleeing Continentals were said to have stopped just to listen to it. After which Washington rallied his men and fought the British to a stalemate (the Brits retreated during the night).

Being ignored for a Greene could have later brought out the worst in the eccentric Lee. Many of the better officers went over the edge while serving with Washington. In the immediate family, all of the better ADCs couldn't take him. Mifflin was particularly upset about the commander's faith in Greene. Reed escaped to his law practice. Even the faithful Hamilton quit for a time.

It took a certain kind of personality to remain calm in the face of Washington's indecisiveness and plodding ways as a general, his fortitude, and all the positives of character his admirers ascribe to him. Greene had it, while Lee went bananas. Greene and Washington had similar sadomasochistic personalities. Greene was just as harsh a disciplinarian as Washington was. They shared an opposition to riflemen sniping at the British in disorganized fashion. They read the same military books, only Greene was a faster study.

"I am exceeding happy," he told Kitty when he was again a right-hand man, with "the full confidence of his Excellency General Washington. . . . The more difficult and distressing our affairs grew," he explained, the more Washington relied upon him.[134]

Greene seemed to go up and down in Washington's mind, like the stock market. It was almost as if there were some market barometer (railroad boxcar loadings, corn or hog belly futures) of that day, as an index to when he was in or out.

---

sented a financial setback to the king's accounts. Every wounded one was three times as costly. (It took two men to carry a wounded one from the battlefield.)

* * *

[28]

Everything seemed to go wrong for Washington in the battles of the next five years. Long Island and New York were the start of a trend in the war that would have hurt other men's reputations. Not the first Teflon man. Nothing stuck.

The people's enthusiasm for the bloodless victory at Boston seemed to sustain them through the next five years of the war, when much of the time nothing happened. He fought no battles the last three years, except the last one, at Yorktown, in 1781. When he fought and lost, he was soundly thrashed, whomped, beaten, mauled, creamed, as the sports pages of the day might have said of the setbacks. But Washington's image always came out unscathed. This phenomenon began at the Battle of Long Island, where the loss, despite his poor management of the troops, was rarely attributed to him.

As Schwartz says, "Newspaper accounts stressed the enemy's numerical superiority and indicated that a retreat was the only alternative to surrender or suicidal counter-attack. Washington's own role in this withdrawal was thought to be heroic. From one eyewitness the nation learned that he 'flew like a guardian angel to protect and bring off his brave troops. . . . The retreat was conducted with the greatest secrecy. . . . There never was a man that behaved better upon the occasion than General Washington; he was on horseback the whole night, and never left the ferry stairs till he had seen the whole of the troops embarked.' " The press was a wonderfully reliable source of information.

After more than two months of further victorious withdrawals, Washington suddenly took his army into New Jersey and dealt the enemy sharp and effective blows. By January 1777, most Americans were convinced that their Washington was a great warrior whose prowess had on three different occasions (at Boston, Trenton, and Princeton) humiliated the numerically superior British veterans. Praise for Washington was boundless.[135]

William Hooper, delegate to Congress from North Carolina, declared him to be "the Greatest Man on Earth."[136] "Had he lived in the days of idolatry," announced a writer in the *Pennsylvania Journal*, "he had been worshipped as a god."[137]

The press, the poets, the portrait painters—the media—and the common people all saw Washington as their hero right or wrong. The greatest man in the world couldn't lose.

So what if his record was 2-9-1, or however you play the numbers game with the war battles. Was Trenton, it could be asked, a battle or a skirmish? With an image like that, he couldn't lose. You can see where the myth came from that he was unbeatable.

[29]

I t's 1781. October 19. Two P.M. Yorktown. Cornwallis has surrendered. "The play, sir, is over," as the Marquis de Lafayette wrote a friend.[138]

It was done in the trenches beside the York River, at the Battle of Yorktown, which would have been a minor engagement if the war hadn't suddenly ended there.

As you know, we won. Otherwise we would all be British today. Not Italian-Americans or Lithuanian-Americans, but true Brits.

It was a miracle. The victory was enough to make one believe in God, or Providence, since the former is a word General Washington didn't use. David had beaten Goliath. God may have saved us, but Marie Antoinette, soon to lose her head over another revolution, and Louis XVI helped.

All the famous faces were there. Henry Knox, Mad Anthony Wayne, Baron von Steuben, the general's favorite Marquis. Lafayette fought valiantly as ever.

The hero of the battle, for me, is Alexander Hamilton. Hammy had a good war record, leading the charge of the letter writer's brigade since 1777: 2,309 boxes of letters, or copies, were his contribution to the war effort. An unprecedented feat in a war. Nobody had written so many letters to his congressmen.

The general and his amanuensis-de-camp had had their fights at headquarters, culminating with a bitter squabble over who kept who waiting on a staircase in HQ one day in 1780, at the end of which Hammy turned in his quill. He obviously wanted out. He wanted combat and fame as a soldier, not as a secretary.

Destiny (and General Washington) brought him back in time for the Big Y, Yorktown, 1781. It was a macho thing for the little colonel leading the charge on the right wing of the banks of the York River. Hammy was so short that he couldn't climb out of the trench and over the palisade. He had to ask another man to bend over, then, leaping on his back, he sprung up on the palisade and hurled over the parapet—to glory.[139] Since Hamilton, as Hughes says,[140] wrote the official account of the attack, with all his brilliant literary skill he managed to make most of the glory his own.

George Washington had displayed his usual courage in battle. I feel glad he finally won one. It must have been depressing losing so often even if you're a god. It was especially wonderful, since he had been against the Yorktown battle. The French had conned him into it.

He was for attacking New York. It was the key to isolating Canada, he had argued. He was fixated on Canada. I think he wanted to invade Saskatchewan, landing his troops at Moose Jaw, then come in with the right button hook from his floating batteries.

He also lobbied vigorously for an amphibious landing in New York.

During the previous year, he had been trying to convince his opposite number, Count de Rochambeau, commander-in-chief of the French forces, to strike at New York, where the count could have led the bloodiest disaster in French military history. But this didn't prevent Washington from taking all the credit for Yorktown.

As even Colonel Flexner says,[141] "Washington's memory, like that of lesser men, was sometimes to edit the past to make it seem more reasonable. In 1788 he played down for publication the fact that Rochambeau, although titularly under his command, had forced him to undertake the Yorktown campaign against his better judgment. However, his contention that he had willingly consented forced him to misstate widely what was the strategic situation when the campaign had started. Since 'our affairs were then in the most ruinous train imaginable . . . I never would have consented to embark in any enterprise wherein, from the most rational plan and accurate calculations, the favorable issue should not have appeared as clear to my view as a ray of light.' "

Yorktown, ray of light and all, was won because of an amazing series of coincidences. The Rochambeau battle plan for Yorktown had all the complexity of a genuine Washington original. It called for the arrival of two French fleets, and no storms or sightseeing excursions, as the French had a tendency to indulge in. It required the arrival of two French armies, plus the rebel Washington armies, from long distances. It required the British armada not to arrive from New York. It required, also, that the Brits under Cornwallis actually stay there so they could be surrounded. And surrender.

And miraculously all the elements fell into place at the same time. *Sacré bleu!* The French fleets arrived. There were no storms. The British armada, which would have lifted the siege, was two days away when Cornwallis threw in the towel.

The British had had enough. They pulled out, like we left Vietnam. The country was divided at home over the war. It was considered a waste of money. Anyway, the important thing to them was India. India was the land of opportunity. The streets of India were paved with jewels and spices.

Yorktown was the *coup de marron glacé.* The French had pulled Washington's chestnuts out of the fire.

To the French, George Washington was only a third-rate farmer-soldier. The Father of the Revolution, the manager, the man they respected and who got them involved was Benjamin Franklin, whom they called the man who "ripped the lightning from the skies and the scepter from the tyrants." Washington returned the lack of respect.

It was one of the greater ironies of history, Hughes says, that Washington "should have owed the ecstasy of this day and all his consequent glories and his elevation over perhaps all other men to the French, who had been his first inveterate enemies; whom, with the exception of one marquis, he never liked; whose language he would never learn; whom he would once more oppose and abhor, bringing on himself unimaginable abuse; against whom he would take the field, in his final year on earth, as their sworn enemy again, thus completing the round."[142]

Since the autumn of 1776 the French court of Louis XVI had been secretly supplying the rebels with guns, ammo, and supplies for troops. Like the U.S. later was supplying the Contras in Nicaragua, the French did it through a covert import/export firm. The contraband arms used to win the battles of Trenton and Princeton I were supplied by the covert trading company set up by Caron de Beaumarchais. How French to put the traffic in arms in the hands of a satirical farce writer, the man who did the book for Mozart's opera *The Marriage of Figaro.*

*

I don't want to be giving the French all the credit here. The British helped, too, by losing the war. It was a tactical error, not sending a gunboat up the Potomac River and threatening to shell Mount Vernon. It was flammable and within gun range. His hen houses and cherry trees? It would have broken his spirit, hit him where it hurt, in his property. This was General Howe's biggest mistake in a series of many miscues.

Among the many bungles the king and his honorable representatives made here, the worst was not issuing an emergency honors list: that is, wartime titles on the spot, like battlefront commissions. The Earl of Mount Vernon to George Washington. The Duke of Back Bay to John Hancock. That would have siphoned off revolutionary zeal. A seat in the House of Lords, this was the standard way the crown corrupted all the opposition greats in Britain. Whigs, bomb-throwing radicals, anti-monarchists, we all settle for a title. That would have ended the war on a highly moral, favorable basis for the British Empire. Very negligent of the colonial office.

And let us not omit the secret factor in Washington's victory. During his Long Island–New York exploits, during the thrilling escapes through Howe's fingers in the retreat through the Jerseys, he had on his side an invisible ally. The fact that the trap was not closed on him so many times was due to Howe's timidity and slowness, it was said, and not to Washington's foresight. What about good old-fashioned luck? The angel who rode by Washington's side all his life had her work cut out for her, as he bungled his way upward to the top.

Part IV

—

The Making of the Reluctant Noncandidate

Being the incredible account of the man who said,
"I'd rather sit under my fig tree than be prefident."

[1]

On October 28, 1783, the general came riding home to what he called "My seat at Mount Vernon." The war was over.

Five-score-and-one months before, when he left "the place of buccolic rest" on May 4, 1775, he had promised to return before Christmas. And now he was fulfilling the pledge—only seven years and ten months late.

In December he was riding north again, but this time to Annapolis to make his retirement from public service official. On December 23 there was a moving ceremony before Congress, which was meeting at the Annapolis statehouse. In a solemn ritual, General Washington handed over his sword and presumably his mighty pen, which had also performed gallantly during the war. At last he was a vet.

Everybody was moved by the event, except the president of Congress, Thomas Mifflin, a former ADC of Washington's and conspirator against him. "The spectators all wept," James McHenry—a member in good standing of the Mount Vernon machine, another former ADC, and the man who had devised the form of the ceremony—wrote to his girlfriend, "and there was hardly a member of Congress who did not drop tears. The General's hand which held the address shook as he read it. When he spoke of the officers who had composed his family, and recommended those who had continued in it to the present moment to the favorable notice of Congress he was obliged to support the paper with both hands. But when he commended the interests of his dearest country to almighty God, and those who had the superintendence of them to his holy keeping, his voice faultered and sunk, and the whole house felt his agitations." [1]

Not since the saying goodbye to his officers at Fraunces Tavern three weeks before had there been such a moving farewell performance. His self-possession also failed him in New York. When "his excellency entered the room," recalled Colonel Benjamin Tallmadge, the Yale classmate of Nathan Hale, Washington's chief intelligence officer, and another member of the Mount Vernon machine, "his emotion was too strong to be concealed." And this failure of concealment, Tallmadge went on to say, "seemed to be reciprocated by every officer."

At the end of his carefully prepared address there was a moment of total confusion. As Schwartz described it, it was when his eyes failed him and he drew from his pocket something few had ever seen him wear: a pair of spectacles. "The simple admission that he had 'not only grown gray but almost blind' in the service of his country produced the effect he sought from the persuasive logic of his speech." [2] The result was "a scene of sorrow and weeping I had never before witnessed," Tallmadge said, "and fondly hope I may never be called upon to witness again."

A similar thing had happened when Washington confronted the mutinous officers at Newburgh, New York, on March 15, 1783. They were bitter about not being paid and other slights. The sight of their glorious commander, who came to them as a weakened, bespectacled supplicant, set the hardest-hearted veterans and the most dedicated mutineers, it was said, to open weeping.

Anyone who attended all three major farewell speeches might have noticed a certain resemblance. At Newburgh, Fraunces Tavern, and Annapolis, there was the address, the manner, the glasses bit, the tears, the shaking of the hands of each soldier or legislator—each a potential voter, which I'm sure was only a secondary consideration. Pulling out the glasses, suggesting the loss of eyesight as well as the graying of his hair in the cause of his country! He did it the way Ronald Reagan would have done it.

It was a magnificent piece of theater and politics that could have won him an Emmy. John Adams was the first to call Washington "the great actor." Adams attributed Washington's hold on the public to a "Shakespearean and Garrickal excellence in Dramatic Exhibitions," and said Washington was "best actor of the Presidency we have ever had." [3]

Few besides Benjamin Rush, the man to whom Adams's words were addressed, would have agreed.

Washington had discovered a great political truth, explains Richard B. Bernstein: "Crying is a lot better than formal arguments." All wore their hearts on their sleeves in the old days. It was not considered shameful to cry. Not a macho thing. Real men cried in the 1780s; it was okay to "lose it."

But I accept the sincerity of the emotions. There was a lot to cry about: sorrow for departed comrades, tears of joy for what had been accomplished.

Washington's great achievement was holding the army together, during the war and then at Newburgh. He was like Ike and the allies in World War II. And he did it with showbiz techniques that Ronald Reagan would have given him a four-handkerchief rating for.

Congress, sitting at Annapolis, was especially thrilled with him, and understandably so. He had, after all, talked his men into setting aside their plans to seize control of the government, it is said, out of respect for him. As James Madison, of the Mount Vernon machine, who originally doubted Washington's ability to put down the mutiny at Newburgh, said of that turning point in the race, "The steps taken by the General to avert the gathering storm, and his profession of inflexible adherence to his duty to Congress and to his Country, excited the most affectionate sentiments toward him." [4]

An understatement if there ever was one. For a Congress that had just had its skin saved, as Schwartz says, [5] and for a society acutely aware that most earlier experiments in republicanism had run the ancient cycle—anarchy, then order through tyranny—Washington's achievement was a victory over history itself. "The moderation of a single character," wrote Jefferson, "probably prevented this Revolution from being closed, as most others have been, by a subversion of that liberty it was intended to establish." Even John Adams, who, as Schwartz says, seemed the only one troubled by Washington as the sole beneficiary of public gratitude, had to admit publicly that the general was in truth an authentically disinterested man: "The happy turn given to the discontent of the army by the General, is consistent with his character, which, as you observe, is above all praise, as every character, whose rule and object are duty, not interest, nor glory, which I think has been strictly true with the General from the beginning, and I trust will continue to the end." [6]

And so it did. By the end of the war, Washington's disinterestedness had already become legendary. Philip Freneau had sung of it as the Virtuous Victor passed through Philadelphia on his way home:

> O Washington!—thrice glorious name,
> What due rewards can men decree—
> Empires are far below thine aim,
> And septres have no charms for thee;
> Virtue alone has your regard,
> And she must be your great reward.[7]

The teary ceremony at the Annapolis statehouse was not witnessed by the general public, Schwartz says,[8] but it was quickly and fully broadcast in the press, and the people at once grasped its significance. Freneau in one of his poems of protest sang: "Thus he who Rome's proud legions swayed / Return'd and sought his sylvan shade." The image lingered, and settled, in the collective consciousness.[9]

He had the strength of character to go back home to start living the life of the proto-yuppie that had been delayed by the war, to tend his house and garden, to dabble in real estate, to sit on the boards of directors of canal companies, and make his millions (in paper profits).

Behind him now were the shameless panic at Kips Bay, the temporary glory of the sneak attack at Trenton, the confusion of Brandywine, the disappointment of Monmouth. Now, like a Cincinnatus, he would quit the walks of public life, "to retire under the shadow of my own vine and my own fig tree," he told the audience at Annapolis. He was becoming, as they say today, "history."

This Cincinnatus image was ingenious in terms of attracting the voters of the day, if he was ever to run for office. People liked the idea of a Roman citizen-soldier giving up the hearth and plow as the crisis starts and turning in the sword and shield for fig and vine as the curtain comes down.

Of course, Washington was not shy about reminding them of his sacrifices for them. In 1778, as Schwartz says, Washington informed the Reverend William Gordon, who just happened to be writing a history of the war, a newly emerging cottage industry, that "the rewards of being Commander-in-Chief meant nothing in comparison with the cost of gaining them." And so, if "a person is found better qualified to answer [the public's] expectation, I shall quit the helm with as much content, as ever the wearied pilgrim felt upon his safe arrival at the holy land."

Even when undertaken for nonpolitical reasons, Schwartz says,[10] "self-denial for the public good was heavy with political implications. To surpass others in self-denial for the public good was to place them under an obligation that could be satisfied only by gratitude and respect; such was the advantage of noblesse oblige. Washington must have realized this himself. As one of the most status-conscious products of his society, Washington never let pass the opportunity to remind his countrymen of what he had renounced for their benefit."

Washington pounded away at this theme, as if the sanctity and importance of his domestic life was a plank in a platform. "I feel myself eased of a load of public care," he wrote at war's end to Governor Clinton of New York. "I will spend the remainder of my days cultivating the affections of good Men, and in the practice of the domestic Virtues."[11] Beautiful. Roger Ailes couldn't have written it down for him better as a position paper for 1789.

[2]

After hanging up his sword at Annapolis, the planter-farmer emeritus of Mount Vernon began leading a life that he described as "an existance of a tavern keeper." This was high praise. For Washington, as we all know now, was very fond of taverns.

Americans have always been devout hero worshipers, and Washington was the hero of the time. Mount Vernon became the shrine of American glory, the mecca of patriotic pilgrimages, the launching pad for mythologizing and adulation. Admirers trooped to the place, and stayed to dinner—governors of states, generals out of service, scientists, high rollers and insiders putting together canal and steamboat deals, diplomats, biographers and paragraph writers, adoring women, borrowers of money, painters of pictures, applicants for jobs.

What he was doing prior to 1789 was running the first of the front porch campaigns, credited by historians one hundred years later to William McKinley.

And it should be noted in any description of Washington's apolitical hermitlike life from 1783 to 1789 that turning Mount Vernon into a Dew Drop Inn was a continuation of the prewar pattern. When he reached home on November 11, 1771, as Colonel Freeman notes,[12] "he found ten guests in the house but he contented himself with listing the names in his diary and with noting thereafter the various departures." He was not inhospitable and, within limits, was glad to have company at Mount Vernon. Later the same year he was to welcome with much pleasure Governor Eden and a group of other Maryland notables,[13] but he probably was beginning to wonder whether he was a planter or an innkeeper.[14]

He told everybody who swarmed into the tavern,* or Mount Vernon, the news that he was not a candidate. All he wanted to do was stay at home, tranquilly glide down the stream of life, and count his slaves and chickens. He was resigning from public service for good. This was the most reassuring news the Washington-for-Prefident movement could get. His denial was tantamount to throwing a tricornered hat into the ring.

He had resigned or threatened to resign from public service at least seven times. His whole life, if there was any truth to John Adams's assessment that George Washington was a great dramatic actor, was a series of farewell performances. Nobody could not be running for something with more sincerity than George Washington. He denied he was a candidate for commander-in-chief. He would soon be denying he would go to the Constitutional Convention, where he was to sit as a figurehead, preparatory to denying he was a candidate for whatever they were going to call the leader of the country.

There was more to these denials than met the ear. It was a code word which politicians understood. Psychologically the denial meant the opposite. It sounds better in the German phrase used by Freud, describing the phenomenon: *"Schlepp mich, ich geh' gern"* (Drag me, I'd like to go).

---

* A conservative politically, he entertained on a liberal scale. One statistically minded historian, Marcus Cunliffe, calculated in the seven years up to 1775, about 2,000 guests visited, most of whom stayed for dinner and a brew or two, and many remained overnight.[15]

The negative method of saying "I'd be honored to serve" was consistent with George Washington's usual honorable personality.

Washington, for a politician, was a direct, honest person, who always said what he meant, or thought he meant. He was consistent. When he said he wasn't a candidate for something, for example, he'd keep repeating it, even when he was taking office. In the mouths of many politicians who follow in his hallowed voiceprints, the sentiment of denial often sounds hollow and hypocritical.

Washington by declining was inaugurating the declining-to-run race, an event which is staged every four years in honor of George Washington.*

Whatever Washington said he was doing, he was practicing the most profound of political strategies, avoiding being the frontrunner. The man with the longest lead in history in the polls—one hundred percentage points—was playing it safe. He knew intuitively, as we see in politics today, everybody gangs up on the frontrunner. Can you imagine Jefferson, Monroe, Adams, Madison, and that ilk ganging up on you as the frontrunner? It's awesome.

As a noncandidate, Washington was avoiding the kind of setbacks that frontrunners face today. Not that such setbacks would have mattered much to Washington. The man had a way of emerging unscathed from disasters. He was the first granite candidate (before Teflon was invented). His talent for passing the Continental dollar (as the buck was then known) was awe-inspiring. Despite losing nearly every battle, he came out of the war a hero. That's understandable, since he won the war. But it is also an illustration of his great talent for politics. Never since, until Dan Quayle parlayed six years in the National Guard as a public relations officer, otherwise known as a secretary, into a great war record, has a candidate done so much with so little.

But that should not be surprising. Washington was a masterful politician. He knew he had to be a hero and he became one before

* Not running for the highest office of the land is a tradition now with many variations. A person can refuse to run, but this doesn't preclude jogging or even walking. Did the candidate say he wouldn't run in the wrong direction for prefident (which is actually toward the prefidency)? Is running laterally allowed? The not-running strategy is complex.

he had done anything heroic. And then he knew that to achieve political success he had to be nonpolitical. And so he became the first noncandidate candidate. By resolutely denying that he wanted to be prefident, he became the first candidate to run against himself. He was always deprecating his ambitions, saying, "I'd rather be a farmer," "I'd rather tend my garden," "I'd rather pursue opportunities in the private sector." But he always conveyed his real message, which was, "Please draft me."

What is more, he had a powerful machine behind him. You won't read about the Mount Vernon mafia, also known as the Family and the Virginia Junta, in the history books, but this group of pioneering pols created a well-oiled campaign apparatus. He had the most brilliant operators of his generation—Madison, Hamilton, and others—working single-mindedly for his election. These men were not only pioneers in the arts of image making, issue dodging, and horse trading, they were brilliantly effective. After all, they engineered the only unanimous electoral college win in history for their candidate. (Dick Nixon came close in 1972 against George McGovern, missing it by only one state, Massachusetts, and the District of Columbia, which says something about unanimity.) The Virginia Junta was the first conservative cabal, the prototype for Ronald Reagan's California kitchen cabinet. At a time when there were supposedly no politics, no factions, no parties, the Mount Vernon machine flattened the opposition.

[3]

The machine had its work cut out for it. The Mount Vernon mafia consisted of men whose different intellectual and political highways came together for a short distance and forked again, like U.S. 1 and 9 through northern New Jersey. Alexander Hamilton, a machine stalwart, was a key player at the Annapolis convention of 1786. But machine lieutenant James Madison took over at Philadelphia in 1787. Men as different as Samuel Adams, Patrick Henry, and Christopher Gadsden worked with the machine in the early days, before they fell or threw themselves from the steam-roller.

The cast of characters in this scenario began assembling in the House of Burgesses in the 1750s, when veteran Virginian politicians first noticed the tall, silent assemblyman from Fairfax County. His early supporters included such political powers as George Mason, the general's first mentor, a states' sovereignty man and idea man with whom the general broke after Washington fell under the influence of the strong central government man, Hamilton; Edmund Pendleton, perennial Speaker of the House of Burgesses and the most successful lawyer in the state; Edmund Randolph, the governor of Virginia; and Benjamin Harrison. A Signer (as they called the 55 immortals who signed the Declaration of Independence), father of one president, and great-grandfather of another, Congressman Harrison was one of the general's closest political cronies, and figures in our story in an alleged incident of womanizing. (See pages 45–46.)

His famiglia had grown larger during the war. It included the aides-de-camp (ADCs) who were to be with him or against him for the rest of his life. His staff during the war was the equivalent of those who were with JFK in the West Virginia primary. The war was the primaries for George Washington, the dark days, when he could have been knocked out of the race and easily have been forgotten like Lincoln (Benjamin) or Artemas Ward. Who knows today that Ward was the first commander-in-chief outside of Boston?

The Washington ADCs were an illustrious group of mostly young Virginia and Philadelphia aristocrats. After graduation from the army they became wealthy merchants, lawyers, and power brokers playing important roles during the campaign and the first administration: Edmund Randolph, Tench Tilghman, George Baylor, Caleb Webb. They also made up his enemies list: Thomas Mifflin, Joseph Reed.

There were two kinds of ADCs: "riding" aides or "writing" aides, according to their inclination for indoor or outdoor duty. A riding aide was a staff officer who could carry a verbal order, or stay on a horse for hours, but who was of little use at a desk. A writing aide was, in effect, a secretary. The writing aides, or secretaries, were to play especially important roles in the making of the prefident. They could make George Washington sound as articulate and bright as Alexander Hamilton.

What remains of his correspondence today fills thirty-seven volumes. During the eight years of the war alone he employed at least thirty-two men (in batches of four and five) to handle his mail. Not all of these had the stature of press secretaries. Some were little more than glorified office boys.

They didn't have mimeograph machines in those days. The numerous duplicate copies of each letter were processed by hand. First there were the copies dispatched to correspondents' friends and associates, who had to be kept abreast of the public figure's latest thoughts and positions. The communications problem was further complicated by the unreliability of the mail. Stagecoaches were robbed; express riders drank and lost letters in transit; ships sank. To cope with the drudgery of sending out duplicate copies of each letter, the man of public affairs hired undersecretaries, or special assistants.

When the political figure called in his press secretary or a special assistant and told him the drift of his thought and allowed him to write the letter or speech himself, this functionary is what we call today a ghostwriter.

One of the men who served in this capacity during the war was operating behind the scenes for the Mount Vernon machine now: a key member of the general's think tank in 1788, a man who was to have a lot of things named after him soon, especially banks, the prominent Wall Street lawyer, Alexander Hamilton. Young Hamilton was in New York functioning as his chief of staff. He was a beloved figure in the extended family, as beloved by John Adams as Bobby Kennedy was by LBJ in the Kennedy administration.

Hammy, as his friends called him (but not to his face), was like a son to Washington. To others he was also known as "a son of a bitch."

This was more than a term of endearment. Hamilton's legitimacy was seriously questioned in the newspapers. The noted political hack J. T. Callender, editor of a *National Enquirer* type of publication, the *National Gazette,* was later to call him "the son of a camp-girl." That was one of the nicer things said about his mother.

As late as 1813, Adams was still calling Hamilton "that bastard brat of a Scotch pedlar." [16]

At least Adams had the decency not to call him a "black

bastard." For Washington's right-hand penman, a bright, ambitious, vicious, opportunistic, social-climbing West Indian bastard, that was a step up the social ladder.*

The discovery of Hamilton by Washington—an event which he recorded in his orderly book on March 1, 1777: "Alexander Hamilton Esq. is appointed Aide de Camp to the Commander in Chief, and is to be respected and obeyed as such"—was a gift from heaven. It was a major turning point in history.† It gave Washington a mind with the lucidity of crystal.

Hamilton was always the villain when I went to high school and first heard about him. He was the *eminence grise*, the little guy behind the throne, the fine Italian (or partly Jewish and black) hand. But history teachers never appreciated his brilliance.

Hamilton was one of those poor people who suffered from a superiority complex. But he was superior in many ways. He could work all day and play all night, manipulate, read, study, try cases, and dash off an op-ed piece to the *New York Gazette*. He could argue a case in court which could establish rights for Tories in postwar New York, as in the *Rutgers Brewery* v. *Waddington* case, and then rush back to the office the same night and write a piece for the papers on the same subject. So it wouldn't confuse anybody raising the "objectivity of the author" issue, he would use a pseudonym like "Phocion," explaining further the legal issue, nailing down points. Hamilton was one of the earliest spinmeisters.[18]

He was a remarkable fellow who could come up with a report

---

* Unthinking people said Hamilton was black. His mother was a Creole, as they called it in the West Indies. As if he didn't have enough social handicaps, she also could be called "Jewish." Her name was Rachel Levine, as it is pronounced today. She was married to a man named Levine, or Lavien, as Schachner says.[17] Alexander Hamilton-Levine-Lavine himself spelled it indifferently: Levine, Lavein, and Lavion, a practice that was later to grow among assimilationist Levines. All of this about Hamilton being a black Jew is absolutely unfounded, political claptrap, tommyrot, bilge. Alexander Hamilton was not black. He was not Jewish. Rachel Faucette La Vien was French Huguenot.

John Michael Levine, a rich, Jewish-Danish planter from Saint Croix, had wed Rachel, a beautiful sixteen-year-old girl-about-the-islands, daughter of the French Huguenot Dr. Faucette. Rachel's mother, Mary, was a bit of a runaround, and Rachel's paternity was questioned by Dr. Faucette, who was a noted drunk himself. It's hard to see the family tree for the forest.

It came to pass that Rachel Levine, née Faucette, left the bed and board of the fat merchant Levine and cross-bred with the handsome black sheep wastrel of a Scotch house named James Hamilton, thus giving to the rebel cause a youth named Alexander Hamilton. It speaks well for illegitimacy.

† The young Captain Hamilton climbed on the Washington bandwagon after turning down two major generals who sought his service as aide-de-camp. He knew where the power was. When Washington invited him to join the family—with a double promotion to lieutenant colonel—he accepted. Hamilton always had an eye for a seat in the first carriage.

on finances or manufacturers that would shape the future of a country. He could see the city of Paterson as a model industrial town in his S.U.M. [Society for Useful Manufactures] prospectus, destroy the Articles of Confederation, and sleep with some rich available beauty all on the same day. One can see why Washington admired and was influenced by him. Hamilton was a man who could run things, a talent in great demand and short supply. He gave workaholics a good name.

The wonderful thing about Washington's non-political activities during the war, with his thirty-two press secretaries and special assistants, ghostwriters, whatever you want to call this cadre, inner circle, family, junta, cabal, is they were all on the public payroll. There was no dividing line between his public duties and private affairs, as we shall see.

In his letters the man of public affairs often asked a correspondent for reports on the popular mood in his immediate area. They would provide answers to specific questions, the equivalent of "If an election was held today, who would you vote for? . . . What issues concern you? . . ." etc. Today such people are known as pollsters. One of the most reliable polls in George Washington's opinion was the Knox Poll, run by General Henry Knox. It was Knox who first told George Washington in 1783 the people wanted him, a theme he was to continue harping on in his reports from the field through the convention in 1787 and election in 1789. His work as the machine pollster was to be rewarded with the job of secretary of war in the first Washington administration.

Chief of finance for the machine in its early period, the Maecenas of the money bags, the wise counselor of Washington in all things, was Robert Morris. He was one of the founding crooked congressmen, a group which included such luminaries as Samuel Chase of Maryland, who was buying up wheat during the Valley Forge years and selling it to the British for gold. "Bobbie" Morris, as he was identified in the political cartoons in the *Pennsylvania Packet* ("Wee Bobbie"), was a political crony of the general, part of the inner circle of card players which rivaled Warren Harding's brain trust.

Robert Morris, "The Signer" (another of the immortals, who signed the Declaration of Independence), was a master of shady deals. One of his impressive achievements in the world of high, medium and low finance was co-founding the Asylum Company, a land development flyer during the first Washington administration that had been established for settling and improving one million acres of Pennsylvania land. Stock units were being sold for two hundred acres at one shilling, and moving briskly. The creative part of the plan was that Morris and his co-partner didn't own the land to start with. That's the kind of crowd the machine attracted.

Let me tell you what a crook Morris was. In 1779 Morris was formally accused of improper speculation in flour. He absolved himself by saying he was acting as agent of the king of France. Our greatest patriot in the financial community, the man whose house Washington stays at in the nation's capital (Philadelphia), at work and play, the Bebe Rebozo of the first administration, said there was nothing unethical about his conduct. He was acting as a secret agent for a foreign power. What a defense! No wonder there is so much morality in Washington today.

Bebe Rebozo Morris was the architect of the new country's finances, starting in the Congress of 1775, which benefited the House of Morris by allowing him to mix private with public business. As head of the Congress's finance committee he merged the country's business with his own companies, a major feat of double, triple and quadruple book-keeping. Basically the complex system Morris set up was like the Secretary of the Treasury paying his American Express bills with taxpayers' money.

His incredible book-keeping did not go unnoticed. In 1779 Tom Paine attacked Robert Morris, insisting that delegates and agents of the United States had no right to engage in commerce and speculation. Paine had many quaint notions, Hughes says.[19] He was on the committee that acquitted Morris of fraud—with a verdict of "Not guilty but don't do it again." Morris had done nothing wrong except to buy a ship's cargo before Congress could, to commit a monopoly and make large profits as a speculator while honored by the public confidence. The committee thought he should have been more patriotic.

The germs of patriotic idealism were just sprouting, Hughes says.[20] Thomas Paine and George Washington set too high a standard. In 1781 Congress tried to make Morris end his commercial connections. He refused and Congress yielded. Sumner says of Morris: "He never gave anything to the public, nor lost anything by the public service."

Washington was pure. He stood above his crooked friends, but he was loyal. It was Morris who wined and dined the planter-soldier when he came to Philadelphia as congressman in 1774. These were the good years, when Morris was a partner with

Thomas Willing in the prestigious banking house of Willing & Morris. He was a lavish host, with good cigars and wine which Washington partook of.

Meanwhile, in 1775 Congress had begun giving Willing & Morris contracts to buy war supplies. Morris was a key member of various secret committees to secure such supplies, and more and more contracts were given to his firm. Morris developed a network of official government partnerships with his commercial friends and associates throughout the United States and overseas, and he continued to do so after he retired from Congress in 1778. In 1781 Congress appointed Morris Superintendent of Finance and gave him virtually unlimited control over finance. The same year, Morris, Thomas Willing, William Bingham (who made a fortune as Congress's and Morris' agent in the French island of Martinique between 1776 and 1780), and other merchants founded the Bank of North America, the first private bank in America,[21] further complicating the nation's finances. Bobbie Morris's operations made Ivan Boesky look like a country bumpkin.

The Patriot Financier's methods of doing business for the country were based on the principles of duplicity, fraud, and malfeasance. As one historian who understood Morris's methodology better than I explained, during and after the war, whether in government contracts or land speculation, Morris's ability to complicate a simple transaction, to postpone settlement by the addition of ancillary deals, defies understanding except as chicanery. But Washington saw nothing wrong with maintaining close ties with this shady operator.

Bobbie Morris shouldn't be confused with Gouverneur Morris, the Bronx native and literary stylist who wrote the Constitution, friend of Washington and prominent one-legged man about Congress. He was the only confidant of Washington's who people said had lost his leg getting out of a boudoir of a house in Philadelphia's Society Hill one step ahead of a husband, by jumping off a balcony. It was one of those stories that could have been true (actually he lost it in a carriage accident).

James Madison, another hero of the machine, was the brilliant strategist and media manipulator. The short, pale, sickly bookworm wrote major parts of the Constitution and kept the single most detailed set of notes on what went on behind closed doors in the so-called miracle at Philadelphia. And saw to it they were not published until forty-three years *after* the event. No wonder they named Madison Avenue for him, although I suspect General

Washington himself would have preferred to call it Hamilton Avenue, after the other Federalist media genius.

Madison was more friendly toward Thomas Jefferson than toward Washington. The master wheeler-dealer in Congress, Jemmie Madison, was in his private life an ascetic who didn't like to gamble, go fox hunting, dance, or sleep in different places, like Washington. Aside from politics, his favorite sport was eating ice cream, the "Hello, Dolly" phase of the story.

There is, in case any movie producer is counting, a cast of thousands.

The candidate's media staff was beyond comparison.

By the 1789 campaign the sound bites about Washington were basically on the theme that he was first in war, first in peace, and first in the hearts of his countrymen. It was at least one-third inaccurate, setting a standard for veracity that subsequent voters have come to expect. Actually, until the battle of Yorktown, Washington was running a distant second in war.

The machine image merchants earlier had given him the best campaign slogan ever coined: "Father of His Country." It is said that Henry Knox wrote it, or borrowed or stole it.

It was Knox who urged his old friend, whatever his doubts and no matter how reluctantly, to go to Philadelphia as a delegate at the Federal Convention in 1787.* Knox added, about the new document he expected to come out of the session, "with your signature, it would be a circumstance highly honorable to your fame, in the judgement of the present and future ages, and doubly entitle you to the glorious epithet—the Father of Your Country." [22]

North Callahan says, "After thorough investigation of the records, it seems safe to state that this was the first time that any person of consequence had definitely bestowed upon George Washington the lasting title 'Father of His Country.' Such a reference to Washington had appeared in 1779 in a German-language newspaper in Lancaster, Pennsylvania, but whether Knox had

---

* Eventually the father of the campaign slogan became an investor and speculator in the Washington mold. The man who was called "the Nabob of Maine" bought and sold 50,000 acres at 50 cents an acre at a time. With Lucy at his side, Knox continued being a man of gargantuan appetite and an entertainer on a lavish scale. He invited an Indian tribe to dinner on his Maine estate; they stayed for a month, eating him out of tepee and home. He died on October 25, 1806, nearly bankrupt, according to the historian North Callahan, "unexpectedly at the age of 56, as a result of swallowing a chicken bone."

seen or heard of it is impossible to say. It would appear that Knox may have gained the expression from his reading, as the title was bestowed upon Cicero in 64 B.C. and on Peter the Great in 1721." [23]

Technically speaking, Washington couldn't be "the father of his country." He was without issue. The truer father of his country would be Conrad Castor, of Brock's Gap, Virginia, a foot soldier in the Continental Army, who had twenty-seven children. Patrick Henry was the father of twenty. Washington himself had no white children. There are strong indications, Colonel Flexner says, "that despite his known denial Washington was sterile." Martha had conceived four children in rapid succession during her first marriage. Nevertheless, Washington, Colonel Flexner tells us, "liked to feel she was somehow responsible for his not having an heir." Since there seems to be no scientific psychiatric literature on the subject, the worried Flexner adds, "it is impossible to guess what effect any anxiety he felt lest this be the case might have on his sexuality." [24]

He could have been called "the founding stepfather of the country," being stepfather to two, and making quite a cock-up of it. He was almost as bad as Martha when it came to spoiling the two Custis children.

Politicians reached the voters in different ways. One form of media was sitting for portraits. While they stood for office, in the British sense, they also sat for office. No matter how busy the general was running the war, he found time to sit for portraits.

They also had the equivalent of TV jingles and spots. Phillis Wheatley, the famous black poet, was one of many members of Poets for Washington, churning out odes, panegyrics, and elegies to the general. A member of the family, an ADC who stayed with the candidate through the inauguration in 1789, was Colonel David Humphreys, a leading Yale poet, and the Robert Frost of the first administration. The general encouraged poets, who responded by inundating him with a deafening crescendo of poetry.

And then there was the day-to-day campaigning, writing letters, the press releases of that day. Once a letter was written, as I said, his legion of secretaries made copies and sent them to newspapers and political friends, spreading his ideas and issues. This was word of mouth, the television of its day.

His media people were the glibbest wordsmiths around. Hammy Hamilton, Jemmy Madison, Harry Knox, could have moved a lot of soap and underarm deodorants in the old days, if they hadn't been selling the revolution, the Constitution, and a strong central government starring Washington and the conservative junta. They make Roger Ailes, David Garth and Lee Atwater look like two-bit hack shyster media guys.

They had a man whose hands shook, who had a weak, effeminate voice, who was a dull writer and speechmaker. He was slow to make up his mind, he drank too much, he was always in debt, and they turned him, through packaging, into a candidate with Washington's image.

And unlike today's political consultants, they didn't tell a lie. These early Federalists really knew how to make a prefident. They wrote the book, as it is said.

[4]

Washington began not running in earnest by sending his famous circular letter of June 8, 1783, to the states. This was a kind of farewell to the troops, the American people. The document, which came to be known as "Washington's Legacy," told the people flat out that he would never again "take any share in public business." He had no personal ambitions along political lines.

Even Colonel Flexner seems to believe he was not sharing with the people all his thoughts on this subject, despite his disclaimer. Flexner says his private belief was that "a convention of the people" should be called to establish "a federal constitution," which would reduce the states to the position of counties. Local problems would go to local legislatures, but "when superior considerations predominate in favor of the whole," local "voices should be heard no more." [25]

On June 19, 1783, eleven days after the issuing of "Washington's Legacy," which had launched this vigorous nonpolitical period, the retiring noninvolved ex-general Washington was elected president-general of the Society of Cincinnati. This was the first veterans organization, a super-American Legion officers-only group, which was a major political action group of its day. One of its first community activities was holding a convention at the same time as the constitutional convention of 1787 in Philadelphia. If ever the country would be taken over by young colonels, the founding paranoids were saying, it would be at a convention of the Cincinnati.

Why didn't Washington follow his own advice and really retire? He had sacrificed a lot for his country, more than any politician. He didn't have to go on. Something was driving him. Was it vanity? Was his so overweening? Did he really think he was essential? Did he have a founding-father-figure complex?

The farmer-planter-soldier emeritus also did other things to keep busy. He ran the farm, for one thing. We're not talking about some farmer who comes into town on the end of a flatbed of a wagon full of watermelons. Here was a man who had sold about 900,000 herring one year, taken from the Potomac.[26] He also was a pioneer in the antismoking movement. He finally realized his tobacco crop was inferior and doomed to low market price, and was getting out of the filthy weed as fast as he could.

As an emerging industrialist, he had established a mill for grinding flour. The General's Mills ground out flour he modestly called "superfine."

The still he had ordered from England in the 1760s was making peach wine. His slivovitz was the talk of the county. However, as Colonel Freeman put it, the brandy was only for sick servants and chilled "laborers."

Schnapps-maker Washington also got to know the voters through his activities as a real-estate operator. George Washington's philosophy about how to make money in real estate was: Buy low and sell high.[27] A corollary of Washington's law was buying it just before people moved on the land. In other words, frontier land. His ambition, it seemed, was to own the United States when he grew up. He fell short of his goal. At the time of his death, he owned only 62,000 acres.

He had conducted a little real-estate business even at Valley Forge. His tent flap was always open to any soldier who wanted to sell land, or script for land given by states in lieu of salary or bounties for enlisting. When land values were somehow depressed, due to his leadership during the war, and men were forced to sell, General Washington was always open to buy. If the price was right.

Most of the awards were not worth much. To hold a valid title the soldier had to have his land surveyed and staked, and the title recorded. Kentucky, where much of the soldiers' land was actually located, was about as accessible from tidewater Virginia at that time as Mexico is from New York today. To the average ex-soldier the process of getting the land made it an impossible pie in the sky. Many of them sold their claims for small amounts of cash. Washington picked up some of these claims at low prices. He wrote to his brother Charles: "As you are situated in a good place for seeing many of the Officers at different times I should be glad if you would (in a joking way rather than in earnest, at first) see what value they set on their lands."

At least he wasn't like those other war vets who squandered their bonus money on food and subsistence. He put his into land.

Washington had started taking land off the hands of his men as early as the French and Indian War. Governor Dinwiddie had pledged in the Council of Virginia in February 1754 to allot 200,000 acres to those who would volunteer "to go to the Ohio to erect and support the fort" to be built at the forks—that is, without which the land wouldn't be the Ohio Company's. The bonus offer included 100,000 contiguous acres, with the other 100,000 to be on or near the River Ohio. As the colonel, Washington was entitled to 5,000 acres; the captains to 3,000; subalterns to 200 acres; and private soldiers to 50 acres each. Not bad pay—eventually—for participation in a stockholders' battle.*

At any rate, the ancient pledge by Virginia to Washington's troops had not been redeemed. Most veterans had forgotten their claims to land in the Ohio valley, crawling with "furr"-bearing animals. It was not going to be easy to get their pay for the job.

While others were writing the matter off as a bad debt, it was Colonel Washington who coincidentally started asking for his re-

---

* To be fair, there was more to this Ohio business than land grabbing or just another sleazy real-estate development deal. There were the fur rights.

The Ohio Company, of which George Washington sat as vice-president in charge of acquisitions, wasn't primarily founded for making Washingtontowns filled with split-level (log) cabins. The big money wasn't in shelter. It was in fur trading. They were "furr," as Washington spelled it, crazy in the pre-Revolutionary War period. The Ohio Company was after the pelts of animals, and they didn't mind taking the pelts of either Indians or whites who interfered with the hope of profits. As Hughes wrote, "If man had been a fur bearing animal, instead of a human fur wearing one, history would have been crowded with the slaughter of men as well as the incomputable butchery and unspeakable cruelty of trapping poor wretched animals for their pelts."[28]

The conflict between the English—that is, the Ohio Company—and the French was like Fred the Furrier's declaring all-out war against Antonovich.

ward for participating in the stockholders' battle. He wheeled and dealed, using his influence and seniority in the House of Burgesses, to revive the claim single-handedly. He had personally surveyed or hired surveyors to examine the tracts, and had chosen among the best for himself. He viewed the obligation of the Ohio Company grant to his soldiers as sacred. In 1770 he was writing to the royal representative Governor Botetourt, the king's latest replacement for Washington's secret business partner Dinwiddie, of it as an "absolute compact" no less good for having lain "in a dormant state for sometime."

He asked for one change in the tract allotted, and ended: "This favor, my Lord, would be conferring a singular obligation on men, most of whom, either in their persons or fortunes, have suffered in the cause of their country; few of them benefited by the service; and it cannot fail to receive the thanks of a grateful body of men, but of none more warmly than of your Lordship's most obedient and humble servant."[29]

His "most obedient," etc., was always diligent in pursuit of foxes and claims for lands due him. There was a "claims pressed while you wait" sign over his desk. And when the destitute old soldiers were fading away, it was Washington who could be counted on to buy up, quietly, at the lowest possible prices below market value, the land which was only to become downtown Pittsburgh.*

His habit of making shrewd bargains was legendary among his neighbors. One time Henry Lee, who was dining at Mount Vernon, mentioned that he wanted to sell a certain blooded horse.

"I'll buy him from you," Washington said.

"Oh, no, I shall not sell him to you" was Light Horse Harry's reply.

"Why not?"

"Because you never pay what anything is worth," Lee explained.

My favorite Washington transaction took place in 1782. While he was traveling in western New York, ostensibly on government business, reconnoitering the enemy, he happened to see a choice piece of New York State, some ten thousand acres in the Mohawk

---

* All in all, he accumulated 10,234 acres of the Ohio Company tract as compensation for his efforts, including much of downtown Pittsburgh, the Gulf Oil Building, and my grandmother's house on Dinwiddie Street.

valley, which he bought in a complex partnership with Governor Clinton of New York. Clinton was later leader of the antiratification, or anti-Washington, forces in New York. Landownership rises above mere partisanship. The Washington-Clinton parcel later became a part of the route for the Erie Canal.

The general also built houses in Alexandria as an early urban renewal project. He noticed in the reports, historians say, that one of his carpenters took six days to pave and sand a cellar. He wrote hotly to his foreman that any workman in Philadelphia would have done as much in six hours. What he doesn't mention, as Woodward suggests, is that in Philadelphia workmen are paid what they call wages, which have been known to motivate even the shiftless yuppies of today. His people, or slaves, had no incentive whatever, except the fear of a whipping.

With his old buddies, he served on the interlocking directorates of the military-industrial complex which founded the country. General Washington had Potomac fever as an investor. On May 17, 1785, he was elected president of the Potomac River Canal Company, in which he possessed fifty shares (and one hundred in the James River Canal Company).[30] He was one of the originators of a plan to make the Potomac navigable from Tidewater to Fort Cumberland. The prospectus called for a canal from the head of navigable water to the foot of the mountains and to provide a road or portage that would cross the Alleghenies to the navigable Ohio. With the settlement of Kentucky and the West, it was thought that this highway would be the great commercial transportation route, the first interstate, between the coast and the back country.*

Canals and steamboats, the jets of their age. The man was transportation crazy. He was a hot investor in the steamboat race of the century, being a leading moneyman in the Robert Fitch steamboat. Unfortunately, it finished second to Robert Fulton and the Cleremont (backed by Chancellor Robert Livingston of the Hudson River Families branch of the Mount Vernon machine, who later was to give Washington the oath of office).

The fact that he sometimes bet on the wrong horse, and bought lands that didn't turn out to be such bonanzas (Dismal

---

* Jedidiah Morse, writing in 1792, says that the cost of the Potomac canal alone was estimated at fifty thousand pounds sterling. At that time part of the canal was completed. Its cost ran eventually far above the original estimate. In its final form it became the Chesapeake and Ohio Canal, which later spawned the railroad of the same name.

Swamp and the Mississippi Company were among the unsuccessful scams he subscribed to) only enhanced his appeal to your average real estate speculator and corporate insider, two of the largest
voting blocs in the nation at the time.

[5]

A number of his other activities had political advantages for a
man not running for office. He spent much time taking care
of his neighbors' problems with debt. Old soldiers came to him for
advice. If he wasn't advising them to sell their land to him, he was
lending them money. Of course, it was Martha's money. But the
First Lady's Bank of Mount Vernon was always open. He was
guarantor of loans, many of which caused him grief and vexation.

He seemed to have a fiduciary relationship with half of Virginia. The other half had him down in their wills as the executor
of their estates. This was a form of campaigning, a higher level of
kissing babies. People indebted to you tend to be loyal, whatever
one might do.

He was also the neighborhood philanthropist. His friend William Ramsay of Alexandria had asked for a loan. As Colonel Freeman says, "he had heard Ramsay speak in praise of New Jersey
College as if it were the wish of the father to have young William
Ramsay attend that school. If expense were the only obstacle,
Washington wanted the boy to have the benefit of college. He
accordingly wrote his friend that he would make twenty-five
pounds a year available for the education of the youth." In what
was the most generous sentence that ever had come from his pen,
Washington wrote: "No other return is expected or wished for this
offer than that you will accept it with the same freedom and good
will with which it is made, and that you may not even consider it
in the light of an obligation, or mention it as such: for be assured
that from me it will never be known." [31]

Somehow it got mentioned in all the books.

The anonymous philanthropist of the year in Northern Neck
also attended his local Masonic lodge meetings. The Alexandria-

Washington Lodge No. 22, A.F. & A.M. of Virginia, was considered his home lodge of the three Freemason groups he was a card-carrying member of, as George Bush would have put it in 1988. Lafayette, Mozart, and other liberal-minded Europeans of the period were Masons, Cunliffe says.[32]

He was also a regular at the meetings of the Cincinnati, the fraternal order of aging young colonels who secretly dreamed about having a monarchy with George Washington as king. The big issue in the pre-1789 period was making membership in the organization hereditary. It reminded some democrats of a higher order, like the knights who sat around the round table with King Arthur. Washington squelched the hereditary membership rule and was cool to all monarchist sentiment in the society.

There were other activities, but nothing that would hurt him if he decided on the off chance to change his mind about running. It's hard to see how it would happen, but you never know.

[6]

On May 25, 1787, picking their way through a driving rain, thirty men representing seven states finally managed to assemble all at one time in the Pennsylvania statehouse, now known as Independence Hall, and Con Con, as I call it, was able to begin.

The assembly wasn't known as the Constitutional Convention until later in history. The delegates didn't know they were coming to rewrite the law of the land without authorization until they got there. Only Providence knew, and the Mount Vernon machine.

Eventually their number grew to fifty-five, representing twelve states. Thomas Jefferson, writing from his post in Paris to John Adams, described the group "as an assembly of demi-gods." The luminaries included many of the nation's top politicians, governors, chief justices, attorney generals, and delegates to the Continental Congress, and several distinguished Americans who had agreed to come out of retirement one last time.

Among the senior citizens who answered what he said was a call to duty was George Washington.

There had been some doubt whether Washington would be coming to Philadelphia. He had said that he was finished with public affairs. In his Annapolis address he had pledged a second time never to return to public life. The first pledge had been made six months earlier, in his "Circular Letter to the Nation's Governors." His letter sounded final, ending on the note "a last farewell to the cares of office and all the imployments of public life."[33]

Given the firmness of his announcement over the years, as Schwartz says,[34] it is no surprise that when Washington was called by Virginia's delegation to lead it to the federal convention in Philadelphia, he found himself in a ticklish situation. If he even attended the convention, let alone accepted its presidency, his *disinterestedness* would be open to question. His earlier professions of desire for private life would be seen as a screen for political appetite, about which many suspicious critics warned the public as his wartime fame grew. "The world and posterity," he feared, "might probably accuse me [of] *inconsistency* and *ambition*."

He announced therefore that he would not go to Philadelphia.[35]

But then, as he writes to Knox, the stout Federalist who has been leaning on him to go, he must let the world see where he, the great Washington stands, or sits, on the issues: "A thought however has lately run through my mind, which is attended with embarrassment. It is wheather my non-attendance in this Convention will not be considered a derilication to republicanism, nay more, whether other motives may not (however injuriously) be ascribed to me for not exerting myself on this occasion in support of it." In short, if Washington had not gone to Philadelphia, if he had refused to participate in an assembly seeking reforms that he himself had endorsed, he would have stood open to charges that he valued his own fame more than the public good. That would have made for an intolerable questioning of his public virtue.[36]

At length Washington decided to attend. "As I have yielded . . . to what appeared to be the earnest wishes of my friends," he explained about his decision to attend, "I will hope for the best."[37]

Once again he had wrestled with his conscience and lost (in a thrilling tag-team bout, starring the Potomac Pummeler vs. his better side).

*

As Washington rode away from his seat at Mount Vernon, due northeast to Philadelphia, in late April 1787, to return to public life, he assured the Lady Washington he would be home by Christmas. It's not known if he specified which one.

[7]

When Jemmy Madison stepped out of the Philadelphia Cannonball—the express coach service from New York—on May 3, he was in good shape for the heavy work that lay ahead in Con Con.

As Brant says,[38] incessant horseback riding and long rambles in the country didn't add any inches to his height, but the frailty and pallor of early youth were gone. The historian Grigsby, who drew part of his accounts from contemporaries, describes his appearance a year later—muscular, well proportioned, ruddy complexioned. He probably was tending toward the habitual black which later ruled his dress, but Grigsby heard of him "handsomely arrayed in blue and buff," his coat single breasted, ruffles at wrist and chest. His hair, combed low to conceal an early recession from the forehead, was dressed with powder and ended with a long queue. He walked with a bouncing step.

Madison had worked hard organizing what was to be the model of a free and closed convention for democratic societies, an open covenant secretly arrived at.

A Virginia Plan had to be written. The Mount Vernon machine made good use of the eleven days between the official and actual starting dates. They had a series of resolutions ready that set the agenda for restructuring the Articles of Confederation government. The opposition was disorganized. They thought they were coming to Philadelphia to do a little sanding on an existing document, rounding off the rough edges, only to find that a whole new ship of state was being built.

It was to be a long, difficult process, with arguments, issues, debates, and points being thrashed out for weeks and months.

Hundreds of books have already been written about "the miracle," which don't make it seem so easy and smooth. But the most important achievement of the machine had been getting George Washington to give up his plow and fig tree and return to Sin City, Philadelphia.

The Federal Convention needed the prestige and authority of Washington's presence. Prior to the meeting, James Monroe, in a letter to Jefferson, suggested that "the presence of General Washington will have great weight in the body itself, so as to overawe and keep under the demon of party [sectional interests], and that the signature of his name to whatever act shall be the result of their deliberations will secure its passage thro' the union. . . . Because a FRANKLIN and a WASHINGTON are among the number of those who gave approbation to it." [39] Alexander Hamilton also expressed confidence that the new Constitution would be ratified because of Washington's presence. [40]

By agreeing to attend, he was in effect sponsoring the convention. Trust me, his presence said. A strong executive is one of the Americans' greatest fears? No limits placed on the president's term? Whatever my boys want, his presence said, it's okay. It sometimes seemed as if the delegates did not want to insult Washington by fixing the incumbency. As South Carolina's Pierce Butler put it in a letter about the executive's powers, "Entre nous, I do not believe they would have been so great, had not many of the members cast their eyes toward General Washington as President; and shaped their ideas of the powers to be given a President, by their opinions of his Virtue." [41]

When Washington arrived in Philadelphia to attend the Federal Convention, Madison noted the enthusiasm with which he was received, and "the affection and veneration which continues to be felt for his character." Delegates' letters reveal their awareness of Washington's reluctance to return to the national scene. And if anyone believed he was acting out a script in order to preserve his image or to prepare groundwork for a power play, Schwartz says, they did not let on.

Only scattered delegates from seven states were present as Madison set up his campaign headquarters at Mary House's house at Fifth and Market streets. George Washington was taken in hand by Robert Morris, the founding con artist, market manipulator, and delegate, who kept his glass and plate full at the Morris town house and country manor for the next five months.

The sophisticated French soldier-philosopher Chastellux was to write of Morris, "It may safely be asserted that Europe affords few examples of perspicacity and facility of understanding equal to his, which adapts itself with the same success to business, to letters, and to sciences." Chastellux described Morris as "a large man, very simple in his manners, but his mind is subtle and acute. . . . His house is handsome closely resembling the houses in London. He lives there without ostentation but not without expense, for he spares nothing which can contribute to his happiness or that of Mrs. Morris, to whom he is much attached. A zealous republican and an epicurean philosopher, he has always played a distinguished part at table and in business." [42]

Morris spared no expense in wining and dining his co-delegate to the convention in the next five months. It was cheap at the price for anyone who wanted the next prefident's ear.

For some time, as Brant says, they lacked a quorum for any business except to dine at Franklin's house and broach a cask of "the best porter they have ever tasted." Or so Franklin reported to the donor of it, while Washington recorded that he drank tea.

The lagging of New England caused Madison to suffer "a daily disappointment," Brant says. [43] But this left time for a breakfast with General Mifflin, who then rode out with Washington, Madison, Rutledge, and others to visit country seats across the Schuylkill. There was time, also, for all the Virginians except Washington to attend mass at the Roman Catholic church on Sunday the twentieth—"more out of compliment than religion, and more out of curiosity than compliment," the Anglican George Mason explained apologetically. The general was at the Morris farm, so a week later he too "went to the Romish church to high mass"—a fact which led the newspapers to praise Father Beeston's excellent sermon.

The key test at Con Con, when it finally began two weeks later, was the first vote for chairman. A leading candidate was General George Washington. Interestingly, he did not show up the first day in uniform. It must have been out to the cleaners. It probably would have had the wrong effect on delegates this time anyway. He was still not a candidate for public office, but he neglected to mention it this day. With seven states voting on May 25, George Washington was elected chairman of the convention.

Suffice it to say now, in the few remaining pages I have left in this book, that the machine had its finest hour at Con Con. Madison, Hamilton, the Morrises, Gouverneur and Bobbie, Charles (Pincky) Pinckney the Younger, James Wilson, and others all performed brilliantly, creating a new government tailor-made for their candidate.

I'm happy to say that my main man at the convention, General Washington, who you recall was worried that his reputation for being "disinterested" would be hurt by his attendance, maintained his integrity by a compromise. He attended the convention, but he didn't say anything. There is no record in James Madison's notes of a single major speech by the general.

For five months he served as the convention's guiding light, sponsor, and never once stepped down from the chair to share his views. He reigned like a king in the statehouse, George the Silent.

What might have he said? As a starter, he might have contributed his thoughts on the slave question. All the states, except South Carolina, wanted to end the slave trade. The historians tell us he was in favor of freeing his slaves. What a maiden speech Washington's proclamation regarding the slave question would have made—especially as reported by his minuteman Jemmy Madison thirty years later. What might, one thinks, Jefferson have done if he had sat in Washington's chair?

Instead, he just sat there, silently counting his slaves, the window "paynes," the flies, whatever. It is said he was not into the Constitution like some of the other founding fathers. I don't think the Constitution bored George Washington so much as he was out of it during those five months in Philadelphia from partying every night with his host Bobbie Morris, at whose country farm (weekends) and town house (weekdays) he was staying. Morris also didn't make a single speech. The two of them sat silent during the whole great proceeding, like two book ends. Wee Bobbie was a bad influence on the future prefident.

[8]

Con Con over, the assembly of demigods dispersed. The leading demigod, the chairman of the board, Bobbie Morris's houseguest, announced he was retiring. He could now resume his life of quiet opulence.

He told himself, as Colonel Freeman says,[44] that he had performed his last public service in the Philadelphia convention and had discharged it at the call of his country and in a willingness to accept all the criticism that might be stirred.[45] "Although I shall not live," he had written Nathaniel Gorham, a Mount Vernon machine stalwart from Massachusetts, delegate to Con Con, and co-owner of six million acres in western New York, "to see but a small portion of the happy effects which I am confident this system will produce for my country, yet the precious idea of its prosperity will not only be a consolation amidst the increasing infirmities of nature and the growing love of retirement, but it will tend to soothe the mind in the inevitable hour of separation from terrestrial objects."[46]

He is retiring again? For the eighth time? This is getting boring. He is sounding like a broken record.

This was his hope, this his expectation, Colonel Freeman says;[47] but discussion of the presidency, which he had tried to disregard in the autumn of 1787, became brisker after the new year. The *Pennsylvania Packet*, one of the two or three most important papers of the country, mentioned Washington frequently as president-to-be—and never once spoke of anyone else for the office. In the New York celebration of Massachusetts' acceptance of the Constitution, one toast—doubtless of deep draught—was, significantly, 'General Washington—may his wisdom and virtue preside in the councils of his country.'[48] "Many towns observed his fifty-sixth birthday with enthusiasm. In the mailbag brought down from Alexandria," Colonel Freeman says, "Washington found letters from old and distinguished friends whose appeals for his acceptance of the presidency he could not ignore. General John Armstrong, comrade of three decades and more, wrote as if the hand of the Almighty had been placed on Washington's head; a letter from Lafayette expressed some alarm over the magnitude of executive powers under the Constitution but voiced the belief that if Washington exercised the authority of the office and found it dangerously great, he would reduce it. For this and other reasons, Washington must consent to be president." [49]

Without any prearrangement, as Colonel Freeman says, [50] the celebration of the Fourth of July, 1788, became in large part a general call for the election of Washington as president. At Wilmington, Delaware, a toast was drunk to "Farmer Washington— may he, like a second Cincinnatus, be called from the plow to rule a great people." [51] Citizens of Frederick, Maryland, lifted their glasses with the sentiment "May the Saviour of America gratify the ardent wishes of his countrymen by accepting that post which the voice of mankind has assigned him." [52] At York, Pennsylvania, loyal participants in the festive ceremony listened to a "new Federal song" in five stanzas, each of which concluded:

> Great Washington shall rule the land
> While Franklin's counsel aides his hand.

At New York City's observance of the Fourth, there was a mass of marching men, pulling floats and emblems, many of which hailed Washington. [53] The Tallow Chandlers, observers said, outdid the others. It was "a flag with thirteen stripes—under them the figure of General Washington, with these words placed over him, 'the illustrious Washington, may he be the first Prefident of the United States.' " [54]

Informed sources—the business of insiders making predictions about the candidate's intentions and future plans was becoming another new cottage industry—began making predictions in earnest. "The opinion seems to be universal that General Washington will be elected President," said a friend and former military aide, poet-in-residence Colonel David Humphreys, in a November 1788 letter. "His inclinations," the letter went on to say, "will certainly lead him to refuse. Should circumstances overcome his inclinations, I know it will occasion more distress to him, than any other event in his life." [55] Several months passed, but the perception of Washington's preferences did not change. Jefferson told a correspondent that "Genl. Washington . . . will undertake the presidency if asked . . . tho' with vast reluctance." [56]

The PR wing of the machine had done its work well.

The machine privately put pressure on him that echoed the

public calls for him to run. Hamilton, from his Wall Street law office, especially leaned on his old boss.

"It is my great and sole desire," he told Hamilton, responding to one of his ex-secretary's many exhortations to run, "to live and die, in peace and retirement, on my own farm." But Hamilton pressed him hard in letter after letter. Without Washington in the presidency, he declared, the ship was sunk before it had even quit port. "The framers of [the Constitution] will have to encounter the disrepute of having brought about a revolution in government, without substituting anything that was worthy of the effort; they pulled down the Utopia, it will be said, to build up another."

Hamilton to the end of Washington's days was always trying to draft him for the presidency. He was still pushing for a third term when Washington died in 1799.[57]

In reply to that friend's argument for the general's acquiescence in the call of the country, according to Colonel Freeman, Washington said: "The event alluded to may never happen, and . . . in case it should occur, it would be a point of prudence to defer one's ultimate and irrevocable decision, so long as new data might be afforded for one to act with the greater wisdom and propriety."[58] Then he admitted a scruple: persons familiar with his inclination would understand why he might consent if a "different line of conduct" proved "indispensable," but after all he had said about retirement from public life, "the world and posterity"—he never forgot posterity in his later years—"might probably accuse [him of] inconsistency and ambition."[59]

Hamilton, of course, regarded Washington's concern as ill founded, though he agreed that prudence justified his old commander in deferring a decision. With his usual persuasive logic, Hamilton reviewed the circumstances and maintained that "every public and personal consideration will demand from you an acquiescence in what will *certainly* be the unanimous wish of your country." Those were challenging words.

The newspapers, too, renewed their appeals, not so much this time in order to win Washington's consent as to assure a unanimous vote for him and to rally weak-kneed doubters and lukewarm patriots with the confident statement that he would accept.[60] The *Pennsylvania Packet* ran a quotation from a letter written at Augusta, Georgia, October 6: "Let it ever be remembered that a Washington is to guide the helm." *Pennsylvania Packet*, November 6, 1788,

p. 3: "The universal voice of America is prepared to call to the chair of president of the United States the venerated President of the Federal Convention." A letter from Massachusetts in the *Packet* on November 13, 1788, p. 2: "General Washington is universally talked of for president of the United States," and the "judicious and sensible" elements in Massachusetts favored John Adams as vice president. A quotation in the *Pennsylvania Packet*, November 25, 1788, p. 2, from a letter to the *Albany Register*, undated, dealt with the "operation of the new government under the auspices of our illustrious Washington" as if he already had been elected.

Such pressure no human being could resist. And, of course, Washington was not human. He was a demigod.

"He did not say he would refuse to accept the presidency," Colonel Freeman points out for the general, "he affirmed only, in effect, that he did not desire the office, that he hoped it would not be offered him, and that if acceptance were unavoidable, it would represent the heaviest possible sacrifice. All this was written with composure, in much the spirit he had displayed many times during the war when he had refused to cross a bridge until he had come to it."

Even before these articles began to appear and letters by the mailbag arrived, Washington had to admit to himself that he almost certainly would be the choice of the electors. "I have always felt kind of gloom upon my mind," he confessed, "as often as I have been taught to expect I might, and perhaps must ere long be called to make a decision" and he added in manifest distress of spirit: "If I should recieve the appointment and if I should be prevailed upon to accept it, the acceptance would be attended with more diffidence and reluctance than I ever experienced before in my life."

It is also true that while he was theoretically making up his mind, examining his options and writing tortured letters gloomily pessimistic about his chances, he was already involved in the fights over the ratification of the Constitution going on in the state conventions. While the general went back and forth in his mind, the ratification campaign went forward. And he was always for the Constitution. Everybody knew the real issue: Who was going to be running the country? The Constitution vote had little to do with the details of government. A vote for the document was a vote for Washington.

On the question of whether the powers of the chief executive office might be abused by one of Washington's successors, William Lewis of Pennsylvania replied, "General Washington lives, and as he will be appointed President, jealousy [suspicion] on his head vanishes." [61]

In Washington we could trust, the machine said. And they were right. That's why it hadn't been necessary to write a seven-thousand page document in Philadelphia defining all the duties of exactly what a prefident would do, a piece of paper they would be throwing out whenever a new group of young colonels came of age.

Everyone knew that Washington presided over the creation of the Constitution and was the first to sign it. Praise of Washington filled pro-Constitution newspapers, exploiting his identification with it. His prestige was invoked at every state convention as, Schwartz says, opponents of the Constitution were obliged to rationalize their disagreement with him. A letter to Jefferson concerning Virginia's ratification bears a conclusion that told which way the wind was blowing on the ratification campaign. "Be assured," wrote James Monroe, "that General Washington's influence carried this government." [62]

While he walked around Mount Vernon, brooding, as Colonel Freeman says, Washington knew exactly how the Constitution vote was going in each of the 13 states, through his internal network of political informants and newspapers. This was not a man who didn't know where the vote stood for the states. He was somebody who counted the number of bricks fired in his kiln on June 25.[63] He kept track of important things.

He knew that New York was in the doubtful column. Governor Clinton, his real-estate partner, was the leader of the anti-Federalists, and had twice as many votes. But Clinton was going to lose to Alexander Hamilton and John Jay. It was to be Hammy's finest hour at Poughkeepsie, proving he was a prophet in his own country.

The Virginia battle was, Bernstein says,[64] one of the classic political battles of American history. The Federalists were led by Jemmy Madison. Having devoted most of his intellectual energies during the spring of Con Con in drafting twelve-point memoranda like "Vices of the Political System of the U.S.," he now generaled the floor fight for the Constitution in the Virginia convention. Also assisting was machine veteran Edmund Pendleton. They were up against anti-Federalists Patrick Henry, George Mason, and the young war vet, James Monroe, who had been with Washington at Trenton.

Washington, who had retired again, stayed above the battle, firing off letters to politicians and newspapers in favor of the Constitution, which of course, in his mind, had nothing to do with him personally. He kept up with the latest gazettes, reading his favorite column, the Federalist Papers.

This was a difficult period for the general as he tried to make up his mind. He had some important political visitors at Mount Vernon he could count bricks with: Madison, Bobbie Morris, and Gouverneur Morris, he lists in his diaries.[65]

Gouverneur Morris, who actually wrote the Constitution (in two days he did the four pages, five thousand words, that have lasted two hundred years), is one of Washington's favorites. He admires his lace shirts and his economics. He studied financial policy under both Morrises. Gouverneur Morris had a sound business head, Colonel Flexner says, "over the elegant lace that beautified his chest."

As the years passed Gouverneur Morris became one of Washington's most intimate friends. He came from a leading family in aristocratic New York, a fiery early patriot. He was witty, chatty, a snob, a dandy, an able political operator with a talent for diplomatic and business intrigue, and a gift as a ladies' man. As reward for his good works, the Mount Vernon machine was later to send Morris, wooden leg, covetous eye and all, as ambassador to the French court, where he became a noted operator in the bedroom of Adelaide de Flahaut, the mistress of the Roman Catholic bishop of Autun, better known to history as Talleyrand. His high spirits, it is said, kept Washington amused.

But the general was not smiling these days. He was sulking as he tried to make up his mind.

How do we know? Guests are leaving Mount Vernon displeased with their host. This is unprecedented. As Francis Adrian van der Kemp, introduced by Lafayette, wrote: "There seemed to me to skulk somewhat of a repulsive coldness, not congenial with my mind, under a courteous demeanor; and I was infinitely better pleased by the unassuming, modest gentleness of the lady, than with the conscious superiority of her consort."[66]

*

Will he run? That was the question on the nation's mind until October 1788. With characteristic reluctance he finally came to a decision. In response to Hamilton's urgings and the urgings of other friends, Washington finally yielded, reluctantly, with fear, while avowing that he would accept only to retire as fast as possible, in order "to pass an unclouded evening after the stormy day of life, in the bosom of domestic tranquillity."[67]

Already he was talking retirement. Pundits could interpret that as the start of his reelection campaign of 1793 (the second term).

Part V

—

Campaign '88

*Being the amazing saga of how the steamroller
chased George Washington over the top.*

[1]

The Mount Vernon machine had been busy since 1775 building up its man, the obscure former Virginia colonel George Wash ington. They had made him into a war hero, despite a losing war record, and tailored a constitution to fit his enhanced stature, according to my very reductionist reading of *The Making of the Constitution*. Now it was time to campaign. What did they have to work with?

There are a lot of basic questions about George Washington, the candidate, that have gone unanswered in the two hundred years since the election. That's because of the historian-meisters' Providence complex—the idea that Washington's election was an act of God.

So much has been written to him, by him, and about him,* and yet we don't even know, for example, if he looked prefidential.

What *did* he look like?

Let's go to the portraits, the videotape of their day (page 241 and following). You put them up against each other and you notice something very strange. They don't look like the same person. They look like the Ten Most Wanted FBI list in the post office, a rogues' gallery. Will the real George Washington stand up?

---

* His personal file of documents—diaries, financial accounts, letters written and received, and so forth—Colonel Flexner says, amounts to 75,000 folios in the Library of Congress; the complete archive was published in 1965 by the Library in 24 reels of microfilm.

Some of these guys wouldn't win even a Washington look-alike contest.

My image, and most people's, if it didn't come from the dollar bill or from postage stamps, came from the portrait of him in Mrs. Jacobs's room, the Gilbert Stuart rendition of 1796. Washington didn't like Stuart. The artist talked all the time. He had been a loyalist during the war, or at least a Tory sympathizer. Also, Washington had new teeth, as leaden as the pose. He was very irritated with the sitting. He looks at us with those forlorn eyes. What Stuart captures, besides the need for a good dentist, is a look in those eyes which says, "When will this man go away?" Washington didn't look like that! All my years growing up I saw the man through Stuart's vision. If an artist can be said to execute a portrait, then Stuart took Washington out and shot him at dawn. And Washington looked like a condemned man.

Just how trustworthy *are* paintings? Look at his shoulders in some of the many portraits. They are as broad as Eric Sevareid's. And look at that chest, swelling with well-deserved pride. The chest is tailor-made. Under the well-padded coat, Dr. Rudolph Marx in "A Medical Profile of George Washington" says, "Washington's chest was flat and somewhat hollow in the center, probably from early rickets. And the shoulders were not as broad as they appeared from the outside." [1]

George Washington was the most widely drawn figure in American history. There are more examples of what he looked like than any other historical figure, and they're all different.

Maybe we should turn to writers for an accurate portrait. They say one thousand words are worth one picture. I particularly like the snapshot of him as a young colonel by his aide-de-camp Captain George Mercer. Somebody in England had asked Mercer for a description of the colonel after he began making the papers in London for his exploits during the French and Indian War. And Captain Mercer, who had a flair as an image maker, sent off a nifty résumé:

Although distrusting my ability to give an adequate account of the personal appearance of Col. George Washington, late Commander of the Virginia Provincial troops, I shall, as you request, attempt the portraiture. He may be described as being as straight as an Indian, measuring six feet two inches in his stockings, and weighing 175 pounds when he took his

Will the Real George Washington Stand Up, Please?

What did the general really look like? Probably not like Grant Wood's portrait of him about to fall out of the boat in the background of this 1932 work, titled *Daughters of Revolution*. He is believed to be the fellow in drag, on the far left, which Wood based on Gilbert Stuart's most famous likeness (the *Athenaeum* portrait).

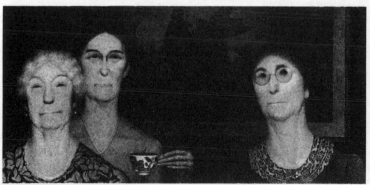

Daughters of Revolution, Grant Wood.

But he could also be any, or all, of the following:

George Washington, Gilbert Stuart.

George Washington,
engraved by R. A. Muller,
from a painting by
C. V. F. de St. Memin.

George Washington, David Edwin.

George Washington,
Charles Willson Peale.

George Washington, Gilbert Stuart.

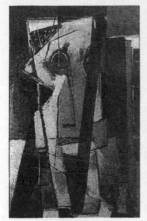

George Washington,
Alfred Maurer.

George Washington (Vaughan portrait), Gilbert Stuart.

George Washington, William James Hubard.

George Washington, John Trumbull.

The Prayer at Valley Forge,
engraving after a painting by Henry Brueckner.

George Washington, Frank Moran.

George Washington, William Williams.

George Washington, Edward Savage.

George Washington's Life Mask.

seat in the House of Burgesses in 1759. His frame is padded with well-developed muscles, indicating great strength. His bones and joints are large, as are his feet and hands.

He is wide shouldered, but has not a deep or round chest; is neat waisted, but is broad across the hips, and has rather long legs and arms. His head is well shaped though not large, but is gracefully poised on a superb neck. A large and straight rather than a prominent nose; blue-gray penetrating eyes, which are widely separated and overhung by a heavy brow. His face is long rather than broad, with high round cheek bones, and terminates in a good firm chin. He has a clear though rather a colorless pale skin, which burns with the sun. A pleasing, benevolent, though a commanding countenance, dark brown hair, which he wears in a cue.

His mouth is large and generally firmly closed, but which from time to time discloses some defective teeth. His features are regular and placid, with all the muscles of his face under perfect control, though flexible and expressive of deep feeling when moved by emotions. In conversation he looks you full in the face, is deliberate, deferential and engaging. His voice is agreeable rather than strong. His demeanor at all times composed and dignified. His movements and gestures are graceful, his walk majestic, and he is a splendid horseman.[2]

But the vital details vary from historian to historian. Take the color of the eyes, which Mercer said are "blue-gray." Others called them "light-blue" or "steel gray." One historian said his eyes tended to be "almost white." Leaping lizards! Clearly orphan George's eyes weren't purple, like Elizabeth Taylor's.

He also had "reddish brown hair," "blond hair," "silver hair," as well as "light brown." Little is said of his wigs, which probably were not made by Dolly Parton's hairdresser.

He was "six feet two or three inches tall," the historians say.

Why did he then invariably announce that he was only "six feet tall" or "six feet in stature"? Was he being modest? Was he shortchanging himself in the height department? A curious error for him to have made, being a surveyor and stickler for minute details.

How tall was Colonel Washington? Six feet, or "6'3½ exact inches," according to the testimony of Tobias Lear, the general's last secretary, who was there when the doctors measured him stretched out after his death?

All agree that George's skin was bad, in contrast to what eye-witness Captain Mercer wrote in his definitive pen portrait. His face was, as historians report, "slightly pocked" or "heavily pocked." (The pockmarks were caused by smallpox, which he caught as a teenager in 1751, during his summer vacation in the Caribbean.)

One thing is certain: Nobody called George Washington "cra-ter face," even if his phiz looked like the far side of the moon. Some may have said, "Come here, pizza face." What I'm trying to say is, the candidate was no Robert Redford. On the other hand, he wasn't entering a beauty contest. American political campaigns hadn't progressed that far in 1789.

What kind of speaker was Washington? What did he really sound like? Well, he didn't talk like he does in the history books. The founding fathers did not leave us audiotapes, only letters. And historians faithfully use the letters as oral histories, re-creating the way they sounded through letters, constructing events with super accuracy by the letters. Even the occasional historical drama on public TV, like "The Adams Chronicles," used letters as dialogue.

Now, letters are very important in our story. They were, as I've explained, campaign speeches. Washington's media blitz consisted of letters, either one-on-one, or the multiple send-ing of letters, the equivalent of the press conference. Letters, however, are not necessarily a clue to the way people sound, even today.

Everybody knows the hardest thing to do when you write an important letter is sound natural. Everybody gets convoluted, tan-gled up in syntax. That's not the way we converse. We put the nib in the mouth, polish and polish, until it gets stiff and tortured. Washington was a prime example of the agonized letter writer, stifled, as if in thumbscrews.

At his loosest and most relaxed, he never sounded like Addi-son, Steele, or Alexander Pope. He was a surveyor who had a way with numbers, figures, things, not words or ideas. Whether he was left hemisphered or right hemisphered, his world of letters was flat, and he was always falling off.

Then what did he sound like in real life? He probably would have had an affected British accent. He was an Anglophile. As we have seen, he wanted everything—clothes, furniture, wallpaper, etc.—to be British. He was a first-class pseud who wanted to be a member of the aristocracy.

An upper-class British accent might have been a drawback with the good ol' boy vote, but Washington handled the problem by not saying much.

[2]

O n the positive side, the machine also had a lot to work with in Washington. He was one of the tallest men in America, and people looked up to him, especially when he was on horse-back. The country had a man-on-the-white-horse complex.

True, he was not one of your traditional handshaking, baby-kissing politicians. Washington had an aversion to handshaking, historians say. He believed that a handshake was beneath his dig-nity. So he always stood by the fireplace and received visitors with a courtly bow. Another theory is that he didn't shake hands for health reasons, like Howard Hughes.

He didn't have that easy familiarity of politicians today. A story is told that during the Federal Convention of 1787, Gouver-neur Morris supposedly offered to bet any man in the statehouse that he could go up to the general and say, "By God, George, I'm glad to see you. You look well, how's it going. . ." all the while slapping him on the back. And live to tell the tale. He did, but barely. Morris said "That moment I think the earth opened up and swallowed me." He swore he wouldn't do it again for £10,000.

George Washington didn't smile much. Of course, founding a new nation is a serious business. What's to smile about? I should point out here that there is no factual basis to the persistent rumor that George Washington wore wooden teeth. Have you ever no-ticed what happens to a toothpick in your mouth after a while? The leading dentists of the day, who were also barbers, not carpen-ters, made his teeth from a pound of lead: the reason he frowned was to hold his teeth in. If he had relaxed his face muscles, the heavily weighted false teeth would have dropped out of his mouth.* Not to mention, possible lead poisoning.

The unsmiling countenance has led to the rumor that the general had no sense of humor. It is probably true Washington did not laugh often. For when he did—for example, the time in 1789 he went to the Dunlap Theatre to see a play called *Poor Soldier*— all the newspapers mentioned the fact that he laughed. It was news. He was a tough audience.

Due to his denture problems, he had difficulty pronouncing "s" words.†

Ill-fitting dentures, furthermore, may have affected policy. His second inaugural address was only one page long. And by the time of his farewell address, he couldn't be bothered to deliver his message in public. He had it printed in the newspaper. Yet another sign of his media savvy, perhaps: You were guaranteed to reach more people with written messages.

General Washington was not glib. In dealing with the press he was a lot like Ronald Reagan in his later years, when questions often left him confused, incoherent, more and more frustrated and angry. All in all, the noncandidate would not have knocked anybody's white silk socks off on TV. But again, Washington's luck held; there was no TV in 1788.‡

He was not a spellbinder on the stump like Patrick Henry or an articulate, fast thinker like John Adams. His public addresses on policy issues were short but rambling, much like his letters, those writ by his own hand. He was Eisenhoweresque in speech.

But none of this mattered to the average American voter. Most of them were disenfranchised, anyway. Washington aimed his campaign at Congress and the Electoral College, which is where the votes were.

Washington, the man of few words, was a man of action, a brave soldier who threw himself into dangerous situations. The

---

* He began to use false teeth in 1789, a campaign device to improve his public image. When Washington sat for Gilbert Stuart, the artist ordered that a special set of teeth be made to fill out his face. The puffiness of his lips in the Gilbert Stuart Athenaeum portrait, and the peasant heaviness of his face in that picture, it was said, are not natural, but come from Stuart's attempt to rectify the distortion of the false teeth by placing wads of cotton around his sitter's gums. Eventually Washington got a set of "sea-horse teeth"—made from hippopotamus ivory—which fitted him much better. Although an artistic success, the new plates were worthless for eating. No wonder he looked so glum in the pictures.

† *Suck* might have come out *fuck*.

‡ Benjamin Frankin had invented TV, a by-product of his experiments in electricity, but he decided not to tell anybody about it on the grounds that it was bad for society.

general had something else going for him, something that transcended appearance and sound and character: he gave the impression of inner depths, of hidden profundity. On meeting Washington for the first time, John Adams's wife, Abigail, quoted to her husband what the Queen of Sheba said on meeting Solomon: "I thought half was not told to me."

General Solomon Washington indeed had something that was special. The Greeks had a word for it: χάριμα.*

Others of the founding fathers were as brave and courageous and loved their country as much, but they lacked the *C* word. John Adams, for example, had minus charisma. A pouterpigeon, a Cornish hen, or a quail of a man, Little Jack Adams was only vice-prefidential material.

And, like President Reagan, Washington looked great in a suit.

[3]

Rather than discuss the issues of Election 1789 (there were none†), I would like to discuss the nonissues—or rather, the should-have-been issues. These are three: (1) war, (2) corruption, and (3) sex.

First, Washington's war record should have been an issue, but as we have seen already, nobody blamed him for what went wrong at the time, and now who cared? Bring up the subject with your average Joe Six-pack in the Philadelphia Tavern, and he would say, "He won the war, didn't he?"

Now, corruption in the administration of the army could have been a hot issue if the investigative reporters of the day had been on their toes. Why, even I as an armchair historian came across a juicy hidden scandal, involving a man close to Washington—none

---

* Charisma. George Washington had charisma, a personal magnetism that inspired trust, love, and political loyalty. It was based on saying nothing, or next to it. He radiated!

† If you don't count the process of implementing the Constitution, and the likelihood of a second Constitutional Convention. These could be called big issues, and the reason why George Washington seemed so perfect as a prefidential candidate.

other than Nathanael Greene, husband of the dance-crazed Kitty. And I'm not only talking about the quartermaster corps' hanky-panky that Congress raked over at the time. It was worse. Thanks to Washington's intervention in his friend's behalf, Greene came out reasonably unscathed, but if there had been a true opposition party in 1788, the Greene scandal would have been another Teapot Dome or Iran/Contra.

Let me pause to tell this inspiring story, which will live in the annals of the patriotic laundering of large sums of money. It is a story of free enterprise, which will bring tears to any patriotic businessman's eyes. It shows how it is possible to profit at the expense of one's country, while having the highest of motives and, as Hughes says, following Saint Paul's advice to avoid even the appearance of evil. I haven't been so moved by a business partnership helping its country since Colonel North described what he and his partners (General Secord, Albert Hakim, et al.) arranged at the Iranscam hearings of 1987.

Our founding fathers were more corrupt than their daughters and sons have told us over the years. "Weeks might be spent in finding an honest industrious person qualified to barter for shoes," Colonel Freeman says. "It was exceedingly difficult, Washington discovered, to get a wagonmaster who, in the later words of the general, 'was not himself above his business.' " Congressmen were on the payroll of the French Foreign Office during the war, Richard B. Morris says.

Still, General Nathanael Greene distinguished himself in the field of wartime profiteering rackets. Everybody seemed to take kickbacks and other goodies in the purchase of supplies for the army. Greene's scams included setting up private companies, which then became favored suppliers of such necessaries as rum and gin, and it was all done secretly. The Greeneing of the army involved a very silent partnership established by General Greene with his commissary general, Jeremiah Wadsworth, one of the most prestigious men in Connecticut, a patriot leader, a pillar of the financial community, a political stalwart, a civilian who was doing his bit for the war effort as commissary, supplying the army necessities, which gave him an honorary title (colonel) and a commission deal.*

---

* He was one of the earliest friends of the revolution, who actually lent Washington a horse as the new general rushed to the front at Cambridge on the expense account. It

A third very silent partner was Barnabas Deane, brother of our old friend Silas Deane, who, by spreading the false rumor about Washington's mythical private army rushing to the relief of Boston, was instrumental in the making of the general.*

This wholesome threesome formed a little company that should inspire every crooked-thinking young American.

As the men and horses kept eating and fighting, or at least staying alive, the sums in Greene & Partners' pockets got larger as depreciation increased. There was a fortune to be made in arbitrage—that is, juggling currency in the world's money markets, and various other rackets, which even I do not understand. Knowing how vicious critics could be, Greene, the Quaker moralist-general, decided that the new partnership "should be kept a secret. . . . The nearest friend I have in the world shall not know it from me, and it is my wish that no mortal should be acquainted with the persons forming the Company except us three. I would not wish Mr. Deane even to let his brother know it . . . he may inadvertently let it out into the broad World . . . however just and upright our conduct may be, the world will have suspicions to our disadvantage."[6]

The first rule of successful corruption is to cover your tracks. General Greene wore sneakers, and walked three feet above the ground.

It was decided the firm should have a fictitious name. The next step was that the members should use cover names in their inter-

---

shocked me to learn in the library of Wadsworth's contribution because Washington in his expense account said[3] he *bought* four other horses. A fifth always came in handy. It also made one ponder about those patriots who sold the horses. War profits are war profits, being philosophical about it.

* Silas Deane would later be accused of unlimited robbery and treason.[4] More than fifty years after his death, Congress paid his heirs money due him since 1778.[5] It pays to have friends in government. The heirs of Haym Salomon, who lent the revolutionary government in Philadelphia money during the financial crisis of 1781–82—without interest—are still waiting.

Salomon, a Polish-born Philadelphia investment banker, lent the rebel government an amount that ranges from $350,000 to $700,000 depending on which historian you read. The funds consisted of his entire fortune, some say. The patriotic financier was given a promissory note from Congress on March 27, 1782, signed by Robert Morris, then superintendent of finance for the Continental government. Salomon, the savior of his country as he was called by the grateful Congress earlier in the war, was never paid back and he died in 1785, impoverished. In the early nineteenth century his heirs made an attempt to have the debt cleared up. Salomon's vouchers, given to a government official for the purpose of verification, were mysteriously lost. The matter of Haym Salomon versus the U.S. government is still unsettled. With interest, the estate is owed approximately 4 billion dollars today. In fairness, the case should be re-opened.

office correspondence. And finally that they should use a 'cipher code, since one of Silas Deane's letters had been intercepted and used as proof that he "has a plan of Land jobbing."[7]

A typical letter from Greene to Wadsworth on a major piece of business went:

> Dear Sir: I returned last night from 2010. The 332 are as great a set of 1012 as ever got together. The 166 of 1292 are 1404, than the former. One of them I am sure is nothing less than a 1286; he . . . is from N 2013. . . . Take care what you 1411, . . . send the information in one letter, and what you say upon it in another.
>
> Yours, You Know Who, N 713[8]

This letter from the quartermaster general becomes as stirring as the Declaration of Independence when decoded, with the knowledge that 2010 means Philadelphia; 332, Congress; 1012, rascals; 166 of 1292, Board of Treasury; 1404, worse; 1286, traitor; 2013, Carolina; 1411, write; 713, Greene.

The letter contained other statements:

> It is the intention of 1292 [the Treasury] not to let any 232 [cash] go through your hands, with a view of saving the 292 [commission]. . . . You may depend upon it that great pains is taking to 240 [censure] you and me. The plan is not to attack us personally; this they know will not answer; but to accuse the 1232 [system] of each. . . . Truth and righteousness is of no account with these 931 [people]. Any claim of merit for past services is not only laughed [at] but the person who should be foolish enough to make it would be severely ridiculed. Be upon the 1367 [watch] and be upon your 718 [guard], for depend upon it the hand of Joab is in all these things.
>
> Yours, You Know Who, etc.[9]

"You Know Who" is you know who (713, aka Greene).

You Know Who, with his flair for secrecy and skill at laundering money, would have been a natural for the post of CIA director in the first Washington administration in 1789.

What a Quaker Greene must have been. A friend of high ethical standards. I now see where Dick Nixon's ethics came from.

Greene was no crook! Furthermore, he was furious that Congress suspected him and was treating him like a crook, without ever knowing about you know what.

The sanctimonious, chatty (in code) silent partner 713 complained to his buddy 692 (Wadsworth) about the congressional probe of corruption in the quartermaster corps: "Certain Members of Congress are endeavoring to spread among the people that the avarice and extravagance of the Staff are the principal causes of all the depreciation of the money. . . . I thought it most prudent to write them . . . I have received no answer to it yet."

Two weeks later he writes to Wadsworth:

The midnight politician which we have often talked about
for his duplicity, who used to lodge with you in the same
house in Philadelphia, thinks and says we are a set of rascals;
that we are folding our arms and swimming with the tide,
secure in our emoluments and regardless of the ruin and fate
of our Country. . . . He further adds, if the people won't
save themselves they may all go to h-- and be damn'd. . . .

Though he offered to serve for a year without pay, to prove his patriotism, the suspicion of Greene went so far and his difficulties were so great that before the year was over he offered his resignation. Congress answered with a commission of investigation and reform.

As late as July 18, 1781, Greene wrote to Wadsworth: "How goes on our Commerce? Please to give me an account by the Table as letters are frequently intercepted."

Greene's name never appeared in the books of the mystery firm. The Congress never knew he was buying rum and gin for the army distilled by his own distillery. Beautiful. The discoverer of all this in the 1920s writes that "the integrity and honor" of the partners was "without stain; nor is there a vestige of evidence that its founders took undue advantage of their official positions to extend the business or increase the profits of the firm." One may well agree with this, Hughes says, yet be dazed at finding Nathanael Greene dealing in government supplies under every possible mask. What would have been thought of him if the secret had come out at the time?

Among the "surprized," when the secret partnership was uncovered, might have been George Washington.

Despite all of Greene's financial empire building under the cover of his military duties, that excellent judge of character (General Washington) vigorously defended You Know Who. Greene eventually had refused to serve under the new system (no percent-age commissions) and showed such high spirit that Congress planned to vacate his regular army commission, publish him as a public defaulter, and prevent his returning to the line, Hughes says. Washington wrote beseeching that no such step be taken. With his usual mingling of evasive courtesy and subordination, he said that, in the absence of the documents, he would "neither condemn or acquit General Greene's conduct for the act of resig-nation." He pleaded that dismissal of Greene would show all the officers

> . . . the uncertain tenure by which they hold their
> commissions. . . . Such an act in the most despotic
> government would be attended at least with loud
> complaints . . .
> If Congress by its mere fiat, without inquiry and without
> trial, will suspend an officer to-day, and an officer of such
> high rank, may it not be my turn to-morrow, and ought I to
> put it in the power of any man or body of men to sport with
> my commission and character, and lay me under the
> necessity of tamely acquiescing, or, by an appeal to the
> public, exposing matters, which must be injurious to its
> interests?

Congress hearkened to his advice and let Greene out quietly, appointing Pickering quartermaster general in his place. Thus Washington received back a valued officer, whom he immediately began campaigning vigorously to send southward with all haste. Fortunately, with Kitty arriving, you know who would be there to hold the fort, so to speak.

[4]

Now let's look at the potential sex issue in the campaign of 1789, which was so smoothly managed not a breath of scandal touched Washington. Who was the winner of the Donna Rice Prize, the founding girlfriend, the woman who of a given night could say with absolute certainty "George Washington slept here"? There are at least eight leading candidates for the honor. Was it *:

a) Lucy Flucker Knox; b) Mrs. Clement Biddle; c) Mrs. George Olney; d) Theodosia Prevost Burr; e) Lady Kitty Alexander Duer; f) Lady Stirling; g) Elizabeth Gates; h) Phoebe Fraunces; i) Elizabeth Willing Powel; j) Mrs. William Bingham; k) Mrs. Perez Morton; l) Kitty Greene; m) Myrna Loy; n) none of the above; o) all of the above?

Is there any truth to the rumor that he had four girls in his New York town house, the nation's first executive mansion, at No. 3 Cherry Street in New York City on inauguration eve? Or did he just go to a massage parlor in Chinatown?

These and other questions about Washington's sex life have baffled historians for 199 years. That's because of the press of the day. Nobody ever asked him such good questions. As I've said, the press wasn't fulfilling its duty in the old days. It was not vigilant. It was busy printing canned op-ed pieces from Madison and Hamilton and Jay on boring constitutional issues, neglecting ever to ask what the people really wanted to know, about whether the nation's first prefidential candidate ever committed adultery. And if he didn't, why not?

The press of that day was soft on the womanizing issue. They also did not bear down on a lot of other issues, I should in fairness point out. They didn't touch on the religious issue. Here was a man who didn't even go to church regularly. They didn't hit him

---

* THE SCORECARD (without which you can't tell the Players):
a) the stout Federalist spendthrift
b) wife of the foragemaster-general of the army, a prominent Federalist flirt
c) who told the general to mind his hands
d) the Belle of Paramus
e) daughter of Lord Stirling and prominent Washington party girl. The Paula Parkinson of her day
f) Lady Kitty's mother, and wife of Lord Stirling, the bogus royal from Basking Ridge, New Jersey, and member of the Washington Social Athletic Club (SAC), who danced regularly with the Big Bopper.
g) wife of Gen. Gates, who favored mannish riding clothes. Is said to have frightened General Charles Lee ("a daemoness," he called her) and possibly the horses
h) serving wench at the tavern of her father, Black Sam Fraunces, who was not Negro
i) Mrs. Mayor of Philadelphia
j) the Perla Mesta of the first administration
k) the rich, gorgeous enchanting poetess, who was such a fan Gilbert Stuart in his portrait painted her fingering a statue of the general, an in-joke of the period
l) well-known Washington aficionado

with the charges of luxurious living, considered a vice for others in that period, and degenerate entertainment (theater-going), both of which issues he looked bad on.

Conflict of interest? Washington was knee-deep in the real-estate game. He was an intimate of every major financial crook and market manipulator, including Bobbie Morris, whose house he made the summer White House in Philadelphia in 1790.

If the *Miami Herald* or the *Washington Post* had been around then, they would have asked bluntly:

"Mr. Prefidential candidate, sir, it is a well-known fact that you never told a lie. And in the light of your background of having slept in so many places, can you tell us then, sire, have you ever committed adultery? And with who, or is it whom?

"And if the answer to the question is no, Mr. Prefidential candidate, are you now, or have you ever been a homosexual?"

Or questions to that effect.

If I happened to be attending a press conference, I would have added, as a follow-up question:

"During this period, Mr. Prefidential candidate, sir, did you ever sleep with Martha, your wife, and how often?"

What would have happened if the Sam Donaldson of his day had called out from a cluster of reporters running after the prefidential noncandidate as he walked to his waiting carriage: "What's this about you and Sally Fairfax, general?"

Dignified silence, a pause for a minute or so. Then he would have turned on his heel. He might have given the member of the press a long quiet look. Maybe he would have put on his magic glasses, the ones that when he put them on at his farewell to the troops at Fraunces Tavern, or his handing in the sword at Annapolis, or quelling the mutiny of his officers at Newburgh, made everybody start to cry.

My guess is that he would have raised up his cane and brought it down on Sam Donaldson's head. Richard B. Bernstein thinks he would have not answered at all. "He wouldn't have understood the question or grasped the interest in the press. Gossip didn't interest the press then."

But who should win the Donna Rice prize for giving the least convincing denial (of the womanizing charges whispered about in 1789)? Who would be the woman most likely to tell Barbara Walters it never happened, whatever the prying journalists implied?

First of all, we have to round up the usual suspects and dismiss them. Sally Fairfax has been the number-one target since 1877, when letters were discovered in a shoe box in England indicating some kind of mufkeying around between her and the general.*

Young George wrote Sally F. several letters as a teenager. Two letters dated September 12, 1758, later turned up. They were printed on March 30, 1877, in the *New York Herald*. They had been found in a shoe box containing the effects of Sally Fairfax, her ancestors in England claimed. The centennial birth of the nation had been finished being celebrated only a few months earlier. The shoe-box cache was a shot heard around the world.

The letters, as John R. Alden says,[11] indicated that George really was not fond of Mrs. Money-Market Martha Custis. They were of the someone-loves-you-know who variety, letters befitting a lovesick youth of sixteen or seventeen, rather than a man Washington's age. The nation almost collapsed from the impact of finding the letters.

Was the sainted Washington attempting a base seduction, the country asked nervously?

Fortunately, historians dismissed the letters as forgeries. The nineteenth-century establishment historians always claimed anything showing Washington to be less than a marble statue to be a forgery; anything fitting in with the standard picture of a tin god passes inspection. Why anybody would go to the trouble of forging letters from Sally Fairfax is something of a mystery. At any rate, looking for Sally Fairfax letters turned into a leading parlor game in FFV (First Families of Virginia) country in honor of Martha Washington's quest.

As should be clear by now, my own investigations have unearthed another suspect—Catharine (Kitty) Greene, holder of the nonstop dancing record with the general. An inspection of General Washington's foot locker by a more aggressive press corps might have found a pinup of her in his collection of Playmates. (See pages 258–259)

The evidence supporting Kitty Greene's claim for the Donna

---

* The latest to be hoodwinked into affirming the existence of a George Washington and Sally Fairfax affair was Colonel Flexner, who was the historical consultant on the TV mini-series[10] which shaped the minds of Americans for the next one hundred years. The TV show clearly indicated that the father of our country had been doing something with Jaclyn (Jackie) Smith, as Sally Fairfax was known in the docudrama.

Sally Cary Fairfax
The girl next door

Eliza Powel
The mayor's wife, at whose house
Washington often slept

Peggy Shippen Arnold
Miss Philadelphia of 1777

Gen. Lafayette
Bosom companion

Girlfriends

Betty Grable
Whoops, wrong war!

Martha Washington
The girl he left behind

Kitty Greene
Washington groupie from Rhode Island

Catherine Duer
Prominent Washington party girl

Mrs. Perez Morton
Ardent Washington supporter and fanatic

Rice Prize includes proof she was sexually active during the period. It is actually mentioned in her letters. This is rare. Nobody's sex life appears in the early United States mail. Judging by the infrequency of sexual contacts in surviving correspondence, it's a miracle the new country didn't go the way of the Shakers.

Ah, that Kitty Greene. "She enlivened many a black night in the revolutionary winter quarters," Colonel Freeman says. I bet she did.

She began in our story at the start of the war as a newly married, fresh, beautiful twenty-two-year-old woman, sociable, engaging, graceful, soft, demure, a notorious flirt, who loved fast chariots and men.

Kitty was the Washington groupie who rushed to the front in New York in 1776, at the time all the other generals' wives were being sent home packing. A retreat was going on, but Kitty was rushing to the city like a matron from Connecticut coming in to a matinee.

At this juncture in history, her activities went unrecorded. That's because the historians in those days were all men. They didn't think women were worth following. Anyway, they saw nothing unusual in a headstrong, tempestuous flirt rushing to the front with her trunks of party gowns and dancing shoes, like a Barbara Hutton.

Kitty was the life of any party, even at grim Valley Forge. It was at Valley Forge, they say, she first slept with the Marquis de Lafayette. Among those who said it was the Marquis. Washington's favorite boy trooper was quite candid about it—even to the point of telling his wife in France how fond he was of Kitty.[12]

Lafayette's *petite l'amour* with Kitty Greene must have ended the rumor that the boy major general was *toujours gai* and cemented the secret alliance with France in a single stroke.

This act of Franco-American friendship on Kitty's part, sleeping with the general's best friend, to her childish mind may have had an ulterior motive, beyond politics, like making the general jealous.

Kitty also mentioned "sleeping with the Marquis." See her letters to Colonel Wadsworth. Wadsworth, horselender to General Washington and commissary general under General Greene, was a Mount Vernon machine member who won election to Congress as a representative from Connecticut in the first election of 1789 and emerged in the nation's capital as a major behind-closed-doors force. He also emerged as a secret admirer of Kitty's. As her contribution to celebrating the first election of George Washington, Kitty began sleeping with her husband's secret business partner in 1788.[13]

She was also sleeping with Major General Mad Anthony Wayne at the time. She was mad about generals.

Kitty Greene, in fact, was involved with so many soldiers between her first visit to the front at Cambridge in 1775 to 1789, we need a road map of her travels (see page 262).

That Kitty was a rascal. One only has to read of her exploits during the last days of the war to be awed.

Nat's Angel rushed to be at his side on the Southern front in 1780. She kept him company with distinction, winning commendation as *plus belle* of the army, while becoming the talk of Charleston and Savannah with her feverish romance on the side with General Anthony (Mad About-the-Girl) Wayne.

The South depressed her. After Yorktown, while her husband was drearily mopping up in South Carolina, she asked him to put her on the first ship headed north, sailing out of Charleston. It was a troopship bound for Philadelphia.

Also aboard the first transport was Col. Kósciuszko, an old friend from the Southern Command whose departure, as the Stegemans say, "broke many a heart in South Carolina. One of the women seeing the colonel off at the dock received a promise that he would return as soon as her husband died."[14]

One woman aboard a troopship, heading for Philadelphia, the city of vice and dissipation, where the government lay. And it turned out to be Kitty Greene. What bliss. Kitty Greene rides again.

And while she was in the Quaker City, she vexed Greene by not writing a line to him while he mopped up the British forces in the South for the next two years.

I am still researching this, but it's starting to seem as if the only one missing in Kitty's game plan to mufkey everybody in the army was you know who, as the late General Greene might have put it. Who else was there? With the possibles and probables, the only one left is the man she danced with three hours without stopping during the terribly cold winter of 1778–79 at Middletown, when they presumably discussed amphibious invasions and floating batteries.

Despite all of the evidence that would hold up in the *National*

Kitty Greene's War Record

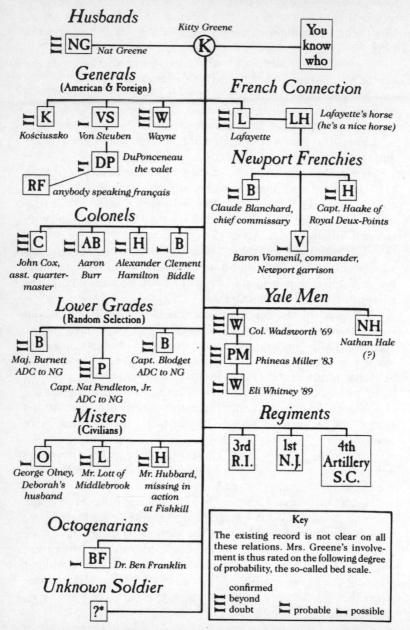

Husbands

Kitty Greene

≡ NG Nat Greene — K — You know who

Generals (American & Foreign)

≡ K Kościuszko ⌐ VS Von Steuben ≡ W Wayne

⌐ DP DuPonceneau the valet

RF anybody speaking français

French Connection

≡ L Lafayette — LH Lafayette's horse (he's a nice horse)

Newport Frenchies

≡ B Claude Blanchard, chief commissary ≡ H Capt. Haake of Royal Deux-Points

V Baron Viomenil, commander, Newport garrison

Colonels

≡ C John Cox, asst. quarter-master ⌐ AB Aaron Burr ⌐ H Alexander Hamilton ⌐ B Clement Biddle

Lower Grades (Random Selection)

≡ B Maj. Burnett ADC to NG ≡ P Capt. Nat Pendleton, Jr. ADC to NG ≡ B Capt. Blodget ADC to NG

Yale Men

≡ W Col. Wadsworth '69 NH Nathan Hale (?)
≡ PM Phineas Miller '83
≡ W Eli Whitney '89

Misters (Civilians)

⌐ O George Olney, Deborah's husband ≡ L Mr. Lott of Middlebrook ≡ H Mr. Hubbard, missing in action at Fishkill

Regiments

3rd R.I. 1st N.J. 4th Artillery S.C.

Octogenarians

⌐ BF Dr. Ben Franklin

Unknown Soldier

?*

Key

The existing record is not clear on all these relations. Mrs. Greene's involvement is thus rated on the following degree of probability, the so-called bed scale.

≡ confirmed beyond doubt ≡ probable ⌐ possible

*The above list is not all-inclusive. Space limitations prevented mentioning everybody. The blank space on the chart by inference includes the remainder of the Continental Army. No slight of an ancestor is intentional, but coincidental.

Enquirer, General Washington definitely did not sleep with Kitty Greene. Absolutely not.

How is this possible? General Washington didn't do that sort of thing, as any historian will tell you. That's what you have lieutenants for, like Hamilton.

My theory is that Kitty Greene had sex with everybody in Washington's official army family, except him. That's my story and I'll stick to it.*

[5]

Having absolved Mrs. Greene, the others I'm not so sure about. Here is my list of top suspects who he may have slept with, once again ignoring Sally Fairfax. This is the "B" List and should not be confused with the "A" list above, both of which are not mutually exclusive. The order of listing is based on the highest probability factor (number of chances, such as sleeping in the same room, or seeing him nude †).

Official Founding Girlfriends List

1. Theodosia Prevost of Paramus, N.J.
2. Mrs. Watkins' daughters (two)
3. Eliza Willing Powel
4. Mrs. John Posey the First of Rover's Delight, Va.
5. Peggy Shippen Arnold
6. Eliza (Polly) Philipse
7. Mrs. Bache
8. Mary McDaniel
9. Mary Gibbons
10. Betsy Ross

---

* I may be wrong about this. He may have been sleeping with her since Cambridge. In which case, I quote the words of that great American historian, Emily Litella: "Never mind."

† Hawthorne doubts anyone ever saw Washington without his clothes on.

Who's Whom

1.–2. The general and his family in the spring of 1780 have been through hell, i.e., the Passaic area of New Jersey. The family is scheduled to stop, Colonel Flexner tells us, at the home of a Mrs. Watkins for the night. They had hardly washed their hands at this modest dwelling when up rode a servant with an invitation for them to stay with Mrs. Theodosia Prevost at Hermitage, her elegant mansion in Paramus. Mrs. P. was the social leader of Paramus. Not wishing to offend Mrs. Watkins, Washington remained with her for dinner. And was rewarded, so his A.D.C. McHenry writes, by having "her two charming daughters sing" several pretty songs in a very agreeable manner.

Then the family moved on to the Hermitage; it is not clear if after or before the charming daughters' encores or other festivities. Here, Colonel Flexner says, they found it was "inhabited by belles of a more prismatic brilliance." . . . Mrs. Prevost is the rich widow of a British army officer who had the decency to die in the West Indies, and is soon to marry Aaron Burr. She had staying with her some fair refugees from New York. With them, McHenry says, "we talked—and walked—and laughed and danced and frolicked and gallanted away the leisure hours of four days and nights."

I don't know how to tell Colonel Flexner about this, but four days and nights of frolicking and gallanting can be hard on a man. The women of New Jersey and New York, if not the whole tri-state area, tend to fall to pieces after *three* days and nights of frolicking and gallanting.

Washington himself, of course, might have spent the four days writing letters with the buxom, sex-starved Madame Bovary of Bergen County sharpening his quill.

3. Mrs. Mayor of Philadelphia, of whom we will hear more later.

4. First wife of Capt. John Posey, Washington protegé and next door neighbor, who was heavily in debt to the squire of Mount Vernon. The latter was said as a teen-ager to have been the father of Mrs. Posey's first son, the other reason why he went to the Caribbean that summer with brother Lawrence Washington, until it blew over. Eventually, the unusually tall son of Posey served under Washington in the army, and was promoted with extreme rapidity.

5. The beautiful, active in the Philadelphia theatre, socialite wife of Benedict Arnold, left behind at West Point temporarily. After the defection, his lovely theatrical wife bared her soul and breasts to Gen. Washington when he came to comfort her with news of her husband's betrayal (also to Col. Hamilton in a similar passionate scene). But she was thought to be temporarily insane with grief from the perfidy, and would do anything. Those who were there praised her mad act.

6. Colonel Flexner says admiringly, "Although slim, Polly was also statuesque; her delicate features were somehow expressive of cool strength; her full mouth was both sensuous and firm."[15] But what George probably admired most about Polly was her wealth. Her father owned Yonkers, and she was the heiress: one of the nine who spurned him during his years as a teenage werewolf who was to come into her life again as supreme commander of her war zone.

7. Mrs. Bache was Benjamin Franklin's granddaughter, who Washington danced the night away with at George and Martha's twentieth anniversary ball at the beautiful Mrs. Powel's house in Philadelphia in the winter of 1778–79.[16] One wonders what Ben Franklin might have made of the Bache–Washington connection.

8. Mary McDaniel, convicted of "robing the cloaths of Mr. George Washington when he was washing in the river" in the summer of 1751, and sentenced to suffer fifteen lashes upon her bare back.

9. "Mary Gibbons," whom he was reportedly "maintaining genteely" in Hoboken, New Jersey, was the person he was supposed to be visiting with his pockets full of state papers, which a friend of hers copied while the girl from New Jersey mufkeyed with the general from Virginia. The friend was possibly Washerwoman Kate. Not related to Edward Gibbons.

10. Unemployed seamstress.

Historians would have us believe it was none of the above. My working thesis is that it may have been all of the above.

Two things you have to know about George Washington. He was "a lusty fellow," as John Alden calls him, and was probably sexually frustrated. He had told Sally Fairfax he had married for money. He was a chaser of girls as a young man, pursuing attractive aristocratic ladies on the Tidewater, and less sophisticated country girls in the mountains. Why would he suddenly change the spots on his coat when he became a soldier and a war hero and the country's most frequent flyer when he traveled around the country as a salesman for the new U.S.A.?

Few women were attracted to Washington during his youth. By 1776 his countenance and physique and appearance had become breathtaking enough to note in diaries. One prominent lady confessed in her diary to "a womanly admiration of a noble exterior." [17]

That was hot stuff in 1776.

It was also a lusty time. If Washington had partook, he would have been a normal American of that period, when procreation and the population explosion were an instrument of policy. The average family had 12.2 children. Americans were the jackrabbits of the British Empire. At the time, the British population rate was declining. The colonists were bursting out of the seams here. It amounted to patriotic duty to have sex often.

Sex was on everybody's mind, especially for an ex-Congress member.

Member of Congress!

Why did they call it that—I ask you?

Traditionally, every war hero has his way with the ladies, camp followers, groupies, hero worshipers. Every Napoleon has his Josephine. (Caesar had his Mrs. Sid Caesar.) Ike had his Kay Summersby. Howe had Mrs. Loring.

With all the accumulated power of his war heroics and political ascendancy, the historians are trying to tell us he didn't have a girlfriend? It would be like a top rock star abstaining the years he is on the charts. The frustrated teenage werewolf with the pick of the nation's ladies had suddenly got a grip on himself.

Historians have several theories about the absence of sex in the stories about Washington:

1. He had the sex drive of a turnip.
2. The country was founded by ascetics.
3. He was a homosexual. There were some great generals in the Turkish army, too. Washington, AC/DC, they could call the seat of government.

How is it the historians never noticed anything sexual going on? First of all, they say, there is no evidence—that is, a letter, a piece of paper—proving Washington did mufkey on such and such a date. There may be two reasons for this:

1. There was nothing noteworthy about sex relations. They were so commonplace nobody thought to mention them.
2. The past has been expurgated.

I know Washington idealized women, put them on a pedestal. But it's hard to believe he went fourteen years of being on the road without a woman or Martha. Yet, I have read a thousand history books, and there is not a single case of an unnatural act— that is, sleeping with somebody, not even Molly Pitcher.

What's going on here: Washington was either 1) a genuine original. They threw away the mold when they made him. Or 2) he had help. There has been a gigantic coverup of Washington's private life because of the special place he had in American psychohistory. They all cleaned house for him, even Martha. Let me jump ahead of our story for a moment.

George Washington died in 1799, historians tell us, from a cold. He caught it while riding his horse in his fields. Others say he caught the fatal chill as a result of jumping out the back window with his pants in his hands "after an assignation with an overseer's wife in the Mount Vernon gardens on a cold afternoon." [18]*

All agree he was, as was the medical custom of the day, bled to death. They did that for everything from boils to astigmatism to cancer to reading too many history books.

Within minutes after his death from a cold, as they say, Martha rushed to his library and started burning papers. His widow burned every letter that she had ever received from him, Woodward in the 1920s said, with the exception of three or four,† a handful that escaped apparently by accident.

No one has ever explained the motive behind this wild letter-burning episode. Martha Washington knew at the time—indeed,

---

* So distinguished a historian as Arnold Toynbee, Colonel Flexner notes,[19] "published the statement that Washington died because of a chill he contracted visiting a black beauty in his slave quarters."

† More conservative historians say it was two.

the whole world knew—that George Washington was a superstar in the field of history, and that every scrap of his writing would be treasured and printed. Did she feel, as Woodward suggests, that his letters to her were so sacred in their intimacy that posterity had no right to read them?

Possibly.

She may have been antidemocratic. The masses should keep their noses out of her drawers. She *was* Lady Washington. Perhaps Lady Washington did not want to cast her husband's pearls before us swine.

"Privacy," explains historian Richard B. Bernstein. "There. You have your explanation."

Did Martha's incendiary hand stop at her own letters? Were there, perhaps, more letters to and from Benjamin Harrison, The Signer, about Washerwoman Kate? Franklin telling him about the belles of Philadelphia or Paris? Were there letters indicating that the Fabius Maximus Gluttus of Virginia was really Caligula?

I'm not saying that. But who knows what she burned?

It was widely assumed that Martha's sudden burst of house-cleaning was aimed at burning his private letters from "you know who," as giddy historian Elswyth Thane says in *Washington's Lady*. Certainly no letters by Sally Fairfax ever turned up in his papers. There were only those two alleged forgeries discovered in London.

My own theory is that the letters Martha was going after were you know who's letters. Kitty Greene's. The so-called Greene mail.

Kitty Greene seems to have pioneered in the extramarital affair, judging from what historians say. Or at least the art of discussing them in her letters. She is the founding co-respondent. Howard Swiggett says, "Her letters being unique in that period of American life when the extramarital affairs between two people of social prominence, though doubtless not unknown, are not even hinted at in anyone's correspondence."

Greene broke new ground in her private letters to Jeremiah Wadsworth (Nat's monkey-business partner during the war) in 1789. While not nearly as passionate as the Lafayette-Washington correspondence (not burned), they are fascinating in their details of dalliance. Her adultery letters to Wadsworth are so smooth, clearly not the first effort of an inexperienced amateur but an old hand at deception. There are two sets, for example: "private letters" covered by simultaneously "public letters." *

Admittedly her husband the cryptologist General You Know Who himself (713), Nathanael Greene, probably would have been even more artful, writing in the ever-romantic numerology. Who could he have possibly been writing love letters to—948? †

Martha was not as dumb as historians make her seem. She knew something was going on between those two. You don't just sit there watching your husband, the big war hero, dance with the same young, trim, beautiful, flirty woman for three hours "without stopping" without its crossing your mind, whatever "it" was.

By burning Kitty's letters to George, Martha the Torch was protecting her own position as the wife of the noblest prefident of all. She had her private humiliation and sorrow, which she didn't want to share with posterity or her next-door neighbors.

Martha, the vandal, wasn't the only one who would go through her late husband's things, neatening the papers, so to speak. First there was Bushrod Washington, the prefident's brother Jack's son, who became a justice of the Supreme Court of the United States and inherited Mount Vernon. It was Bushrod who first tore out the pages of Washington's diaries and records by the handfuls and gave them away as souvenirs to casual visitors.[21]

Then the historians got at them. The Harvard historian Jared Sparks was the first to organize and publish the prefidential papers in the 1830s, and tamper with the text. I don't care if he did become president of Harvard: What he did with the papers was

---

* It makes one blush to read the exchanges between this wholesome, flirtatious, frisky, beautiful, life-of-any-party woman and the solid Hartford banker and pillar of society. But on April 4, she wrote privately:

> I have a thousand things to communicate but my little secret hope of seeing you soon makes me forego my propensity—perhaps in a month you will see me in New York. Nothing but the fear of unnecessary expense will prevent me from declaring in person how much affection I feel for you. I am, your devoted,
> C. Greene
> P.S. I believe I forgot to mention my noble lover to you. The Marquis of ———, I forget what, but he had very serious propositions.[20]

This is steamy prose for the period.

For anyone's prurient interest aroused by the unusual Greene–Wadsworth papers, they are in the smutty letters wings of the Jeremiah Wadsworth Papers, in the Connecticut Historical Society, and the Wadsworth Athenaeum in Hartford.

† Martha.

despicable. Sparks cut up the manuscript letters, sending parts of the letters to different people. The signatures were favorite gifts. He crossed out certain things. Marcus Cunliffe says, "He omitted or altered passages that might be regarded as vulgar."[22] For example, "But a flea-bite at present" was changed to "totally inadequate to our demands at this time." No wonder Washington sounds so boring. Anything that didn't fit the image of the man and the monument was excised.

Sparks corrects spelling and suppresses sections of letters, including one to George's friend Robin (about Sally F.) on the grounds that it is "imperfect and of very little importance." Can you imagine what Sparks might have done if he had found one of Kitty's playful letters?

> *Dear Georgie Porgie—*
> *. . . Did we have a great time bonking in Brandywine.*
> *Or what? . . . Save the last dance for me.*
>
> *Signed:*
> *Meow!*
>
> Or:
> *Dear Tall, Light, and Handsome—*
> *You are the most gallant stallion in the forces raised*
> *outside Philadelphia. . . .*
>
> *Signed:*
> *Dirty Dancer.*

How do we know Sparks didn't find them?

Or perhaps something in code. She probably played the numbers game too, taught to her by you know who.

So few details of Washington's private life surfaced in the papers. Jared Sparks must have used the first desktop dust-buster on them. It's the natural inclination of scholars who want to clean up things to fit their preconceived premises. Too bad there wasn't a Liz Smith or *Spy* magazine. Some subclerk would have leaked the out-takes, thus guaranteeing a fuller historical record.

Still, what Jared Sparks and others of his ilk did was a lot better than the earlier spin-meister historians, like Parson Weems, who invented anecdotes to fill in the numerous gaps in his private life, such as chopping down the cherry tree and the never-telling-a-lie story. Most of the few things we all know about Washington as a fact come from Weems's seminal work of historical fiction. *A History of the Life and Death, Virtues and Exploits of General George Washington* was published in 1800 by Mason L. Weems, who, as you may have guessed, was not a real parson.

The historical vandalism continued, with each generation bowdlerizing or censoring the papers and diaries in their own way. In the twentieth century, J.P. Morgan bought Washington letters for his library.* He burned what he said were the smutty ones.

What these well-meaning scholars were doing was working as free-lance image makers. As a result, what there is left of Washington is a plaster saint, an alabaster marble piece on a purple fruited plain. Modern politicians and prefidents do the same thing. LBJ, until his death, Doris Kearns tells us, was busy in his library rewriting his government memoranda, taking out all traces of his special charm. LBJ in his papers is the George Washington of the Pedernales.

I'm of two minds on this issue. On the one hand, I've been taught that Washington was a god. He was the most virtuous, moral man who ever lived, a paragon, a man of stainless steel purity, the coldest fish in the Potomac. I was a little puzzled by the Washington monument, the content of that symbolism and hidden psychological statue. What did that phallus mean? What did it have to do with George Washington, the man, the monument, or the bridge?

Still, I always believed that George Washington didn't fool around. As the historians said, he was a man of marble without flaws. Of course, I never thought that Warren Harding did either. Or Grover Cleveland. There was a sanctity of the office that protected prefidents from human shortcomings. Oh, maybe Woodrow Wilson had a girlfriend. You can't trust these guys with rimless glasses who look like ministers. But not Washington. He was above womanizing. That's what I was taught. I can't help it. That's one of my limitations as a scholar.

But I'm also a reporter. When I read his wife burned the letters, then historians cleaned up what they didn't discard, that the whole establishment for 199 years or so worked as a well-oiled machine to say certain things about Washington, well, this raises the hackles.

What we have here is a situation where the experts, the his-

* If you have to ask how much a collection of Washington letters costs, you can't afford one.

torians, know very well that evidence is missing (starting with Martha the Torch's work in the field of scholarship), and on the basis of the incomplete record they have built a character who has no flaws.

So why are they cheating my man Washington of his reputation? He could be the biggest stud in Virginia, unbeknownst to his adoring public. Yet another conspiracy against his memory, like saying he was not a great politician. Here was this young, dashing, adventure-loving soldier, who goes back and forth between the jungle, the assembly ballroom, and the state assembly, who is dancing and drinking his way through the Bible belt, with all those poor decadent overheated aristocratettes and country girls wasting away in the heat and monotony of the bush . . . and he's totally devoid of a sex life? Odd. These historians could do the life story of John F. Kennedy and make it sound like he spent his years as senator and prefident in a Trappist monastery.

The problem may be that historians today are Victorians. They are writing history with an asexual bias. Their personal feelings about sex may determine the telling of history. There is something evil about sex the way they write about it.

Good guys don't have sex. He's away from Martha for fifty weeks at a time; that's it. But it's okay for the bad guys to have sex. General Lee is allowed to have sex during the war. He was a disgusting lout to historians like Colonel Flexner. They all tell that sickening story of how this contemptible worm sneaked a woman into his quarters. It was at Valley Forge, and his room was right behind Lady Washington's sitting room, and he had brought the hussy in from Philadelphia by a back door. Lee, as I said, was a satirist. This was his idea of a private joke, perhaps. Besides, what else is there to do in Valley Forge in the winter, for Providence's sake? Take cold showers? Dance the night away?

The attitude toward Lee and the strumpet is very revealing of the new Victorians.

Hamilton also can have sex. He is the bad guy of the Washington administration. They even tell of a long-term flirtation Colonel Hamilton had with his sister-in-law, Angelica Schuyler Church. When she comes to visit New York from England, he pays for her lodgings and lists the love nest in his account book, Richard B. Morris says, as a bill for Angelica's "music master." "One may pardonably speculate that a consuming passion covered these cryptic entries," Morris adds. "It was all very furtive but not uncharacteristic of the way Hamilton arranged his extra marital affairs." [23]

Aaron Burr could also do anything. He was *the* Gary Hart of the American political scene of 1789.

It's like those two great figures in modern history, Elizabeth Taylor and Marilyn Monroe. Certain people are allowed to have sex with anybody; others, like Ingrid Bergman, are not. One affair with Roberto Rossellini and she's run out of the country. Life in the United States is funny that way.

George Washington was one of those short-changed. He is not allowed to have had sex. Zero contacts a year. It leaves one unconsciously disappointed in Washington. So many prefidents seemed to have done it. "Camelot" turned out to be "the Six Wives of JFK." Warren Harding had Nan Britton in the closet with the umbrellas in the White House. Grover Cleveland had an illegitimate daughter. FDR loved Lucy. Thomas Jefferson, they say, dated his slave girls. What was *wrong* with Washington?

Part VI

—

The Last Huzzah

or, the Man Who Wouldn't Be King

[1]

Surprise. Washington was elected preſident on April 6, 1789. He received 69 votes. That was less than the 638 I received in New Hampshire 175 years later. But his were Electoral College votes, where they really counted; mine were in the Republican party primary.* Of course I didn't have a machine behind me like he did.

When the ballots cast by the electors on February 4 were officially opened on April 6, he had carried ten states. New York, North Carolina, and Rhode Island didn't vote for various reasons. For example, the great state of Rhode Island, the home of paper money, the Rhode Island Reds (hens), and Kitty Greene, "Rogue Island," as General Washington called it, didn't ratify the Constitution until 1790.

All told, there were supposed to be 72 electors from ten states. Of these, two in Maryland and one in Virginia failed to appear, so that the total vote was 69. Washington received every vote.

Sixty-nine out of 69? Amazing. It was a landslide. The polls had been right.

These are the 69 heroes of '89, who made the preſident. Each is a member in good standing of the Mount Vernon machine, and should have had his hand shaken by the successful candidate, which unfortunately he couldn't do because of his sense of dignity

* In New Hampshire in 1964, a race in which I managed to lose to Harold Stassen (1209 votes) among others, thus ensuring my becoming a footnote to history. You can look it up.

277

or cleanliness obsession. But all are enshrined in the Hall of Fame of American machine politics. Their names, which should be memorized by every schoolboy and girl in the land, are:

Presidential Electors, February 4, 1789

New Hampshire
Benjamin Bellows
John Pickering
Ebenezer Thompson
John Sullivan
John Parker

Massachusetts
Caleb Davis
Samuel Phillips, Jr.
Francis Dana
Samuel Henshaw
William Sever
David Sewall
Walter Spooner
Moses Gill
William Cushing
William Shepard

Connecticut
Samuel Huntington
Richard Law
Matthew Griswold
Erastus Wolcott
Thaddeus Burr
Jedidiah Huntington
Oliver Wolcott, Sr.

New Jersey
David Brearley
James Kinsey
John Neilson
David Moore
John Rutherfurd
Matthias Ogden

Delaware
Gunning Bedford, Sr.
George Mitchell
John Baning

Pennsylvania
James Wilson
James O'Hara
David Grier
Samuel Potts

Alexander Graydon
Collinson Read
Edward Hand
George Gibson
John Arndt
Laurence Keene

Maryland
John Rogers
William Tilghman
Alexander Contee Hanson
Philip Thomas
Robert Smith
William Matthews
George Plater*
William Richardson*

Virginia
John Pride, Jr.
John Harvie
Zachariah Johnston
John Roane, Jr.
David Stuart
William Fitzhugh
Anthony Walke
Patrick Henry
Edward Stevens
Warner Lewis*
James Wood, Jr.

South Carolina
Christopher Gadsden
Henry Laurens
Edward Rutledge
Charles Cotesworth Pinckney
John F. Grimké
Thomas Heyward, Jr.
Arthur Simkins

Georgia
George Handley
John King
George Walton
Henry Osborne
John Milton

* Did not vote.

They are also the first class in the electoral college, the nation's newest institution of higher learning, whose quadrennial convocations were not without the frivolity of a frat party on other campuses. Some newspaper accounts survive of the meeting of that first class of electors of 1789, according to Matteson.[1] A Boston account dated February 4 declared that the electors met and balloted unanimously for Washington and Adams, "without a single debate on the subject."[2] This meeting was at ten o'clock in the senate chamber of the statehouse in Boston. The report from Annapolis closed with "We shall be excused for closing this account with a wish that the people of America may have many other such opportunities of reassuring this great man of their love and attachment."[3] From Augusta, Georgia, came the statement that after the balloting the electors "politely acknowledged" that the vote had been unanimous for Washington.[4] A letter from Reading, Pennsylvania, of February 5, said: "Yesterday the Electors for Pennsylvania met at this place. . . . Having proceeded to the Court-house, . . . they balloted. The business of the day being over they returned to Witman's, the Federal Inn, of the borough; and dined with a number of gentlemen who were in their suite. A few other gentlemen of the place supped with the electors, and concluded the evening with great hilarity, circulating the glass in honor of the Constitution, General Washington and Doctor Adams. I believe there can be no doubt that the former will be the President and the latter Vice President, which God in his infinite mercy grant."[5]

The victory had been less than unanimous for the veep, John Adams. He had carried his native state, Massachusetts (10 votes), and New Hampshire (5) unanimously.

Connecticut gave him 5, New Jersey 1, Pennsylvania 8, and Virginia 5. John Jay had 3 votes in Delaware and 5 in New Jersey, undoubtedly in accordance with a previous understanding, Matteson says. Hancock had 2 in Pennsylvania. All the six attending electors of Maryland gave their second vote to Robert Hanson Harrison of that state. The other 5 votes in Virginia were 3 to Clinton, 1 to Hancock, and 1 to Jay; while all the South Carolina and Georgia votes went to various local men, except 1 to Hancock and 1 to Lincoln. In Georgia one of the electors received 2 votes. The 3 votes for Clinton are all that can be called really anti-Federalist, one of them undoubtedly being Henry's vote.[6]

Doctor Adams's total of 34 votes was not even a majority. Not what his polls were anticipating. He had run into Alex the Knife.

At least 16, and probably 27, scattered votes would, without what Matteson calls "the Hamilton manipulation," have gone to Adams.

Washington–Adams was not the party ticket in 1789. Technically there were no parties in 1789, although Washington and Adams were Federalists, as any true Federalist knew.*

Whether there were parties or not, Washington was against them. His reason for running for prefident was to eliminate party strife. Everybody would be behind him. So they didn't need any parties.

Adams wasn't, of course, running. As Colonel Freeman says, Benjamin Lincoln and others had been working industriously and with political skill to have John Adams chosen as vice-president, and they sounded out Washington on his attitude toward the Massachusetts leader.[8] The general's answer was that Massachusetts might reasonably be expected to supply the vice-president. Any "true Federalist" who sufficiently enjoyed the confidence of faithful Americans to be named to that office could not be "disagreeable" to the General. "I would most certainly treat him," said Washington of his hypothetical vice-president, "with perfect sincerity and the greatest candor in every respect. I would give him my full confidence and use my utmost endeavors to cooperate with him, in promoting and rendering permanent the national prosperity; this should be my great, my only aim, under the fixed and irrevocable resolution of leaving to other hands the helm of the

---

* "The term Federalists was used to designate the Constitution's supporters and Anti-Federalists to designate the Constitution's opponents," Bernstein says. "This nomenclature arose in the early 1780s when disputes over proposals to give the Confederation Congress more power divided the nation into Federalists—those favoring additional power for the federal government—and Anti-Federalists. Thus, when the Constitution's supporters adopted the name Federalists, they could claim consistency with the word's earlier usage. But the Constitution's opponents argued that they had at least as valid a claim to be called Federalists. Invoking the traditional distinction between federal and national government, they denounced the Constitution as a nationalizing, consolidating charter that would destroy the sovereignty of the states, individual liberties, and republican government. However, the Constitution's supporters won the tug-of-war over nomenclature by linking the Constitution with the idea of Union; they maintained that the American people could preserve the Union only by adopting the Constitution. The next step in this war of words, which they portrayed as simply a logical consequence of celebrating the Constitution as the bulwark of Union and Federalism, was that the new charter's opponents, the Anti-Federalists, were willing or even eager to dissolve the Union. These terms soon passed into general usage. However, neither the Federalists nor the Anti-Federalists were modern political parties as we understand them. . . . Though some historians maintain that the Federalists and Anti-Federalists of 1787–88 evolved into the Federalists and Republicans of the 1790s, the course of party development was more complicated and the continuities between the two sets of parties were much more attenuated than the traditional wisdom would suggest."[7]

State, as soon as my services could possibly with propriety be dispensed."[9]

The Adams camp took that as a strong endorsement from the noncandidate. Adams was acceptable on Washington's vice-prefident short list. It balanced the ticket. I, myself, would have preferred Sam Adams, Father of the Revolution, running with the Father of the Country, an all-father ticket. Or a woman, preferably a black. Somebody like Betty Davis, who worked for General Washington during the campaign, without pay (she was a slave). Since it was to be a largely ceremonial, symbolic post, a slave would fit right in, especially one who could clean up the mess in the White House which we'd often hear about later on.

Betty Davis was an obsession of his, like amphibious invasions. His letters to Mount Vernon during the setting up of a new government in 1789 include: "By the Reports I perceive also, that for every day Betty Davis works she is laid up two.—If she is indulged in this idleness she will grow worse and worse, for she has a disposition to be one of the most idle creatures upon earth; and is, besides, one of the most deceitful."

This Negress evidently continued her deceit and idleness, for a month later he wrote: "What kind of sickness is Betty Davis's? . . . If pretended ailments, without apparent causes, or visible effects, will screen her from work, I shall get no service at all from her;—for a more lazy, deceitful and impudent huzzy, is not to be found in the United States than she is."

Imagine having the mighty George Washington on one's case.

The prefident's race may have been apolitical, but the VP was political as all get-out. Jay, Adams, Charles (Pincky) Pinckney, and George Clinton, the anti-Federalist candidate and Washington's real-estate partner, were all being boosted for the job.

People allied against Adams wanted to give him a negative admonition to remind him, Bernstein says, he wasn't the king pin he thought he was. Still, the negative vote got out of hand.

Having engineered the presidency to his satisfaction, Miller says,[10] Hamilton had turned his attention in 1788 to the more knotty problem of the vice-presidency. It was generally agreed that the second office of the government ought to go to a Northerner, inasmuch as the presidency was to be given to a Virginian. The leading contender for the post was John Adams of Massachusetts. A Signer of the Declaration of Independence, American minister to Holland and Great Britain, and the author of an influential book on political science, Adams was one of the most distinguished statesmen in the United States.

Nevertheless, in Hamilton's scale of values, these qualifications were outweighed by Adams's quirks of personality, the "wrongheadedness" of which he was sometimes guilty, and the low esteem in which he was reputed to hold George Washington. In his long political career, Adams had distinguished himself as the very archetype of the civilian: during the Revolutionary War, he freely criticized the American generals, insisted upon the subordination of the military to the civilian government, and advocated the annual election of commanding officers by the Continental Congress. Understandably, therefore, John Adams was not a popular figure at Washington-for-Prefident headquarters.

Hamilton suspected that this crusty, intractable, and opinionated New Englander had helped to make life miserable for the army during the war and that he had conspired to remove Washington as commander in chief, Miller says. Certainly it was true that Adams was jealous of Washington: he felt that the commander in chief, together with Benjamin Franklin, had monopolized the glory of the revolution. For these reasons, Hamilton feared that if Adams were placed in the vice-presidency, he would intrigue against Washington and the administration would be rent by the "broils and contentions" of its two highest officers.[11]

It was therefore "deemed an essential point of caution," Hamilton later said, "to take care, that accident, or an intrigue of the opposers of the government, should not raise Mr. Adams instead of General Washington, to the first place."

Hamilton's method of avoiding a miscarriage in the Electoral College was to make sure that the electors voted unanimously for Washington and that votes were withheld from John Adams. To accomplish his second objective he induced a few prominent politicians in Connecticut, Pennsylvania, and New Jersey to throw away the electoral votes of those states. From Hamilton's point of view, the plan worked to perfection: Washington received a unanimous vote in the Electoral College; John Adams fell far short of unanimity.[12]

John Adams did not take kindly to this jockeying of the vote in the Electoral College: he swore that there was a "dark and dirty intrigue . . . to spread a panic lest John Adams should be President." Fortunately for Hamilton, the irascible New Englander did not know (at the time) who was responsible for his discomfiture.

Adams didn't figure out what hit him in '89 until several elections later.

When the split in the Federalist party came in 1800, Matteson says,[13] Hamilton explained: "Great was my astonishment and equally great my regret, when, afterwards, I learned from persons of unquestionable veracity that Mr. Adams had complained of unfair treatment in not having been permitted to take an equal chance with General Washington, by leaving the votes to an uninfluenced current." On his part, Hamilton could not forgive the man he had injured for displaying such peevishness, jealousy, and vanity as to complain because a few votes were withheld from him to make certain that George Washington would be elected president.[14]

So what if Adams almost finished third?

Unfortunately, Doctor Adams hadn't read Hamilton's letter to Madison (November 23, 1788), in which he saw danger in too great an agreement on Adams. He wrote Madison: "If it should be thought expedient to endeavour to unite in a particular character, there is a danger of a different kind to which we must not be inattentive—the possibility of rendering it doubtful who is appointed President . . . it would be disagreeable even to have a man treading close upon the heels of the person we wish as President. May not the malignity of the Opposition be in some instances exerted even against him? Of all this we shall best judge when we know who are our electors: and we must in our different circles take our measure accordingly." Hamilton took his measures very effectually, as it turned out: raised a fear before the election and indeed prevented Adams from receiving even a majority of the votes, and, according to his own statement, which finds support in the opinion of later members of the Adams family, incurred Adams's own antagonism thereby.[15]

Jonathan Trumbull wrote Adams after the election:

In the choice of V.P. you had certainly no rival. All that could be done by your enemies was to deprive you of a number of votes. Many of your friends were duped on that occasion. I will inform you how it was managed in Connecticut. On the day before the election Colonel [S. B.] Webb came on express to Hartford, sent, as he said, by Colonel Hamilton, &c. who, he assured us, had made an exact calculation on the subject, and found that New Jersey was to throw away three votes, I think, and Connecticut two, and all would be well. I exclaimed against the measure, and insisted that it was all a deception; but what could my single opinion avail against an express, armed with intelligence and calculations?

Hamilton played hardball.

Jeremiah Wadsworth wrote to Hamilton: "Our Votes were given agreeably to your wishes." It is to be noted here, Matteson says, that even in that early day the electors were not looked upon as entirely free agents. Hamilton, Madison, Carrington, Sedgwick, Trumbull, Wadsworth, none of them was an elector; all were, however, political leaders in their states, and their judgment evidently was potent upon the minds of the actual vote casters. Wadsworth's "our votes" meant that the vote of the state was settled before the presidential electors assembled. Adams's son or grandson wrote many years later: "What he [John Adams] did complain of, and very reasonably too, was, the secret effort made to reduce the votes for him everywhere." [16]

Adams's troubles began, anyway, after his election to a job which he was later to describe with considerable disgust as "the most insignificant office that the invention of man ever contrived, or his imagination conceived." Adams was the first victim of the vice-presidency. The man, who thought he was going to be King Washington's prime minister in the Senate, had the bad luck to be playing second fiddle to the biggest national hero in American history. It must have been torture for him in the Senate, what Nixon went through as Ike's number two. The veep could never figure out what his duties were.

[2]

On April 14, Washington heard a strange horse clattering up the serpentine drive. The clattering turned out to be the hoofbeats of the secretary of Congress, Charles Thomson. The ax had fallen. The trapdoor sprung. In the banquet hall of Mount

Vernon at about 1:00 P.M. Thomson gave him the latest election results:

> Sir,
> The president of the Senate chosen for the special occasion having opened and counted the votes of the Election in the presence of the Senate and House of Representatives, I was honored with the commands of the Senate to wait upon your Excellency with the information of your being elected to the office of Prefident of the United States of America. This commission was intrusted to me on account of my long being in the confidence of the late Congress and charged with the duties of one of the principal civil departments of government. I have now, sir, to inform you that the proofs you have given of your patriotism and of your readiness to sacrifice domestic separation and private enjoyments to preserve the liberty and promote the happiness of your country did not permit the two Houses to harbour a doubt of your undertaking this great, this important office to which you are called not only by the unanimous vote of the electors, but by the voice of America. I have it therefore in command to accompany you to New York where the Senate and House of Representatives are convened for the dispatch of public business. In executing this part of the commission where personal gratification coincides with duty I shall wait your time and be wholly governed by your convenience.[17]

The general, who had been denying he was a candidate for several years, whipped out his acceptance speech from his pocket (some say a drawer in the credenza):

> Sir, I have been long accustomed to entertain so great a respect for the opinion of my fellow-citizens, that the knowledge of their unanimous suffrages having been given in my favor, scarcely leaves me the alternative for an option. Whatever may have been my private feelings and sentiments, I believe I cannot give a greater evidence of my sensibility for the honor they have done me, than by accepting the appointment.
> I am so much affected by this fresh proof of my country's esteem and confidence, that silence can best explain my gratitude—while I realize the arduous nature of the task

which is conferred on me, and feel my inability to perform it, I wish there may not be reason for regretting the choice. All I can promise is, only that which can be accomplished by an honest zeal.[18]

The clearest sign that Washington knew the election results well in advance was a letter he wrote to General Knox in February shortly after the meeting of the Electoral College. He had seen an ad that "Superfine American Broadcloth" was on sale in New York. He had asked big Harry to buy him sufficient yardage for a suit, and while he was at it, make him a riding habit for Martha.[19] The candidate of the vested interests had decided to be inaugurated in a plain civilian suit, whether or not he received a campaign contribution from the American Broadcloth PAC.

[3]

The condemned man, sorry, the prefident-elect, left Mount Vernon at ten o'clock on the morning of April 16. His inaugural travel party consisted of Colonel David Humphreys, the Yale literary man who had moved into Mount Vernon as poet-in-residence, ad hoc speechwriter, and acting majordomo, and Tobias Lear, Harvard '83, Washington's first secretary. They rode in a coach with four horses, Matteson says,[20] "but there were also led horses for riding." One was a white horse for city travel. Washington always rode through cities on a white horse. It was an image thing.

Among those missing from the party was Mrs. Washington. Unlike the Bush campaign of 1988, nobody was asking "Where was George?" But the people should have been asking "Where was Martha?" She did not leave home until mid-May, Matteson says. She arrived in the nation's capital in June. This is most odd.

What's so important going on at Mount Vernon that she had to stay at home for six weeks before going to New York?

Maybe she had to wait for the decorator? They were delivering the wallpaper and she had to tell them where to put it up.

That's not woman's work. Washington did that kind of important thing.

Did he tell her, "Oh, it's nothing. You know, business. You'll only be bored," as many men today tell their wives about business meetings and conventions in far-off cities? What could be so interesting for Martha in New York anyway? Her husband is only being inaugurated as the new country's first prefident. Most wives I know of would be there even if they had to crawl North.

Didn't historians find it strange, the way Martha stayed away from the inaugural? How often does a man found a country or become a first prefident? It is a rather important time in the life of your average founding husband and his country.

When you think of first ladies today, like Nancy Reagan and Eleanor Roosevelt, Martha was really sort of uninvolved in his career, wasn't she? Or was she ideologically against democracy and all its trappings? Was she the sort of person who would say, in the privacy of the bed chamber, "I want to be queen"?

"But I can't do that, Patcy dearest. I have to be prefident."

"I don't care. If you love me, you'll make me queen . . . NOW."

Or did he even tell her he had been elected?

He had been saying so often and so passionately he was retiring. Maybe she hadn't kept up with the latest change in policy. What was it between the beloved couple that historians aren't telling us about?

Martha was always praised for her duty and devotion, and the way she was discommoding herself to be with her man several weeks a year during the black days of the war. The *Pennsylvania Packet* (May 26, 1789, p. 3) spoke for all when it hailed Martha Washington for having "contributed to relieve the cares of our beloved Chief, and to soothe the anxious moments of military concern."

She was a comfort to him, the historians all say. Staying at home. Not coming after him, seeing where he is every night, not pestering him, agreeing to stay at home, where he knows she'll be safe.

Martha missed all the preliminary inaugural "bawls," the celebrations and drinking bouts, from Alexandria to Baltimore, Philadelphia, Trenton. A trail of Madeira bottles marked the triumphant progression of the prefident-elect to New York. It gives one a hangover to read of the festivities en route to where he will soon be standing shakily on the balcony in New York, taking the oath of office with—and no one could blame him—a glazed expression.

How come historians didn't notice the six-week gap? They are sexists. They think history is made up only of things men do. The men make all those important speeches and write letters, but the woman's side is ignored.

At any rate, Martha, with her usual haste, didn't leave the plantation until May 16, giving the new prefident a head start to complete any pressing unfinished business in the nation's new capital, ample time to conduct his affairs, whatever they were.

As Gloomy George headed for his inaugural in New York, he may have wished that his mother had been there to see him now, if his wife couldn't be. He had said good-bye to her, for the last time, before he left Mount Vernon in April, probably on March 7, when he rode up to Fredericksburg to tell her the good news that he might have been elected, and if he had been, it would only be temporary. He would be retiring any day now.

This was the period when he had actually forbidden his mom to come to Mount Vernon. It would hurt his image, with all the important visitors like the Marchioness de Bréhan, the French minister's slut,* to have her wandering around in her negligee, or "dishabille," as he put it to the pipe-smoking, perhaps tobacco-chewing mother of the country. But the historians put it in a positive way.

"It was part of the independent nature of Mary Washington," Colonel Freeman says, "to live in her own establishment and to dress, eat, sleep, and manage her servants in her own way, even though her son was willing to do everything possible for her. In the same letter he had said frankly that he did not believe residence at Mount Vernon would ever 'answer [her] purposes in any shape whatsoever.' 23 The house was 'to be compared to a well resorted tavern, as scarcely any strangers who are going from

* The so-called Marchioness de Bréhan was accompanying her brother-in-law, the new French minister to the United States, Éléanor-François Élie, the Comte de Moustier, on the second of November, with her son and their escort, Victor Marie du Pont. 21 Washington previously had written the minister a letter on the possible development of trade between the United States and France, 22 a letter that was most carefully prepared because it was understood that de Moustier was not pleased with America. The minister and the marchioness tried Washington's legs and perhaps his patience by a seven-mile walk around Mount Vernon.

North to South, or from South to North, do not spend a day or two at it.' If she lived there, he said, she would always have to be dressed for company, or appear in 'dishabille,' or remain in her room."

At other times, he told her to just forget the idea of dropping by for a visit. She would not understand the people who were around him, and they would not understand her; she would be miserable in such society, and it would make him unhappy. That was no way to treat a mother, as my mother would have told George.

He would address her in his letters as "Honoured Madam." And that is in one of his intimate personal letters, responding to a complaining letter when she heard from his brother that he was volunteering for Braddock's command. "Dear Mother" was too sentimental for her son the colonel. When he wrote to her, Woodward says, he seemed to be addressing a public meeting.

There was a rift as large as the Cumberland Gap between the founding son and the founding mom. Maybe it was because he was always turning to some man for advice, never listening to his mother like a good son should, as my mother told me to do.

But he was too upwardly mobile. He was probably embarrassed by her. Remember, Mother Washington smoked a pipe, like Mammy Yokum in "L'i'l Abner." She also was a worse speller than he was in her letters, which were always harping to him and others how her son, the rich man, was neglecting his own mother's welfare. In 1787 she wrote to her other son John Augustine about George's neglect of his responsibility:

Dear Johnne,

I am going fast, and it, the time, is hard. I am borrowing a little Cornn—no Cornn in the Cornn house. I never lived soe, poore in my life. Was it not for Mr. French and your sister Lewis I should be almost starved, but I am like an old almanack quite out of date.

Mother Washington was not broke. She just said she was. George's mom was what one historian has called a "kvetch." At one time in the 1780s, she was accepting gifts from her neighbors. She complained so incessantly of her poverty that a movement was started in the Virginia Assembly to give the old lady a pension. When the news of this reached Washington, he wrote to a friend in the Assembly to stop the agitation by all means. He said that he was confident "that she has not a child that would not divide the last sixpence to relieve her from real distress. This she had been repeatedly assured of by me; and all of us, I am certain, would feel much hurt, at having our mother a pensioner, while we had the means of supporting her; but in fact she has ample income of her own."

Their relations were never warm.

And when he was running for prefident, she wasn't too impressed. I think she would have preferred him, all in all, to be a doctor.

His other official act before departing was, in effect, picking up his traveler's checks from the special interests. He was, as the expression goes today, overdrawn at the bank. Matteson says, "He was as always, after the Revolution, in need of current cash, and was forced to borrow in order to leave home from obligations and to have the funds necessary for the journey and the requirements of his exalted office." Not that there were many checks to pick up on the way North, as we shall see.

He would need, Colonel Freeman says, "£500 or £600 to pay pressing debts and the expenses of a journey to New York. On the very day the wheels of the new government were supposed to turn for the first time, March 4, Washington applied for a loan from a wealthy citizen of Alexandria, Richard Conway, the merchant prince, and offered security and 6 percent interest." [24]

Can you imagine a man who they say was the richest man in the country actually not having the wherewithal to get to his own inaugural? It's probably not indictable, but it doesn't look nice.

In August Washington confided to Dr. Craik: "I never felt the want of money so sensibly since I was a boy of 15 years old as I have done for the last twelve months and probably shall do for twelve months more to come." [25] To his humiliation he had to put off the sheriff of Fairfax County three times when that official came to collect the money due on Mount Vernon,[26] and he had received warning that his lands in Greenbriar County would be sold unless his taxes there were paid.[27] He could not remit the whole of what he owed Dr. Craik for medical attendance;[28] the rector of his church was to send in November for pew rent of five pounds, which should have been forwarded on August 29.[29]

George Washington hadn't thought of raising money by charging people $10,000 to have breakfast with him, as politicians do today. It sure would have helped balance his budget.

Colonel Freeman says the special reasons for Washington's more acute financial distress at this time were the failure of his grain crop and the necessity of laying out at least five hundred pounds for corn to make good the shortage.[30]

It didn't help, either, that he had a tendency to spend money like a drunken sailor. His continued extravagant living and unending entertainment, however, were campaign expenses, if he was running for anything.

And there was an inability to sell his Western lands at the kind of excess profit he thought reasonable.[31] He was, in effect, land rich and cash poor. Fortunately, the merchants of Alexandria, who were soon to receive the boondoggle of all time, in the placing of the federal district (the nation's capital) on its doorstep, helped him out in a neighborly way.

[4]

The first stop of the Washington Inaugural Express was at Alexandria, as Matteson says,[32] he being met some miles outside by an escort of citizens, and partaking of an early dinner at Wise's Tavern, with thirteen toasts, which set the tone and rate of alcoholic intake. The Inaugural train roared north on the momentum of the Madeira, practically flying into Baltimore.

The George Washington Schlepped Here Tour, as constitutional and legal historian Richard B. Bernstein refers to the first inaugural parade from Mount Vernon to New York, was a travelling political carnival show, everywhere a big hit. Every town Washington passed through was plastered with flags, emblems, slogans, and thirteen-toast politicians. Mounted escorts were sent out to receive him. At the sound of the clattering entourage, Schwartz says, applause; at the sight of the man himself, pandemonium. Then the addresses, the toasts, the fetes. Then the farewell, to the roar of crowds and cannon. As the procession worked its way North, the crowds grew bigger and the ceremonies more elaborate. Twenty thousand people witnessed his passage through Philadelphia.[33]

Colonel Freeman says the advance men who had come out from Philadelphia must have brought with them "a finely caparisoned white horse for the general, and acceptable mounts for Humphreys, Lear, and Secretary Thomson. These animals were provided in order that Washington might be seen by everyone when he entered Philadelphia and not remain half hidden from public view in his coach. He obediently went to the head of a column that steadily was growing longer, and from Chester he took the familiar road to the Lower Ferry Bridge across the Schuylkill. Ahead was the bridge at Gray's Ferry."[34] Then the prefident-elect beheld what the bridge owners, the brothers Gray, had planned as a surprise for him and, so it shouldn't be a total loss, as an advertisement for the crossing.

With the help of Charles Willson Peale, Colonel Freeman continues in awe, they had "adorned amazingly the unstable structure." At each end of the bridge was an arch of laurel; the sides were lined with more of that shrub and with cedar. The ferry boats and the ferry barge were anchored in the stream. All the approaches were graced with large billboards—one proclaimed "The New Era," another portrayed the rising sun of empire. A white standard expressed the motto "May Commerce Flourish," and a fourth, under a tremendous Liberty cap, was blazed with the familiar warning "Dont Tread on Me." Along the north side of the bridge were banners for each of the eleven states that had ratified the Constitution; on the south side, midway the crossing, the flag of the American Union rode high. Such a scene it was, an observer wrote in enthusiastic hyperbole, "that even the pencil of a Raphael could not delineate it."[35]

Washington observed, admired, and rode to the western end of the bridge. Just as he came under the first arch, a child in garlanded dress let go a wreath that descended, unobserved by the general, to a point not far above his head. One Philadelphia paper, Colonel Freeman says, reported that Angelica Peale, daughter of Charles Willson Peale, "lowered on the hero's brow a wreath of laurel." The detailed contemporary accounts in the newspapers did not mention Angelica by name. One journalist told of a "child, clad in white," who lowered the wreath. Another eyewitness report included reference to "a lad, beautifully ornamented with sprigs of laurel," who "let drop above the Hero's head, unperceived by him, a civic crown of laurel." Nothing in these descriptions warrants the statement sometimes made that the wreath was dropped *on* Washington's head. "He was spared that embarrassment," Colonel Freeman says in his footnote.[36] Another reporter said that as he passed under this structure a concealed mechanism was operated so that a wreath was lowered by a wire until it rested on Washington's head.[37]

That was the closest Washington ever got to being crowned. Philadelphia was going wild for Washington. After he crossed the river and came to the stretch between the Susquehanna and the city, Washington found "every fence, field and avenue" lined with people of every age and station. More cannon barked,* the church bells rang, vessels in the river ran up all their flags and joined in the salute, Colonel Freeman says.[39] He rode flawlessly, as always, and bowed again and again when spectators cheered or clapped their hands or shouted their welcome. He kept astride the white horse, down Market and Second streets to the City Tavern, the prefident-elect's old stomping ground.

A great dinner had been prepared at the expense of private citizens, the Mount Vernon machine's Philadelphia chapter, who invited "all the clergy and respectable strangers in the city." Approximately 250 men gathered at three o'clock while a band played and waiters uncorked the wine for fourteen toasts. Federalist toasts, stout and uncompromising—"the members of the late General Convention" and "May those who have opposed the new Constitution be converts, by the experience of its happy effects" and a final "Government without oppression, and liberty without licentiousness!"

Among those joining the fun in Philadelphia was Washington's dear Eliza Powel, the mayor's wife, who has been called by Colonel Flexner "his favorite female friend." He had stayed at her house whenever possible during the war. And she never stopped sending him those enigmatic notes, dear to the hearts of historians and the Mount Vernon Ladies Association.†

---

*Jacob Hiltzheimer, the Philadelphia livery stable owner and a Mount Vernon machine stalwart, who at that moment was in the town of Bristol on his way home from Trenton, reported that even at such a distance he could hear "the great guns" in Philadelphia sounding their welcome.[38]

† A typical cryptic message from dear friend Eliza to the office of the Prefident of the United States:[40]

Dear Sir,
   Feeling myself incapable of nourishing an Implaccable Resentment; and in conformity with your letter & dispassionate Judgement—I have after maturely considering all that passed Yesterday, determined to dine with you Tomorrow, when I will endeavor to meet your Ideas with Fortitude.
   With Sentiments of Respect & Affection,
      I am Sir
         Your sincere Friend
         Eliza Powel

Also fighting to get a piece of the social action was Mrs. William Bingham, the wife of one of the wealthiest speculators in lands and public securities, and a Federalist sachem. She was the great society leader of Philadelphia, which was the social and financial center of the country, who was delighted to know the government would soon be settling there for a ten-year stay.

Also a leading Federalist, Mrs. Bingham reportedly was a slender, shimmering beauty, a skittish lady who shocked her puritanical guests with dainty little oaths that would have reminded soldiers of the Monmouth Courthouse performance by the new prefident-elect. Said to be a superb hostess, and a woman of culture and political acumen, she was also, it seems, an admirer of the sedate Washington. And she even tried to admire Martha, so thoroughly were she and her husband bound up in Federalist politics. Mrs. Bingham was a great value to the Federalist cause, to the party of high finance and speculation. Her dinners, balls and other social events were an instrument of policy, keeping wavering delegates or Senators in line during the first hundred days of the Washington administration.

Many a woman he danced with or who had fantasies about him in the long campaign had shown up for the party. Every flirty dirty one who had rejected him in his salad days now had the thrill of realizing she had cast out the first prefident.

Washington remained to the end of the dinner in Sin City and, "as usual, captivated every heart," as Colonel Freeman says, "though he must have been weary long before the last clinking of the glasses. From the tavern he went directly to the home of Robert Morris and probably to the very chamber he had occupied in the summer of 1787, when he had wondered what sort of government the members of the Convention would offer the country." [41]

With the formation of the national government, Morris went to New York as senator from Pennsylvania. To the other Pennsylvania senator, William Maclay, the diarist, Morris was "the greatest blackguard in the way (of depravity) I ever heard open a mouth," and John Adams, seeing him at what he called "the Republican Court," was revolted by him and his cronies. His senatorial career was mainly notable for his unsuccessful effort to have the national capital built on land he owned along the Delaware.

The overnight visit by the new prefident was such a serious business that Wee Bobbie, the First Host, stayed away from his desk in the Senate from April 11 to May 12. [42]

Well, I say it's lucky the prefident-elect didn't fall in the Susquehanna and drown. Or be busted by the New Jersey State Police DWI patrol on the way to Trenton, after partaking of the splendors of Bobbie Morris's house and cellar.

The crowning achievement of the Big Schlep took place at this wettest Battle of Trenton. As Matteson says, "again there was a triumphal arch, this time on thirteen pillars, erected under the direction of the ladies of the town, who attended on the bridge. As the General passed beneath the arch an original song was rendered by a female chorus." There were thirteen young maidens and prominent matrons of Trenton, each dressed up to represent one of the thirteen states. They had come at General Washington as he crossed the bridge, as if from a twin-flanking enfilade from either side of the roadways, these little girls in white, young ladies in spring costume, and the most prominent matrons of Trenton in living exemplification of the words written on the arch: "The Hero Who Defended the Mothers Will Protect the Daughters."[43] Schwartz explains, "The slogan reminded those present of the atrocities committed by British soldiers against American women, and of the American soldiers' determination to 'free the land from rapine, devastation, and burnings, and female innocence from brutal lust and violence.' "[44]

And then the white-robed choir of ladies serenaded him with a ballad as they strewed blossoms in his path:

> Virgins fair, and Matrons grave,
> Those thy conquering arms did save,
> Build for thee triumphal bowers
> Strew, ye fair, his way with flowers—
> Strew your Hero's way with flowers.[45]

The Trenton poem was written for the occasion by Mrs. Richard Stockton, noted Washington lover and poetess, whose husband, The Signer, is remembered for the gas station named for him on the New Jersey Turnpike (our state's highest honor).

She had previously sent Washington some verses about himself as the national hero, Woodward says. His reply to her letter accompanying the verses is one of the few epistles in which he comments on a literary subject. He wrote:

> Fiction is to be sure the very life and soul of Poetry—
> all Poets and Poetesses have indulged in the free and

indisputable use of it, time out of mind. And to oblige you to make such an excellent Poem on such a subject, without any materials but those of simple reality, would be as cruel as the Edict of Pharaoh which compelled the children of Israel to manufacture Bricks without the necessary ingrediants.

Martha would have loved it, especially that white-robed choir of nubile New Jersey maidens.

The toasting and celebrations continued all the way to the barges, across the Upper New York Bay. As they approached Bedloe's Island on the left, Colonel Freeman says,[46] a finely handled sloop came up on the starboard bow, under full sail. When she was close in, Washington saw preparations aboard her, and then in the wind he heard a familiar tune with new words—"God Save the King" with five stanzas of welcome and of praise directed to him.[47] Washington and his party lifted their hats; the gentlemen aboard the sloop returned the compliment,[48] while the sopranos and the contraltos doubtless beamed. This was not the end of song. From another craft, which pulled directly to the stern of the barge, the foremost of about a dozen male passengers leaned forward and handed the coxswain a number of copies of an ode, which the gentlemen on the rear boat began immediately to render in four parts.[49] A few minutes later, porpoises began to play around the prow of the barge[50] as if these forefathers of Flipper wished to do honor to the tall man in the cocked hat, the blue suit and the buff underdress. Not until the eighty-eight pianos playing Gershwin in the 1984 Olympics in L.A. had America had such a production number.

In the welcoming procession, also a predecessor of the Op Sail of the 1980s, was the schooner *Columbia*, with the revolutionary poet Philip Freneau on the bridge as master. Freneau's ship was "dressed and decorated in the most superb manner," the *Daily Advertiser* said on April 24, 1789 (p. 3).

Close now to the landing, Colonel Freeman says, Washington looked at thousands and thousands of New Yorkers. The city virtually stopped work for the day;[51] everyone crowded in at the fort to see the prefidential barge dock. When cannon of the Battery fired another salute of thirteen guns, the spectators gave three huzzahs and then nearly all of them started to Murray's Wharf, at the bottom of Wall Street, to see the general. So great was the din, after the landing salute had been fired, that probably few heard the church bells, which loyally were to be rung for half an hour. The smoothly piloted chief executive barge tied up sometime between two and three o'clock; the committees climbed out and started up the carpeted steps, the rails of which had been draped with crimson. Then, after a fitting pause, Washington went ashore and mounted to the landing, where the top New York politician, Governor George Clinton, and lesser state, county and city officials welcomed and congratulated him. Washington thanked them with his dignified regard for each individual.[52]

It was, as Elijah Fisher of the commander's guard might have concurred, a real "bawl." "The whole city of all descriptions were out to meet him," wrote Samuel B. Webb, "and in all my life I never saw such unfeigned joy in every countenance."[53]

Advance man Joseph Jones wrote Madison on May 10: "The General's journey to N. York shews the people still retain the same respect and veneration for his person and character they heretofore entertained and altho' he is little captivated by ceremonial distinctions yet he could not fail of being sensibly gratified by such universal demonstrations of affection as were exhibited through his progress, among them none I conceive could be more pleasing than his reception at Trenton bridge."

Washington's accounts state simply that the journey cost him $182.78.[54] It really moved him.

[5]

There is universal joy in New York on this April 30. Inauguration Day. The capital had been New York City since 1785. The dying Confederate Congress could not agree on where the new country's capital should be, so they left it in New York City for the time being to get the country started, waiting for the first Congress to decide this matter. And what a deal the Mount Vernon machine struck the next year (1790).

New York first (for one year), then Philadelphia (for ten years), and finally they all move to a tract of mosquito-infested land not too far from Alexandria, where the prefident owns some property, but his friends own lots and lots. What a wonderful compromise. Three different real-estate markets boom. Hamilton and Madison and Jefferson worked it out with the Philadelphia and New York and Virginia interests. What will the new federal district be called? Oz? Ruritania? How about Washington?

The town quivered with the roar of cannon, and the golden voices of bells. Flags and ribbons flashing in the breeze. Artists sketching on pads of paper. People clinging to roofs. Carriages creeping perilously through the jam of humanity. Wall-to-wall people. The city had virtually come to a standstill, closed down for the occasion, except for the taverns and shops.

There was a boom in inaugural souvenirs. Ye shoppes had new inaugural tankards with remarkable unlikenesses of the prefident with a big nose, appropriate to toast "the Greatest Man on Earth." There were George Washington inaugural blazer buttons made out of silver (I have a set myself, reproductions from the Smithsonian), and cuff links.

The merchandising blitz included Washington watch fobs, inaugural plates, textiles, and inaugural medals.* There were Washington brooches being worn by fashionable, politically active ladies. Many contained lockets of the president's hair.

Thousands of citizens, so dense in their assemblage as to make movement difficult, Schwartz says,[55] pressed for a sight of their hero. A few people were heard to say that they could die content, having cast their eyes at last on the savior of their country. Others shuddered at the sublimity of the occasion itself. The *Gazette of the United States* said it was "beyond any descriptive powers of the pen to do justice to—How universal—and how laudable the curiosity—How sincere—and how expressive the sentiments of respect and veneration." [56]

The people were thrilled and awed. "I have seen him!" exclaimed a young lady in the crowd, "and though I had been entirely ignorant that he was arrived in the city, I should have known at a glance that it was General Washington: I never saw a human being that looked so great and noble as he does. I could fall down on my knees before him." [57]

At fifty-seven, the man who had them on their knees still was an awesome, imposing figure, nothing like the picture most of us have of him. This is the 1796 portrait by Gilbert Stuart, drawn, not

---

* Examples of the first inaugural merchandise—the start of what Jean Shepherd calls slob art—are on display at the University of Hartford Political Memorabilia Museum.

well, from life after two administrations, when he almost died from illness twice and was totally exhausted and beaten down, trying to mediate between his prime ministers without portfolio Hamilton, Madison, Adams, and Jefferson.

He was always careful about his appearance and had started considering what his costume would be at the inaugural, as I've explained, even before he knew he would be there. The costume chosen was the American-made brown broadcloth suit, spun at Hartford,* that he asked General Knox about, starting a precedent in free inaugural clothing we thought may have started with Nancy Reagan.

It was a political statement as well as a fashion statement. The suit also turned out to be a political favor, arranged for by Jeremiah Wadsworth, representative-elect from Connecticut, who was in New York conducting closed hearings with widows of Revolutionary War heroes, starting with Kitty Greene. He had used his political influence with the Mount Vernon machine to get the prefident-elect to wear the cloth of a Hartford mill. They, in turn, could now affix to their advertisements a note, something to the effect of being "purveyors of suits to His Mightiness the Prefident" (or "We Gave him the Suit on his Back").

Wearing American broadcloth was designed to show the administration's support for American business. It was also a homespun way for the administration to re-proclaim its belief in American liberty, since the buttons had a wingspread eagle. The American-made nature of the garment was proclaimed proudly by every newspaper.

Little was said about the new prefident's white silk stockings, from London.

The rest of the costume of the homespun chief executive included silver shoe buckles, while at his side there hung a steel-hilted sword. His hair was powdered and worn in a bag, or queue, behind, which indicated his continuing ties with the nation's hairdressers (the Mr. Charlotte vote).

*

* Daniel Hinsdale from the Hartford manufactory wrote Washington on March 23 that he was sending "a pattern of fine Cloth of our Fabrick which the Company flatter themselves Your Excellency will Receive as a Token of their Respect & Esteem." Washington on April 8 acknowledged the receipt of the cloth, with "best thanks" and praise for its quality, as well as pleasure over the dawning "spirit of industry economy and patriotism" which the making of such fabrics in America indicated.[58]

As the prefident-elect stood on the balcony of Federal Hall looking out at the gathered multitude at the corner of Wall and Broad streets, his thoughts may have gone back to the week's banquets since his arrival without Martha. He was the adored hero-general-prefident, the lionized rock star of the century, idolized as no political figure, returning war hero, or recipient of a ticker-tape parade up lower Broadway had ever been.

We have no special information on Washington's actions during the week that ensued before the inauguration, Matteson says, curiously, except that he received many calls of respect from congressmen, officials, and others; paid calls of ceremony on the congressmen, at least; and even this early was made aware of the necessity of scheduling his time. Maclay mentions the call on himself, the general coming on horseback and not sitting down.

"I had dressed and was about to set out," Maclay writes in his diary for April 28, 1789, "when General Washington the greatest Man in the World paid me a visit. I met him at the foot of the stairs. We asked him to take a seat. He excused himself on Acct. of the number of his visits. We accompanyed him to the door. He made us complaisant bows, one before he mounted and the other as he went away on horseback." [59]

When you are founding a country, I tell you, there isn't time to sit down, much less lie down.

He may have retraced his footsteps to all the places he had slept in New York City, mostly without Martha, who was usually at home, not beside her man. And his thoughts probably went to his plow and his fig tree and his vine, to which he would be returning within days or weeks, as soon as he got this colt of a country on its feet.

But now it was time for him to go cheerlessly as to the gallows, as he spoke and wrote of his new job.

The prefident-elect's preparation for the moment had begun early that day, as Colonel Freeman says. "By the time he had completed his toilet and had eaten his breakfast, the bells of city churches began to ring, some of them merrily at first and then all of them solemnly in a summons to prayer at nine or nine-thirty o'clock. The general and his assistants doubtless listened sympathetically, but they were busy with last-minute details that had to be set in order before the ceremonies began."

Washington's inaugural address was not a concern, Colonel Freeman says. It was in final form, ready for delivery. He had prepared for his first inaugural a long statement of needed legislation. He (or, probably, David Humphreys, the staff poet) had written it some weeks before at Mount Vernon for presentation to Congress. History would have called it the First First Hundred Days. It would have taken that long to read. But his advisers had him throw it out. In its place, there was a new, shorter, digest version. It was a paper that could be read at unhurried pace in less than twenty minutes.

The address was largely personal, with one recommendation and that one carefully couched. No further change in the text was considered now. The sheets of the digest version of the speech were folded and in the coat pocket of the specially-made-in-the-USA inaugural brown suit.

Nothing went smoothly. There was a lack of planning and central organization at the inaugural festivities. After all, they had never done it before. If the inaugural had been on TV, there would have been a lot of dead air, interrupted by comments from anchorman to correspondents: "Dan, where is he? What's going on now?"

"Walter, we're down here on the floor of the Senate," Dan might have said. "There is not a sign of General Washington. He was expected an hour ago. Back to you, Walt."

There had been days of parliamentary maneuvering, and intricate debates about who, what, where, and when the swearing-in would take place. Small details were forgotten such as a Bible. The new country was improvising.

"Walter," the voice might have broken in, "the senators are finally leaving for the Federal Hall balcony upstairs."

Cut to the balcony. "Jeremiah, what's happening up there?"

"Walt, we're on the balcony still waiting for the general."

A remote at his house at No. 3 Cherry Street, the first executive mansion, now a pier of the Brooklyn Bridge, would show the greatest man on earth and his party piling into the executive carriage. There would be lots of talk between the commentators about the arms on his carriage. And then the cameras would have followed the prefident-elect's party through the jammed narrow streets of what is now the financial district to Wall and Broad Streets.

On the balcony, when the invited dignitaries and guests were in their latest assigned places, as Colonel Freeman says, "Washington perceived that the historic moment was at hand. He arose and came forward again, close to the iron rail and in unobstructed view of the crowd." Opposite him stood Chancellor Robert R. (Steamboat) Livingston, patron saint and leader of the Hudson River

Family section of the Mount Vernon Machine, who had cast his vote for Washington for general in the 1775 Congress. Samuel Otis, the small, short secretary of the Senate, lifted the Bible and the red cushion from the table and took his station between Washington and the chancellor. Otis stood with his face to the throng; the judge and the president were in profile when seen from the street. After the briefest of pauses, when Washington saw that the judge was ready, he put his right hand on the Bible.* "Do you solemnly swear," asked the chancellor, "that you will faithfully execute the office of President of the United States and will, to the best of your ability, preserve, protect, and defend the Constitution of the United States?"

"I solemnly swear," Washington answered—and repeated the oath. Reverently he added, "So help me God." He bent forward as he spoke and, before Otis could lift the Bible to his lips, he kissed the book.

"It is done," Livingston announced, and, turning to the crowd, he made a broad gesture with his hand and shouted, "Long live George Washington, Prefident of the United States!" The roar of the throng came back, like instant replay. "Joyful and sustained," Col. Freeman says. Livingston's cry was taken up, and with it came clearly, "God bless our Prefident." Washington bowed. The answering cheers were louder and more emotional than ever. While the rejoicing continued, many eyes were lifted to the cupola of the Federal Hall, where the flag was being raised. It was a signal to the Battery, which answered quickly with the bang-bang of thirteen guns. Soon this was amplified: According to Colonel Freeman, *Galveston*, the Spanish sloop of war in the harbor, loosed her fire. In the intervals of this bombardment, keener ears than those of Washington heard again the church bells of the city.

The prefident had not intended to address the crowd, as Colonel Freeman says, and, "if he had planned to do so, he could not have made his voice audible above the congratulatory din." He bowed his acknowledgments, which evoked even wilder cheers.

With the ovation still ringing in his ears, the new prefident was whisked off stage, back down the stairs to the Senate chamber to deliver his inaugural address. And guess what. The doors were shut. There were no TV cameras. The show was over.

---

* A large, elegant one, hastily procured at the last moment, Matteson says, from Saint John's Masonic Lodge nearby.

There was no inaugural address for the public to be bored by. It was carried in the newspapers a few weeks later. There was no inaugural parade. There wasn't a series of inaugural balls that night. Somebody threw a party a week later. It made some of the diaries, the equivalent of the Liz Smith columns of the day.

From inside reports, since published, we know what happened behind the closed doors of the Senate.

The crowd had given three cheers, Senator William Maclay wrote in his diary.[60] Then Pref. Washington took his seat on the dais and waited for the members and their guests to resume their places.

After a pause, he got on his feet to read his inaugural address. The assembled rose with him and, after he had bowed again, the crowd sat down in awe and respect. "Fellow Citizens of the Senate and House of Representatives," Washington began in a deep, low voice and with manifest embarrassment, "Among the vicissitudes incident to life, no event could have filled me with greater anxiety than that of which the notification was transmitted by your order. . . ."[61]

It was to be another one of his spellbinders!

Colonel Freeman was very moved by the speech. But the reviews were mixed.

During his inaugural address Washington appeared to be flustered, or overcome with emotion. Woodward says he kept putting his hand in his pockets and taking them out again. His hands trembled, and his papers got mixed.

He seemed to be in the grip of stage fright, Schwartz says. His gestures were awkward; his voice barely audible; his delivery flawed by an apparent inability to make out the words of his own prepared speech.

Washington had not yet learned ease, if he ever did, Matteson says, as a speaker, and the solemnity of the occasion had evidently affected him deeply.

Maclay, who was there, called the 1,500-word address "heavy." He wrote in his diary:

[T]his great Man was agitated and embarrassed more than ever he was by the levelled Cannon or pointed Musket. He trembled, and several times could scarce make out to read, tho it must be supposed he had often read it before. He put part of the fingers of his left hand, into the side, of what I think the Taylors call the fall, of his Breetches. Changing the paper into his left hand, after some time, he then did the same with some of the fingers of his right hand. When he came to the Words *all the World,* he made a flourish with his right hand, which left rather an ungainly impression. I sincerely, for my part, wished all set ceremony in the hands of the dancing Masters. And that this first of Men, had read off, his address, in the plainest Manner without ever taking his Eyes off From, the paper. For I felt hurt, that he was not first in every thing.[62]

Madison loved it. Of course, he wrote it. Historians say he was the one who convinced Washington to cast aside the first draft of the longer inaugural speech by Humphreys.

Madison also drafted Congress's reply to the inaugural. Previously, he had sent a note inviting the prefident to deliver it. Then he drafted the acceptance for the president, and the Congress's reply. Jemmy was one very busy man in that Congress.

Did the new prefident warn them about the coming of parties, the continuing absence of which was a prime goal of his in the coming out of retirement? What this country needed was no parties. "Let George do it" was his platform in 1789.

The first inaugural address in history was a simple statement of generalities, about the future of the nation, interlaced with personal remarks such as his being inadequate to the task at hand. He took the liberty of reminding the two houses in the senate chamber that they were welcoming to office a man of "inferior endowments"—the Washington touch.

Ineptitude, self-depreciation—those were his *shticks.* And the American people loved him for it. As his career as a general was a triumph of mediocrity, his inaugural address seemed to say he would be applying the same skills to government.

The most significant part of the speech was his first fiscal recommendation. He told Congress that he wanted no compensation as chief executive, desiring only that they pick up his expenses during the first administration. He "must decline as inapplicable to myself, any share in the personal emoluments, which may be indispensably included in a permanent provision for the Executive Department; and must accordingly pray that the preliminary estimates for the Station in which I am placed, may, during my continuance in it, be limited to such actual expenditures as the public good may be thought to require."

It was the same deal he had offered the country after his election as general. He was, again, *volunteering* without pay. The offer was especially interesting in the light of his current financial condition—that is, the shortage of ready cash back home. Congress—perhaps having gotten around to reading his wartime expense sheets, or having noticed he had already eighteen servants* in the executive mansion at No. 3 Cherry Street, a tiny dwelling, where it was said they were so numerous they bumped into each other—declined the generous offer. There was probably nothing to prevent him from turning back into the treasury such amounts as he considered excessive. But, as Matteson says, he never did this, and indeed declared that the salary was "inadequate to the expense of living." [63]

Words as usual had failed him. His inaugural address was a disaster by today's artistic standards, but it didn't hurt him politically. That his hands shook and they couldn't hear his voice was interpreted as a positive.

"It was a very touching scene," wrote Representative Fisher Ames, then the greatest orator in Congress. "His aspect grave, almost to sadness; his modesty, actually shaking; his voice deep, a little tremulous, and so low as to call for close attention; added to the series of objects presented to the mind, and overwhelming it, produced emotions of the most affecting kind upon the members. I, Pilgarlic,† sat entranced. It seemed to me an allegory in which virtue was personified, and addressing those whom she would make her votaries. Her power over the heart was never greater, and the illustration of her doctrine by her own example was never more perfect."

Washington, a self-controlled and resolute military commander, had lost his composure during a rite of passage to induct him into his nation's highest and most powerful civil office, as Schwartz says. [64] "The flaw in his performance at this ritual, as the audience saw it, betokened not stage fright or embarrassment but awe—and the revelation of this sentiment induced the audience

---

* Plus a valet, a coachman, a secretary, an assistant, and three aides.

† A member of the peeled garlic family.

to recognize in Washington its own respect for the sanctity of the station he was about to assume. Not polish but sincerity, not boldness but diffidence, is what Americans found appealing in Washington's inaugural performance."

"Washington's traits were superior to the inflations of vanity, and they furnish a model of humility," the Reverend Abiel Holmes told his Boston congregation later, as a eulogy. Meekness is a virtue he shared with Moses, Alexander MacWhorter said before his listeners.[65]

As I said, the man couldn't lose for winning. Whatever he does wrong becomes a positive. We hadn't seen anything like that until President Reagan coined the phrase "There you go again, bringing up the past," during the Carter–Reagan debates of 1980, and the Reagan first inaugural address, in which he promised to balance the budget by increasing defense spending and cutting taxes.

How was he going to do that?

As Rich Little said: "Two sets of books."

I, myself, think he did rather well, under the circumstances. The scene was enough to make anybody nervous, even a demigod. The most self-assured man would be apprehensive. And Washington was known to lack confidence when he faced new challenges. They gave him the shakes. He told his diary that the "display of boats . . . the decorations of the ships, the roar of cannon, and the loud acclamations of the people . . . filled my mind with sensations as painful (considering the reverse of this scene, which may be the case after all my labors to do good) as they are pleasing."[66]

In a similar manner, the British kings were not always spellbinding in their public addresses. King George III, who still had quite a following in the old country, spoke with a German accent. King George VI, highly popular in our time, stuttered.

Eventually, Washington solved the problem of speaking in public. His famous farewell address of September 17, 1796—one of Hamilton's masterpieces—was a one-page statement sent directly to the newspapers (the *Philadelphia Daily American Advertiser* had it first), which printed it without fumbling hands, a radical but effective solution to packaging the prefident in the media.

[6]

Spellbinding or not, what New York was seeing that day was more a coronation, albeit a republican coronation, than an inauguration, and the historians have been afraid to tell us. Not knowing about it has caused problems to this day. From the earliest days (1775), when he took command of the army in Cambridge, Washington looked majestic. "Not a king from Europe," reported the *Morning Post and Daily Advertiser* of London, "but would look like valet de chambre by his side."

William Sullivan, the lawyer who had many opportunities for observing Washington, said of his royal demeanor, "His mode of speaking was slow and deliberate, not as though he was in search of fine words, but that he might utter those adapted to his purpose. . . . His deportment was invariably grave; it was sobriety that stopped short of sadness. His presence inspired a veneration, and a feeling of awe, rarely experienced in the presence of any man."

He was, as we have already seen, the kind of man who doesn't shake hands, who has no gossip, who is not at all anxious to hear what one has to say, who listens to your best jokes with a solemn face, and says coolly, "Is that so?" That was Washington. No wonder he was awe-inspiring.[67]

Who would be surprised to learn that after fourteen years of veneration the likes of which were unprecedented and perhaps unjustifiable, given his war record, he thought he *was* king? He didn't need James McHenry, his erstwhile military secretary, reminding him on March 29, 1789: "You are now a king, under a different name; and, I am well satisfied, that sovereign prerogatives have in no age or country been more honorable obtained; or that, at any time they will be more prudently or wisely exercised. . . . That you may reign long and happy over us, and never for a moment cease to be the public favorite is a wish that I can truely say is congenial to my heart."[68]

This sort of talk could go to a prefident's head. There were young colonels who wanted him to be king. At the critical juncture, at Newburgh in 1782, when mutiny was soon to be threatened by the officers, Colonel Nicola, who is described by Schwartz[69] as "a patriot with a distinguished record of service against the British," outlined to Washington in writing the merits of monarchy, and recommended to Washington that he allow himself to be crowned king of America. He received a fast and stinging reply. The colonel's plan was viewed by the would-be king "with abhorrence and reprehended with severity."[70] But no mention of the letter was made to Congress, nor to any private party.

King Washington hadn't turned the colonel in, the way he ratted on the Reverend Duche, who had written a similar letter in 1779.

Pseudoroyalty was trendy. There was a leading newspaper called the *Gazette of the United States*, a semi-weekly which started up in April 1789 in New York. It was the first of the national papers, the grandfather of *USA Today*, under the editorship of a crusading, fearless journalist named John Fenno, fearless except maybe when it came to George Washington. His paper viewed Washington as a god as well as a king. At the mere mention of Washington, Fenno would break into a poem. Typical utterances were an eleven-stanza "ode" styled "The Visitation," said to have been written soon after Yorktown (May 16, 1789, p. 3); and an "ode" sung at a meeting of the Ancient and Honorable Artillery of Boston with this extraordinary quatrain (June 10, 1789, p. 2):

> Fill the bowl, fill it high
> First born son of the sky,
> May he never, never die
> Heaven shout, Amen.

Absurd as much of this now seems, Fenno was by no means the sole culprit. It seems to have been overlooked, Colonel Freeman says, that other editors went as far as he did, though less persistently. A few examples for closet monarchist-hunters are: *Maryland Journal* (Baltimore), Apr. 24, 1789, p. 4, a ninety-one-line "ode" to Washington; *Daily Advertiser*, May 8, p. 2, copied in Fenno's issue of May 13, 1789, p. 2, a seven-stanza poem in honor of the prefident; *Daily Advertiser*, June 26, 1789, p. 2, a fifty-eight-line effusion by a "young lady of New York" on Washington's arrival there. The climax was:

> The man's divine—let angels write his name
> In the bright records of eternal fame.[71]

Fenno and the *Gazette* regularly addressed Mrs. Washington as "Lady Washington." And when Martha came to New York, the principles of the court were applied in a list of "the principal ladies of the city" who, "with the earliest attention and respect, paid their devoirs to the amiable consort of our beloved President." Fenno began with "The Lady of His Excellency the Governor" and proceeded with "Lady Stirling, Lady Mary Watts, Lady Kitty Duer, La Marchioness de Brehan, the Ladies of the Most Hon. Mr. Langdon, and the Most Hon. M. Dalton, the Mayoress"— and only at this point did he drop to plain "Mrs." in naming the wives of New Yorkers and of members of Congress who called on the "President's consort."

Think of what pressure there must have been inside the summer White House (Mount Vernon) or No. 3 Cherry Street. Any wife who comfortably accepts being called Lady, as if it is her due, can only wonder how long it will be until she is promoted up the scale. There was no future in it for a Virginia farmer's upwardly mobile chubby little rich wife.

Admittedly, George Washington had a taste for grandiloquent titles. When he was a mere militia colonel in backwoods Virginia he was calling himself "Colonel of the Virginia Regiment & Commander in Chief of all Forces Now Raised & to be Raised for the Defence of This His Majesty's Colony." [72]

It's ridiculous, of course, pure rubbish, to say that Washington dreamed of being king when he grew up. One can argue that he thought titles were a good thing. The people should respect their leader, and titles helped. At most, it was just, as his good friend Gouverneur Morris declared, that an "inordinate love of fame was Washington's greatest moral weakness."

There was no chance he would be king. He was almost allergic to such proposals. Besides, being called "King George" would be political suicide. (If his Christian name had been Melvin, Sidney, or Wanda . . . who knows?)

Still, there was a lot of formality about the first administration. Washington did not say "nay" to being called "His Mightiness the President of the United States," as advocated by John Adams.* The speaker of the House laughed at this title, and was never forgiven by Washington. It was finally decided to call him simply "The President of the United States."

No matter, Woodward says, titles were of rubber and there

---

* John Adams had been first in the running for prime minister, as he originally perceived his role as vice-president. But because of his pushing for titles such as "His Mightiness," his laughing stock rose in the first administration, but not his workload.

were plenty of people to stretch them. Some called Washington "Mr. Prefident"; others continued to prefer "His Excellency"; and still others went as far as to say "His Majesty."

Hamilton believed that "the public good requires as a primary object the dignity of the office should be supported," Schwartz says. Mindful of the negative reactions they might arouse, Hamilton nevertheless recommended that certain ceremonial forms followed by European courts be adopted in carrying out the affairs of the American presidency. Prominent among these forms was the levee, an arrangement for receiving visitors that required the president to appear weekly for half an hour and, as Hamilton put it, "converse cursorily on indifferent subjects with such persons as shall strike his attention and at the end of that half hour disappear." There were also weekly tea parties and official dinners, all formal affairs whose every detail was reported in the Federalist press and read with great interest.[73] It was like the Royal Calandar in the *Times* of London.

The first presidential levee, or reception, must have been an awkward affair. It was arranged by Colonel Humphreys, the administration's poet and image-maker. The scene: People standing around the sides of a room, gentlemen and ladies in full dress. Humphreys enters the door, which is flung wide open by flunkies, and announces: "The Prefident of the United States." Washington enters, and everybody curtsies. All remain standing in silence. Washington goes around the room, stopping before each person and saying a few words.

That is the way it was, and it displeased Washington. When it was over he said to Humphreys, "By God, you've taken me in once, but you shall never do it again." After that his receptions were not so ceremonious, but they were never informal.[74]

The honeymoon ended early. On June 15, 1789, only three months into the first administration, an observer in New York's *Daily Advertiser* complained that "Levees, Drawing Rooms &c. are not such strange, incomprehensible distant things as we have imagined; and I suppose, that in a few years, we shall have all the paraphernalia yet wanting to give the superb finish to the grandeur of our AMERICAN COURT!"[75] As the end of Washington's first term approached, the antimonarchist antilevee tempest grew more intense. In the *National Gazette,* one "Cornelia" in capitals spoke of "THE DRAWING ROOM" before exhorting readers to "fashion men to virtue, but not to the servility and adulation of royalty."[76] As another correspondent a month later in the same newspaper put it:

> It appears from some late publications, that a new order of citizens has been created in the United States, consisting only of the *officers* of the federal government.—The privileges of this order, it is said, consist in sharing, exclusively, in the profits of the 25,000 dollars a year allowed for the Prefident's table, and in the honor of gazing upon him once a week at his levees.—It remains only to give this new order a name, and assign it a proper coat of arms and insignia; I shall therefore propose that it be *called the most noble order of the goose.*[77,78]

"The creatures that surround him," William Maclay, the Harrisburg lawyer and first senator from Pennsylvania, said in his *Journal*, "would place a crown on his head, that they may have the handling of its jewels."[79]

What ultimately may have saved the prefidency was Washington's infertility, or birth control measures he practiced, as I like to think, or whatever method he used for not having a line of dukes or dukettes. For, as John Adams was heard to grumble in 1787, contemplating the on-rushing Washington prefidential express steamroller, if the great man had a child of his own, he or she would be "demanded for marriage by one of the royal families of France or England, perhaps by both. So great an impression would this invitation make on the pride and vanity of Americans, Adams thought, that every precept of republicanism would be sacrificed to its acceptance."[80]

The country to this day does seem royalty deprived. Why did the American public go bonkers over the visit of the royal couple—everybody's favorite ex-kindergarten teacher and her unemployed husband with big ears—in 1985? They are as American as English muffins.

Robert Morley, then British Airways spokes-fat-person, speaking to David Hartman on "Good Morning, America" the morning of the Di-Charles wedding, said, "You will be back into the Empire in twenty years." I sometimes think it will be sooner.

[7]

B ut I digress.

Martha finally did arrive in the nation's capital on May 27, a month or so after the inaugural festivities started, but she didn't get into the social whirl. Lady Washington arrived with Molly Morris, the wife of the Patriarch Financier and prefidential counselor, who shortly will be on the threshold of debtors' prison, Robert Morris. The First Lady did not seem to like New York and its prefidential splendor. She wrote: "I lead a very dull life here and know nothing that passes in the town. I never goe to any publick place,—indeed I think I am more like a state prisoner than anything else, there is certain bounds set for me which I must not depart from—and as I cannot doe as I like I am obstinate and stay at home a great deal." [81]

What was the prefident doing while Martha imagined she was a state prisoner? He conducted his affairs, whatever they may have been.

He had to fight off job seekers. These had not taken seriously his denials of being a candidate and had been applying for years for openings in his first administration, in which there was a 100 percent vacancy rate in 1789.

Typical of those with hat in hand was Benjamin Harrison, the Signer and ex-governor of Virginia, who had been one of the earliest machine members. Unfortunately, he had opposed the Constitution in the Virginia convention of '88. But this didn't prevent him from asking his old drinking buddy from those wild prewar bachelor nights in Philadelphia where they served as congressmen while their wives served at home. On March 9, 1789, Washington wrote what Matteson calls "a characteristic answer":

> In touching upon the more delicate part of your letter (the communication of which fills me with real concern) I will deal by you, with all that frankness, which is due to friendship, and which I wish should be a characteristic feature in my conduct through life. I will therefore declare to you, that, if it should be my inevitable fate to administer the government (for Heaven knows, that no event can be

less desired by me; and that no earthly consideration short of so general a call, together with a desire to reconcile contending parties as far as in me lays, could again bring me into public life) I will go to the chair under no pre-engagement of any kind or nature whatsoever. But, when in it, I will, to the best of my Judgement, discharge the duties of the office with the impartiality and zeal for the public good, which ought never to suffer connections of blood or friendship or intermingle, so as to have the least sway on decisions of a public nature.[82]

I'm sure Washington resisted to the end such appeals for political favoritism from low people who had been accused of procuring washerwomen for his old buddy during the war.[83]

The importunities, Matteson adds, were not confined to Washington. The correspondence of the time shows that others believed to have the ear of the general were solicited by many to use influence in their behalf. The correspondence of Knox, for instance, contains letters to this effect from Nathaniel Gorham, who with Jeremiah Wadsworth as a partner had just bought six million acres of New York State,* Edward Carrington, Benjamin Lincoln, Henry Jackson, John Brooks, Sebastian Bauman, and various other interested and willing patriots. Representative Sedgwick wrote his wife on August 1, 1789: "This city is indeed crowded with the candidates who expect to obtain the means of subsistence under a government, whose adoption they wished for that very end. By this herd I have been pestered incessantly ever since I arrived in town."[85]

The business community was quivering in anticipation of the takeover by the Federalists, with the government physically in Wall Street and Mr. Wall Street himself, "Hammy" Hamilton, in the government. High finance in America was born during Hamilton's years in the Treasury during the Washington administration. Speculation became the chief activity of the day. Land gave way to money. Paper fortunes came into existence—wealth created through sleight-of-hand tricks with paper and ink.

George Mason—the former friend of Washington—said that

* The land was Genesee Country, the part of New York lying west of Seneca Lake, jointly claimed by Massachusetts and New York, and a political plum tart for any friend of the Mount Vernon machine. Senator Morris and his partners in 1790 took all but 700,000 acres off Gorham and Wadsworth's hands.[84]

Alexander Hamilton had done more harm to America than the British armies. And that's why Mason didn't last long in the machine, being one of the first to fall to the wayside in the Virginia dust.

Nobody could suspect Washington or his machine of corruption. Who would they corrupt? The whole business community of speculators was already corrupt; the country, it could be argued, was founded on corruption in the manipulation of the war debt.

Consider Hamilton's exploits as secretary of the treasury. As Professor Morris says,[86] he was accused by political foes of using intermediaries to purchase Revolutionary War veterans' certificates secretly, at a huge discount. His defense was that this was nonsense—he was being blackmailed for sleeping with the wife of one of the speculators. "My real crime is an amorous connection with his [James Reynolds's] wife," he would one day publicly admit in response to articles in a newsmagazine, *The History of the United States for the Year 1796*, which was somewhere between *Time* and *The Star*. It is evident from this sordid incident that, whether it was true or fictional, Hamilton was prepared to go to the limit to protect his public honor, even at the sacrifice of his private life.

With that flair for dashing off op-ed pieces on pressing issues of the day, Hamilton decided to publish a pamphlet entitled *Observations on Certain Documents contained in Nos. V and VI of The History of the United States for the Year 1796, in which the Charge of Speculation against Alexander Hamilton, late Secretary of the Treasury, is fully refuted. Written by himself*. In this pamphlet Hamilton laid bare his shame for his stunned wife, Elizabeth, and all the world to see.

It took tremendous courage thus to avert the charge of speculation by an open confession of his private disgrace, Schachner says. His friends shook their heads and wondered whether he had not been precipitately rash. After the publication of his widely read pamphlet, he was still suspected as a speculator, and now he was a confessed philanderer as well.

His major weakness seemed to be writing reports. Washington, Madison, and others in the machine could control Hamilton by asking him to write reports. "It was his favorite thing in life," Bernstein says. "Like being asked to do whatever *your* favorite thing is." He didn't make money from his reports (on the bank, assumption of the debt). He was not a wealthy man, and did not seem to be interested in making money the way so many others in the machine were. He certainly could have amassed a fortune. Alexander Hamilton was honest. He maintained his integrity by not personally profiting from the buying and selling of government securities in the assumption-of-debt bill period. His friends and his wife's rich relatives did profit. The worst thing you could say about Hamilton is that, like many a person whose origins are murky, he had a need to be well liked by his social betters. He shut his eyes, in some ways, to corruption around him: the "I can't believe it, and I don't want to know" school of morality. He was no crook, just a bad judge of character.

The machine with Hamilton at the throttle had worked hard to make America safe for property and 10 percent interest, and things looked bright in 1789.

How did Washington relax from the cares of giving his friends jobs and protecting their investments?

First of all, he never relaxed. According to historians, he worked all the time. He was a grind. A concern of Washington's first days in New York, Colonel Freeman says,[87] was the ceaseless flow of visitors in numbers for which even his long service as unlicensed and unrequited tavern keeper at Mount Vernon had not prepared him. "I was unable," the general testified later, "to attend to any business whatsoever; for gentlemen, consulting their own convenience rather than mine, were calling from the time I rose from breakfast, often before, until I sat down to dinner."[88] Some public affairs demanded attention, regardless of hours. Official visits had to be returned, at least while he remained a private citizen. Lear probably told the literal truth when he said, "There has not been a moment unemployed."[89]

One of Washington's specific queries was pitiful, Colonel Flexner says:[90] Could he sometimes slip out inconspicuously to have tea with a friend?

George Washington was against parties. But not social functions. They were the staff of life. His advisers on protocol recommended establishing two occasions a week when any respectably dressed person could, without introduction, invitation, or any prearrangement, be ushered into his presence. One was the president's levee, for men only, every Tuesday from three to four. The other was Martha's tea party, for men and women, held on Friday evenings.

Although Washington's levees were usually dull, Colonel

Flexner says,[91] Martha's weekly tea parties were gay. The general, who on these more informal occasions appeared without hat or sword, was a different man. He relaxed in the presence of the fair sex. Female elegance appealed to him, and the ladies of New York (as later in Philadelphia), having no more elaborate presidential parties to attend, did not spare the milliners and hairdressers. They wore their hair low, with pearls and bandeaux, *à la grecque,* or rolled moderately skyward, *à la Pompadour.* It was noted that when his duties as a host left him free to circulate, Washington passed the men by and spent all his time with the ladies.[92]

He would never miss Mrs. Washington's tea parties, which for a busy man like him must have been like attending women's night at the Turkish or Ukrainian bath on the Lower East Side.

Sullivan, who was there, writes:

> It was the usage for all persons in good society to attend Mrs. Washington's levee every Friday evening. He was always present. The young ladies used to throng around him and engage him in conversation. These were some of the well-remembered belles of that day, who imagined themselves to be favourites with him. As these were the only opportunities which they had of conversing with him, they were disposed to use them. One would think that a gentleman and a gallant soldier, if he could ever laugh, or dress his countenance in smiles, would do so when surrounded by young and admiring beauties. But this was never so; the countenance of Washington never softened, or changed its habitual gravity.

[8]

What is Prefident Washington so glum about? Of course, it is assumed it is some affair of state. But could his secret service intelligence have discovered that Kitty Greene was dating Congressman-elect Wadsworth?

*

Washington had every reason to expect the president of his fan club, Kitty Greene, to be in town for the inaugural festivities that month. His feet could be expected to have the itch. She had never been known to have not jumped into her phaeton whenever there was a chance to be near the presidential action party in the past. She loved to dance, and now she was a gay widow.

The country suffered an irreparable loss when Nathanael Greene died at Mulberry Grove, his plantation in Georgia, on June 19, 1786. He was prevented from playing a leading role in the final act of the Mount Vernon machine production of 1789, like his wartime buddies Hamilton and Knox. Kitty would have been the administration's first Madame Pompadour.

George and Martha were saddened by Kitty's loss. The general tried to console the widow by taking over the education of his namesake, George Washington Greene, whom Kitty actually called "Washington." *

When Congress adjourned in the autumn, George Washington left Martha at No. 3 Cherry Street and departed New York for the first presidential tour of the New England states. What's for Martha to do on a business trip, a monotonous repetition of addresses of welcome, banquets and balls, poems, arches, and young girls with flowers throwing themselves at the national hero?

George Washington seems to have been principally a figurehead, Woodward says,[93] a symbol. He was almost as impersonal at the top of the government as a statue on top of a monument would have been. But when he went on the Northern tour the tumultuous welcomes revived him.

The people still thought of Washington in terms of royalty. A merchant named Barrell wrote a letter describing Washington's visit to Boston, in which he said: "His Majesty, while here, went to the manufactory of oilcloth, and was exceedingly pleased. The spinning for the manufactory is done by a number of girls who were dressed clean, and in general are likely. His Majesty made himself merry on this occasion, telling the overseer he believed they collected the prettiest girls in Boston."

---

* It was amazing how many of the high command sought to console the widow. The Marquis de Lafayette offered to take young Washington (George W. Greene) into his château in the Paris suburbs for a study-abroad scholarship underwritten by the Washingtons. Madame de Lafayette must have been thrilled to have the boy, in the light of the Marquis's confessions about his sleeping with Mother Greene during the war.

After making merry, Thayne says, "George returned from the New England tour restored in health and spirits." Nothing like getting away from Martha, and shaking hands with a few thousand shopgirls.

While away, he also found time to pay his respects to, and console, widow Greene, whom he hadn't seen since New York. As Thayne said, "She was still a bright, beguiling creature, with pretty clothes and the ability to evoke laughing memories of the grim old days in Jersey and Pennsylvania. She enjoyed dining with the Washingtons and attending the theater in the president's box." [94] The prefident was such a dependable, incredibly loyal, devoted friend to his old army buddies and/or their wives.

The young and attractive widow with four small children, whom she was in the habit of packing off to live with relatives or at boarding schools, and the prefident had tea, his diary said. And I'm sure they talked over old dances of the past. Like an early Fred Astaire and Ginger Rogers.

In May of 1791, Prefident Washington, on a nonpolitical campaign swing through the South, again found time to stop off and call on Kitty at the Greene plantation, Mulberry Grove, which adjoined the plantation of another wartime friend, General Mad Anthony Wayne. Martha was otherwise disposed.

A typical event Martha missed on this southern trip was a dinner in Charleston, attended, Schwartz says, by local, state, and foreign dignitaries. Washington's table was set under an imposing triumphal arch, and as toasts were drunk to his government, cannon volleys were fired off. On the third night, he attended a public ball at the Exchange Building. Within clear sight of that building, in Charleston harbor, a ship, brightly illuminated, displayed the letters *VW* (for *Vivat Washington*—Long Live Washington) on its largest sail. The entrance to the building itself was decorated by his portrait, along with the inscription "Deliciis Patriae" (Delight of the Nation). Inside, the pillars were entwined with laurel, and throughout the great hall were placed messages in English, Latin, and French: "With grateful praises of the hero's fame/We'll teach our infants' tongues to lisp his name"; "Magnus in bello" (Great in war); "Hominis jura, defendit et curiat" (The law of man defended and preserved); "Diogène aujourd'hui casserait sa lanterne" (Today Diogenes would throw down his lamp). As

Washington greeted each of the 250 ladies in attendance, he noticed other pictures of himself, and other inscriptions, embroidered on their dresses and ribbons.[95]

After being feted and dined and wined in Savannah by the local Cincinnati, with enough toasts to stop a lancer, Washington went down the river to Mulberry Grove for what Thayer calls a "family dinner,"[96] hosted by the widow Greene.

In addition to beauty, Mrs. Greene still possessed personal charm, intuitive perception, and a very acquisitive intellect and nature. "This power of rendering her intellectual stores," Mrs. Ellet says, "combined with a retentive memory, a lively imagination, and great fluency of speech, rendered her one of the most brilliant and entertaining of women."[97]

Adversity had overtaken this brilliant woman, and her estate problems (which Representative Wadsworth was trying to straighten out) were further entangled by private debts due to mismanaged speculation engaged in by her new business management.[98]

Among the more newly tangled affairs that General Washington might have discovered at this time in Kitty's life was that she was sleeping with the children's tutor, a Yale man named Phineas Miller, whom she had met in Philadelphia on her way South from New York after the general's first New England tour (1789). Miller was Wadsworth's agent, and he lent her two hundred dollars from the Connecticut moneymaker's accounts. He was later promoted to her business manager, and husband.

Her contributions to higher education also included her setting up another Yale scholar in her barn amongst the magnolia trees. She had, as I said, a predisposition for Yale men. This old Eli, named Eli Whitney, was then in his early twenties. He stayed in Kitty's barn for several years, and with her money invented the cotton gin.

The Greene plantation was being turned into a regular frat house. Boola boola. It is not known whether Whitney was a good dancer. But the great inventor fell in love with Kitty, or Caty as Catharine was now known, having outgrown the "Kitty" of her youth. She was the older woman in young Whitney's life, and the affair went on for twenty-five years. He wasn't able to marry another until after her death in 1814. She must have been some lady to have had such an effect on heroes of both the American and industrial revolutions.

Colonel Freeman says of Washington's entry in his journal

about the visit (which must have been an eye-opener), "as echoing a deliberate but awkward effort to disregard the melancholy emotions the visit might have stirred."

"In my way down the river," he wrote quaintly, "I called upon Mrs. Green [sic], the widow of the deceased General Green [sic] (at a place called Mulberry Grove) and asked her how she did." [99]

She was doing quite well, with all those Yalies lurking about.

In the brief time Washington had for this first call on her in her Southern home, Colonel Freeman says, he could not discuss her business affairs, nor would he have talked of them, probably, had his stay been longer, because it was likely he might be called upon, as prefident, to sign or to disapprove legislation for her relief.

And where did George Washington sleep that night, 1,287 miles from New York City in the midst of the Georgia rice mangrove swamps?

Oh, in a nearby tavern, Thayer says, "with due regard for *les convenances*." [100]

Eli Whitney is in the barn with his cotton gin. General Mad Anthony Wayne is in her gazebo. Phineas Miller, the children's tutor, is in the bedroom. And the prefident of the United States, a man with whom she danced three hours without stopping while the world was crumbling, only a few years earlier, she is going to send away because of a fear of what the neighbors would say?

Would Kitty Greene allow the Prefident of the United States to sleep in a common roadhouse? What an insult to her reputation as a Southern hostess. I'm sure no matter how crowded her schedule, she saved the last dance for him.

Acknowledgments

I have limited the number of actual footnotes in the preceding pages to a minimum. Hollywood will not buy anything with footnotes. Nevertheless, I want to thank all the historians who have so thanklessly given to this work their words, sentences, thoughts, sometimes without sufficient footnotal credit. I will try to get you all parts in the miniseries or musical.

A complete list of those to whom I am so indebted for borrowings, gleanings, or research is appended (see Bibliography).

I want to thank specifically the legendary Richard B. Morris, Gouverneur Morris Professor of History at Columbia University, for allowing me to audit his course, G6662y ("The Era of the American Revolution, 1754–1789"), in preparation for writing this book. His death in 1989 has kept him from seeing the nitpicking faults other scholars might find with my scholarship.

I am grateful to Richard B. Bernstein, the legal, constitutional and bicentennial scholar, for reading the current manuscript in its rawest form. He pointed out numerous minefields I was blithely walking across, thus allowing me to escape if not unscathed then scathed. To my questions about glaring omissions in the oft-told story of the 1789 presidency, it was Bernstein who said, "We have trouble explaining some things, and many omit what they cannot explain."

Among other members of the academic community, I want to thank Mrs. Getz, my fifth-grade history teacher who undid some of the damage done by Mrs. Jacobs in the fourth grade at PS 186.

I want to thank Alan Alda, who graciously made available to

me his private library, the early American history wing, near the tennis courts, used in connection with his writing the script to "Sweet Liberty."

The Leonia (New Jersey) Public Library, of which I am a member, was very helpful in securing research materials. Librarian Harold Ficke and his staff were supportive in linking the resources of the Bergen County Library through the New Jersey Access Center interconnect with OCLC.

I would like to thank James C. Roberts and his staff at the reference section of the Library of Congress; Thomas Dunnings of the New-York Historical Society; Mark Herzel-Colvson of the Historical Society of Pennsylvania; Hilliard Beller of the Rhode Island Publications Society; Peter Drummey at the Massachusetts Historical Society; and the others who were helpful in providing copies of key letters, papers, and manuscripts.

I want to thank, also, all the foundations and universities that did not give me a grant to work on this project over the years, thus preventing me from deviating from my search for truth. I understand. Nobody gets grants or tenure trying to find out who George Washington was dancing with.

Writing this book was a difficult time in my life. I have continued doing my important cultural work as the TV critic for *Newsday*. I would go back and forth every day from the 1780s to the 1980s as if in a time machine. I felt like a character in a TV series saying, "Beam me up, Scotty." A number of people in my crew made it possible.

I want to thank Victoria Johnson, my trusty super assistant, who, in her spare time, was in charge of typing and keeping track of the manuscript, facts, sources, bibliography, and the hundreds of other details that went into the production of a big book like this.

I want to thank my editors, a cross section of American publishing today, starting with Richard Kluger and Dan Green, and most recently Arthur H. Samuelson, Daniel Bial, and Richard Lingeman. I am especially grateful to Lingeman, my speechwriter in my campaign for the presidency in 1964. (He first suggested the slogan "I'd rather be President than write.") He continues to be the leading authority on understanding what I'm trying to say and helping me get there.

I want to thank my wife, Carol, for her support, patience, and understanding that was second only to Martha Washington's in a project that took almost as long as the making of the presidency itself. She is a true daughter of the Industrial Revolution (D.I.R.).

Suzy Kitman, my daughter, first inspired me to try to explain the first election. She also served as the art historian who located the pictures in the current volume. My son, Jamie Lincoln Kitman, the lawyer and rock band manager, contributed many insights and quips. So did my daughter, A. J. Kitman, the fashion stylist.

Dr. Erika Freeman made it possible to finish this quarter of a century labor by helping me resolve and appreciate my founding father complex.

Victor Navasky, my campaign manager who almost got me the nomination at the Republican Presidential Convention in 1964 (I managed to tie Harold Stassen: we both got zero votes, only two less than Henry Cabot Lodge), has been a source of satirical inspiration. Annie Navasky is my stockbroker. My friends Barbara Ginsberg and Howard Ginsberg offered advice, sanctuary, historical conversation, and good wine at the completion of the work.

I want to thank Jane Dystel, my agent, for her help in dealing with those two great Americans, Harper & Row; John Brancato, for designing the edifice in which the book was written, thus cleaning up my environment; and Robin Brancato for putting up with it all.

Finally, I want to thank George Washington. Spending so much time with him has resulted in his being a real person. His headquarters and the family were like characters in "M*A*S*H." I would ask him to stand up and take a bow if he were able.

I have been a little hard on George Washington, especially as a military man. But that's only natural—the enlisted man's tendency to be biased against the officers. (George Washington forgot one basic thing they taught us in the army at Fort Dix: Don't volunteer for anything. Keep your mouth shut and your eyes forward. Don't call attention to yourself.)

In all fairness, he was not a professional soldier. That is the amazing thing about him. He did better as an amateur than most executives would. Think of Lee Iacocca leading an army for eight years. Think of how William Howard Taft would have been leading the invasion of Nicaragua by U.S. Marines in 1912. Or Jimmy Carter personally rescuing the hostages in Iran in 1979. That's the perspective.

Washington was a born chief executive, not a soldier.

All those faults I have found, mostly in the general's military strategy and policies, are small potatoes indeed. The great thing you can say about him was he was no Caesar, no conquistador or proconsul, making war to acquire personal wealth or power. He was not evil, Machiavellian—like leaders usually are in the circumstances thrusted upon them, or self-thrusted. For once there was a leader of whom it could be said: What you see is what you get. This was a man who was an exception to Lord Acton's rule that power corrupts.

If not for Washington, we would have been another banana republic, working out our differences with bullets at the polls. Viva George Washington!

He was a great man who could take criticism. You don't have things such as the nation's capital, a state, a bridge, 7 mountains, 8 streams, 10 lakes, 33 counties, 9 colleges, 121 cities and villages, and 1 monument named after you unless you're someone special.

The true moral I have drawn from his life is that one can dress gorgeously and indulge in every luxury and vice, including shopping, dancing, the theater, and cracking walnuts; one can drink and gamble and still manage to go down in history as a pillar of rectitude, temperate, moderate, thoughtful, honest, and wise. All of these are in my personal rules of civility now.

Notes

Preamble: Note on Source Materials

1. Joseph Dillaway Sawyer, *Washington*, vol. 1, as quoted in Rupert Hughes, *George Washington: The Rebel and the Patriot* (New York: William Morrow, 1927), p. 65.

2. For a partial inventory of the nineteenth-century literature, see William S. Baker, *Bibliotheca Washingtoniana* (Philadelphia: R. M. Lindsay, 1889).

3. Clinton Rossiter, *Six Characters in Search of a Republic* (New York: Harcourt Brace, and World, 1953), p. 207.

Part I: The Making of the General

1. Don Higginbotham, *George Washington and the American Military Tradition* (Athens, Ga.: University of Georgia Press, 1985), p. 77.

2. J. P. Kennedy and H. R. McIlwaine, eds., *Journal of the House of Burgesses of Colonial Virginia, 1758–1761* (Richmond, Va.: 1909), pp. 66–67.

3. Dr. Louis K. Koontz, *The Virginia Frontier, 1754–1763* (Baltimore: Johns Hopkins University Studies, 1925), p. 131.

4. Douglas Southall Freeman, *George Washington: Planter and Patriot* (New York: Charles Scribner's Sons, 1951), p. 426.

5. Ibid., p. 293n.

6. John C. Fitzpatrick, ed., *George Washington Papers*, vol. 3 (Washington, D.C.: Library of Congress, 1931–1944), p. 339.

7. Ibid., p. 362.

8. Ibid., p. 357.

9. Ibid., p. 333.

10. W. E. Woodward, *George Washington: The Image and the Man* (New York: Boni and Liveright, 1926), p. 89.

11. James Thomas Flexner, *George Washington in the American Revolution (1775–1783)* (Boston: Little, Brown, 1967), p. 12.

12. Letter of September 10, 1774, to Mrs. Deane; Edmund C. Burnett, ed., *Letters of Members of the Continental Congress*, vol. 1 (Washington, D.C.: Carnegie Institution of Washington, 1921–1936), p. 28.

13. Charles Francis Adams, ed., *The Works of John Adams*, vol. 2 (Boston: C. C. Little, J. Brown, 1850–1856), p. 360.

14. John Adams, August 31, 1774; L. H. Butterfield, ed., *Diary and Autobiography of John Adams*, vol. 3 (Cambridge, Mass.: Harvard University Press, 1961–1962), p. 308.

15. William Wirt, *Sketches of the Life and Character of Patrick Henry*, as quoted in Douglas Southall Freeman, *George Washington: Planter and Patriot*, p. 422.

16. C. D. Bowen, *John Adams and the American Revolution* (Boston: Little, Brown, 1950), pp. 529–532.

17. Carl and Jessica Bridenbaugh, *Rebels and Gentlemen: Philadelphia in the Age of Franklin* (New York: Oxford University Press, 1962), p. 21.

18. Ibid., p. 22.

19. Quoted from the *Pennsylvania Gazette* in John C. Fitzpatrick, ed., *Diaries of George Washington*, vol. 2 (Boston and New York: Houghton Mifflin, 1925), p. 164.

20. W. E. Woodward, *George Washington: The Image and the Man*, pp. 153–154.

21. W. J. Rorabaugh, *The Alcoholic Republic: An American Tradition* (New York: Oxford University Press, 1979), p. 18.

22. G. W. Chase and H. B. Dawson, eds., *Diary of David How* (Morrisania, N.Y., 1865), p. 5.

23. R. T. Barton, *The First Election of Washington*, vol. 11 (Virginia Historical Collection), p. 123.

24. Ibid., p. 124.

25. Arthur M. Schlesinger, *The Birth of a Nation* (Boston: Houghton Mifflin, 1981), pp. 216–217.

26. Paul Leland Haworth, *George Washington, Country Gentleman* (Indianapolis, n.d.), p. 286.

27. Carl and Jessica Bridenbaugh, *Rebels and Gentlemen: Philadelphia in the Age of Franklin*, p. 222.

28. Charles Francis Adams, ed., *The Works of John Adams*, vol. 2, p. 62.

29. Charles Francis Adams, ed., *The Works of John Adams*, vol. 3, p. 35.

30. Carl and Jessica Bridenbaugh, *Rebels and Gentlemen: Philadelphia in the Age of Franklin*, p. 209.

31. E. Powel to Bushrod Washington, Jan. 1, 1785, manuscript, Mount Vernon.

Part II: The Making of the General, II

1. Rupert Hughes, *George Washington: The Human Being and the Hero* (New York: William Morrow, 1926), p. 89.

2. Ibid., p. 99.

3. Horace Walpole, *Memoirs of the Last Ten Years of the Reign of George II*, vol. 1, edited by Lord Holland (London, 1847), p. 347.

4. George Washington Greene, *The Life of Major General Nathanael Greene*, vol. 1 (Boston: Houghton Mifflin, 1878–1890), p. 252.

5. Charles Francis Adams, ed., *The Works of John Adams*, vol. 2 (Boston, C. C. Little, J. Brown, 1850–1856), pp. 416–418.

6. Kenneth Silverman, *A Cultural History of the American Revolution* (New York: T. Y. Crowell, 1976), p. 356.

7. Michael Pearson, *The Revolutionary War: An Unbiased Account* (New York: Capricorn Books, 1973), p. 21.

8. Arthur M. Schlesinger, *The Colonial Merchants and the American Revolution, 1763–1776* (New York: Atheneum, 1968), p. 262.

9. George F. Scheer and Hugh F. Rankin, *Rebels and Redcoats* (Cleveland and New York: World, 1957), p. 21.

10. W. E. Woodward, *George Washington: The Image and the Man* (New York: Boni and Liveright, 1926), pp. 235–237.

11. Frank Moore, *The Diary of the American Revolution*, vol. 1 (New York: Charles Scribner's Sons, 1860), pp. 105–106.

12. Belknap, "Journal of My Tour to the Camp," vol. 4 (Massachusetts Historical Society Proceedings, 1858–1860), pp. 82–83.

13. Letter of Sept. 19, 1775, to Benjamin Rush; *The* [Charles] *Lee Papers*, vol. 1 (New York Historical Society Collections, 1871–1874), p. 207.

14. Horace Walpole, *Last Journals*, vol. 1 (London, 1910), pp. 404–5.

15. J. T. Austin, *The Life of Elbridge Gerry*, vol. 1 (Jersey City, N.J.: Da Capo Press, 1970), p. 79.

16. Worthington C. Ford, et al., eds., *Journals of the Continental Congress, 1774–1789*, vol. 2, pp. 97–99.

17. Rupert Hughes, *George Washington: The Rebel and the Patriot* (New York: William Morrow, 1927), p. 222.

18. Douglas Southall Freeman, *George Washington: Planter and Patriot* (New York: Charles Scribner's Sons, 1951), p. 385.

19. General George Washington and Marvin Kitman, PFC (Ret.), *George Washington's Expense Account* (New York: Simon and Schuster, 1970), p. 24.

20. Charles Francis Adams, ed., *The Works of John Adams*, vol. 2, p. 92.

21. Ibid.

22. Ibid., p. 456.

23. Douglas Southall Freeman, *George Washington: Planter and Patriot*, p. 434n.

24. Ibid., p. 416.

25. George F. Scheer and Hugh F. Rankin, *Rebels and Redcoats*, p. 68.

26. Charles Francis Adams, ed., *The Works of John Adams*, vol. 2, pp. 415–416.

27. Ibid., pp. 416–418.

28. Ibid.

29. Ibid.

30. Douglas Southall Freeman, *George Washington: Planter and Patriot*, vol. 3, p. 437n.

31. John C. Fitzpatrick, ed., *Diaries of George Washington*, vol. 2 (Boston and New York, 1925), p. 199.

32. Douglas Southall Freeman, *George Washington: Planter and Patriot*, p. 437n.

33. John C. Fitzpatrick, ed., *George Washington Papers*, vol. 3 (Washington, D.C.: Library of Congress, 1931–1944), p. 293n.

34. Worthington C. Ford, et al., eds., *Journals of the Continental Congress, 1774–1789*, vol. 2, p. 92.

35. George F. Scheer and Hugh F. Rankin, *Rebels and Redcoats*, p. 72.

36. John C. Fitzpatrick, ed., *George Washington Papers*, vol. 3, pp. 292–293. (The bracketed phrase is in Washington's handwriting.)

37. Peter Force, *American Archives* (4th series), vol. 2 (Washington, D.C., 1837–1853), pp. 1849, 1847.

38. General George Washington and Marvin Kitman, PFC (Ret.), *George Washington's Expense Account*, pp. 1–285.

39. Charles Atherton, *An Eulogy on George Washington*, as quoted in Barry Schwartz, *George Washington: The Making of an American Symbol* (New York: Free Press, 1987), p. 126.

40. George W. Corner, ed., *Autobiography of Benjamin Rush* (Princeton, N.J.: Princeton University Press, 1948), p. 141.

41. Abigail Adams to John Adams, March 2, 1776, as quoted in L. H. Butterfield, ed., *Adams Family Correspondence*, vol. 1 (Cambridge, Mass.: Harvard University Press, 1963–1973), p. 353.

42. Barry Schwartz, *George Washington: The Making of an American Symbol*, p. 5.

43. Thomas Jefferson to Walter Jones, January 2, 1814, as quoted in Paul Leicester Ford, ed., *The Writings of Thomas Jefferson*, vol. 11 (New York: G. P. Putnam's Sons, 1904–1905), p. 375.

44. Rupert Hughes, *George Washington: The Rebel and the Patriot*, p. 244.

45. Sept. 12, 1987, Kaplan's Deli at the Delmonico.

46. Worthington C. Ford, ed., *The Writings of George Washington*, vol. 2 (New York & London, 1889–1893), p. 487.

47. Ibid., p. 1031.

48. John C. Fitzpatrick, ed., *George Washington Papers*, vol. 4, p. 359.

49. Thomas Thatcher, *An Eulogy on George Washington* (Dedham, Mass.: Mann, 1800), p. 10.

Part III: The Making of the War Hero

1. Edmund C. Burnett, ed., *Letters of Members of the Continental Congress*, vol. 2 (Washington, D.C.: Carnegie Institution of Washington, 1921–1936), pp. 405–406; John C. Fitzpatrick, ed., *The Writings of George Washington* (Washington, D.C.: United States Government Printing Office, 1931–1944), vol. 7, pp. 100n, 133 and vol. 8, p. 160n.

2. John C. Miller, *Alexander Hamilton and the Growth of the New Nation* (New York: Harper & Row, 1964), p. 221.

3. Worthington C. Ford, ed., *The Writings of George Washington*, vol. 2 (New York, 1889–1893), p. 440n.

4. Michael Pearson, *The Revolutionary War: An Unbiased Account* (New York: Capricorn Books, 1973), pp. 157–158.

5. *The* [Charles] *Lee Papers*, vol. 1 (New York Historical Society Collections, 1871–1874), p. 207.

6. Rupert Hughes, *George Washington: The Human Being and the Hero* (New York: William Morrow, 1926), p. 17.

7. Ibid., pp. 17–18.

8. Marcus Cunliffe, *George Washington: Man and Monument* (Boston: Little, Brown, 1958), p. 31.

9. John C. Fitzpatrick, ed., *Diaries of George Washington*, vol. 2 (Boston and New York: Houghton Mifflin, 1925), p. 161.

10. James Thomas Flexner, *George Washington: The Forge of Experience* (Boston: Little, Brown, 1965), p. 353.

11. Paul Leicester Ford, *The True George Washington* (Philadelphia: Lippincott, 1909), p. 85.

12. *Tyler's Quarterly Historical and Geneological Magazine* (Richmond, Va.), January 4, 1926, p. 176.

13. Rupert Hughes, *George Washington: The Human Being and the Hero*, p. 359

14. R. W. G. Vail, ed., "A Dinner at Mount Vernon." From the unpublished journal of Joshua Brookes, *New-York Historical Society Quarterly*, XXXI (1947), p. 74.

15. Rupert Hughes, *George Washington: The Human Being and the Hero*, p. 448.

16. John C. Fitzpatrick, ed., *George Washington Papers*, vol. 2 (Washington, D.C.: Library of Congress, 1931–1944), p. 397.

17. John R. Alden, *George Washington: A Biography* (New York: W. W. Norton, 1963), p. 84.

18. W. E. Woodward, *George Washington: The Image and the Man* (New York: Boni and Liveright, 1926), p. 101.

19. Rupert Hughes, *George Washington: The Human Being and the Hero*, p. 454.

20. Ibid., p. 455.

21. Ibid., p. 480.

22. W. E. Woodward, *George Washington: The Image and the Man*, p. 108.

23. John C. Fitzpatrick, ed., *The Writings of George Washington*, vol. 37 (Washington, D.C.: United States Government Printing Office, 1931–1944), pp. 536–537.

24. Rupert Hughes, *George Washington: The Rebel and the Patriot* (New York: William Morrow, 1927), p. 111.

25. Ibid.

26. John C. Fitzpatrick, ed., *George Washington Papers*, vol. 2, pp. 417–418.

27. General George Washington and Marvin Kitman, PFC (Ret.), *George Washington's Expense Account* (New York: Simon and Schuster, 1970), p. 105.

28. Washington to Congress, June 16, 1775; John C. Fitzpatrick, ed., *The Writings of George Washington*, vol. 3, p. 292.

29. Arthur M. Schlesinger, Sr., "Patriotism Names the Baby," *New England Quarterly*, vol. 14 (1941), pp. 611–618.

30. Arthur M. Schlesinger, Sr., *Prelude to Independence: The Newspaper War on Britain* (New York: Vintage, 1965), p. 34.

31. Andreas Wiederholdt, "Tagebuch des Capt. Wiederholdt von 7 October 1776 bis Dezember 1780." M. D. Learned and C. Grosse, eds., in *America Germanica*, vol. 4 (New York: London and Berlin, 1902).

32. Thomas Jones, *History of New York During the Revolutionary War*, vol. 1 Edward Floyd DeLancey, ed. (New York: Printed for the New York Historical Society, 1879), p. 55.

33. Douglas Southall Freeman, *George Washington: Planter and Patriot* (New York: Charles Scribner's Sons, 1951), p. 463.

34. John C. Fitzpatrick, ed., *George Washington Papers*, vol. 3, p. 330.

35. Allen French, *The First Year of the American Revolution* (New York: Octagon Books, 1968), pp. 300–301.

36. George F. Scheer and Hugh F. Rankin, *Rebels and Redcoats* (Cleveland and New York: World, 1957), p. 84.

37. John C. Fitzpatrick, ed., *George Washington Papers*, vol. 3, p. 313.

38. George F. Scheer and Hugh F. Rankin, *Rebels and Redcoats*, p. 88.

39. Charles Knowles Bolton, *The Private Soldier Under Washington* (Port Washington, N.Y.: Kennikat Press, 1902, 1964), p. 25.

40. "Aaron Wright's Revolutionary Journal," *Historical Magazine*, July, 1862, p. 209.

41. Charles Knowles Bolton, *The Private Soldier Under Washington*, p. 127.

42. George F. Scheer and Hugh F. Rankin, *Rebels and Redcoats*, p. 84.

43. Charles Knowles Bolton, *The Private Soldier Under Washington*, p. 173.

44. North Callahan, *Henry Knox: General Washington's General* (New York: Rinehart, 1958), p. 33.

45. W. E. Woodward, *George Washington: The Image and the Man*, p. 269.

46. Douglas Southall Freeman, *George Washington: Planter and Patriot*, p. 444.

47. Arthur B. Tourtellot, *Lexington and Concord* (New York: W. W. Norton, 1963), p. 202.

48. Kenneth Silverman, *A Cultural History of the American Revolution* (New York: T. Y. Crowell, 1976), p. 286.

49. "Journal," *Connecticut Historical Society Collection*, vol. VII, pp. 128–131.

50. North Callahan, *Henry Knox: General Washington's General*, p. 62.

51. Douglas Southall Freeman, *George Washington: Planter and Patriot*, p. 529.

52. *Magazine of American History*, July–Dec. 1890, p. 189; James Thacher, "Military Journal," p. 31.

53. John C. Fitzpatrick, ed., *George Washington Papers*, vol. 23, p. 511.

54. Theodore Thayer, *Nathanael Greene: Strategist of the American Revolution* (New York: Twayne, 1960), p. 69.

55. George Washington Greene, *The Life of Major General Nathanael Greene*, vol. 1 (Boston: Houghton Mifflin, 1878–1890), pp. 109–111.

56. General George Washington and Marvin Kitman PFC (Ret.), *George Washington's Expense Account*, pp. 167–169.

57. W. E. Woodward, *George Washington: The Image and the Man*, p. 279.

58. Theodore Thayer, *Nathanael Greene: Strategist of the American Revolution*, p. 73.

59. George Washington Greene, *The Life of Major General Nathanael Greene*, p. 142.

60. Allen French, *The First Year of the American Revolution*, p. 300.

61. Ibid., p. 655.

62. North Callahan, *Henry Knox: General Washington's General*, p. 40.

63. Alexander C. Flick, "General Knox's Ticonderoga Expedition," *New York State Historical Association Quarterly Journal*, vol. 9, no. 2 (April 1928): pp. 124–125.

64. North Callahan, *Henry Knox: General Washington's General*, p. 53.

65. Kenneth Silverman, *A Cultural History of the American Revolution*, p. 208.

66. William M. Dwyer, *The Day Is Ours* (New York: Viking Press, 1983), p. 232.

67. North Callahan, *Henry Knox: General Washington's General*, pp. 48–49.

68. Henry Knox, "Diary," *New England Historical and Genealogical Register*, vol. XXX, pp. 324–325, as quoted in Henry Steele Commager and Richard B. Morris, eds., *The Spirit of Seventy-Six* (New York: Harper & Row, 1967), pp. 175–176.

69. Ibid.

70. North Callahan, *Henry Knox: General Washington's General*, p. 54.

71. Ibid.

72. Knox's "Account Book."

73. North Callahan, *Henry Knox: General Washington's General*, pp. 156–157.

74. Worthington C. Ford, ed., *Correspondence and Journals of Samuel Blachley Webb* (New York: Burnett, 1894), pp. 129–132, as quoted in Henry Steele Commager and Richard B. Morris, eds., *The Spirit of Seventy-Six*, pp. 176–177.

75. Theodore Thayer, *Nathanael Greene: Strategist of the American Revolution*, p. 80.

76. Worthington C. Ford, ed., *Correspondence and Journals of Samuel Blachley Webb*, vol. 1, pp. 129–132.

77. Harold Murdoch, ed., "Letter of Reverend William Gordon, 1776," *Proceedings* (1927), vol. LX, pp. 361–364.

78. Michael Pearson, *The Revolutionary War: An Unbiased Account*, p. 147.

79. James Thomas Flexner, *George Washington in the American Revolution (1775–1783)* (Boston: Little, Brown, 1967), p. 75.

80. Ibid., pp. 76–77.

81. Allen French, *The First Year of the American Revolution*, pp. 659–660.

82. James Thomas Flexner, *George Washington in the American Revolution (1775–1783)*, p. 75.

83. Michael Pearson, *The Revolutionary War: An Unbiased Account*, pp. 146–147.

84. Kenneth Silverman, *A Cultural History of the American Revolution*, pp. 334–335.

85. Rupert Hughes, *George Washington: The Savior of the States* (New York: William Morrow, 1930), appendix on Howe.

86. Kenneth Silverman, *A Cultural History of the American Revolution*, pp. 334–335.

87. Allen French, *The First Year of the American Revolution*, pp. 341–342.

88. E. F. DeLancey, notes to Thomas Jones, "History of New York During the Revolutionary War," *New-York Historical Society*, vol. II, p. 424.

89. Rupert Hughes, *George Washington: The Rebel and the Patriot*, p. 377.

90. Kenneth Silverman, *A Cultural History of the American Revolution*, pp. 377, 500.

91. Barry Schwartz, *George Washington: The Making of an American Symbol* (New York: Free Press, 1987), p. 21.

92. For a more sustained but equally passionate statement, see Philip Freneau's "American Liberty" (1775) in Fred L. Pattee, ed., *The Poems of Philip Freneau*, Vol. 1 (Princeton, N.J.: Princeton University Press, 1902–1907), pp. 142–152.

93. George R. Stewart, *Names on the Land* (Boston: Houghton Mifflin, 1967), pp. 164, 192; Walton C. John and Alma H. Preinkert, eds., "The Educational Views of George Washington," in *History of the George Washington Bicentennial Celebration*, vol. 1 (Washington, D.C.: George Washington Bicentennial Celebration, 1932), p. 553.

94. Rupert Hughes, *George Washington: The Rebel and the Patriot*, p. 375.

95. Barry Schwartz, *George Washington: The Making of an American Symbol*, p. 35.

96. Supreme Executive Council of the Commonwealth of Pennsylvania, Minutes of the Supreme Executive Council 2 (January 8, 1779), p. 671.

97. Freeman's Journal, Sept. 12, 1781, cited in "Report of the American Historical Association," 1896, vol. 1, p. 194.

98. Barry Schwartz, *George Washington: The Making of an American Symbol*, p. 34.

99. Paul K. Longmore, *The Invention of George Washington* (Berkeley, Ca.: University of California Press, 1988), pp. 206–208.

100. Barry Schwartz, *George Washington: The Making of an American Symbol*, pp. 28–29.

101. See "New Jersey and You . . . Perfect Together" road map: State of New Jersey official transportation map and guide, 1984.

102. Howard Swigget, *The Forgotten Leaders of the Revolution* (Garden City, N.Y.: Doubleday, 1955), p. 70.

103. John C. Fitzpatrick, ed., *George Washington Papers*, vol. IX, p. 207, in James Thomas Flexner, *George Washington in the American Revolution (1775–1783)*, p. 215.

104. Worthington C. Ford, *The Writings of George Washington*, vol. VII, p. 481, in Rupert Hughes, *George Washington: The Savior of the States*, p. 510.

105. Ibid., p. 515.

106. W. C. Bruce, *John Randolph of Roanoke*, vol. I; Rupert Hughes, *George Washington: The Savior of the States*, p. 652.

107. In Rupert Hughes, *George Washington: The Savior of the States*.

108. "Elijah Fisher's Diary," in Dr. Carlos E. Godfrey, *The Commander-in-Chief's Guard* (Washington, D.C.: Stevenson-Smith Company, 1904), p. 280.

109. *Pennsylvania Magazine of History and Biography* 65 (July, 1941), pp. 362–370.

110. Hornor in *Pennsylvania Magazine of History and Biography* 65 (July, 1941), p. 364.

111. Theodore Thayer, *Nathanael Greene: Strategist of the American Revolution*, p. 270.

112. George Washington Greene, *The Life of Major General Nathanael Greene*, vol. 2, pp. 161–162.

113. Elswyth Thane, *The Fighting Quaker: Nathanael Greene* (New York: Hawthorn Books, 1972), p. 44.

114. Theodore Thayer, *Nathanael Greene: Strategist of the American Revolution*, p. 95.

115. Knox Papers, vol. 2, Massachusetts Historical Society, p. 146.

116. Douglas Southall Freeman, *George Washington: Leader of the Revolution*, p. 131.

117. Theodore Thayer, *Nathanael Greene: Strategist of the American Revolution*, p. 95.

118. George Washington Greene, *The Life of Major General Nathanael Greene*, vol. 1, p. 368.

119. E. J. Lowell, *The Hessians in the Revolutionary War* (Williamstown, Mass.: Corner House, 1970; reprint from 1884), p. 56.

120. William M. Dwyer, *The Day Is Ours*, p. 10.

121. Theodore Thayer, *Nathanael Greene: Strategist of the American Revolution*, p. 107.

122. George Washington Greene, *The Life of Major General Nathanael Greene*, vol. 1, p. 220.

123. John C. Fitzpatrick, ed., *Writings of George Washington*, vol. VI, p. 243; William B. Reed, *Life and Correspondence of Joseph Reed*, vol. I (Philadelphia: Lindsay and Blakiston, 1847), p. 256; in James Thomas Flexner, *George Washington in the American Revolution (1775–1783)*, p. 152.

124. Theodore Thayer, *Nathanael Greene: Strategist of the American Revolution*, p. 105.

125. James Thomas Flexner, *George Washington in the American Revolution (1775–1783)*, p. 145.

126. Theodore Thayer, *Nathanael Greene: Strategist of the American Revolution*, p. 229.

127. Ibid., p. 227.

128. Ibid., p. 229.

129. Ibid., p. 259.

130. Henry Steele Commager and Richard B. Morris, eds., *The Spirit of Seventy-Six*, p. 1126.

131. Nathanael Greene to Catharine Greene, n.d., Rhode Island Historical Society Collection, vol. XX (Oct. 1927), pp. 106–107.

132. Elswyth Thayne, *The Fighting Quaker: Nathanael Greene*, p. 176.

133. Henry Steele Commager and Richard B. Morris, eds., *The Spirit of Seventy-Six*, p. 265.

134. George Washington Greene, *The Life of Major General Nathanael Greene*, vol. 1, pp. 310–311.

135. Pennsylvania Gazette, Sept. 4, 1776; Virginia Gazette, Jan. 24, 1777.

136. Hooper to Morris, Feb. 1, 1777, Paul H. Smith, ed., *Letters of Delegates to Congress, 1774–1789*, vol. 6 (Washington, D.C.: Library of Congress, 1976–1983), p. 191.

137. Pennsylvania Journal, Feb. 9, 1777, reprinted in Frank Moore, ed., *Diary of the American Revolution*, vol. 1 (New York: Charles Scribner's Sons, 1860), p. 397.

138. George F. Scheer and Hugh F. Rankin, *Rebels and Redcoats*, p. 495.

139. Isaac Q. Leake, *Life and Times of John Lamb* (Albany, N.Y.: J. Munsell, 1857), p. 279.

140. Rupert Hughes, *George Washington: The Savior of the States*, p. 669.

141. John C. Fitzpatrick, ed., *Writings of George Washington*, vol. XXX, pp. 26–27, as quoted in James Thomas Flexner, *George Washington in the American Revolution (1775–1783)*, p. 440.

142. Rupert Hughes, *George Washington: The Savior of the States*, p. 335.

Part IV: The Making of a Reluctant Noncandidate

1. McHenry to Caldwell, Dec. 23, 1783, "Letters of Members of the Continental Congress," vol. 7, pp. 394–395.

2. Barry Schwartz, *George Washington: The Making of an American Symbol* (New York: Free Press, 1987), p. 154.

3. Ibid., 153.

4. Madison to Randolph, March 17, 1783, *The Writings of James Madison*, Gaillard Hunt, ed., vol. 1 (New York: G. P. Putnam's Sons, 1900–1910), p. 407.

5. Barry Schwartz, *George Washington: The Making of an American Symbol*, p. 136.

6. Adams to Livingston, June 16, 1783, *Works of John Adams*, vol. 8, p. 73.

7. Henry Hayden Clark, *Poems of Freneau* (New York: Harcourt Brace, 1929), p. 89.

8. Barry Schwartz, *George Washington: The Making of an American Symbol*, p. 143.

9. Fred L. Pattee, ed., *The Poems of Philip Freneau*, vol. 2 (Princeton, N.J.: Princeton University Press, 1902–1907), p. 228.

10. Barry Schwartz, *General Washington: The Making of an American Symbol*, p. 122.

11. Washington to Clinton, Dec. 28, 1783; in John C. Fitzpatrick, ed., *The Writings of George Washington*, vol. 27 (Washington, D.C.: United States Government Printing Office, 1931–1944), p. 288.

12. Douglas Southall Freeman, *George Washington: Planter and Patriot*, vol. 3 (New York: Charles Scribner's Sons, 1951), p. 285.

13. Ibid., p. 44.

14. John C. Fitzpatrick, ed., *The Diaries of George Washington*, vol. 2 (Washington, D.C., 1931–1944), pp. 40–41.

15. Marcus Cunliffe, *George Washington: Man and Monument* (Boston: Little, Brown, 1958), p. 52.

16. Adams to Jefferson, 1813; *Historical Magazine*, July, 1870.

17. Nathan Schachner, *Alexander Hamilton* (New York: A. S. Barnes, 1961), p. 5.

18. Richard B. Bernstein with Kym S. Rice, *Are We to Be a Nation?* (Cambridge, Mass.: Harvard University Press, 1987), p. 78.

19. Rupert Hughes, *George Washington: The Savior of the States*, p. 450.

20. Ibid., pp. 450–451.

21. Merril Jensen and Robert A. Becker, eds., *The Documentary History of the First Federal Election 1778–80*, vol. 1 (Madison, Wis.: University of Wisconsin Press, 1976), p. 422.

22. Knox to Washington, March 19, 1787, John C. Fitzpatrick, ed., *George Washington Papers* (Washington, D.C.: Library of Congress, 1931–1944) in North Callahan, *Henry Knox: General Washington's General* (New York: Rinehart, 1958), p. 259.

23. North Callahan, *Henry Knox: General Washington's General*, p. 259.

24. James Thomas Flexner, *George Washington: Anguish and Farewell (1793–1799)* (Boston: Little, Brown, 1972), p. 492.

25. James Thomas Flexner, *George Washington in the American Revolution (1775–1783)* (Boston: Little, Brown, 1967), p. 514.

26. Douglas Southall Freeman, *George Washington: Planter and Patriot*, p. 294.

27. Ibid., p. 185.

28. Rupert Hughes, *George Washington: The Human Being and the Hero* (New York: William Morrow, 1926), pp. 74–75.

29. Worthington C. Ford, *Writings of George Washington*, vol. 2 (New York, 1889–1893), p. 272.

30. James Thomas Flexner, *George Washington: Anguish and Farewell (1793–1799)*, p. 199.

31. Douglas Southall Freeman, *George Washington: Planter and Patriot*, p. 211.

32. Marcus Cunliffe, *George Washington: Man and Monument*, p. 16.

33. Washington to the States (Circular Letter), June 8, 1783, John C. Fitzpatrick, ed., *The Writings of George Washington*, vol. 26, pp. 486–487, 495.

34. Barry Schwartz, *George Washington: The Making of an American Symbol*, p. 143.

35. Washington to Hamilton, Aug. 28, 1788, John C. Fitzpatrick, ed., *The Writings of George Washington*, vol. 30, p. 67.

36. Washington to Knox, March 8, 1787, John C. Fitzpatrick, ed., *The Writings of George Washington*, vol. 29, p. 171.

37. Washington to Randolph, April 9, 1787, ibid., p. 198.

38. Irving Brant, *James Madison: Father of the Constitution* (Indianapolis: Bobbs-Merrill, 1941–1961), p. 14.

39. Monroe to Jefferson, July 27, 1787, Julian P. Boyd, ed., *The Papers of Thomas Jefferson*, vol. 11 (Princeton, N.J.: Princeton University Press, 1950–1982), p. 6.

40. Hamilton, in recollection of the New York State (Ratification) Convention, March 7, 1789, Harold C. Syrett, ed., *Papers of Alexander Hamilton*, vol. 5 (New York: Columbia University Press, 1961–1979), p. 291.

41. Clinton Rossiter, *The American Presidency* (New York: New American Library, 1960), p. 76. See also Jackson Turner Main, *The Anti-Federalists* (New York: W. W. Norton, 1974), p. 141.

42. François Jean, Marquis de Chastellux, *Travels in North America*, vol. 1 (London: Printed for G. G. J. and J. Robinson, 1787), pp. 136, 301.

43. Irving Brant, *James Madison: Father of the Constitution*, p. 18.

44. Douglas Southall Freeman, *George Washington: Patriot and President* (New York: Charles Scribner's Sons, 1954), p. 145.

45. Letter of Aug. 16, 1788, to Charles Pettit, ibid., p. 42.

46. Letter of July 21, 1788, ibid., p. 24.

47. Douglas Southall Freeman, *George Washington: Patriot and President*, p. 145.

48. See especially the Pennsylvania Packet of Feb. 22, 1788, p. 2.

49. Letter of Jan. 1, 1788: Louis Gottschalk, ed., *The Letters of Lafayette to Washington, 1777–1799* (New York: Privately printed by Helen F. Hubbard, 1944), pp. 334–335, as quoted in Douglas Southall Freeman, *George Washington: Patriot and President*, p. 146.

50. Douglas Southall Freeman, *George Washington: Patriot and President*, p. 147.

51. *Pennsylvania Packet*, July 12, 1788, p. 2.

52. Ibid., July 19, 1788, p. 3.

53. Ibid., Aug. 6, 1788, p. 2.

54. Ibid., Aug. 7, 1788, p. 2.

55. Humphreys to Jefferson, Nov. 29, 1788, Julian P. Boyd, ed., *Papers of Thomas Jefferson*, vol. 14, p. 302.

56. Jefferson to William Carmichael, March 4, 1789, ibid., vol. 14, p. 615.

57. John C. Miller, *Alexander Hamilton and the Growth of the New Nation* (New York: Harper & Row, 1964), p. 219.

58. Douglas Southall Freeman, *George Washington: Patriot and President*, p. 148.

59. Letter of Aug. 28, 1788, John C. Fitzpatrick, ed., *Writings of George Washington*, vol. 30, pp. 66–67.

60. *Pennsylvania Packet*, Nov. 3, 1788, p. 3.

61. Lewis to Thomas Shippen, Oct. 11, 1787, in Julian P. Boyd, ed., *The Papers of Thomas Jefferson*, vol. 12, p. 23.

62. Letter dated July 12, 1788, ibid., vol. 13, p. 351.

63. John C. Fitzpatrick, ed., *The Diaries of George Washington*, vol. 3, p. 377.

64. Richard B. Bernstein with Kym S. Rice, *Are We to Be a Nation?*, p. 210.

65. John C. Fitzpatrick, ed., *The Diaries of George Washington*, vol. 3, pp. 384, 387–388.

66. Louis Gottschalk, ed., *The Letters of Lafayette to Washington, 1777–1799*, pp. 334–335; Francis Adiran van der Kemp, 1752–1829; an Autobiography, ed. Helen L. Fairchild, p. 116. (The visit was on July 29, 1788.)

67. Washington to Hamilton, Oct. 3, 1788; Worthington C. Ford, ed., *Writings of George Washington*, vol. XI, pp. 328–332, in Nathan Schachner, *Alexander Hamilton*, pp. 231–232.

Part V: Campaign '88

1. *American Heritage*, Aug. 1955, p. 43.

2. J. M. Toner, "George Washington as an Inventer and Promoter of the Useful Arts," cited in William Spohn Baker, *Early Sketches of George Washington* (Philadelphia: J. B. Lippincott Company, 1894), p. 13.

3. General George Washington and Marvin Kitman, PFC (Ret.), *George Washington's Expense Account* (New York: Simon and Schuster, 1970), p. 105.

4. Rupert Hughes, *George Washington: The Savior of the States* (New York: William Morrow, 1928), p. 447.

5. J. Hammond Trumbull, "A Business Firm in the Revolution," *Magazine of American History*, vol. XII, p. 7.

6. Ibid., p. 20, in Rupert Hughes, *George Washington: The Savior of the States*, p. 447.

7. Rupert Hughes, *George Washington: The Savior of the States*, p. 448.

8. J. Hammond Trumbull, "A Business Firm in the Revolution," p. 26.

9. Rupert Hughes, *George Washington: The Savior of the States*, p. 449.

10. "George Washington: The Forging of a Nation," on CBS, which first played September 21, 1986.

11. John R. Alden, *George Washington: A Biography* (New York: W. W. Norton, 1967), p. 81.

12. Theodore Thayer, *Nathanael Greene: Strategist of the American Revolution* (New York: Twayne, 1960), p. 233.

13. Howard Swiggett, *The Forgotten Leaders of the Revolution* (Garden City, N.Y.: Doubleday, 1955), pp. 49–54.

14. John F. Stegeman and Janet A. Stegeman, *Caty: A Biography of Catharine Littlefield Greene* (Providence, R.I.: Rhode Island Bicentennial Foundation, 1977), p. 106.

15. James Thomas Flexner, *George Washington: The Forge of Experience (1732–1775)* (Boston: Little, Brown, 1965), p 146.

16. James Thomas Flexner, *George Washington in the American Revolution (1775–1783)* (Boston: Little, Brown, 1967), p. 336n.

17. Lydia Minturn Post, *Personal Recollections of the American Revolution, 1774–1776*, ed. Margaret W Willard (Port Washington, N.Y.: Kennikat Press, 1968), p. 228.

18. Karal Ann Marling, *George Washington Slept Here* (Cambridge, Mass.: Harvard University Press, 1988), p. 249.

19. James Thomas Flexner, *George Washington: Anguish and Farewell* (Boston: Little, Brown, 1972), p. 492n.

20. Howard Swiggett, *Forgotten Leaders of the Revolution*, pp. 51–52.

21. W. E. Woodward, *George Washington: The Image and the Man* (New York: Boni and Liveright, 1926), p. 19.

22. Marcus Cunliffe, *George Washington: Man and Monument* (Boston: Little, Brown, 1958), p. 11.

23. Richard B. Morris, *Witnesses at the Creation* (New York: Henry Holt, 1985), p. 39.

Part VI: The Last Huzzah

1. David M. Matteson, *The Organization of the Government Under the Constitution* (New York: Da Capo Press, 1970), p. 76.

2. *Pennsylvania Packet*, Feb. 16, 1789.

3. Ibid., Feb. 21, 1789.

4. Ibid., March 20, 1789.

5. Ibid., Feb. 7, 1789.

338 / Notes

6. David M. Matteson, *The Organization of the Government Under the Constitution*, p. 76.

7. Richard B. Bernstein with Kym S. Rice, *Are We to Be a Nation?* (Cambridge, Mass.: Harvard University Press, 1987), pp. 201–202.

8. Lincoln to Washington, Sept. 24, 1788, Papers of George Washington, vol. 241, pp. 104–105, Library of Congress; Lincoln to Washington, Oct. 25, 1788, vol. 242, ibid.

9. Letter of Oct. 26, 1788, Papers of George Washington, vol. 30, p. 121.

10. John C. Miller, *Alexander Hamilton and the Growth of the New Nation* (New York: Harper & Row, 1964), pp. 220–221.

11. Hamilton, *Writings* (Lodge), vol. VIII, p. 311; vol. IX, pp. 452–454; Madison, *Writings* (Hunt), vol. V, p. 270.

12. Channing, *History*, vol. IV, pp. 170–171; Hamilton, *Writings* (Lodge), vol. VIII, pp. 315–316; R. L. Brunhouse, *The Counter-Revolution in Pennsylvania* (Harrisburg, 1942), p. 218.

13. David M. Matteson, *The Organization of the Government Under the Constitution*, p. 76.

14. John C. Miller, *Alexander Hamilton and the Growth of the New Nation*, p. 221.

15. David M. Matteson, *The Organization of the Government Under the Constitution*, p. 74.

16. Ibid., p. 75.

17. Thompson to John Langdon, April 14, 1789; 21 Early New Hampshire State Papers, pp. 865–866. The original of this famous document is in Papers of George Washington, vol. 243, Library of Congress, p. 19.

18. Thompson to the President of the Senate, April 24, 1789; American State Papers, vol. I, p. 506.

19. Douglas Southall Freeman, *George Washington: Patriot and President* (New York: Charles Scribner's Sons, 1954), p. 157.

20. David M. Matteson, *The Organization of the Government Under the Constitution*, p. 128.

21. John C. Fitzpatrick, ed., *Diaries of George Washington*, vol. 3 (Boston and New York: Houghton Mifflin Company, 1925), p. 441.

22. John C. Fitzpatrick, ed., *Writings of George Washington*, vol. 30 (Washington, D.C.: United States Government Printing Office, 1931–1944), p. 43.

23. Letter of Feb. 15, 1787; *Writings of George Washington*, vol. 29, pp. 160–161, in Douglas Southall Freeman, *George Washington: Patriot and President*, p. 159.

24. Letters to Richard Conway, ibid., vol. 30, pp. 220–223, in ibid.

25. John C. Fitzpatrick, ed., *Writings of George Washington*, vol. 30, p. 36; cf. ibid., vol. 29, p. 335.

26. Ibid., p. 379; cf. ibid., p. 468.

27. Ibid., pp. 500–501; Ledger B, f. 267.

28. John C. Fitzpatrick, ed., *Writings of George Washington*, vol. 30, p. 36.

29. David Griffith to Washington, Nov. 3, 1788; John C. Fitzpatrick, ed., *Papers of George Washington*, vol. 2 (Washington, D.C.: Library of Congress, 1931–1944), p. 242, as quoted in Douglas Southall Freeman, *George Washington: Patriot and President*, p. 144.

30. John C. Fitzpatrick, ed., *Writings of George Washington*, vol. 29, pp. 294, 303, 459–460.

31. Douglas Southall Freeman, *George Washington: Patriot and President*, p. 144.

32. David M. Matteson, *The Organization of the Government Under the Constitution*, p. 128.

33. Barry Schwartz, *George Washington: The Making of an American Symbol* (New York: Free Press, 1987), p. 49.

34. Douglas Southall Freeman, *George Washington: Patriot and President*, p. 172.

35. Philadelphia papers, as supra, n. 18.

36. Douglas Southall Freeman, *George Washington: Patriot and President*, p. 172.

37. W. E. Woodward, *George Washington: The Image and the Man* (New York: Boni and Liveright, 1926), p. 431.

38. *Extracts from the Diary of Jacob Hiltzheimer*, 1765–1798, ed. J. C. Parsons, p. 152.

39. Douglas Southall Freeman, *George Washington: Patriot and President*, p. 173.

40. James Thomas Flexner, *George Washington and the New Nation* (Boston: Little, Brown, 1969), p. 342.

41. Douglas Southall Freeman, *George Washington: Patriot and President*, p. 173.

42. David M. Matteson, *The Organization of the Government Under the Constitution*, p. 131

43. Ibid.

44. Barry Schwartz, *George Washington: The Making of an American Symbol*, p. 217.

45. *The Gazette of the United States*, April 29, 1789.

46. Douglas Southall Freeman, *George Washington: Patriot and President*, p. 180.

47. Boudinot letter, op cit., p. 162. The *Gazette of the United States* printed this ode, seven lines to the stanza, in its issue of April 25, p. 3. Authorship was attributed, Col. Freeman says, to " 'Mr. L.' that is, to Samuel Low."

48. Boudinot letter, op. cit., p. 162.

49. Ibid.

50. Ibid., p. 163.

51. *Daily Advertiser*, April 24, 1789, p. 2.

52. Douglas Southall Freeman, *George Washington: Patriot and President*, pp. 180–181.

53. Correspondence and Journals of Samuel Blachley Webb, vol. V, p. 128, as quoted in Douglas Southall Freeman, *George Washington: Planter and Patriot*, vol. 3, p. 488n.

54. David M. Matteson, *The Organization of the Government Under the Constitution*, pp. 133–134.

55. Barry Schwartz, *George Washington: The Making of an American Symbol*, pp. 49–50.

56. *The Gazette of the United States*, April 29, 1789.

57. Dixon Wector, *The Hero in America: A Chronicle of Hero-Worship* (Ann Arbor, Mich.: University of Michigan Press, 1972), p. 125.

58. David M. Matteson, *The Organization of the Government Under the Constitution*, p. 121.

59. Kenneth R. Bowling and Helen E. Veit, eds., *The Diary of William Maclay and Other Notes on Senate Debates* (Baltimore, Md.: Johns Hopkins University Press, 1988), p. 98.

60. Ibid., p. 13.

61. Douglas Southall Freeman, *George Washington: Patriot and President*, p. 193.

62. Kenneth R. Bowling and Helen E. Veit, eds., *The Diary of William Maclay and other Notes on Senate Debates*, p. 13.

63. David M. Matteson, *The Organization of the Government Under the Constitution*, p. 138.

64. Barry Schwartz, *George Washington: The Making of an American Symbol*, pp. 154–155.

65. Abiel Holms, *A Sermon . . . Occasioned by the Death of General George Washington* (Boston: Samuel Hall, 1800), p. 16; MacWhorter, *A Funeral Sermon*, p. 2.

66. Donald Jackson and Dorothy Twohig, eds., *The Diaries of George Washington*, vol. 5 (Charlottesville, Va.: University of Virginia Press, 1976–1979), p. 447.

67. W. E. Woodward, *George Washington: The Image and the Man*, pp. 347–348.

68. Washington Papers, vol. 242, in David M. Matteson, *The Organization of the Government Under the Constitution*, p. 120.

69. Barry Schwartz, *George Washington: The Making of an American Symbol*, p. 134.

70. Washington to Nicola, May 22, 1782, *Writings of George Washington*, vol. 24, p. 272.

71. Douglas Southall Freeman, *George Washington: Patriot and President*, p. 212, footnote 70.

72. Don Higginbotham, *George Washington and the Military Tradition* (Athens, Ga.: University of Georgia Press, 1985), p. 14, note 11.

73. Barry Schwartz, *George Washington: The Making of an American Symbol*, p. 61.

74. W. E. Woodward, *George Washington: The Image and the Man*, pp. 436–437.

75. (New York) *Daily Advertiser*, June 15, 1789.

76. *National Gazette*, Dec. 26, 1792.

77. Ibid., Jan. 30, 1793.

78. Barry Schwartz, *George Washington: The Making of an American Symbol*, p. 62.

79. Douglas Southall Freeman, *George Washington: Patriot and President*, p. 371n.

80. Adams to Jefferson, Oct. 9, 1787, Julian P. Boyd, ed., *Papers of Thomas Jefferson*, vol. 12 (Princeton, N.J.: Princeton University Press, 1950–1982), p. 220.

81. W. E. Woodward, *George Washington: The Image and the Man*, p. 436.

82. Writings of George Washington, Library of Congress, vol. 30, p. 224, in David M. Matteson, *The Organization of the Government Under the Constitution*, p. 124.

83. See letter, Benjamin Harrison to Washington on p. 45.

84. Shaw Livermore, *Early American Land Companies* (New York: Octagon Books, 1968), pp. 196–203.

85. Massachusetts Historical Society, Sedgwick Papers, vol. 5, in David M. Matteson, *The Organization of the Government Under the Constitution*, p. 124.

86. Richard B. Morris, *Witnesses at the Creation* (New York: Henry Holt, 1985), p. 40.

87. Douglas Southall Freeman, *George Washington: Patriot and President*, p. 186.

88. John C. Fitzpatrick, ed., *Writings of George Washington*, vol. 31, p. 53; cf. vol. 30, p. 361.

89. Letter of May 1789, to George Augustine Washington, as cited supra, n. 3.

90. James Thomas Flexner, *George Washington and the New Nation 1783–1793*, (Boston: Little, Brown, 1967), p. 196.

91. Ibid., p. 200.

92. Anne H. Wharton, "Washington's New York Residence in 1789," *Lippincott's Magazine*, XXXIV (1889), pp. 741–745, in James Thomas Flexner, *George Washington and the New Nation*, p. 200.

93. W. E. Woodward, *George Washington: The Image and the Man*, p. 447.

94. Elswyth Thayne, *Washington's Lady* (New York: Dodd, Mead, 1960), p. 289.

95. *Gazette of the United States*, May 21, 1791, in Barry Schwartz, *George Washington: The Making of an American Symbol*, p. 74.

96. Theodore Thayer, *Nathanael Greene: Strategist of the American Revolution* (New York: Twayne, 1960), p. 281.

97. Mrs. Elizabeth F. Ellet, *The Women of the American Revolution* (New York, 1849), cited in Archibald Henderson, *Washington's Southern Tour, 1791* (Boston: Houghton Mifflin, 1923), p. 206.

98. Douglas Southall Freeman, *George Washington: Patriot and President*, p. 316.

99. John C. Fitzpatrick, ed., *Diaries of George Washington*, vol. 4, p. 176.

100. Theodore Thayer, *Nathanael Greene: Strategist of the American Revolution*, p. 281.

Bibliography

"Aaron Wright's Revolutionary Journal." *Historical Magazine,* July 1862: 209.

Adams, Charles Francis, ed. *The Works of John Adams, Second President of the United States.* 10 vols. Boston: C. C. Little, J. Brown, 1850–1856.

Alden, John R. *George Washington: A Biography.* New York: W. W. Norton, 1963.

Austin, J. T. *The Life of Elbridge Gerry.* Vol. 1. Jersey City, N.J.: Da Capo Press, 1970.

Baker, William Spohn. *Early Sketches of George Washington.* Philadelphia: J. B. Lippincott Company, 1894.

Barton, R. T. *The First Election of Washington.* Vol. 11. Virginia Historical Collection.

Belknap. "Journal of My Tour to the Camp." *Massachusetts Historical Society Proceedings* 4 (1858–1860): 82–83.

Bernstein, Richard B., with Kym S. Rice. *Are We to Be a Nation?* Cambridge, Mass.: Harvard University Press, 1987.

Billias, George Athan, ed. *George Washington's Generals.* New York: William Morrow, 1964.

Bolton, Charles Knowles. *The Private Soldier Under Washington.* Port Washington, N.Y.: Kennikat Press, 1902, 1964.

Bowen, C. D. *John Adams and the American Revolution.* Boston: Little, Brown, 1950.

Bowling, Kenneth R. and Helen E. Veit, eds. *The Diary of William Maclay and Other Notes on Senate Debates.* Baltimore, Md.: Johns Hopkins University Press, 1988.

Boyd, Julian P. *The Papers of Thomas Jefferson.* 14 vols. Princeton, N.J.: Princeton University Press, 1950–1982.

Boylan, Brian Richard. *Benedict Arnold: The Dark Eagle.* New York: W. W. Norton, 1973.

Brant, Irving. *James Madison: Father of the Constitution.* Vol. 3 of *James Madison.* Indianapolis: Bobbs-Merrill, 1941–1961.

Bridenbaugh, Carl, and Jessica Bridenbaugh. *Rebels and Gentlemen: Philadelphia in the Age of Franklin.* New York: Oxford University Press, 1962.

Brunhouse, R. L. *The Counter-Revolution in Pennsylvania.* Harrisburg, 1942.

Burnett, Edmund C., ed. *Letters of Members of the Continental Congress.* 8 vols. Washington, D.C.: 1921–1936.

Butterfield, L. H., ed. *Diary and Autobiography of John Adams.* Vol. 3. Cambridge, Mass.: Harvard University Press, 1961–1962.

———. *Adams Family Correspondence.* Vol. 1. Cambridge, Mass.: Harvard University Press, 1963–1973.

Cady, Edwin H., ed. *Literature of the Early Republic.* New York: Rinehart, 1950.

Callahan, North. *Henry Knox: General Washington's General.* New York: Rinehart, 1958.

———. *George Washington: Soldier and Man.* New York: William Morrow, 1972.

Chase, G. W., and H. B. Dawson, eds. *Diary of David How.* Morrisania, N.Y.: 1865.

Chastellux, Francois Jean, Marquis de. *Travels in North America.* London: Printed for G. G. J. and J. Robinson, 1787.

Clark, Henry Hayden. *Poems of Freneau.* New York: Harcourt Brace, 1929.

Commager, Henry Steele, and Richard B. Morris, eds. *The Spirit of Seventy-Six.* New York: Harper & Row, 1967.

Cooke, Jacob E., ed. *Alexander Hamilton: A Profile.* New York: Hill and Wang, 1967.

Corner, George W., ed. *Autobiography of Benjamin Rush.* Princeton, N.J.: Princeton University Press, 1948.

Cunliffe, Marcus. *George Washington: Man and Monument.* Boston: Little, Brown, 1958.

DeLancey, E. F. "History of New York During the Revolutionary War." *New-York Historical Society,* vol. 2.

Drimmer, Melvin. *Black History.* Garden City, N.Y.: Doubleday, 1968.

Dwyer, William M. *The Day Is Ours.* New York: Viking Press, 1983.

Ellet, Elizabeth. *Women of the American Revolution.* 3 vols. New York: Corner House, 1848.

Fitzpatrick, John C., ed. *Writings of George Washington.* 39 vols. Washington, D.C.: United States Government Printing Office, 1931–1944.

———. *Diaries of George Washington.* 4 vols. Boston and New York: Houghton Mifflin Company, 1925.

———. *George Washington Papers.* Washington, D.C.: Library of Congress, 1931–1944.

Flexner, James Thomas. *George Washington: The Forge of Experience (1732–1775).* Boston: Little, Brown, 1965.

———. *George Washington in the American Revolution (1775–1783).* Boston: Little, Brown, 1967.

———. *George Washington and the New Nation (1783–1793).* Boston: Little, Brown, 1969.

———. *George Washington: Anguish and Farewell (1793–1799).* Boston: Little, Brown, 1972.

Flick, Alexander C. "General Henry Knox's Ticonderoga Expedition." *New York State Historical Association Quarterly Journal*, vol. 9, no. 2 (April 1928).

Forbes, Esther. *Paul Revere and the World He Lived In*. Boston: Houghton Mifflin, 1942.

Force, Peter. *American Archives*. 4th series, 5 vols. Washington, D.C.: 1837–1853.

Ford, Paul Leicester. *The True George Washington*. Philadelphia: Lippincott, 1909.

———, ed. *The Writings of Thomas Jefferson*. Vol. 11. New York: G. P. Putnam's Sons, 1904–1905.

Ford, Worthington C., et al., eds. *Journals of the Continental Congress, 1774–1789*, 97–99, 34 vols.

———, ed. *Writings of George Washington*. 14 vols. New York: 1889–1893.

Freeman, Douglas Southall. *George Washington*. 7 vols. New York: Charles Scribner's Sons, 1948–1954.

French, Allen. *The First Year of the American Revolution*. New York: Octagon Books, 1961.

Godfrey, Dr. Carlos E. *The Commander-in-Chief's Guard*. Washington, D.C.: Stevenson-Smith Company, 1904.

Gottschalk, Louis, ed. *The Letters of Lafayette to Washington, 1777–1799*. New York: Privately printed by Helen F. Hubbard, 1944.

Greene, George Washington. *The Life of Major General Nathanael Greene*. 3 vols. Boston: Houghton Mifflin, 1878–1890.

Gruber, Ira D. *The Howe Brothers & The American Revolution*. New York: Atheneum, 1972.

Haworth, Paul Leland. *George Washington, Country Gentleman*. Indianapolis, n.d.

Henderson, Archibald. *Washington's Southern Tour, 1791*. Boston: Houghton Mifflin, 1923.

Higginbotham, Don. *George Washington and the American Military Tradition*. Athens, Ga.: University of Georgia Press, 1985.

Holmes, Abiel. *A Sermon . . . Occasioned by the Death of General George Washington*. Boston: Samuel Hall, 1800.

Horner. *Pennsylvania Magazine of History and Biography* 65 (July, 1941): 364.

Hover, Herman D. *Fourteen Presidents before Washington*. New York: Dodd, Mead, 1985.

Hughes, Rupert. *George Washington: The Human Being and the Hero*. New York: William Morrow, 1926.

———. *George Washington: The Rebel and the Patriot*. New York: William Morrow, 1927.

———. *George Washington: The Savior of the States*. New York: William Morrow, 1930.

Hunt, Gaillard, ed. *The Writings of James Madison*. 9 vols. New York: G. P. Putnam's Sons, 1900–1910.

Jackson, Donald, and Dorothy Twohig, eds. *The Diaries of George Washington*. 6 vols. Charlottesville, Va.: University of Virginia Press, 1976–1979.

Jamieson, Kathleen Hall. *Packaging the Presidency: A History and Criticism of Presidential Campaign Advertising*. New York: Oxford University Press, 1984.

Jensen, Merrill, and Robert A. Becker, eds. *The Documentary History of the First*

Federal Election 1788–80. Vol. 1. Madison, Wis.: University of Wisconsin Press, 1976.

John, Walton C., and Alma H. Preinkert, eds. "The Educational Views of George Washington." In *History of the George Washington Bicentennial.* Vol. 1. Washington, D.C.: George Washington Bicentennial Celebration, 1932.

Jones, Thomas. *History of New York During the Revolutionary War.* Vol. 1. Ed. Edward Floyd DeLancey. New York: Printed for the New-York Historical Society, 1879.

"Journal." *Connecticut Historical Society Collection* 7:128–131.

Kennedy, J. P., and H. R. McIlwaine, eds. *Journal of the House of Burgesses of Colonial Virginia, 1758–61.* Richmond, Va.: 1909.

Koontz, Dr. Louis K. *The Virginia Frontier, 1754–1763.* Baltimore: Johns Hopkins University Studies, 1925.

Leake, Isaac Q. *Life and Times of John Lamb.* Albany, N.Y.: J. Munsell, 1857.

Learned, M. D., and C. Grosse, eds. *America Germanica.* Vol. 4. New York: London and Berlin, 1902.

Livermore, Shaw. *Early American Land Companies.* New York: Octagon Books, 1968.

Lodge, Henry Cabot, ed. *Complete Works of Alexander Hamilton.* 12 vols. New York: Putnam, 1904.

Longmore, Paul K. *The Invention of George Washington.* Berkeley, Ca.: University of California Press, 1988.

Lowell, E. J. *The Hessians in the Revolutionary War.* Williamstown, Mass.: Corner House, 1970. Reprint from 1884.

Macclintock, Sammuel. *An Oration Commemorative of the Late Illustrious General Washington.* Portsmouth, N.H.: Charles Pierce, 1800.

Main, Jackson Turner. *The Anti-Federalists.* New York: W. W. Norton, 1974.

———. *Political Parties before the Constitution.* New York: W. W. Norton, 1974.

Malone, Dumas. *Jefferson the Virginian.* Boston: Little, Brown, 1948.

Marchione, Margherita, trans. *Philip Mazzei: Jefferson's "Zealous Whig."* New York: American Institute of Italian Studies, 1975.

Marling, Karal Ann. *George Washington Slept Here.* Cambridge, Mass.: Harvard University Press, 1988.

Matteson, David M. *The Organization of the Government Under the Constitution.* New York: Da Capo Press, 1970.

McDonald, Forrest. *Alexander Hamilton: A Biography.* New York: W. W. Norton, 1982.

Miller, John C. *Alexander Hamilton and the Growth of the New Nation.* New York: Harper & Row, 1964.

Mirsky, Jeanette, and Alan Nevins. *The World of Eli Whitney.* New York: Macmillan, 1952.

Moore, Frank. *The Diary of the American Revolution.* 2 vols. New York: Charles Scribner's Sons, 1860.

Morris, Richard B. *Witnesses at the Creation.* New York: Henry Holt, 1985.

———. *The Forging of the Union.* New York: Harper & Row, 1987.

Murdoch, Harold, ed. "Letter of Reverend William Gordon, 1776." *Proceedings* 60 (1927): 361–364.

Pattee, Fred L., ed. *The Poems of Philip Freneau*. Vol. 1. Princeton, N.J.: Princeton University Press, 1902–1907.

Pearson, Michael. *The Revolutionary War: An Unbiased Account*. New York: Capricorn Books, 1973.

Post, Lydia Minturn. *Personal Recollections of the American Revolution, 1774–1776*. Ed. Margaret W. Willard. Port Washington, N.Y.: Kennikat Press, 1968.

Reed, William B. *Life and Correspondence of Joseph Reed*. 2 vols. Philadelphia: Lindsay and Blakiston, 1847.

Rorabaugh, W. J. *The Alcoholic Republic: An American Tradition*. New York: Oxford University Press, 1979.

Rossiter, Clinton. *The American Presidency*. New York: New American Library, 1960.

———. *The First American Revolution*. Part I of *Seedtime of the Republic*. New York: Harcourt, Brace and World, 1953.

———. *Six Characters in Search of a Republic*. Part II of *Seedtime of the Republic*. New York: Harcourt, Brace and World, 1953.

———. *1787: The Grand Convention*. New York: Macmillan, 1966.

Schachner, Nathan. *Alexander Hamilton*. New York: A. S. Barnes, 1961.

Scheer, George F., and Hugh F. Rankin. *Rebels and Redcoats*. Cleveland and New York: World, 1957.

Schlesinger, Arthur M., Sr. "Patriotism Names the Baby." *New England Quarterly* 14 (1941): 611–618.

———. *Prelude to Independence: The Newspaper War on Britain 1764–1776*. New York: Vintage, 1958.

———. *The Colonial Merchants and the American Revolution 1763–1776*. New York: Atheneum, 1968.

———. *The Birth of a Nation*. Boston: Houghton Mifflin, 1981.

Schwartz, Barry. *George Washington: The Making of an American Symbol*. New York: Free Press, 1987.

Shaw, Peter. *The Character of John Adams*. Chapel Hill, N.C.: University of North Carolina, 1976.

Shy, John. *Toward Lexington*. Princeton, N.J.: Princeton University Press, 1965.

Silverman, Kenneth. *A Cultural History of the American Revolution*. New York: T. Y. Crowell, 1976.

Smith, Paul H. *Letters of Delegates to Congress, 1774–1789*. 6 vols. Washington, D.C.: Library of Congress, 1976–1983.

Stegeman, John F., and Janet A. Stegeman. *Caty: A Biography of Catharine Littlefield Greene*. Providence, R.I.: Rhode Island Bicentennial Foundation, 1977.

Stewart, George R. *Names on the Land*. Boston: Houghton Mifflin, 1967.

Swiggett, Howard. *The Forgotten Leaders of the Revolution*. Garden City, N.Y.: Doubleday, 1955.

Sydnor, Charles S. *American Revolutionaries in the Making: Political Practices in Washington's Virginia*. New York: Macmillan, 1965.

Syrett, Harold C., ed. *Papers of Alexander Hamilton.* Vol. 5. New York: Columbia University Press, 1961–1979.

Thane, Elswyth. *Washington's Lady.* New York: Dodd, Mead, 1960.

———. *The Fighting Quaker: Nathanael Greene.* New York: Hawthorn Books, 1972.

Thatcher, Thomas. *An Eulogy on George Washington.* Dedham, Mass.: Mann, 1800.

Thayer, Theodore. *Nathanael Greene: Strategist of the American Revolution.* New York: Twayne, 1960.

Tourtellot, Arthur B. *Lexington and Concord.* New York: W. W. Norton, 1963.

Treacey, M. F. *Prelude to Yorktown (The Southern Campaign of Nathanael Greene, 1780–81).* Chapel Hill, N.C.: University of North Carolina, 1963.

Trumbull, J. Hammond. "A Business Firm in the Revolution." *Magazine of American History* 12: 7.

Vail, R. W. G. "A Dinner at Mount Vernon." From the unpublished journal of Joshua Brookes. *New-York Historical Society Quarterly* 31 (1947): 72–85.

Van Tyne, Claude Halstead. *The Loyalists in the American Revolution.* Gloucester, Mass.: Macmillan, 1902, 1959.

Vidal, Gore. *Burr: A Novel.* New York: Random House, 1973.

Walpole, Horace. *Memoirs of the Last Ten Years of the Reign of George II.* Vol. 1. Ed. Lord Holland. London: 1847.

———. *Last Journals.* Vol. 1. London: 1910.

Washington, General George, and Marvin Kitman, PFC (Ret.). *George Washington's Expense Account.* New York: Simon and Schuster, 1970.

Wector, Dixon. *The Hero in America: A Chronicle of Hero-Worship.* Ann Arbor, Mich.: University of Michigan Press, 1972.

Woodward, W. E. *George Washington: The Image and the Man.* New York: Boni and Liveright, 1926.

Zobel, Hiller B. *The Boston Massacre.* New York: W. W. Norton, 1971.

Index

Adams, Abigail, quoted on meeting
    Washington, 249
Adams, John
    criticism by, of George Washington, 88–
      90
    description of, 76–77
    expense accounts and, 87n, 88
    flaws of, as politician, 89
    letter to, from Jonathan Trumbull, 281–
      82
    in Paris, 90
    political considerations of, 75–76
    quoted
      on card playing, 42n
      on General Washington's retirement,
        203
      on John Hancock, 64
      on opposition to Washington for
        General, 82
      on Philadelphia, 36
      on Washington raising an army, 26
    speech by, on Washington for General,
      80
    as Vice President, 277–82
Adams, Samuel, 77–79
    Boston Massacre and, 68, 68n
Administration, first, formality about, 307–
    8
Aides-de-camp (ADCs)
    as machine behind Washington, 209–
      10
Alcoholic beverages
    at camp outside Boston, 133
    use of, 31–34
Alexa, Frances, 105, 105n
Alexandria, Virginia, on way to
    inauguration, 289

Allen, Ethan, quoted on Joshua Loring, Jr.,
    164
America, representation in, 99
American people
    manipulation of, 128
    as patriots, 98
    as Tories, 98
American Revolution. *See* Revolution,
    American
American Revolutionaries in the Making:
    Political Practices in Washington's
    Virginia (Sydnor), 32–33
Ames, Fisher (Representative), quoted on
    inaugural address, 303
Anti-federalists, description of, 278n
Anti-Washington movement, Pendleton
    and, 76
Apollo Room, 28, 29
Army payroll, 86
Arnold, Benedict, idea for cannon from
    Ticonderoga by, 147n
"Athenaeum, The," 5–6
Augustine, John, letter from Mary
    Washington to, 287

Battle of Bunker Hill, 54, 54n
Belknap, Jeremy, quoted on Charles Lee,
    70
Bernstein, Richard B., quoted on men
    crying, 203
Bingham, Mrs. William, at inauguration
    party, 292
Bland, Mary, 104n
Boston, Massachusetts
    arrival at, 129
    camp outside of, 133–38

Boston, Massachusetts (cont.)
    cannonading of, 157
    hurricane at, 158–59, 160
    invasion of, by sea, 159–60
    population of, 133n
    trip to, in 1756, 23
Boston Cadets, 65–66
Boston Massacre, 68
Boston Tea Party, Sons of Liberty and, 66–
    67
Braddock's Massacre, 63, 63n
Brehan, Marchioness de, 286, 286n
Bridenbaugh, Carl
    quoted on Philadelphia, 38
    Rebels and Gentlemen, 37, 324
British troops, New World fighting and,
    192
Burns's Tavern, location of, 83n
Burr, Aaron, as secretary to General
    Washington, 172

Campaigning
    alcohol and, 31–34
    dancing and, 35–36
Campbell, Alexander, portrait by, of
    General Washington, 168–69
Cannon
    bursts of, on inauguration route, 291,
        291n
    from Fort Ticonderoga, 148–54, 148–49n
    idea for, 147, 147n
    instructions for, 149–50
    travel difficulties and, 150–54
Card playing, John Adams quoted on, 42n
Carrol, Ann, 106
Cary, Mary, 104
Cincinnati, membership in, 223
City Tavern, 28, 29–30
Clinton, Henry (Sir), quoted on Sir William
    Howe, 161–62
Clothing. See also Uniform(s)
    inaugural, 297, 297n
    prewar fashions, 44
    shopping for, 21–22
Coehorn(s), from Ticonderoga, 148–54,
    148–49n
    description of, 148
Connecticut, presidential electors from,
    276
Constitutional Convention, 223–25
    chairman of, 227–28
    Washington's attendance at, 224–25
Continental Army
    alcohol abuse in, 133–35
    appearance of, 140
    bathing in, 135
    camp for, at Cambridge, 133
    choosing of officers in, 135–36
    corruption in administration of, 249–54

count of troops in, 132–33
    discipline in, 138
        after, 139
        before, 140
    dissension in, 138
    enlistment in, 141
    first court martial in, 136–37
    flaws in deployment of troops in, 170–71
    flogging in, 137–38, 137n
    General Washington's plan for, 140
    inactivity of, 141–42
    orders to, for fortification of Dorchester
        Heights, 156
    powder shortage for, 143–44
    punishment in, 137–38, 137n
    reenlistment in, 140–41
    relationship between officers and men in,
        136
    retreats under General Washington in,
        194–95
    rifle companies in, 142–43
    saluting in, 136
    sickness in, 180, 180n
Continental Congress, First, 17–18
    City Tavern during, 30
Continental Congress, Second, 15–17
    City Tavern during, 30
    Congressman George Washington at, 15–
        16
        committee assignment for, 19
    debates of, 16
    Virginia delegation to, 16–17
Corruption, potential campaign issue of,
    249–54
Council of War, meetings of, 142
Crime(s), punishment for, in Continental
    army, 134–38, 137n
Crying. See Weeping
Custis, Martha. See also Washington,
        Martha Dandridge
    financial holdings of, 113–14
    George Washington meeting with, 108–
        10

Dancing
    campaigning and, 35–36
    at Valley Forge, 177–79
Dandridge, Martha. See Custis, Martha
        Dandridge; Washington, Martha
        Dandridge
Davis, Betty, 279
Deane, Barnabas, 251
Deane, Silas, 251, 251n
    quoted on Washington raising an army,
        25
DeJumonville (French Ambassador), death
    of, 58–59
Delaware, presidential electors from, 276
Delegations, divisions among, 75

Dinwiddie, Robert (Lt. Governor of
Virginia)
Ohio Company and, 56–58
stock in, 61–62
Dorchester Heights
fortification of, 155–59
effect of, 160–61
preparation for, 156
work activities on, 161
Drunkenness. *See also* Alcoholic beverages
in Continental army, 135, 135n
punishment for, 134
du Motier, Marie-Joseph-Paul-Yves-Roche-
Gilbert. *See* Lafayette, Marquis de
Duer, William, 184
Dwight, Timothy, poems of Washington
by, 167, 167n

East India Tea Company, 66
Election 1758, alcoholic beverages during,
32–33
Election 1789
issues of, 249, 249n
nonissues of, 249–54
results of, 283
statistics on, 275–78
Electoral college. *See* Presidential electors
Etiquette, George Washington and, 107–
8
Expense account(s)
of George Washington, 7, 87–88
of Paul Revere, 86n

Fairfax, Sally, 106
comparison of, 116
George Washington and, 257, 257n
Martha Washington's friendship with,
115–16
Fairfax, Thomas (Lord), 106–7
Fairfax family, land owned by, 102
Fauntleroy, Betsy, 105n
Federalists, description of, 278n
Fenno, John, ode by, to President
Washington, 306
Fevers, loss of men from, 180
First Continental Congress. *See* Continental
Congress, First
Fisher, Elijah, quoted on life-style at
Valley Forge, 176
Flexner, James T. (Colonel), 9
on Congressman Washington's uniform,
24
George Washington: The Forge of Experience,
10
Flour mill business, 218
Fort Necessity, 59–60, 62
Fort Ticonderoga, cannon brought from,
148–54, 148–49n

idea for, 147, 147n
instructions for, 149–50
Fort Washington, 182–83
fall of, 184
Fourth of July celebrations, 230
Fox hunting, 42
France, supplies for rebels from, 197
Frances Alexa, 105, 105n
Franklin, Benjamin, Battle of Yorktown
and, 197
Freemasons, 56
French, Allen, quoted on work activities on
Dorchester Heights, 161
French armies
Battle of Yorktown and, 197
encounters with, 57–59
French and Indian War, 16, 16n
start of, 59
Freneau, Philip
portrayal of American soldiers by, 140
song for General Washington by, 203–4
in welcoming procession for
inauguration, 294

Gambling, George Washington and, 39–42
Gazette of the United States, quoted on first
inauguration day, 296
*Gentleman's Compleat Military Dictionary,
The*, 156
George III, King of England, 98n
American revolution and, 98
George III and the Mad Business (Macalpine
and Hunter), 98n
George Washington: The Forge of Experience
(Flexner), 10, 327
George Washington: The Image and the Man
(Woodward), 10, 323
George Washington's Expense Account
(Washington and Kitman), 7, 325
George Washington's Generals (Shy), 171
Georgia, presidential electors from, 276
Gloucester Hunting Club, 43
Great Britain, representation in, 99
Greene, Catharine (Kitty)
aboard troopship, 259
Anthony Wayne and, 259
estate problems of, 317
George Washington and, 145, 257–61,
261n
dancing with, 178–79
Jeremiah Wadsworth and, 258–59
letters to, 266–67, 267n
knowledge of French language, 186
Marquis de Lafayette and, 258
Martha Washington and, 146
in New York, 181–82
Phineas Miller and, 317
President Washington and, 317–18
qualities of, 317

Greene, Catharine (Kitty) *(cont.)*
son of, 315, 315*n*
as widow, 315, 316
Greene, George Washington, 315, 315*n*
Greene, Nathanael (Major General), 145
appointment to quartermaster general,
186–88
assignment to South Carolina, 188, 189–
91
corruption and, 250–54
death of, 315
investments in real estate by, 187
letters to Wadsworth by, 252
as scapegoat of Fort Washington defeat,
185
Gruber, Ira D., *Howe Brothers and The
American Revolution, The*, 162*n*
Grymes, Lucy, 104*n*

Hamilton, Alexander
Battle of Yorktown and, 195–96
discovery of, by Washington, 211, 211*n*
Elizabeth Schuyler and, 113
ethnic background of, 210–11, 211*n*
high finance and, 311–13
honesty of, 312–13
Itinerarium, 29
John Adams for vice president and, 279–
82
letter from Jeremiah Wadsworth, 282
as machine behind Washington, 208,
210–12
*Observation of the United States for the Year
1796, in which the Charge of
Speculation against Alexander
Hamilton, late Secretary of the
Treasury, is fully refuted. Written by
himself*, 312
quoted on Philadelphia taverns, 29
as secretary to General Washington, 172–
73
as secretary of the treasury, 312–13
superiority of, 211–12
Washington for president pressure from,
231
Hancock, John
Boston Cadets and, 65–66
reaction to Washington's nomination for
General by, 81
running for general by, 64–69
as smuggler, 65
Sons of Liberty and, 66–67
wealth of, 64–65
Harrison, Benjamin
description of, 45
friendship with, 45
as job seeker, 310
Washington's reply to, 310–11
as machine behind Washington, 209

Haslet, John (Colonel), quoted, 184
Hawkins, Francis, *Youth's Behaviour, or
Decency in Conversation Amongst Men*,
107
Henry, Patrick, quoted on defense and
arms, 26
Hessian Grenadiers, 183
Hiltzheimer, Jacob, cannon bursts on
inauguration route and, 291*n*
Hinsdale, Daniel, Washington's inaugural
clothes and, 297, 297*n*
*History of the Life and Death, Virtues and
Exploits of General George Washington*
(Weems), 102, 269
House of Burgesses. *See* Virginia House of
Burgesses
How, David, 134–35
Howe, William (General)
description of, 162–63
Elizabeth Loring and, 163*n*, 163–65
*Howe Brothers and The American Revolution,
The* (Gruber), 162*n*
Howitzer(s), from Fort Ticonderoga, 148–
54, 148–49*n*
Hughes, Rupert, *Washington*, 10
Humphreys, David (Colonel)
as machine behind Washington, 216
quoted on Washington as president,
230
Hunter, Richard, *George III and the Mad
Business*, 98*n*
Hurricane, at Boston, 158–59, 160

Inaugural address, 298–99, 301–4
first fiscal recommendation, 302–3
in privacy, 301
Washington's discomfort during, 301–
2
Inauguration Day, 298–304
celebrations on way to, 284–86
description of New York City, 296–97
disorganization at, 299
oath of office, 300
souvenirs of, 296, 296*n*
week preceding, 298
welcome to New York for, 294–95
Itinerarium (Hamilton), 29

Jefferson, Thomas
opinion of Philadelphia, 38
quoted on General Washington's
retirement, 203
Job seekers, 310–11
Johnson, Thomas, Washington's
nomination for General and,
82*n*
Jones, Joseph, quoted on welcome for
Washington, 295

Kitman, Marvin
  George Washington's Expense Account, 7
  Number One Best Seller, The, 7n
Knox, Henry (General)
  celebration hosted by, 177
  description of, 150, 150n
  George Washington and
    friendship with, 146–47
    machine behind, 215–16, 215n
  monuments to, 154
Knox, Lucy Flucker, 177

Lafayette, Marquis de
  education of George Washington Greene
    and, 315n
  Kitty Greene and, 258
  as secretary to General Washington, 173–
    75
Leary, Lewis, *That Rascal Freneau a Study
  in Literary Failure*, 249n
Lee, Charles (General)
  background of, 191–92
  bluntness of, 192
  campaign for general by, 72
  character of, 71–72
  description of, 70
  hot temper of, 71, 72
  letters on titles by, 97
  love of dogs by, 70
  love of Shakespeare by, 70
  political support for, 72
  running for general by, 69–72
  tongue-lashing by General Washington,
    193
  understanding of leadership by, 192
  as writer, 70–71
Letter(s)
  burned by Martha Washington, 265–
    67
  from George Washington
    to fellow officers of Fairfax militia
      companies, 91
    on his attendance at Constitutional
      Convention, 224
    to Martha, 117
    to Sally Fairfax, 116–17
    historical vandalism to, 269
    to Robert Cary & Company, 121–22,
      123, 124
  on titles, by General Charles Lee, 97
Littlefield, Catharine. *See* Greene,
  Catharine (Kitty)
London Magazine (Walpole), 62
Loring, Elizabeth Lloyd
  American Revolution and, 164, 165
  Sir William Howe and, 163–64
Loring, Joshua Jr., 164
  penal administration of, 164–65
Lowland Beauty, 104–5, 104–5n

Lyman, Simeon, quoted on reenlistment,
  141
Lynch, Thomas (Congressman), 28
  quoted on Washington raising an army,
    25–26

Macalpine, Ida, *George III and the Mad
  Business*, 98n
Madison, James
  arrival at Constitutional Convention by,
    225
  at General Washington's retirement, 203
  as machine behind Washington, 208,
    214–15
Manners, George Washington and, 107–8
Marriage, of George and Martha
  Washington, 112
Maryland, presidential electors from, 276
Mason, George, as machine behind
  Washington, 209
Masons. *See* Freemasons
Massachusetts, presidential electors from,
  276
McDaniel, Mary, 106
McHenry, James, quoted on Washington's
  position, 305
Mercer, George (Captain), written
  description of Washington by, 240,
  245
Mercer, Hugh, quoted on George
  Washington, 63n
Mifflin, Thomas (Major), 129
Miller, Phineas, Kitty Greene and, 317
Mobility, definition of, 80n
Monument(s)
  to Henry Knox, 154
Morris, Gouverneur, 214, 307
  friendship with George Washington, 234
Morris, Robert
  at Constitutional Convention, 226–27
  home of, on way to inauguration, 292–
    93
  as machine behind Washington, 212–14
Mount Vernon, home improvement for,
  120–21
Mount Vernon machine. *See* Washington,
  George, machine behind
Myths, about George Washington, 4–5

Nash, Michael, 134
New Hampshire, presidential electors
  from, 276
New Jersey, presidential electors from, 276
New York City
  as country's capital, 295
  Inauguration Day in, 296–97
    arrival for, 294–95
  population of, 133n

New York State, land purchases in, 220–21

Number One Best Seller, The (Kitman), 7n

Oath of office, 300
Observation of the United States for the Year 1796, in which the Charge of Speculation against Alexander Hamilton, late Secretary of the Treasury, is fully refuted. Written by himself (Hamilton), 312
Ohio Company, 56–59
    land purchases from, 219–20, 219n, 220n
    stockholders in, 61–62
Olney, Deborah, scandalous behavior by, 176–77
Olney, George, 176
Oppression, 128
Otis, Samuel, oath of office given by, 300

Paine, Thomas, attack on Robert Morris by, 213
Patience, George Washington and, 18
Patriots
    American people as, 98
    division between Tories and, 99
Payroll, army, 86
Peale, Charles Willson, portrait of General Washington by, 20–21, 169
Pearson, Michael, quoted on Admiral Lord Howe's communication with Washington, 96–97
Pendleton, Edmund
    anti-Washington movement and, 76
    as machine behind Washington, 209
Pennsylvania, presidential electors from, 276
Pennsylvania Packet, 229
    on Martha Washington, 285
    on Washington as president, 231–32
Philadelphia, Pennsylvania
    Constitutional Convention at, 223–25
    as country's capital, 295
    decadence in, 38
    description of, 36–38
    gambling in, 39
    inaugural celebrations in, 289–92
    population of, 36–37
    Second Continental Congress at, 15–17
    size of, 37
    taverns in, 29
    theater in, 43–44
Pittsburgh, Pennsylvania, 56–57, 57n
    land purchases in, 220, 220n
Politics, theater and, 202
Port, Jane, 47
Portrait(s), 241–44
    by Charles Willson Peale, 20–21

by Gilbert Stuart, 5–6
    reliability of, 239–40, 245–47
Potomac River Canal Company, 221, 221n
Powel, Elizabeth Willing, 48–49
    at inauguration party, 291
    letters
        to George Washington from, 291n
Powel, Samuel, 47–48
Presidency
    acceptance of nomination for, 235
    acceptance speech for, 283–84
    discussion of, 229–30
Presidential electors, 276, 277
Presidential receptions, 308–9
Prize fights, 42
Punishment, for drunkenness, 134
Putnam, Israel (General)
    running for general by, 69
Putnam, Rufus, fortification of Dorchester Heights and, 156

Quartermaster
    duties of, 186
    General Greene's appointment to, 186–88

Raleigh Tavern, 28, 29
Randolph, Edmund, as machine behind Washington, 209
Randolph, Peyton, 64
Real-estate business, 218–22
Rebel(s), 96n
Rebels and Gentlemen (Bridenbaugh), 37
Rebels and Redcoats (Scheer and Rankin), 67
Reed, Joseph (Colonel), 129
Regulars, New World fighting and, 192
Religion, voting and, 99
Representation, issue of, 99
Revere, Paul
    engraving by, 68, 68n
    expense account of, 86n
    ride by, 67–68
Revolution, American
    cannons in, 148–54, 148–49n
        idea for, 147, 147n
    economics of, for Great Britain, 192–93, 192–93n
    Elizabeth Loring and, 164, 165
    fortification of Dorchester Heights, 155–59
    John Adams and, 98–99
    King George III and, 98
    the people and, 98
    slogan of, 99
Revolutionary War. *See* Revolution, American
Riflemen, in Continental Army, 142–43

Rising Sun Tavern, 28–29
Robert Cary & Company, London, letters
    to, 121–22, 123, 124
Rossiter, Clinton
    1787: The Grand Convention, 113
    Six Characters in Search of a Republic,
    11
Royalty, American public and, 309

Salomon, Haym, 251*n*
Schlesinger, Arthur Sr., quoted on slogans
    and propaganda, 128
Schuyler, Elizabeth, Alexander Hamilton
    and, 113
Schuyler, Philip (Major General), 129
Second Continental Congress. *See*
    Continental Congress, Second
Secretaries, of General Washington, 172–
    75
Self-consciousness, George Washington
    and, 21
Seven Years War, 16, 16*n*
1787: The Grand Convention (Rossiter), 113
Sex
    history writing and, 270–71
    potential campaign issue of, 254–61
Shy, John, *George Washington's Generals*, 171
Six Characters in Search of a Republic
    (Rossiter), 11
Smallpox, 180
Sons of Liberty, Boston Tea Party and, 66–
    67
South Carolina, presidential electors from,
    276
Souvenirs, inaugural, 296, 296*n*
Sparks, Jared, altering of presidential
    papers by, 267–68
Spirit of Seventy-Six, The (Commager and
    Morris), 157
Stockholders, in Ohio Company, 61–62
Stockton, Mrs. Richard
    letter from Washington to, 293–94
    poem for Washington by, 293
Stuart, Gilbert, portrait of George
    Washington by, 5–6, 240
Sullivan, William, quoted
    on Martha's weekly tea parties, 314
    on Washington's royal demeanor, 305
Sydnor, Charles S.
    *American Revolutionaries in the Making:
    Political Practices in Washington's
    Virginia*, 32–33

Tavern(s), in Philadelphia, 29. *See also*
    specific taverns
Taxation, issue of, 99
"Taxation without representation," 99
Tears. *See* Weeping

*That Rascal Freneau a Study in Literary
    Failure* (Leary), 294*n*
Theater, 43–44
Thomson, Charles, 282–83
Titles, 306–8, 307*n*
Tobacco, 46*n*
Tories
    American people as, 98
    division between patriots and, 99
Trenton, New Jersey, on way to
    inauguration, 293–94
Trumbull, Jonathan, letter to John Adams
    from, 281–82
Typhoid fever, 180
Typhus, 180
Tyranny, 128

Uniform(s)
    George Washington and, 19–24
        designing of, 21, 21*n*
        love of, 21
    for trip to Boston, 23
Uniontown, Pennsylvania, 59–60

Valley Forge
    "bawling" at, 176–77
    bitter winter of 1777–78 at, 175–79
    General Washington at, 175–79
Vice President, electoral votes for, 277–
    78
Virginia
    delegation to Second Continental
        Congress from, 16–17
    House of Burgesses, 17
    presidential electors from, 276
Virginia Gazette, on pro-Washington
    sentiment, 74
Virginia House of Burgesses, 17, 18
Voting, 99

Wadsworth, Jeremiah, 250, 250–51*n*
    Kitty Greene and, 258–59
    letters
        from Kitty Greene, 266–67, 267*n*
        by Nathanael Greene, 252
        to Alexander Hamilton, 282
    Washington's inaugural dress and, 298
Walpole, Horace, *London Magazine*, 62
War, potential campaign issue of, 249
Ward, Artemas (General), 139
Washerwoman Kate Affair, 45
    play inspired by, 46
Washington, D.C., as country's capital,
    295–96
Washington, George
    ability of, to blame others, 185
    admiration for, 95–96, 205

Washington, George *(cont.)*
alcohol consumption by, 31–34
appearance of, after the war, 202
arrival of
at Cambridge, 132
at Constitutional Convention, 226–27
at front lines in Boston, 129–31
at New York, 130, 310
as assistant surveyor, 103–4
babies named after, 168
birthday of, 101
celebration of, 168
birthplace of, 101–2
businesses of, 218
card playing and, 39–42
wins and losses at, 40–41
charisma of, 249
childhood of, 102
childlessness of, 216
Cincinnati membership of, 223
clothes-consciousness of, 21–22
clothing stolen from, 106
as Colonel, 16–17
complexion of, 246
as Congressman
at First Continental Congress, 17–18
at Second Continental Congress, 15–16
Constitutional Convention and
chairman of, 227–28
need for attendance at, 226
criticism of, by John Adams, 88–90
death of, 265, 265n
education of, 103
engagement of, 109–10
expense account of, 7, 87–88
eyes of, 245
false teeth of, 247–48, 248n
favorite poems of, 167
financial distress of, 288–89
financial holdings of
after marriage to Martha, 114–15
before marriage to Martha, 115
fox hunting and, 42–43
Freemason membership of, 56
friendships of
with Lord Fairfax, 107
with Kitty Greene, 145
with Benjamin Harrison, 45
with Henry Knox, 146–47
with Marquis de Lafayette, 173–75
with Gouverneur Morris, 234
gambling and, 39–42
as General
acceptance speech for, 83–85, 90
Battle of Yorktown, 196
battles lost by, 170–71
deployment of troops by, flaws in, 170–71
discipline of troops, 134–38, 137n

encounters with French, 57–59
gold medal for, 165–66
headquarters of, 132
in New York, 180–85
nomination for, 73–82
number of troops under, 132–33
offer to raise an army, 24–27
orders to troops, 156
plan for Continental Army, 140
"providential intervention," 169–70
push for attack of British, 142
of rebel forces, 53–54
secretarial family of, 171–75
strength as, 180–81
at Valley Forge, 175–79
victorious withdrawals, 194–95
George Washington's Expense Account, 7
hair color of, 245
hatred for tobacco by, 46n
height of, 245–46
household servants of, 119–20, 120n
humility of, 91–92
information about, 239, 239n
interior decorating and, 120–21
Kitty Greene dancing with, 178–79
land purchases by
in future Pittsburgh, 220, 220n
in New York State, 220–21
from Ohio Company, 219–20, 219n, 220n
letters, 10
alteration of, 267–68
burned by Martha, 265–67
to fellow officers of Fairfax militia companies, 91
from Eliza Powel, 291n
historical vandalism to, 269
of love, to Sally Fairfax, 116–17
to Martha, 117, 125–26
to Mrs. Richard Stockton, 293–94
to Robert Cary & Co., 121–22, 123, 124
to Sally Fairfax, 116–17
life of, after retirement from public service, 204–8
literature on, 10
love affairs of
Frances Alexa, 105, 105n
Mary Cary, 104
Sally Fairfax, 106, 116–19
Kitty Greene, 145, 257–61, 261n
Lowland Beauty, 104–5, 104–5n
machine behind, 227–28
mail order shopping by, 121–25
manners and, 107–8
map drawing and, 103
Martha Custis meeting with, 108–10
Martha's name for, 119
mathematics and, 103

Washington, George *(cont.)*
  military career of
    early, 54–56
    first turning point in, 56–59
    volunteer duty with General
      Braddock, 63
  military record of, 8*n*
  military studies by, 55–56
  moral from life of, 322
  mother of, 286–88
  Mount Vernon and, guests at, 206, 206*n*
  myths about, 4–5
  not-running strategy of, 207–8, 207*n*
  odes to, by John Fenno, 306
  Ohio Company and, stock in, 61–62
  patience of, 18
  places named after, 168
  political considerations about, 75–77
  popularity of, 27
  portraits of, 168–69, 241–44
    by Charles Willson Peale, 20–21
    reliability of, 239–40, 245–47
    by Gilbert Stuart, 5–6, 240
  as President
    acceptance of nomination for, 235
    acceptance speech, 283–84
    dinner in Charleston, 316–17
    election results, 282–83
    election statistics, 275–78
    inaugural clothing, 297, 297*n*
    job seekers, 310–11
    media staff of, 215–17
    tour of New England states, 315–16
    trip through the south, 316–18
    weekly reception for men, 313–14
    widow Greene and, 317–18
  pressure on, to run for president, 230–32
    from General John Armstrong, 229
    from Alexander Hamilton, 230–31
    from public, 230
  prize fights and, 42
  qualities of, 108
  quoted, on inauguration day, 304
  real estate business of, 218–22
  refusal of pay by, 86–87
  religion and, 73
  as representative of the people, 100
  retirement of
    from chairman of Constitutional
      Convention, 229
    from public srvice, 201–2
  royal demeanor of, 305
  Second Continental Congress and,
    committee assignment at, 19
  self-consciousness of, 21
  sex life of, 255–71
    absence of stories about, 264–65
    probability list, 261–63
    Sally Fairfax and, 257, 257*n*
  slogans for, 293

    songs for, 167, 293
    speaking ability of, 17–18
    as surveyor, 103–4
    taste for titles by, 307
    as teenager, 106
    teeth of, 247–48, 248*n*
    theater and, 43–44
    travel to Boston, 127–29
    unsmiling countenance of, 248
    veneration of, 88–89
    voice of, 246–47
    wealth of, 87
    wearing of uniform by, 19–24
    wedding of, 112–13
    welcome for, at New York, 130
    womanizing by, 45–46
    wreath placed on head of, 290–91
    written description of, 240, 245
      questions about, 245–47
Washington (Hughes), 10
Washington, Lawrence, 55
  Ohio Company and, 61*n*
Washington, Martha Dandridge
  arrival at New York, 310
  comparison of, 116
  description of, 110
  financial holdings of, 113–15
  friendships of
    with Sally Fairfax, 115–16
    with Kitty Greene, 146
  George's name for, 119
  greatest asset of, 111–12
  missing from inaugural party, 284–86
  papers burned by, 265–67
  Pennsylvania Packet on, 285
  personality of, 111
  titles for, 97, 306–7
  trip to Cambridge by, 144–46
  virtues of, 111
  weaknesses of, 111
  wedding dress of, 112
  weekly tea parties of, 313–14
Washington, Mary, 286–88
  letter to John Augustine by, 287
Washington Monument, 269
"Washington's Legacy," issuance of, 217–18
Wayne, Anthony (Major General), Kitty
  Greene and, 259
Webb, Samuel B. (Lieutenant), quoted
  on fortification of Dorchester Heights,
    155
  on New York welcome for Washington,
    295
  on Washington's orders to troops, 156
Weedon, George, 29
Weems, Mason L.
  *A History of the Life and Death, Virtues and
    Exploits of General George Washington,*
    269

Weems, Mason L. *(cont.)*
  information about Washington by, 268–
    69
Weeping, upon retirement from public
    service, 202–3
Wheatley, Phillis
  as machine behind Washington,
    216
  poem for General Washington by, 166–
    67
Whitney, Eli, Kitty Greene and, 317

Willing, Elizabeth. *See* Powel, Elizabeth
    Willing
Wine(s). *See* Alcoholic beverages
Womanizing, 45–46
Woodward, William, *George Washington: The
    Image and the Man*, 10

Yorktown, Virginia, victory at, 195–98
*Youth's Behaviour, or Decency in Conversation
    Amongst Men* (Hawkins), 107

COPYRIGHT ACKNOWLEDGMENTS